DAISUKE ASHIHARA

I never thought that over-the-counter medicir
for me, so I never trusted medicine in genera
painkillers I got from the hospital are work
Meds are awesome! Here's *World Trigger* volu

—Daisuke Ashil

Daisuke Ashihara began his manga career at
27 when his manga *Room 303* won second pl
75th Tezuka Awards. His first series, *Super Dog*
began serialization in *Weekly Shonen Jum*
World Trigger is his second serialized work
Shonen Jump. He is also the author of seve
works, including the one-shots *Super Dog*
Trigger Keeper and *Elite Agent Jin*.

WORLD TRIGGER

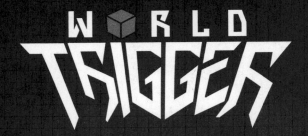

WORLD TRIGGER VOL. 15
SHONEN JUMP Manga Edition

STORY AND ART BY DAISUKE ASHIHARA

Translation/Toshikazu Aizawa
Touch-Up Art & Lettering/Annaliese Christman
Design/Sam Elzway
Editor/Marlene First

First published in Japan in 2013 by SHUEISHA Inc., Tokyo.
English translation rights arranged by SHUEISHA Inc.

Printed in the U.S.A.

Published by VIZ Media, LLC
P.O. Box 77010
San Francisco, CA 94107

10 9 8 7 6 5 4 3 2 1
First printing, April 2017

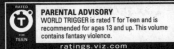

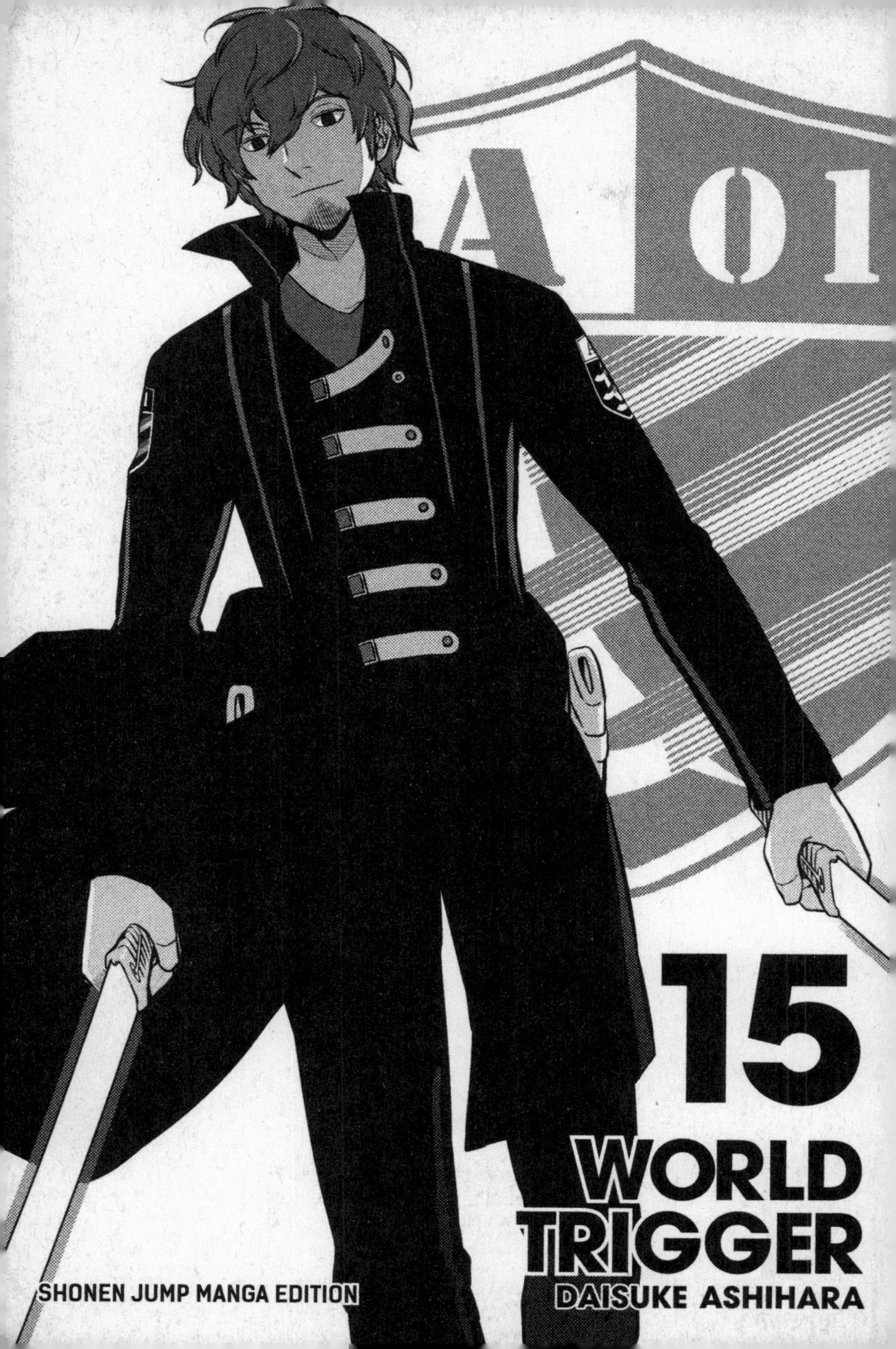
A 01
15
WORLD TRIGGER
DAISUKE ASHIHARA
SHONEN JUMP MANGA EDITION

Invasion NEIGHBOR

Invaders from another dimension that enter Mikado City through Gates. Most "Neighbors" here are Trion soldiers built for war. The Neighbors who actually live on the other side of the Gates are human, like Yuma.

RRRM

H-HEY, IT'S COMING THIS WAY!

WHOA... WAAA

→ Trion soldier built for war. ►

...ARE PEOPLE, LIKE US.

THE NEIGHBORS WHO LIVE ON THE OTHER SIDE OF THE GATE...

GALOPOULA

One of the two countries that are Aftokrator's subordinates. They invaded under orders from Aftokrator.

NOW THEN...

GOOD WORK.

I'M FINISHED, SIR.

TIME TO GO OVER THE MISSION DETAILS ONE LAST TIME.

AFTOKRATOR

The most powerful military nation in the Neighborhood. Also known as "the Holy Land," the country is ruled by four houses that are constantly fighting for power. Each house is invading other worlds to find the next god.

BORDER

An agency founded to protect the city's peace from Neighbors. Agents are classified as follows: C-Rank for trainees, B-Rank for main forces, A-Rank for elites and S-Rank for those with Black Triggers. A-Rank squads get to go on away missions to Neighbor worlds.

Resistance

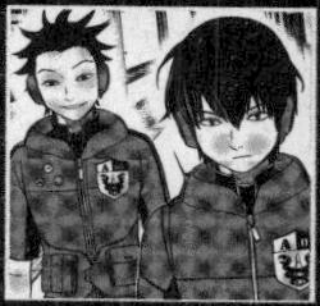

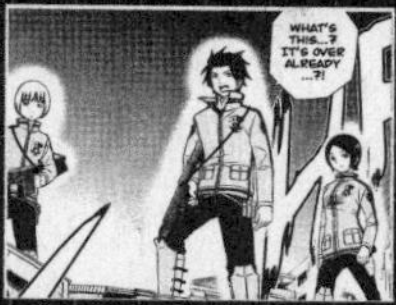
WHAT'S THIS...? IT'S OVER ALREADY ...?!

A-Rank: Arashiyama Squad, Miwa Squad

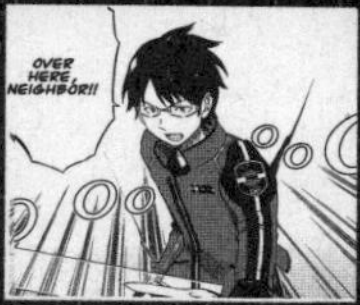
OVER HERE, NEIGHBOR!!

B-Rank: Osamu

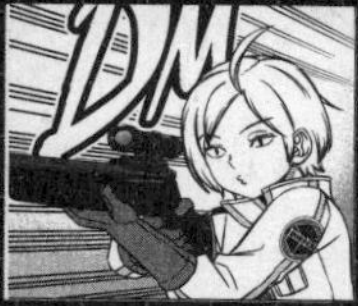

C-Rank: Izuho

Trigger

A technology created by Neighbors to manipulate Trion. Used mainly as weapons, Triggers come in various types. Border classifies them into three groups: Attacker, Gunner, and Sniper.

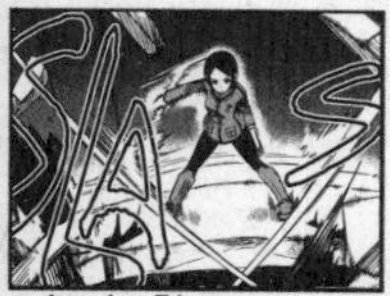

▲Attacker Trigger

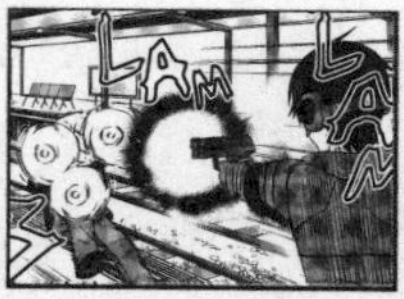

▲Gunner Trigger

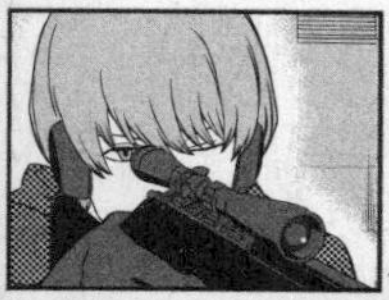

◀Sniper Trigger

Black Trigger

A special Trigger created when a skilled user pours their entire life force and Trion into a Trigger. Outperforms regular Triggers, but the user must be compatible with the personality of the creator, meaning only a few people can use any given Black Trigger.

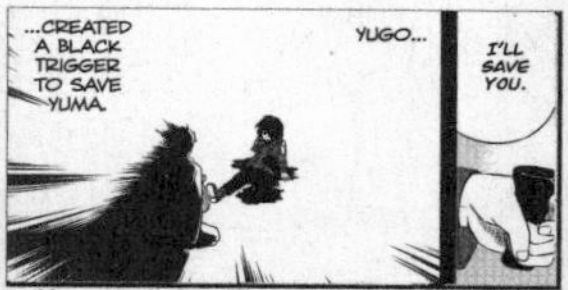
I'LL SAVE YOU.
YUGO...
...CREATED A BLACK TRIGGER TO SAVE YUMA.

▲Yuma's father Yugo sacrificed his life to create a Black Trigger and save Yuma.

STORY

About four years ago, a Gate connecting to another dimension opened in Mikado City, leading to the appearance of invaders called Neighbors. After the establishment of the Border Defence Agency, people were able to return to their normal lives.

Osamu Mikumo is a junior high student who meets Yuma Kuga, a Neighbor. Yuma is targeted for capture by Border, but Tamakoma branch agent Yuichi Jin steps in to help. He convinces Yuma to join Border instead, then gives his Black Trigger to HQ in exchange for Yuma's enlistment. Now Osamu, Yuma and Osamu's friend Chika work toward making A-Rank together.

Aftokrator, the largest military nation in the Neighborhood, begins another large-scale invasion!! Border succeeds in driving them back, but over thirty C-Rank trainees are kidnapped in the process. Border implements more plans for away missions to retrieve the missing Agents.

Osamu's squad, Tamakoma-2, enters the Rank Wars for a chance to be chosen for away missions. The fifth round is about to begin when Border HQ comes under attack by Galopoula, Aftokrator's subordinate nation. Border secretly assembles a small, elite force to handle the threat.

WORLD TRIGGER CHARACTERS

TAMAKOMA BRANCH

Understanding toward Neighbors. Considered divergent from Border's main philosophy.

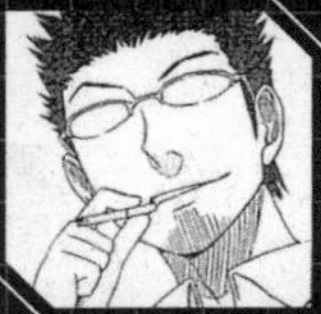

TAKUMI RINDO

Tamakoma Branch Director.

TAMAKOMA-2

Tamakoma's B-Rank squad, aiming to get promoted to A-Rank.

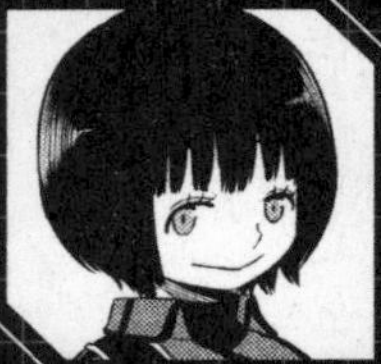

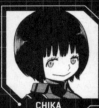

CHIKA AMATORI

Osamu's childhood friend. She has high Trion levels.

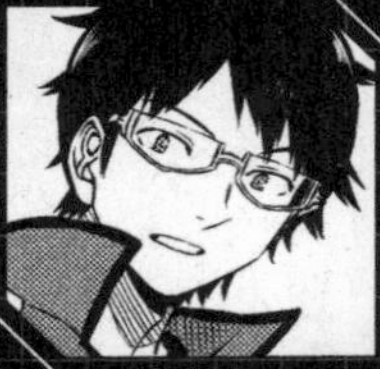

OSAMU MIKUMO

Ninth-grader who's compelled to help those in trouble. Captain of Tamakoma-2 (Mikumo squad).

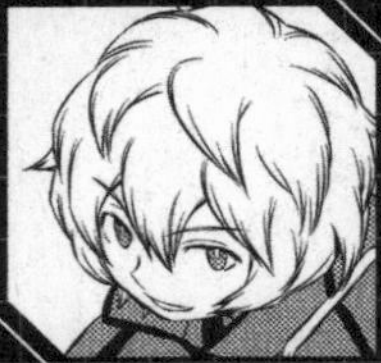

YUMA KUGA

A Neighbor who carries a Black Trigger.

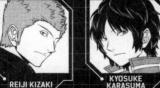

TAMAKOMA-1

Tamakoma's A-Rank squad.

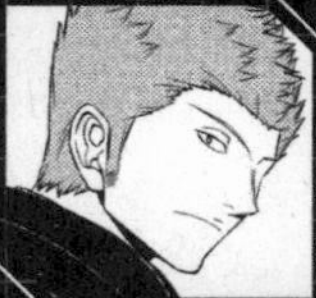

REIJI KIZAKI

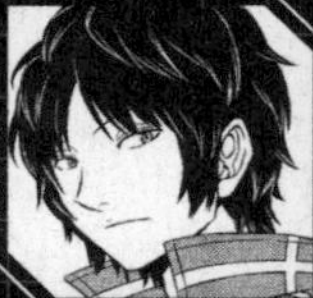

KYOSUKE KARASUMA

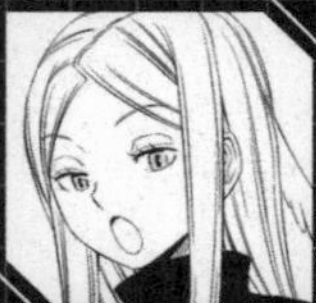

KIRIE KONAMI

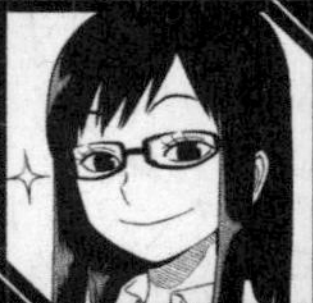

SHIORI USAMI

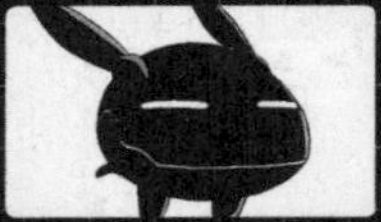

REPLICA

Yuma's chaperone. Missing after recent invasion.

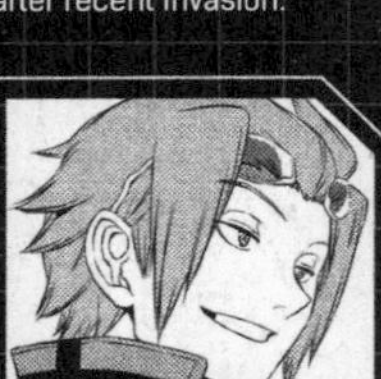

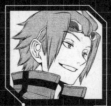

YUICHI JIN

Former S-Rank Black Trigger user. His Side Effect lets him see the future.

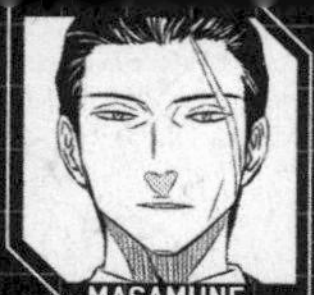

MASAMUNE KIDO
HQ Commander

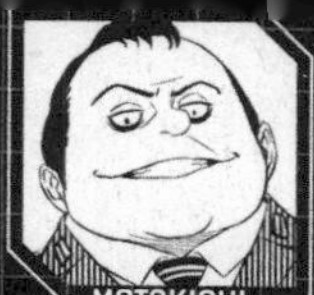

MOTOKICHI KINUTA
R&D Director

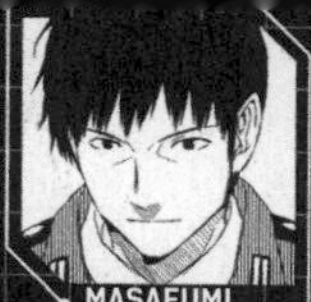

MASAFUMI SHINODA
HQ Director and Defense commander.

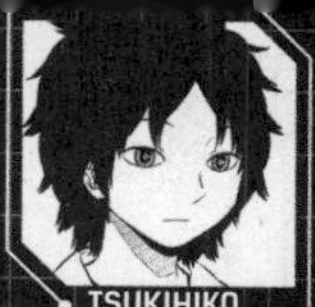

TSUKIHIKO AMO
S-Rank Agent. His Side Effect allows him to recognize an enemy's strength with colors.

A-RANK AGENTS

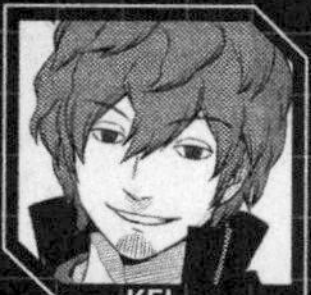

KEI TACHIKAWA
A-Rank #1
Tachikawa Squad captain and #1 Attacker

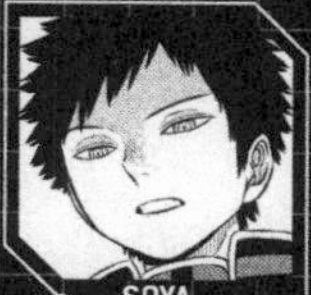

SOYA KAZAMA
A-Rank #3
Kazama Squad captain and #2 Attacker

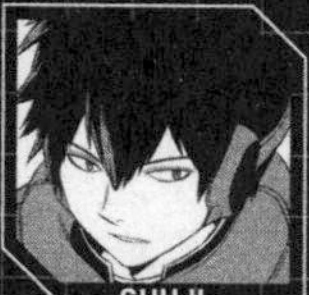

SHUJI MIWA
A-Rank #7
Miwa Squad captain and All-Rounder

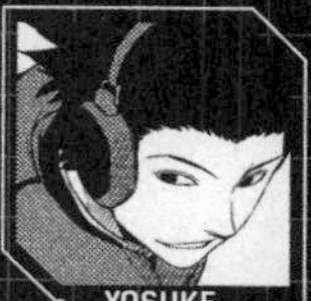

YOSUKE YONEYA
A-Rank #7
Miwa Squad Attacker

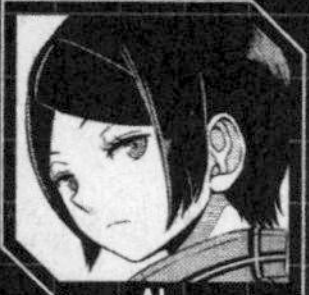

AI KITORA
A-Rank #5
Arashiyama Squad All-Rounder

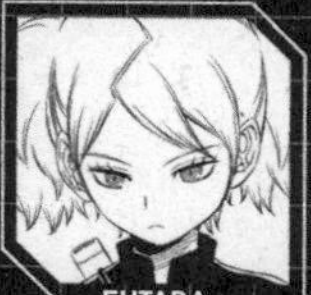

FUTABA KUROE
A-Rank #6
Kako Squad Attacker

B-RANK AGENTS

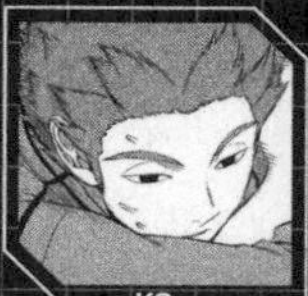

KO MURAKAMI
B-Rank #6
Suznari-1 Attacker

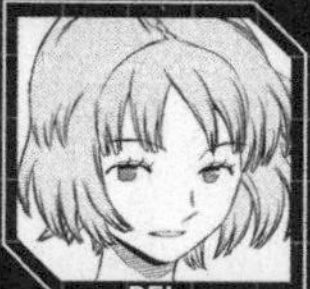

REI NASU
B-Rank #12
Nasu Squad Captain and Shooter

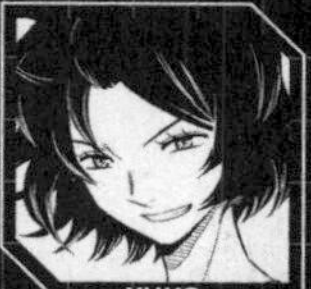

YUKO KUMAGAI
B-Rank #12
Nasu Squad Attacker

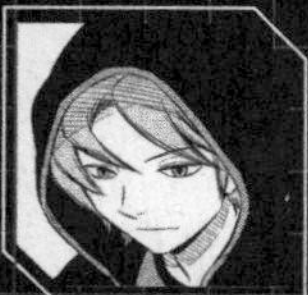

HYUSE
A Neighbor from Aftokrator left behind in the invasion.

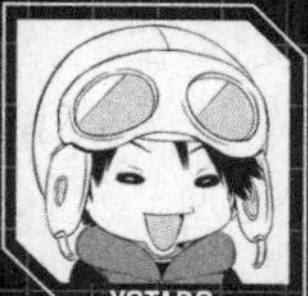

YOTARO RINDO
Tamakoma Branch kid

WORLD TRIGGER
CONTENTS

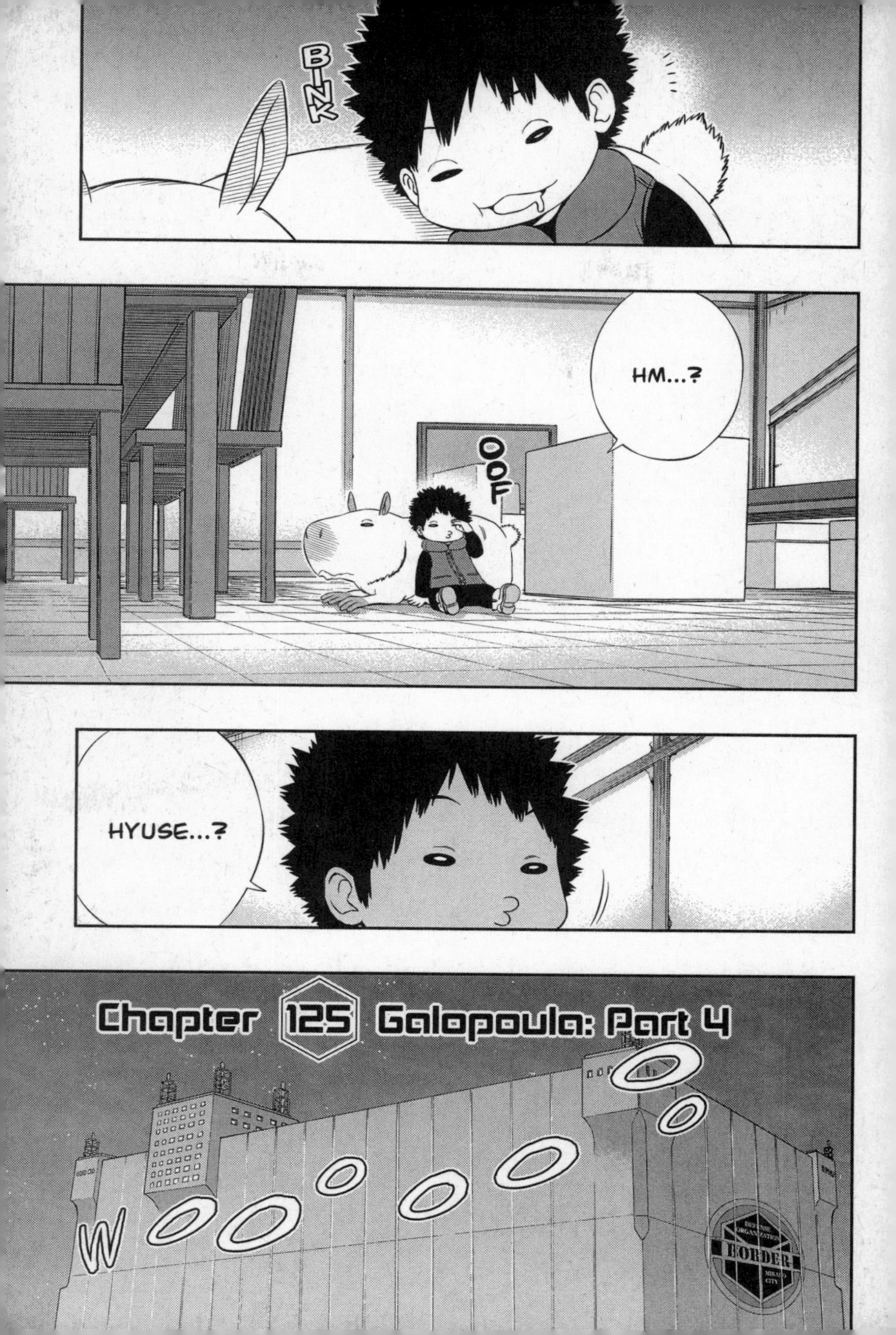
BLINK
HM...?
OOF
HYUSE...?
Chapter 125 Galopoula: Part 4
WOOOOOOOO
DEFENSE ORGANIZATION BORDER MIKADO CITY

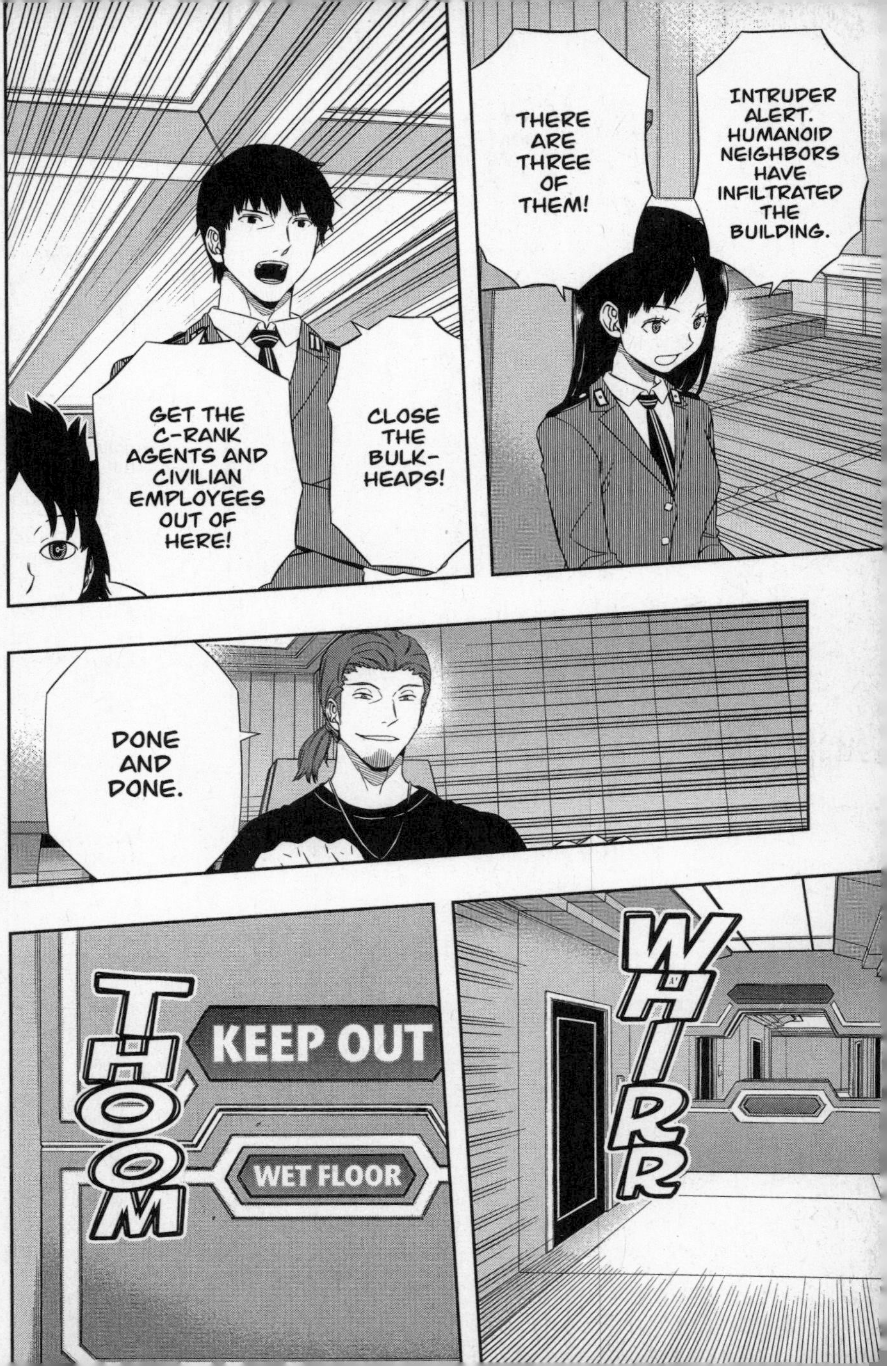
INTRUDER ALERT. HUMANOID NEIGHBORS HAVE INFILTRATED THE BUILDING.
THERE ARE THREE OF THEM!
CLOSE THE BULK-HEADS!
GET THE C-RANK AGENTS AND CIVILIAN EMPLOYEES OUT OF HERE!
DONE AND DONE.
WHIRR
THOOM
KEEP OUT
WET FLOOR

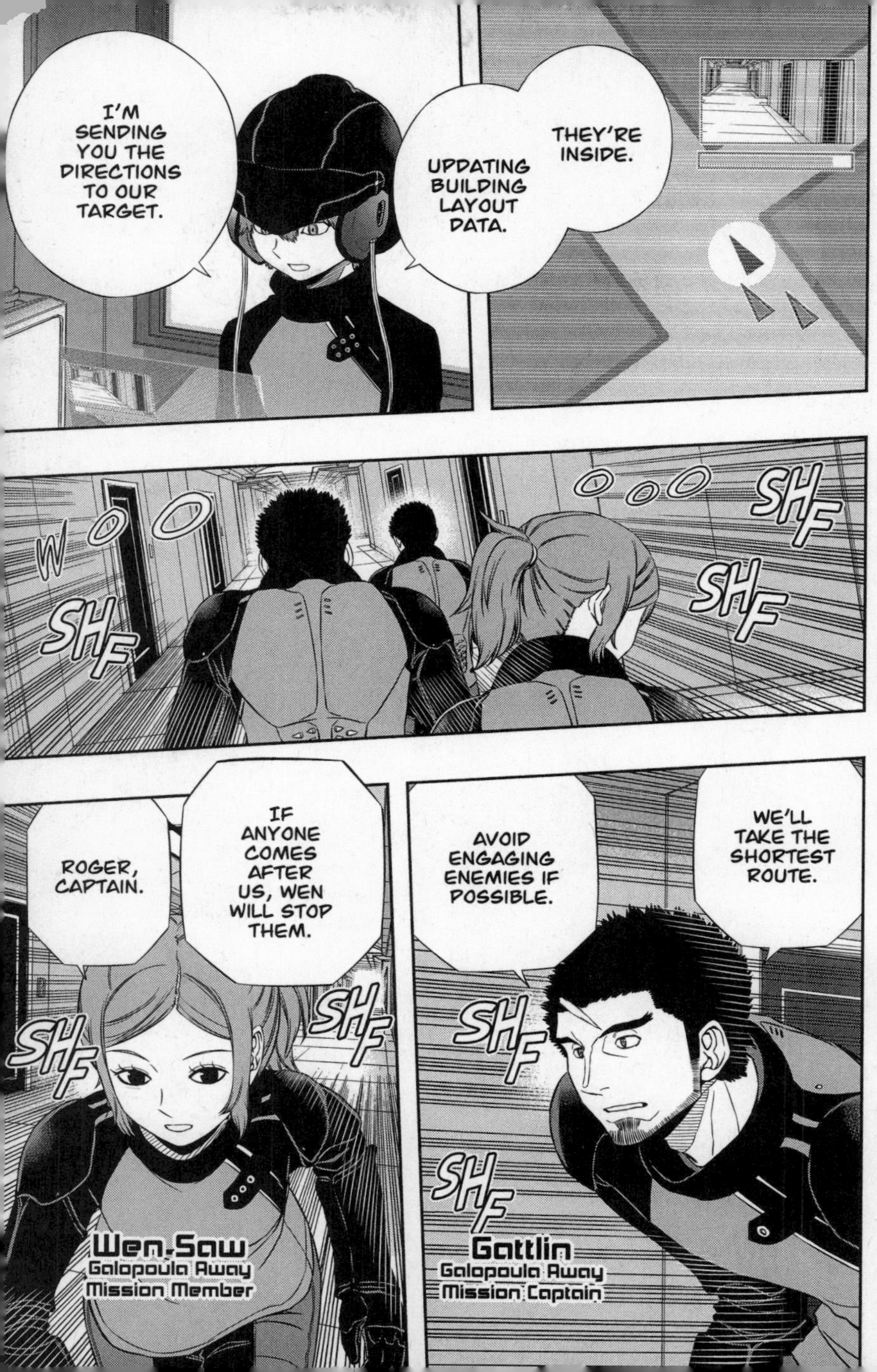
THEY'RE INSIDE.
UPDATING BUILDING LAYOUT DATA.
I'M SENDING YOU THE DIRECTIONS TO OUR TARGET.
OOO SHF
SHF
WOOO
SHF
WE'LL TAKE THE SHORTEST ROUTE.
AVOID ENGAGING ENEMIES IF POSSIBLE.
SHF
SHF
Gattlin
Galopoula Away Mission Captain
IF ANYONE COMES AFTER US, WEN WILL STOP THEM.
ROGER, CAPTAIN.
SHF
SHF
Wen Saw
Galopoula Away Mission Member

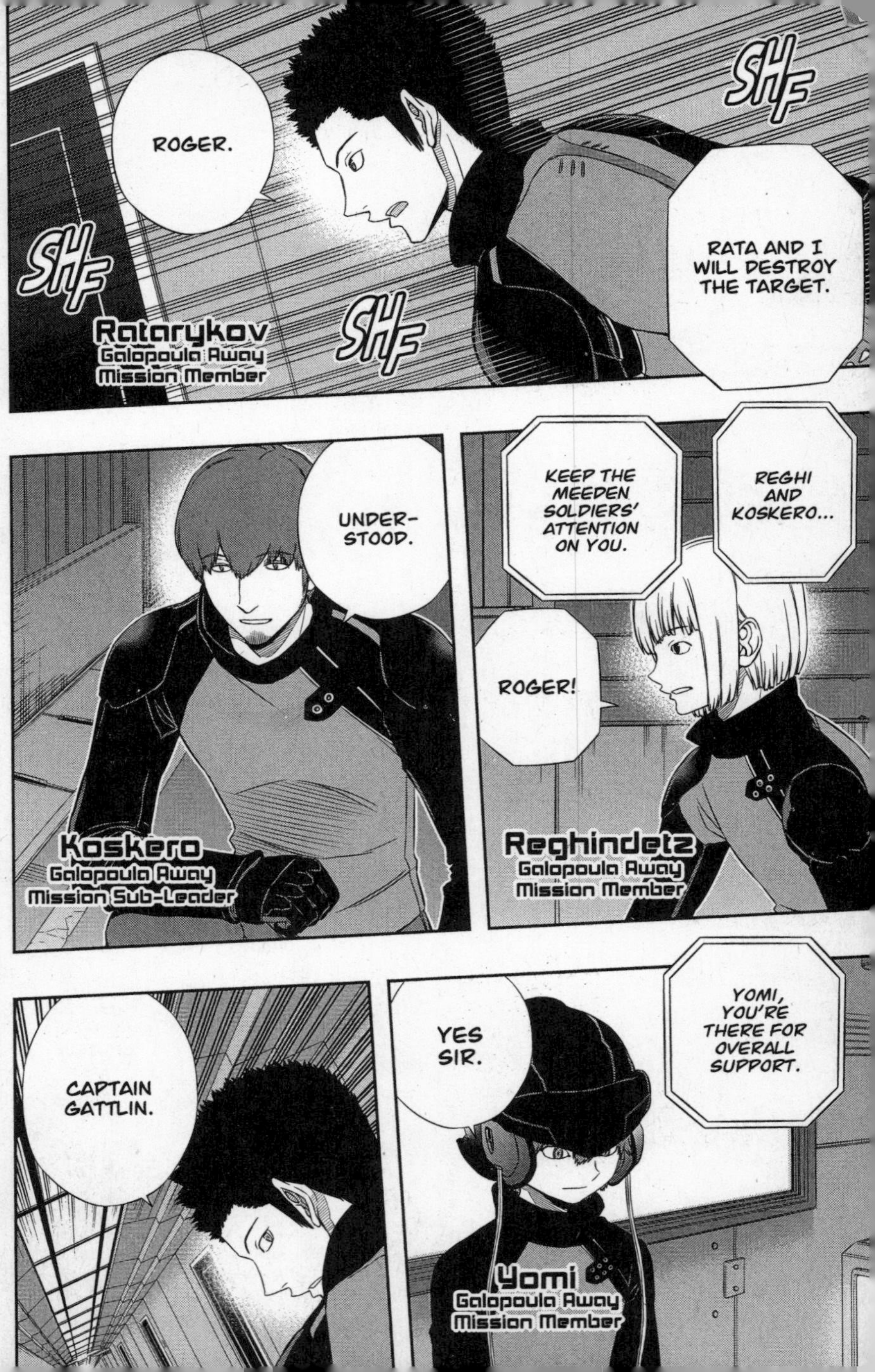
RATA AND I WILL DESTROY THE TARGET.
SHF
ROGER.
SHF
SHF
Ratarykov
Galopoula Away Mission Member
REGHI AND KOSKERO...
KEEP THE MEEDEN SOLDIERS' ATTENTION ON YOU.
ROGER!
Reghindetz
Galopoula Away Mission Member
UNDER-STOOD.
Koskero
Galopoula Away Mission Sub-Leader
YOMI, YOU'RE THERE FOR OVERALL SUPPORT.
YES SIR.
Yomi
Galopoula Away Mission Member
CAPTAIN GATTLIN.

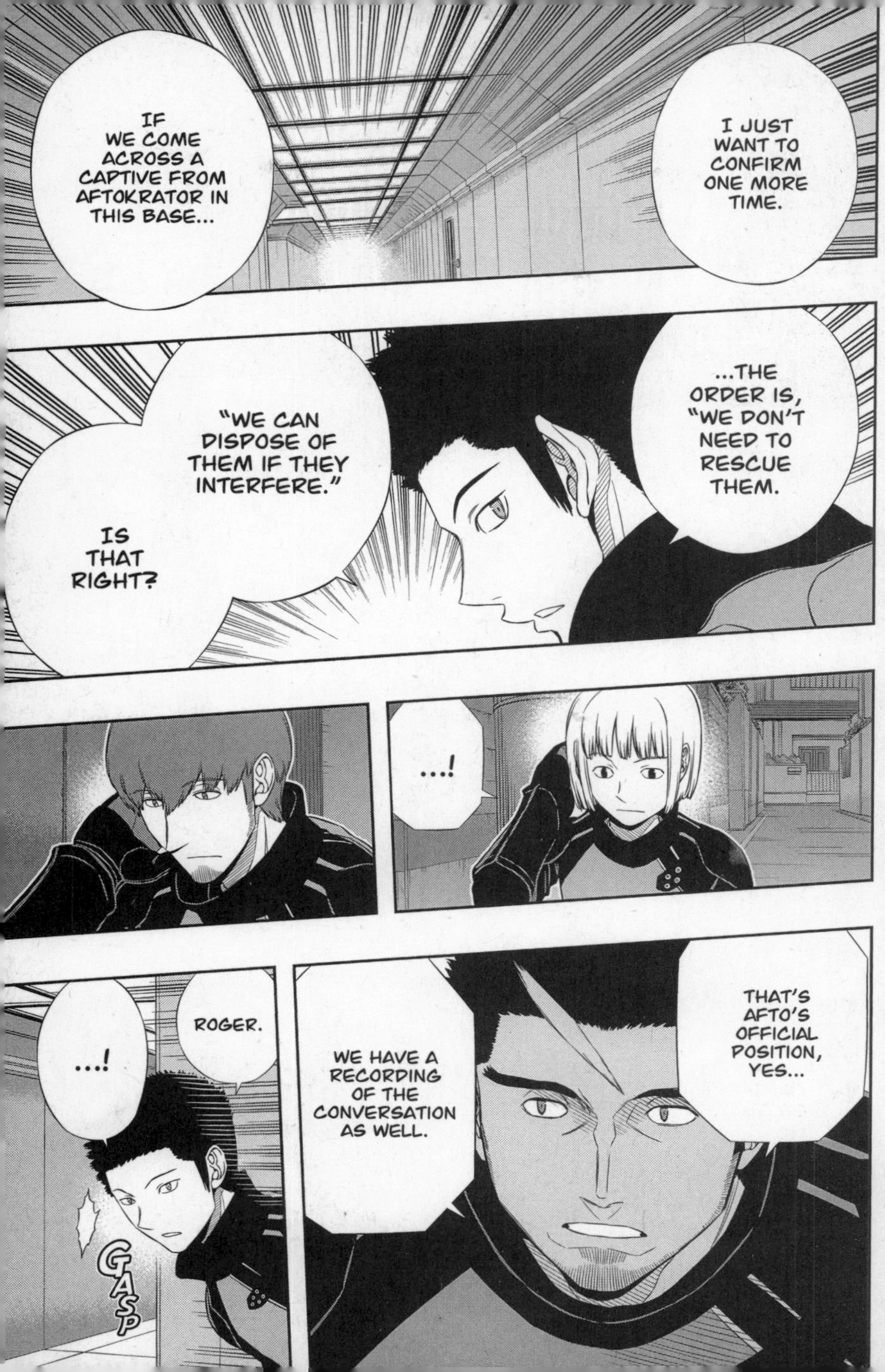
I JUST WANT TO CONFIRM ONE MORE TIME.
IF WE COME ACROSS A CAPTIVE FROM AFTOKRATOR IN THIS BASE...
...THE ORDER IS, "WE DON'T NEED TO RESCUE THEM.
"WE CAN DISPOSE OF THEM IF THEY INTERFERE."
IS THAT RIGHT?
...!
THAT'S AFTO'S OFFICIAL POSITION, YES...
WE HAVE A RECORDING OF THE CONVERSATION AS WELL.
ROGER.
...!
GASP

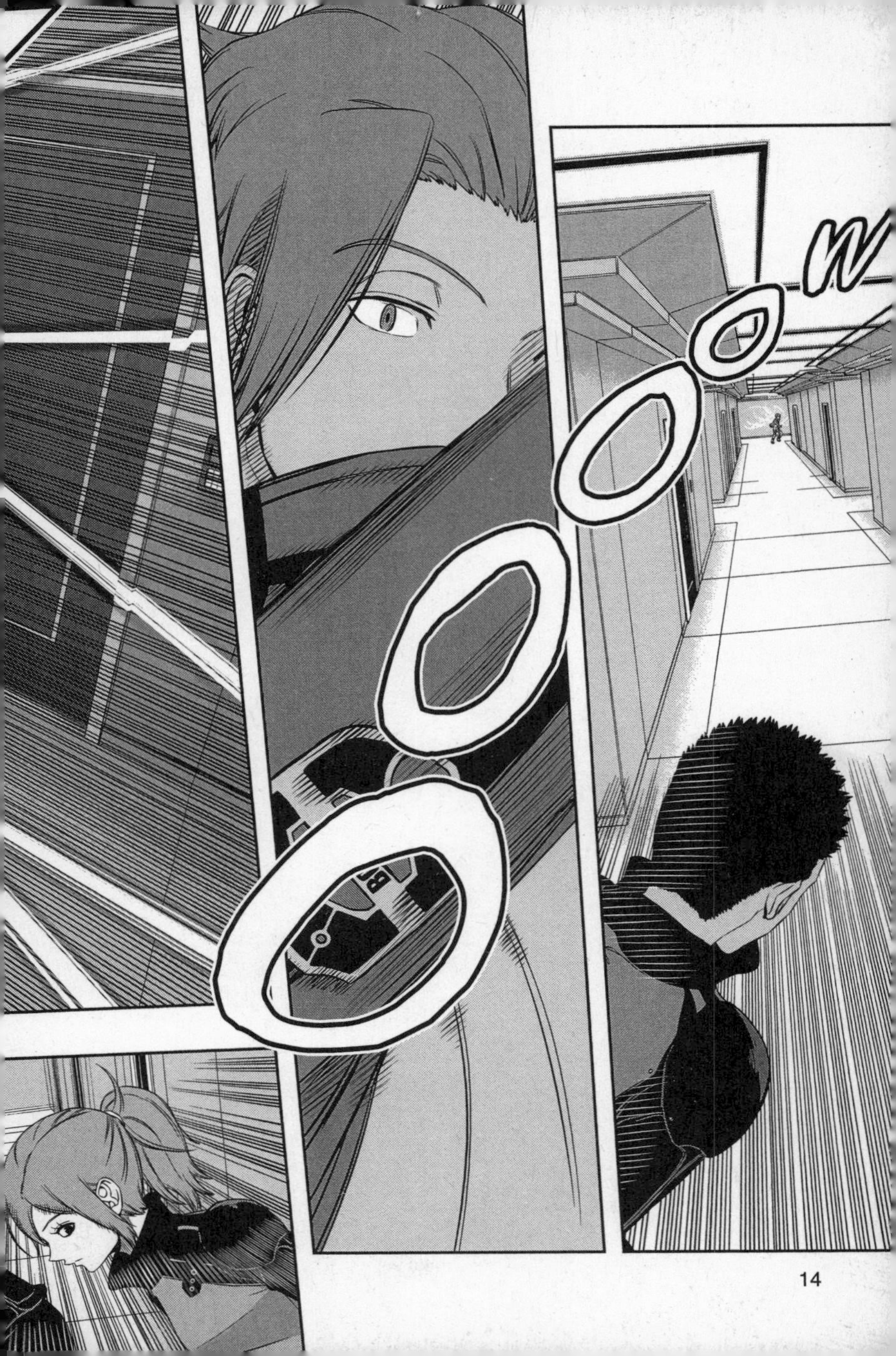

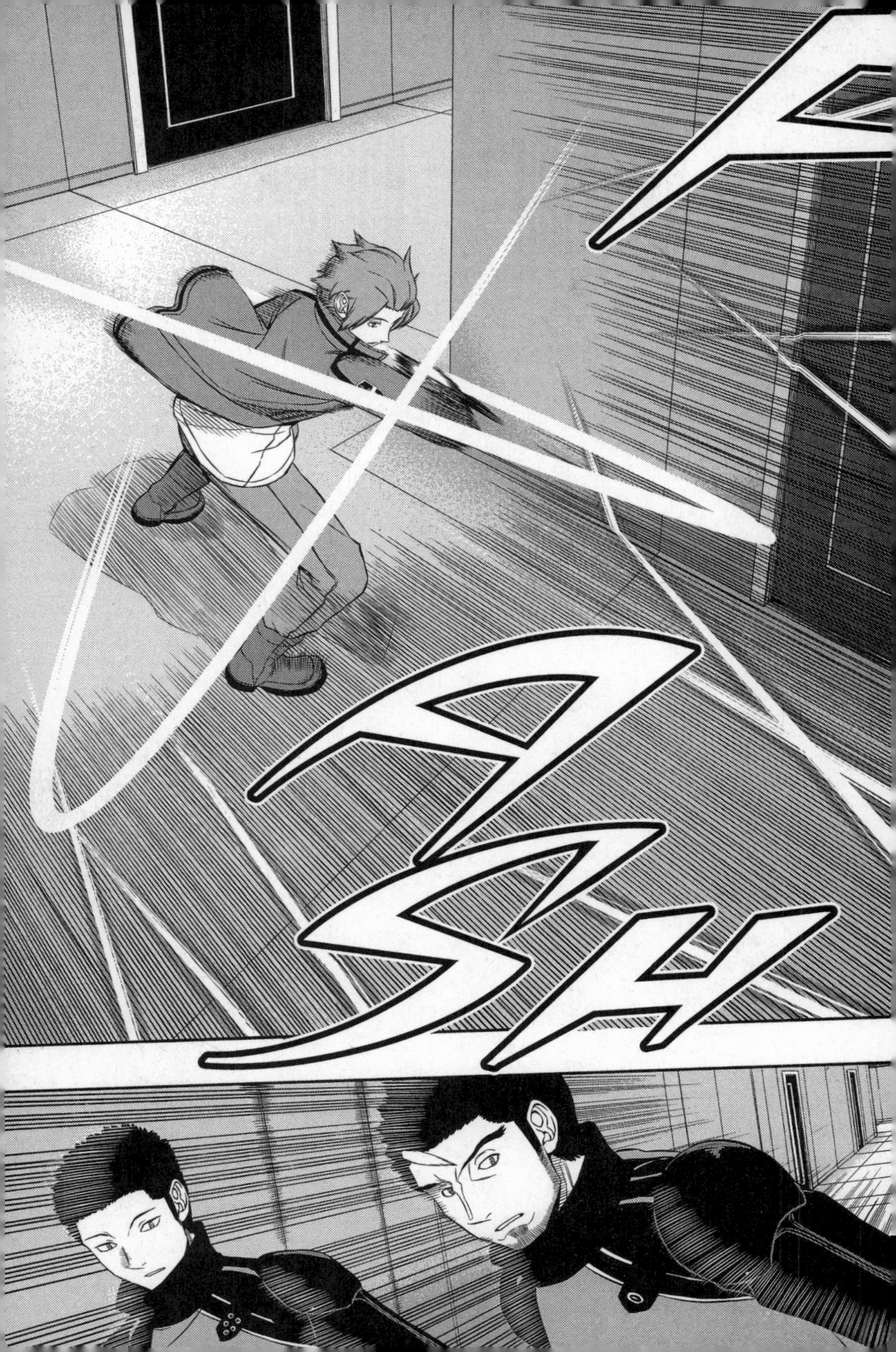
SSH

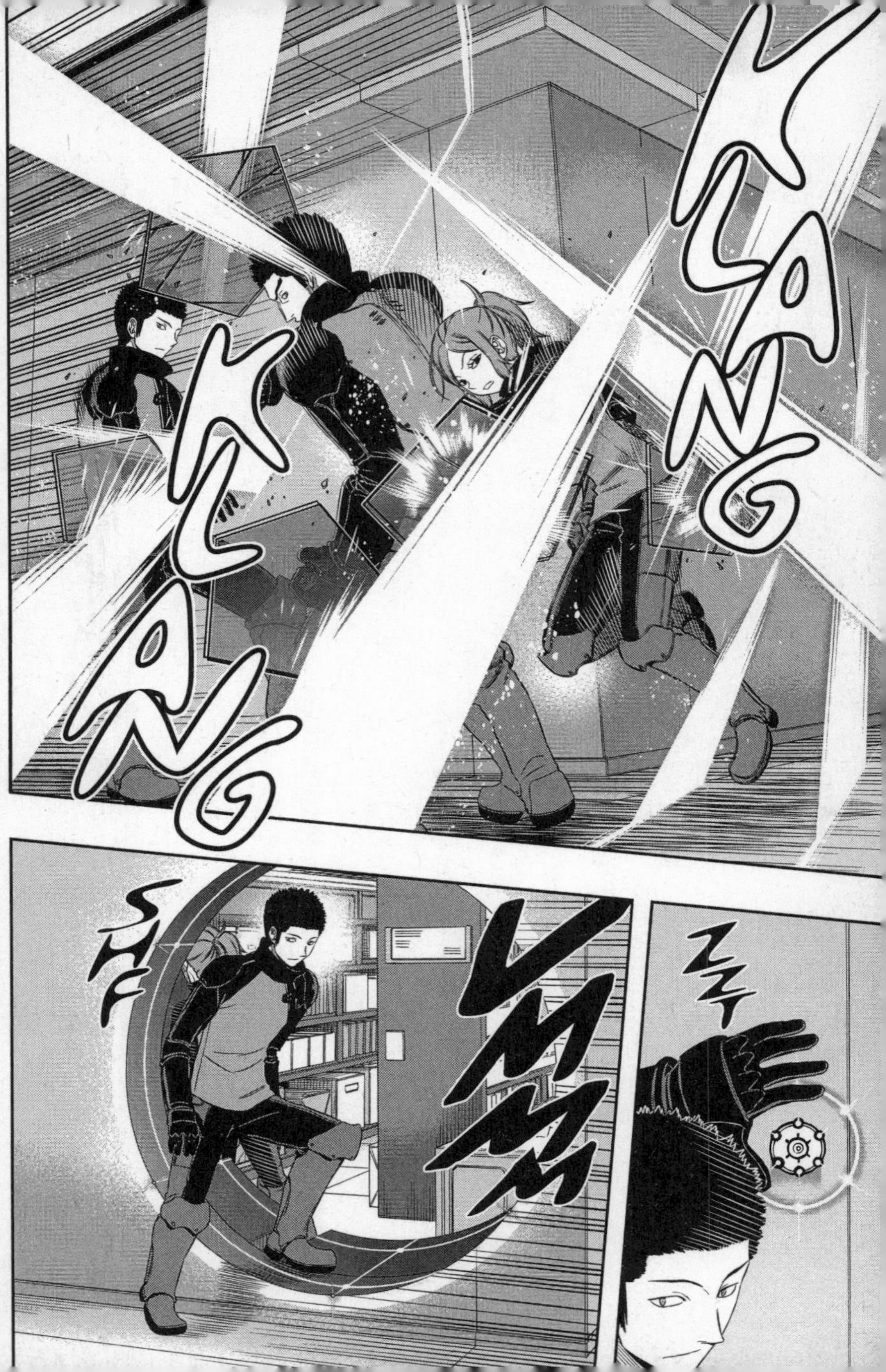
KLANG
KLANG
ZZT
VMMM
SHF

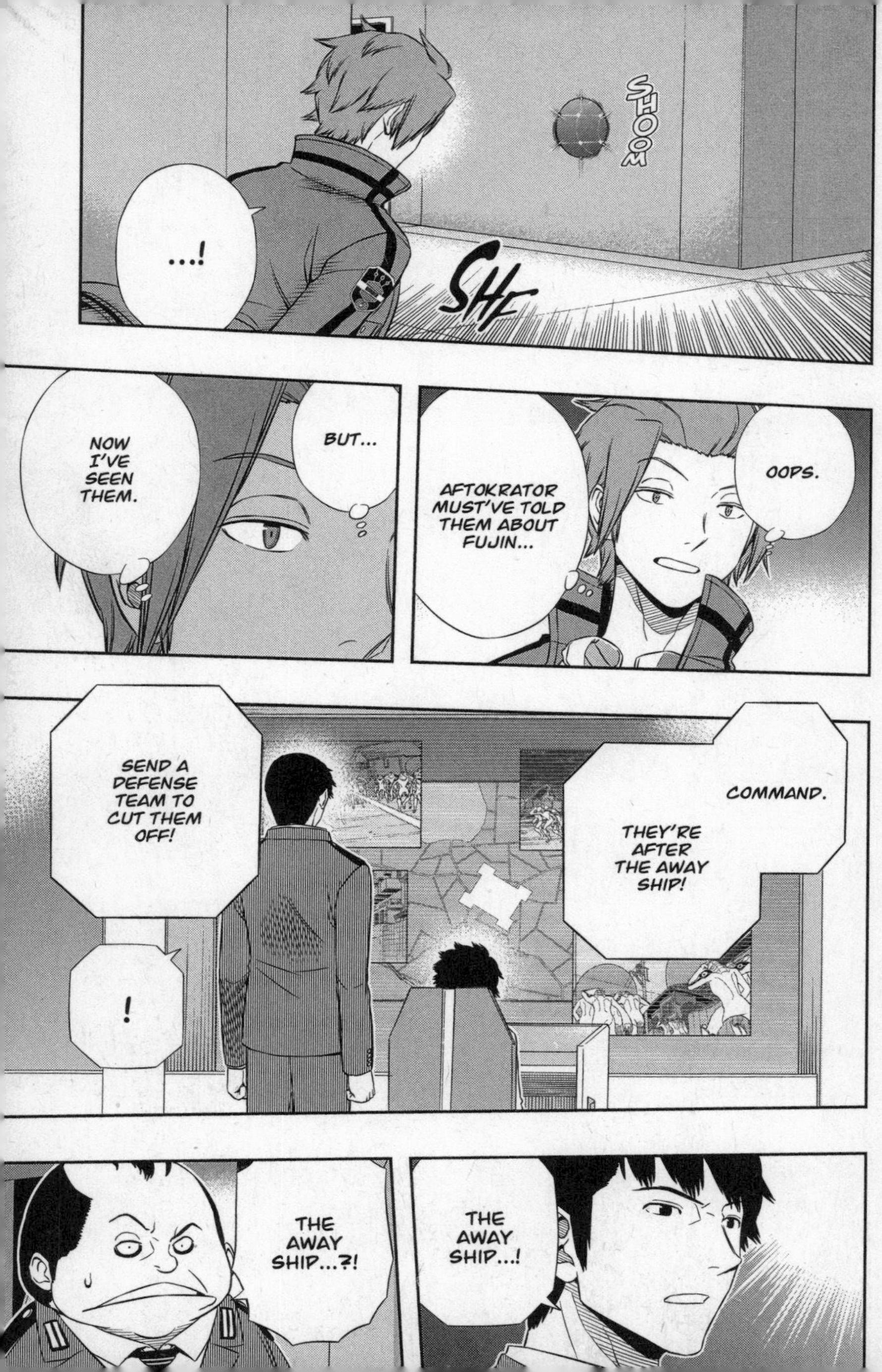
SHOOM
SHF
...!
OOPS.
AFTOKRATOR MUST'VE TOLD THEM ABOUT FUJIN...
BUT...
NOW I'VE SEEN THEM.
COMMAND.
THEY'RE AFTER THE AWAY SHIP!
SEND A DEFENSE TEAM TO CUT THEM OFF!
!
THE AWAY SHIP...!
THE AWAY SHIP...?!

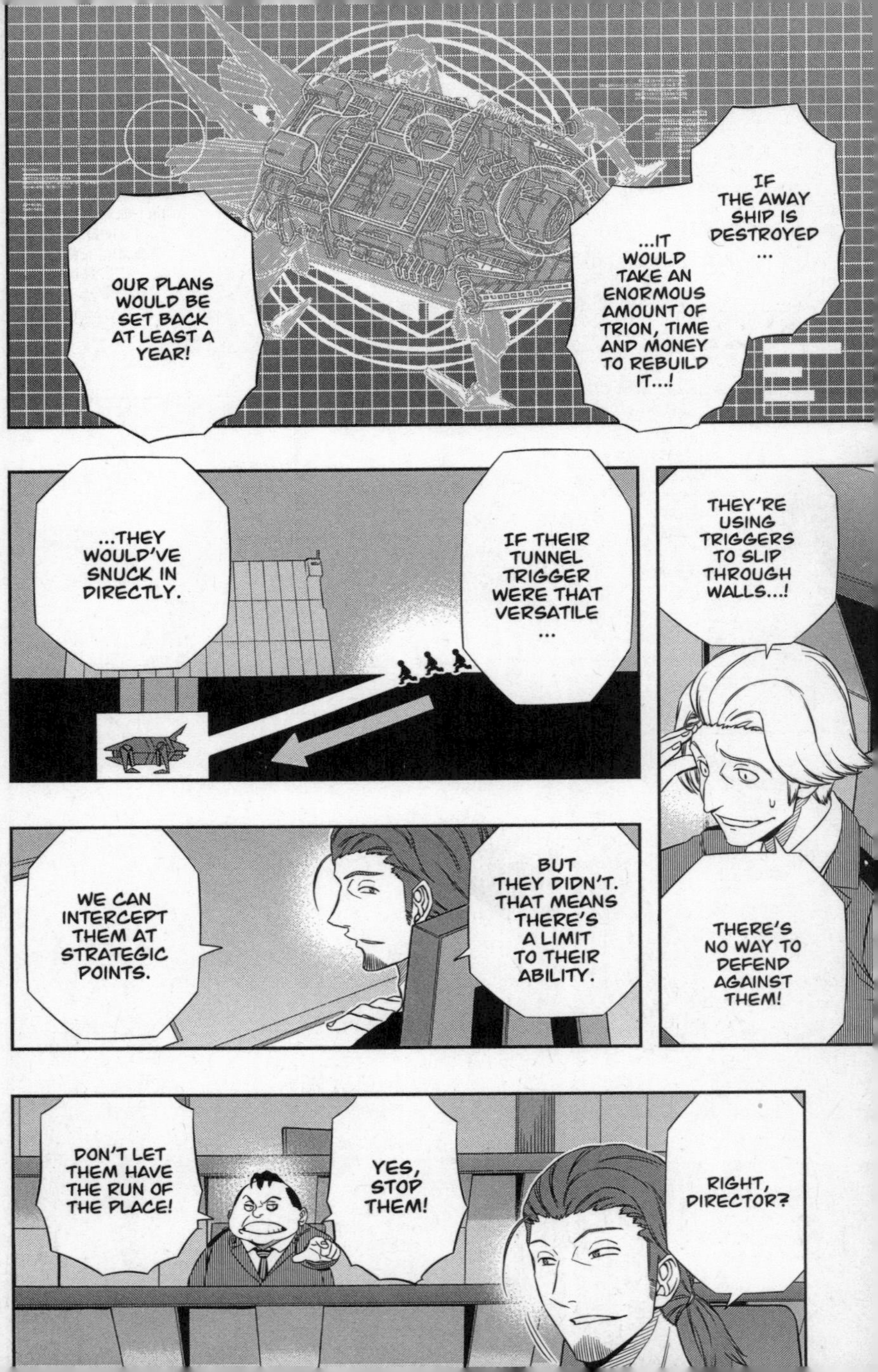
IF THE AWAY SHIP IS DESTROYED...
...IT WOULD TAKE AN ENORMOUS AMOUNT OF TRION, TIME AND MONEY TO REBUILD IT...!
OUR PLANS WOULD BE SET BACK AT LEAST A YEAR!
THEY'RE USING TRIGGERS TO SLIP THROUGH WALLS...!
THERE'S NO WAY TO DEFEND AGAINST THEM!
IF THEIR TUNNEL TRIGGER WERE THAT VERSATILE...
...THEY WOULD'VE SNUCK IN DIRECTLY.
BUT THEY DIDN'T. THAT MEANS THERE'S A LIMIT TO THEIR ABILITY.
WE CAN INTERCEPT THEM AT STRATEGIC POINTS.
RIGHT, DIRECTOR?
YES, STOP THEM!
DON'T LET THEM HAVE THE RUN OF THE PLACE!

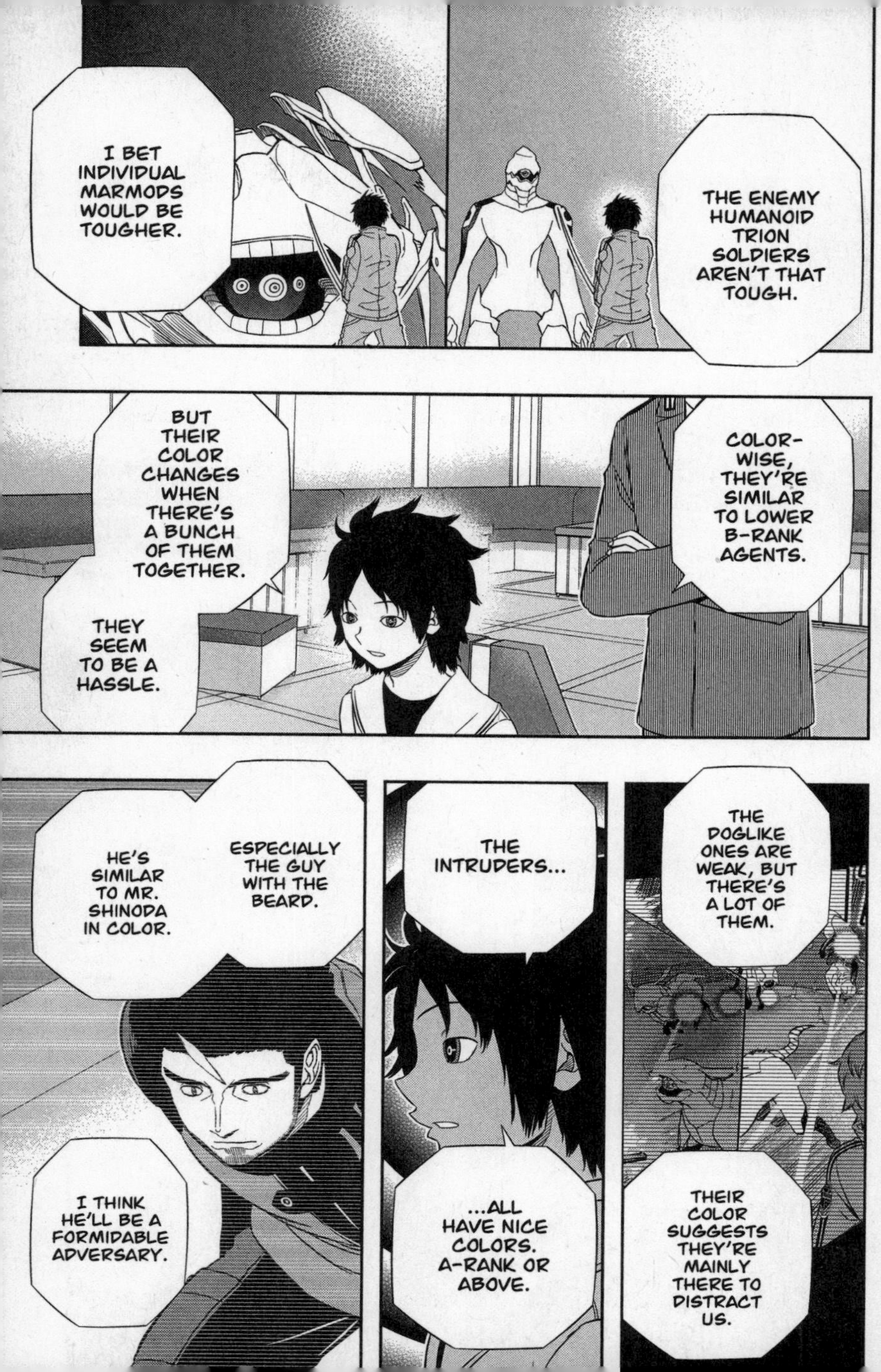
THE ENEMY HUMANOID TRION SOLDIERS AREN'T THAT TOUGH.
I BET INDIVIDUAL MARMODS WOULD BE TOUGHER.
COLOR-WISE, THEY'RE SIMILAR TO LOWER B-RANK AGENTS.
BUT THEIR COLOR CHANGES WHEN THERE'S A BUNCH OF THEM TOGETHER.
THEY SEEM TO BE A HASSLE.
THE DOGLIKE ONES ARE WEAK, BUT THERE'S A LOT OF THEM.
THEIR COLOR SUGGESTS THEY'RE MAINLY THERE TO DISTRACT US.
THE INTRUDERS...
...ALL HAVE NICE COLORS. A-RANK OR ABOVE.
ESPECIALLY THE GUY WITH THE BEARD.
HE'S SIMILAR TO MR. SHINODA IN COLOR.
I THINK HE'LL BE A FORMIDABLE ADVERSARY.

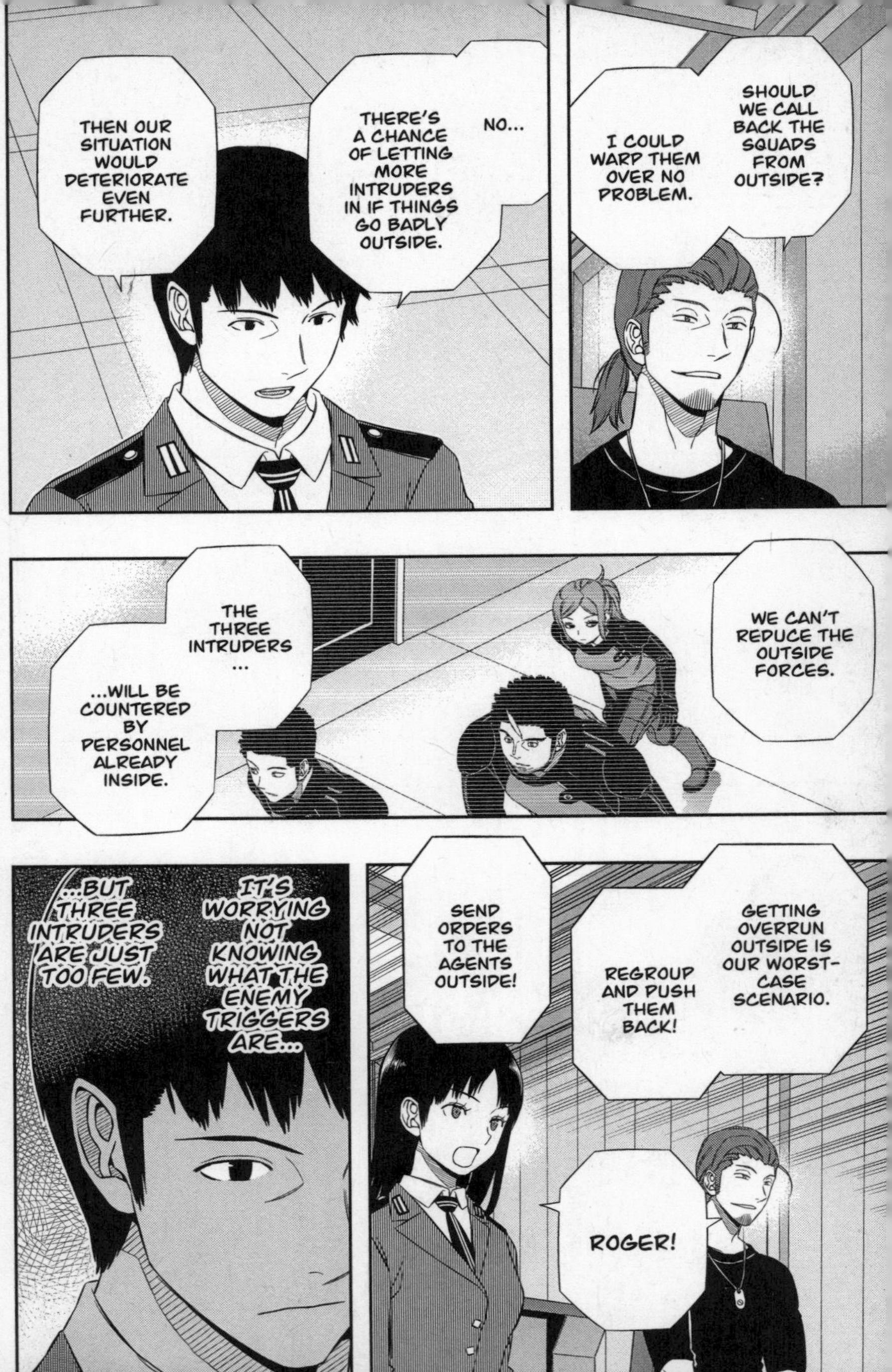
SHOULD WE CALL BACK THE SQUADS FROM OUTSIDE?
I COULD WARP THEM OVER NO PROBLEM.
NO...
THERE'S A CHANCE OF LETTING MORE INTRUDERS IN IF THINGS GO BADLY OUTSIDE.
THEN OUR SITUATION WOULD DETERIORATE EVEN FURTHER.
WE CAN'T REDUCE THE OUTSIDE FORCES.
THE THREE INTRUDERS...
...WILL BE COUNTERED BY PERSONNEL ALREADY INSIDE.
GETTING OVERRUN OUTSIDE IS OUR WORST-CASE SCENARIO.
REGROUP AND PUSH THEM BACK!
SEND ORDERS TO THE AGENTS OUTSIDE!
ROGER!
IT'S WORRYING NOT KNOWING WHAT THE ENEMY TRIGGERS ARE...
...BUT THREE INTRUDERS ARE JUST TOO FEW.

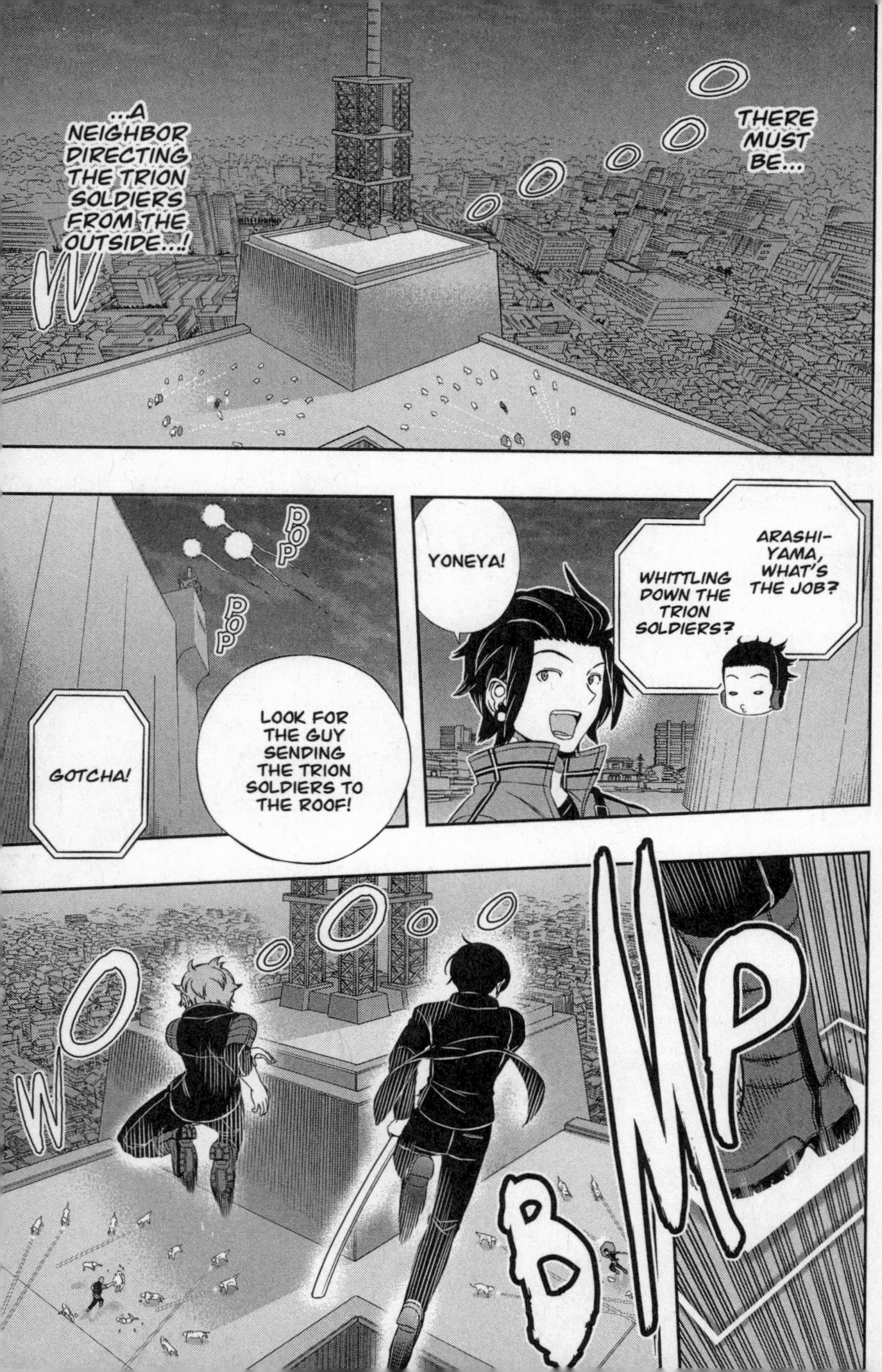
THERE MUST BE...
...A NEIGHBOR DIRECTING THE TRION SOLDIERS FROM THE OUTSIDE...!
WOOOOO
ARASHI-YAMA, WHAT'S THE JOB?
WHITTLING DOWN THE TRION SOLDIERS?
YONEYA!
POP
POP
LOOK FOR THE GUY SENDING THE TRION SOLDIERS TO THE ROOF!
GOTCHA!
BOMP
WOOOOO

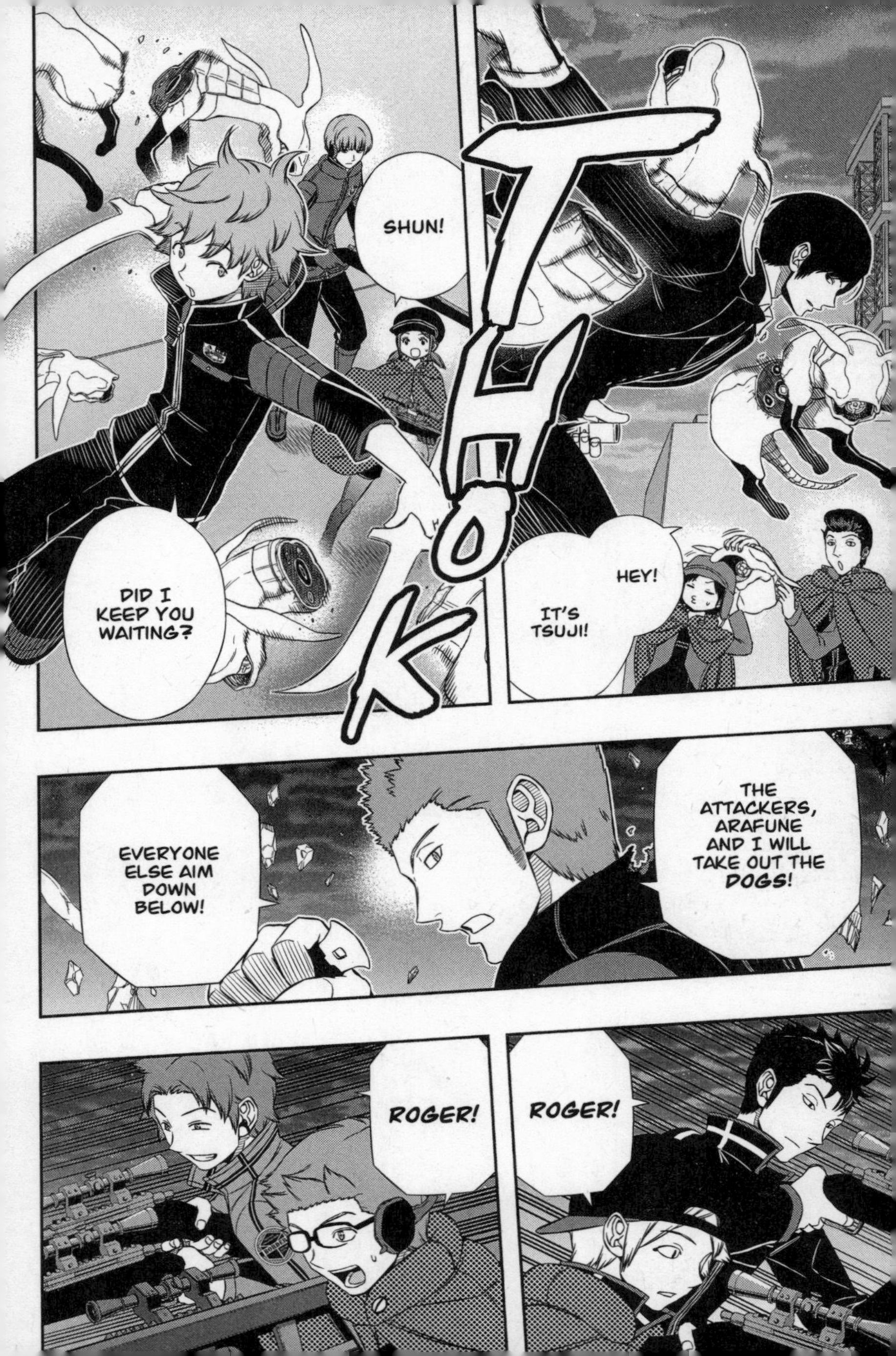
THOK
HEY!
IT'S TSUJI!
SHUN!
DID I KEEP YOU WAITING?
THE ATTACKERS, ARAFUNE AND I WILL TAKE OUT THE DOGS!
EVERYONE ELSE AIM DOWN BELOW!
ROGER!
ROGER!

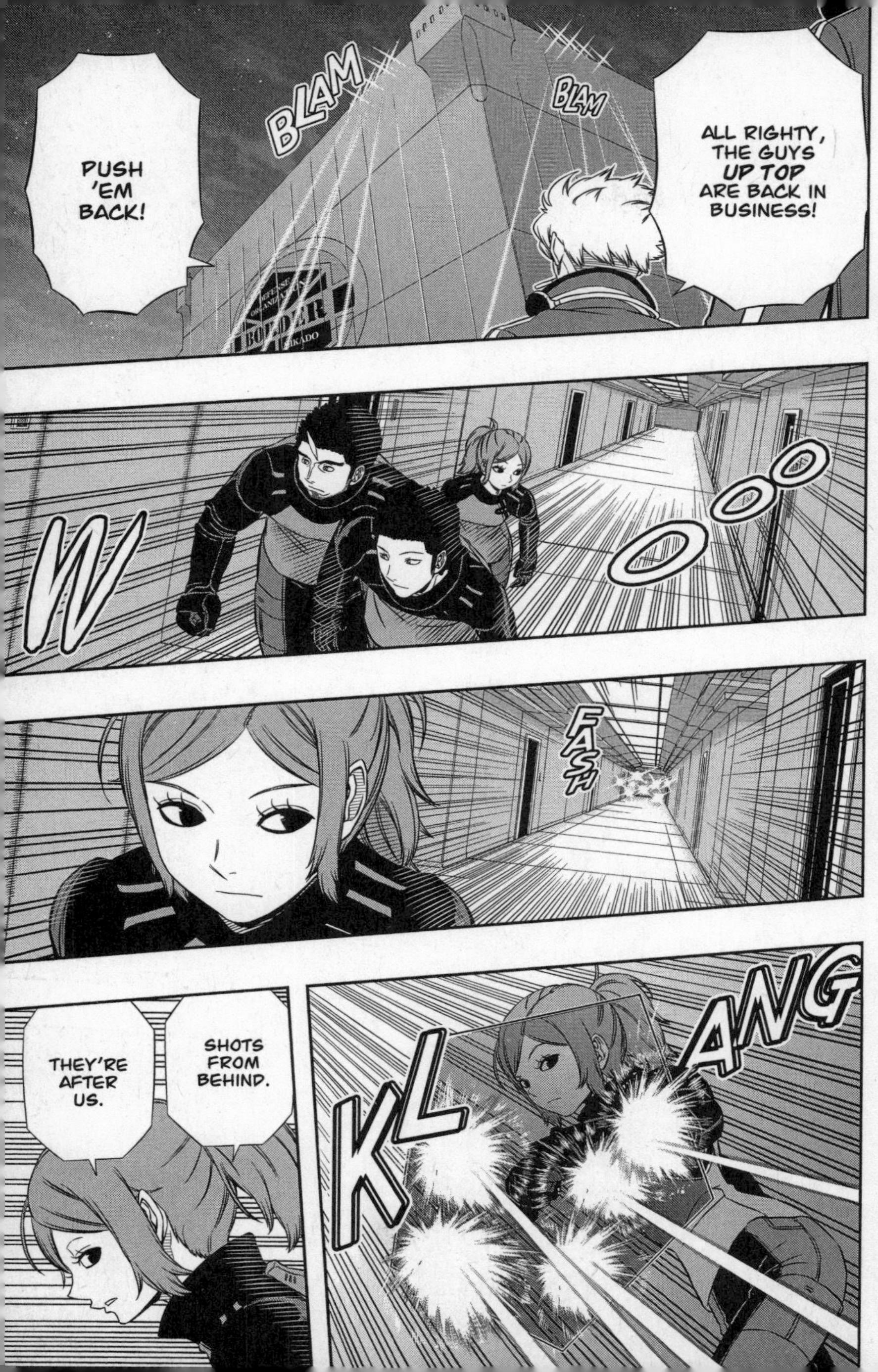
ALL RIGHTY, THE GUYS *UP TOP* ARE BACK IN BUSINESS!
BLAM
BLAM
PUSH 'EM BACK!
BORDER
WOOOO
FASH
KLANG
SHOTS FROM BEHIND.
THEY'RE AFTER US.

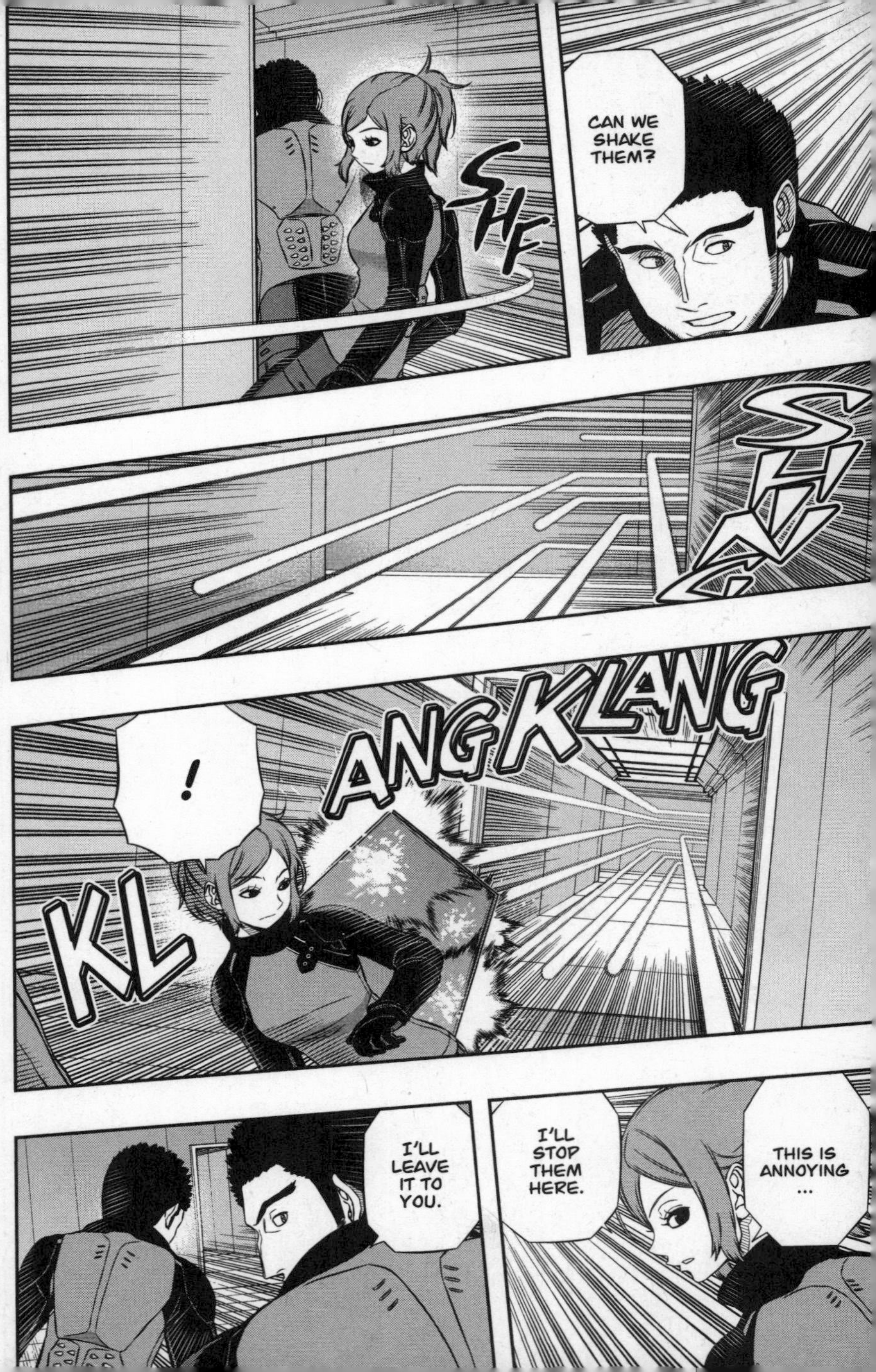
CAN WE SHAKE THEM?
SHF
SHNG
KLANG KLANG
!
THIS IS ANNOYING ...
I'LL STOP THEM HERE.
I'LL LEAVE IT TO YOU.

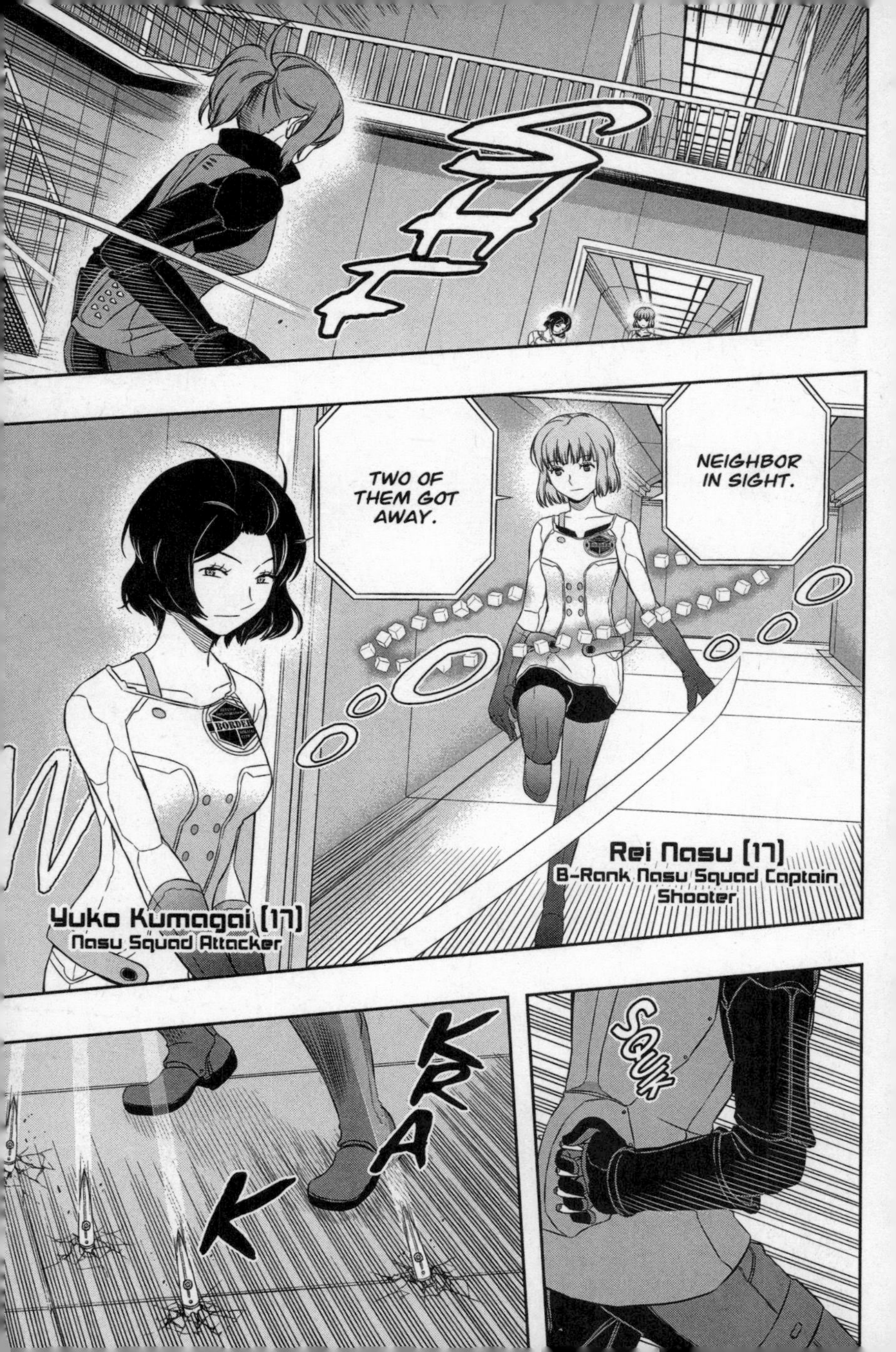
SHF
NEIGHBOR IN SIGHT.
TWO OF THEM GOT AWAY.
Rei Nasu (17)
B-Rank Nasu Squad Captain
Shooter
Yuko Kumagai (17)
Nasu Squad Attacker
SQUIK
KRAK

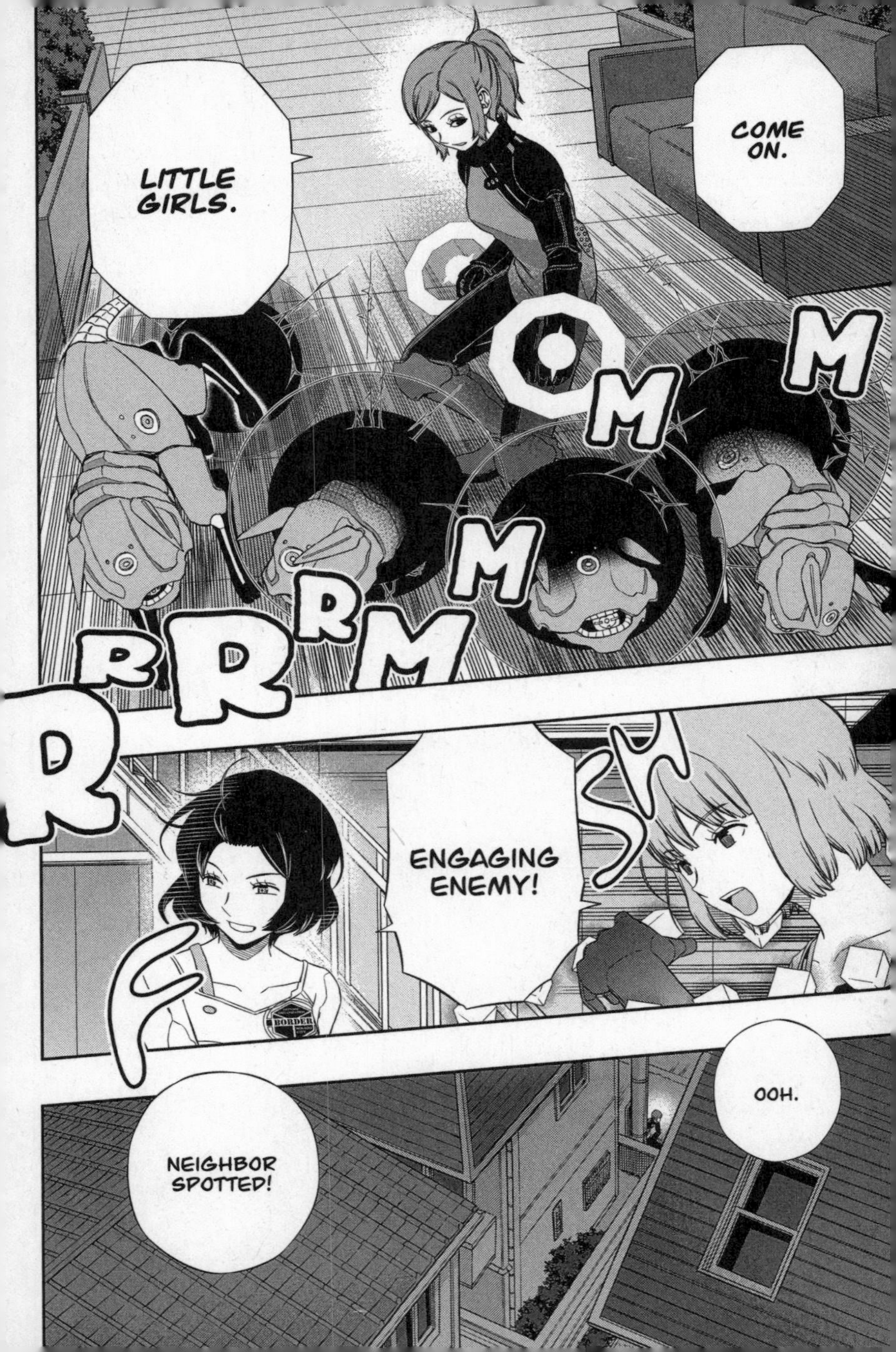
COME ON.
LITTLE GIRLS.
ENGAGING ENEMY!
OOH.
NEIGHBOR SPOTTED!
BORDER

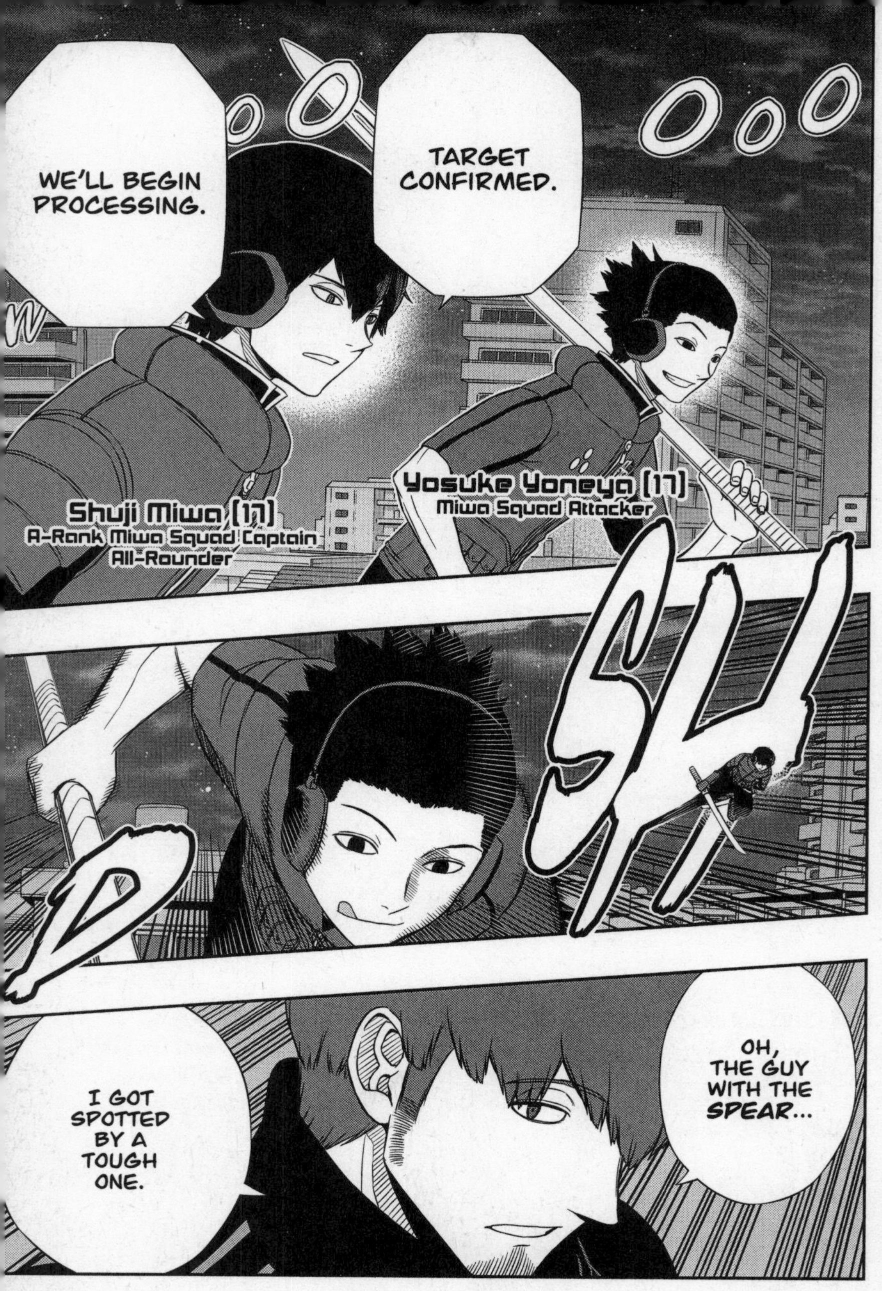
TARGET CONFIRMED.
WE'LL BEGIN PROCESSING.
Yosuke Yoneya (17)
Miwa Squad Attacker
Shuji Miwa (17)
A-Rank Miwa Squad Captain
All-Rounder
SH
D
OH, THE GUY WITH THE SPEAR...
I GOT SPOTTED BY A TOUGH ONE.

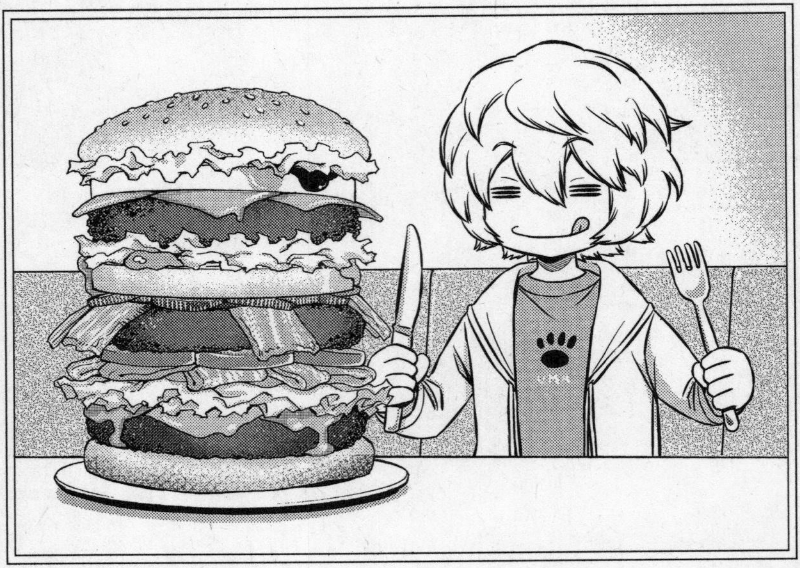

■ 2016 *Weekly Shonen Jump* 21/22 combined issue cover

This was for the 21/22 cover illustration. The concept was to create a complete puzzle. Each piece depicts a *Shonen Jump* character doing something for Golden Week. The assigned task for *World Trigger* was "Yuma taking on a giant hamburger." That's exactly what this is!

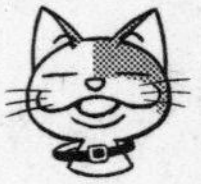

Chapter 126
Galopoula: Part 5

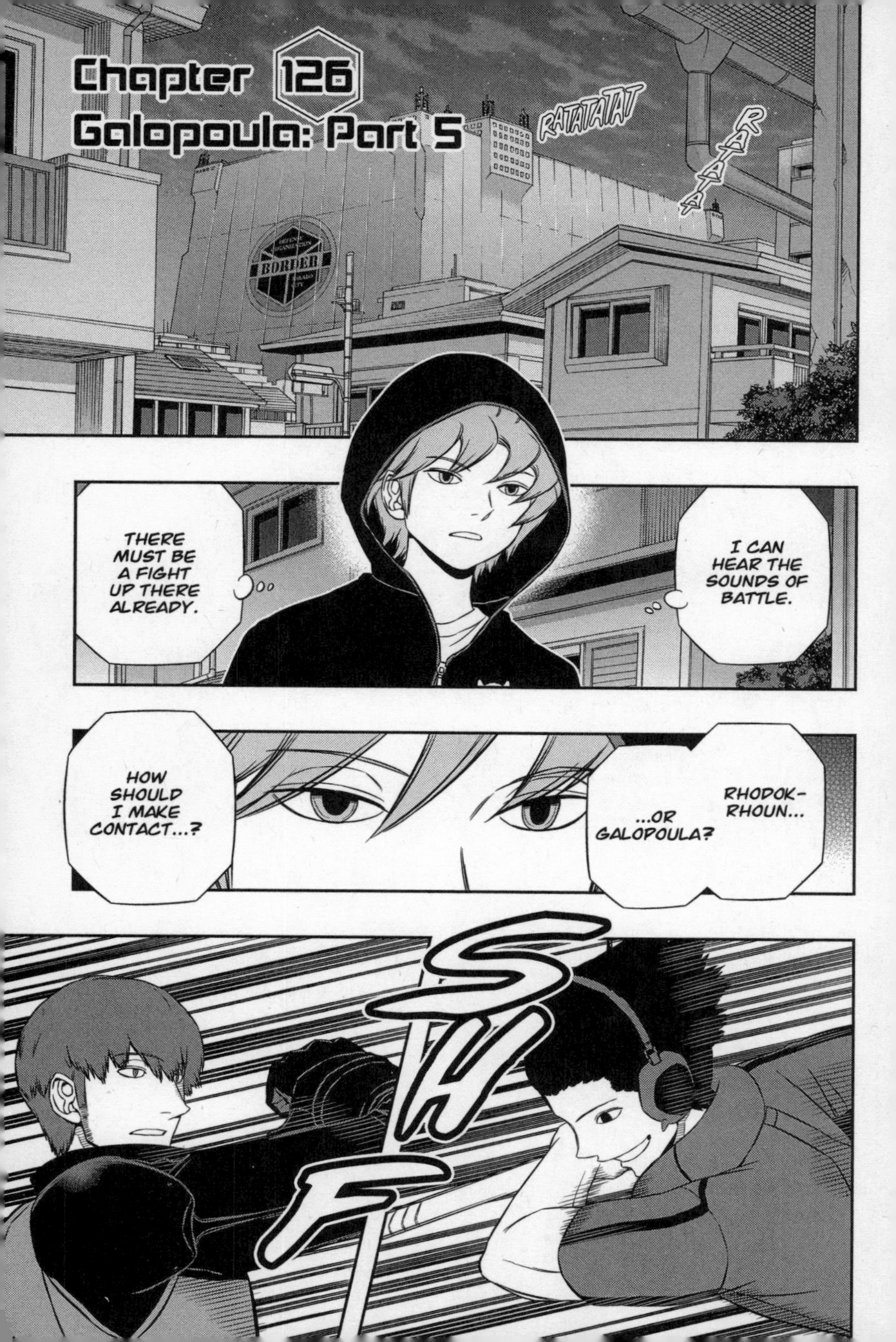
RATATATA
RATATATAT
I CAN HEAR THE SOUNDS OF BATTLE.
THERE MUST BE A FIGHT UP THERE ALREADY.
RHODOK-RHOUN...
...OR GALOPOULA?
HOW SHOULD I MAKE CONTACT...?
SHF

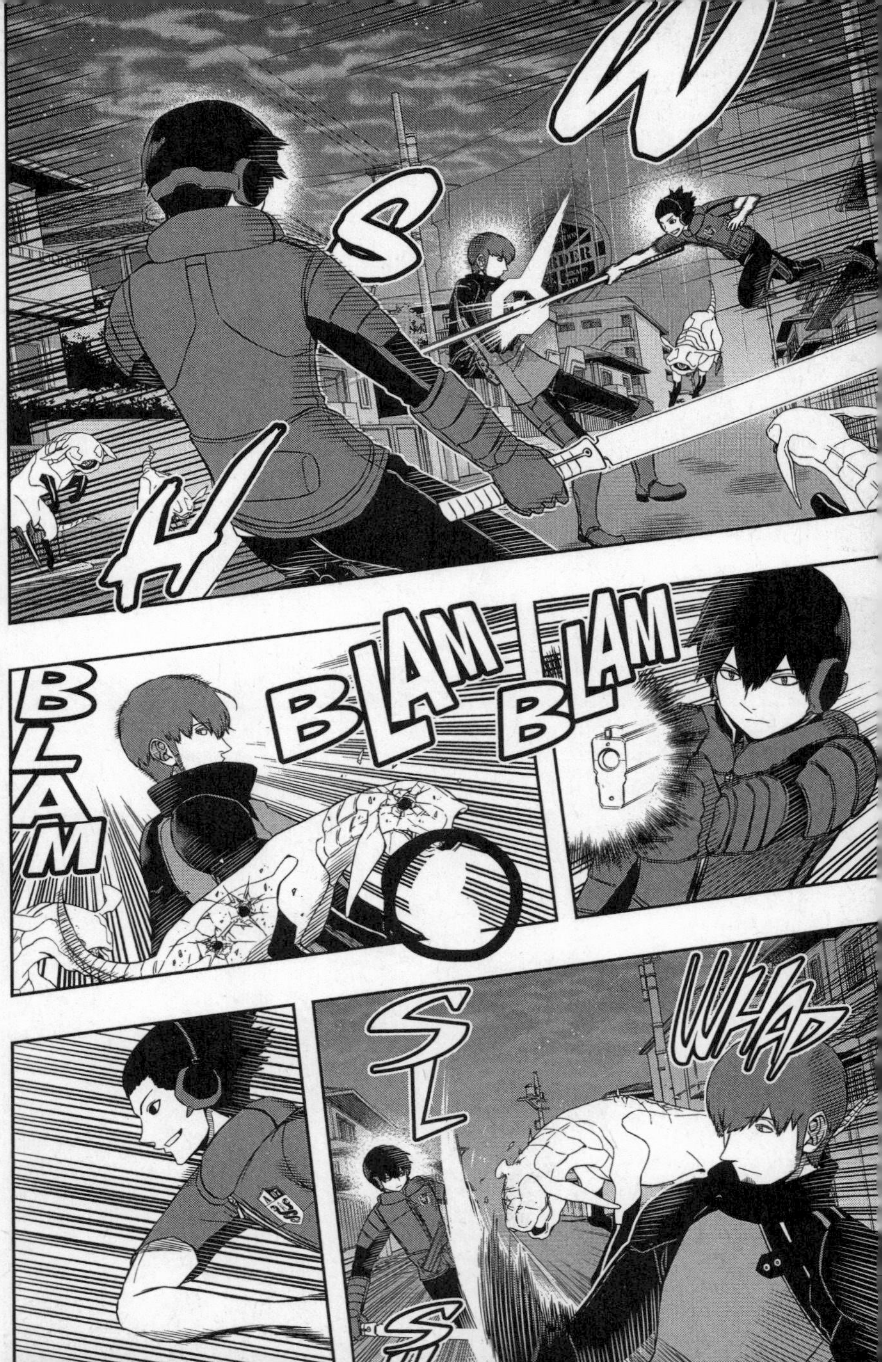

W
S
H
BLAM
BLAM
BLAM
WHAP
S
L
S

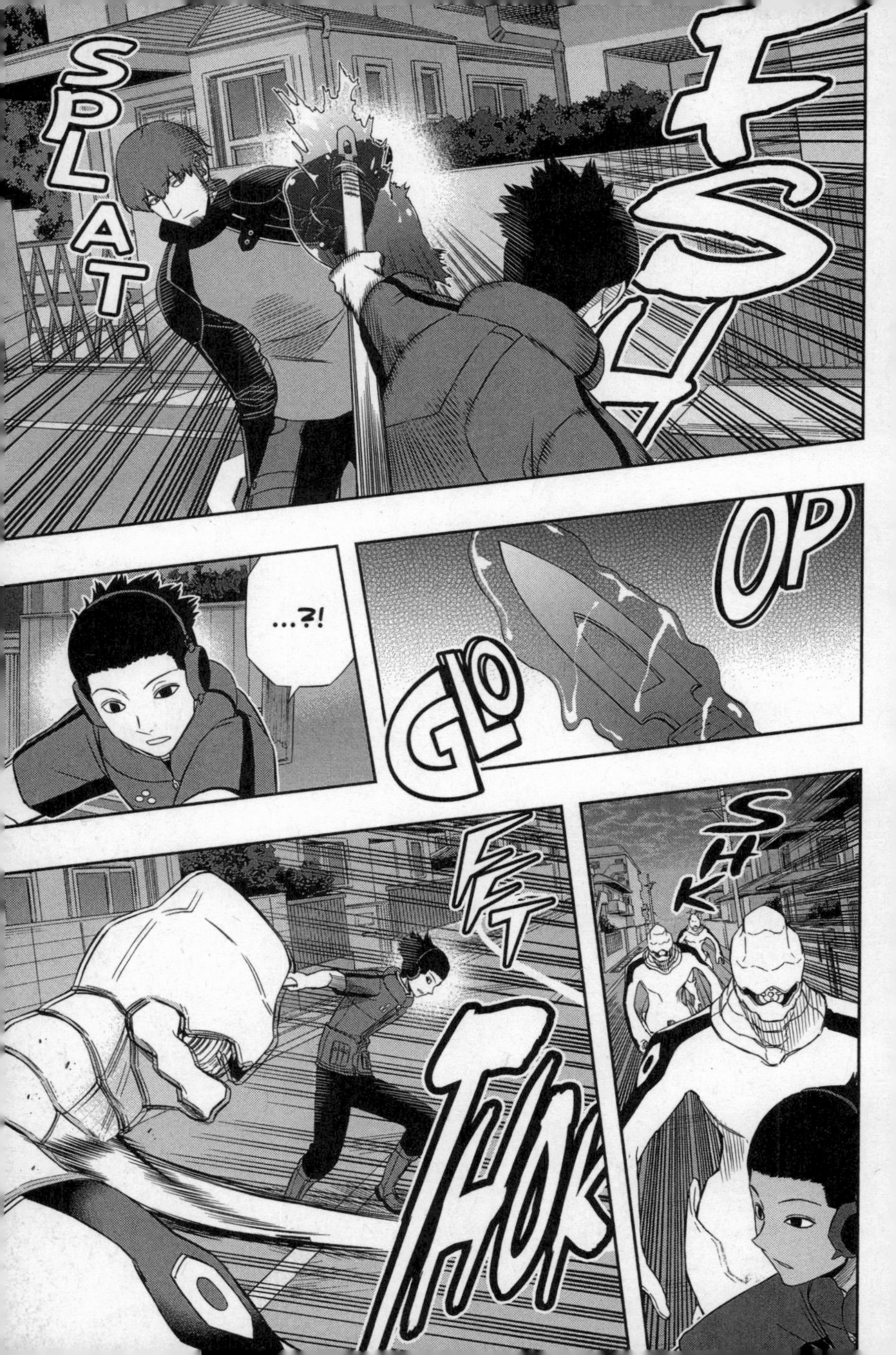
SPLAT
GLO
OP
...?!
SHK
FFT
THOK

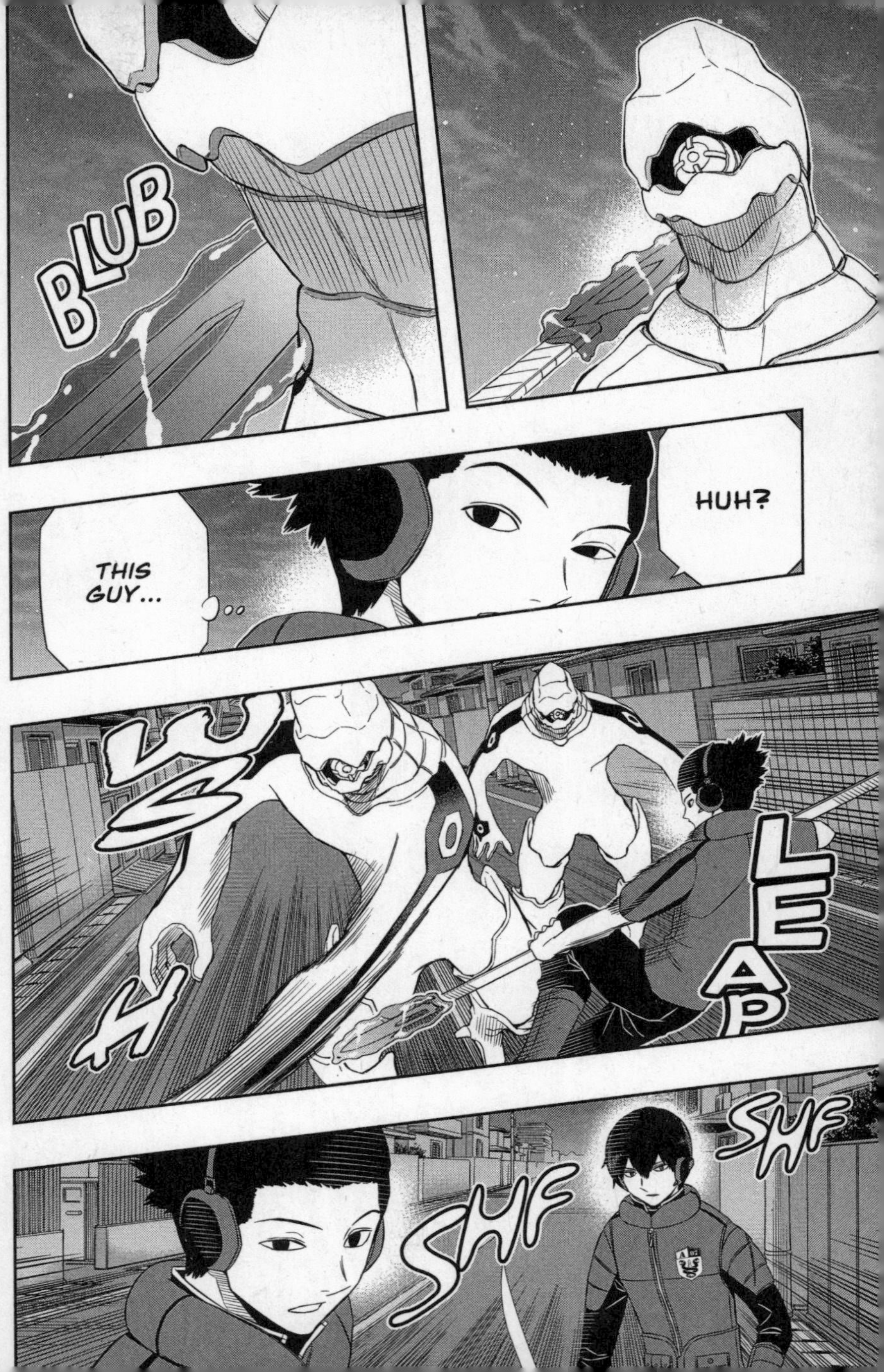
BLUB
HUH?
THIS GUY...
LEAP
SHF
SHF

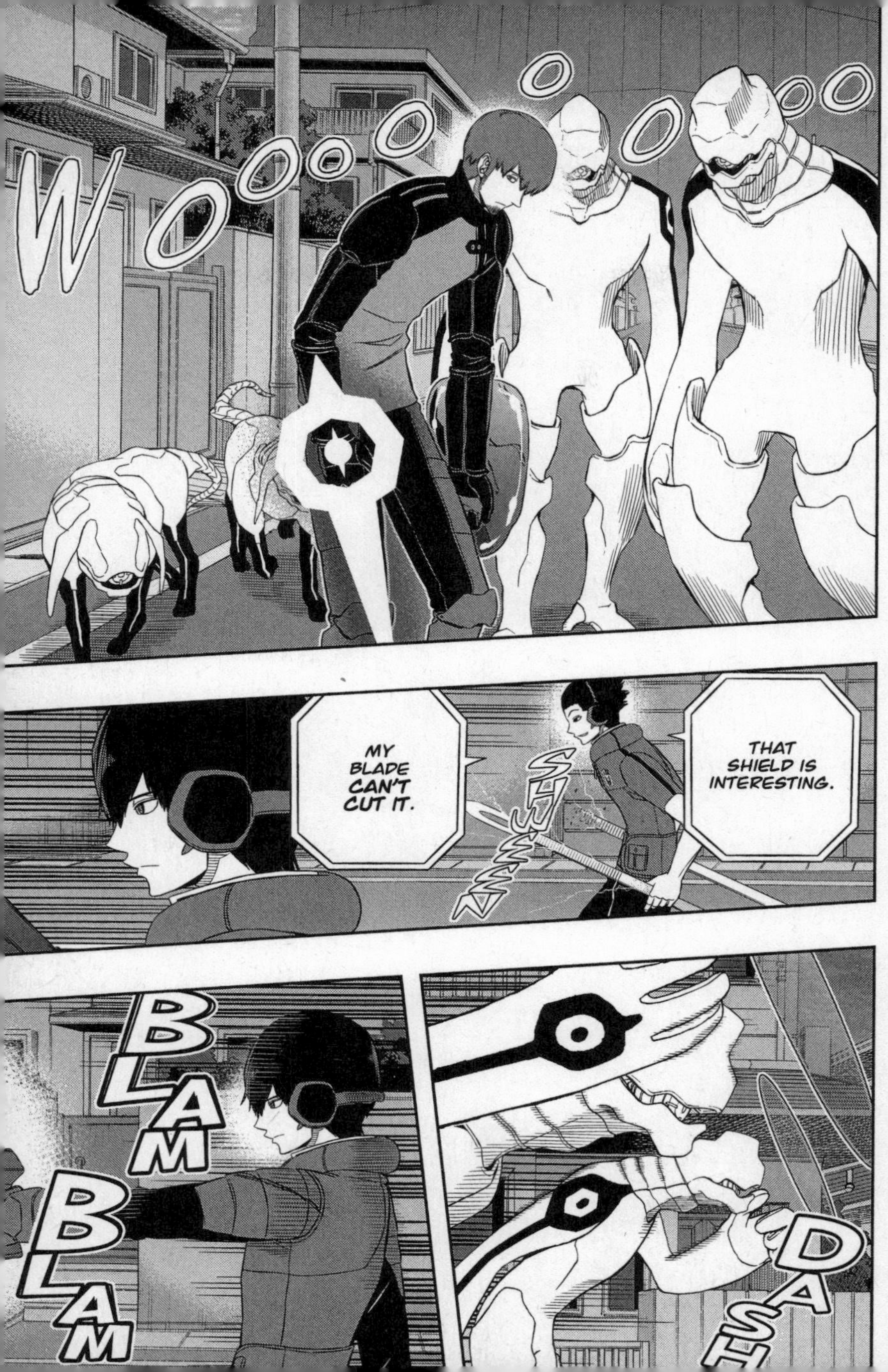
WOOOOOOOOOOO
THAT SHIELD IS INTERESTING.
SHUWWWN
MY BLADE CAN'T CUT IT.
DASH
BLAM
BLAM

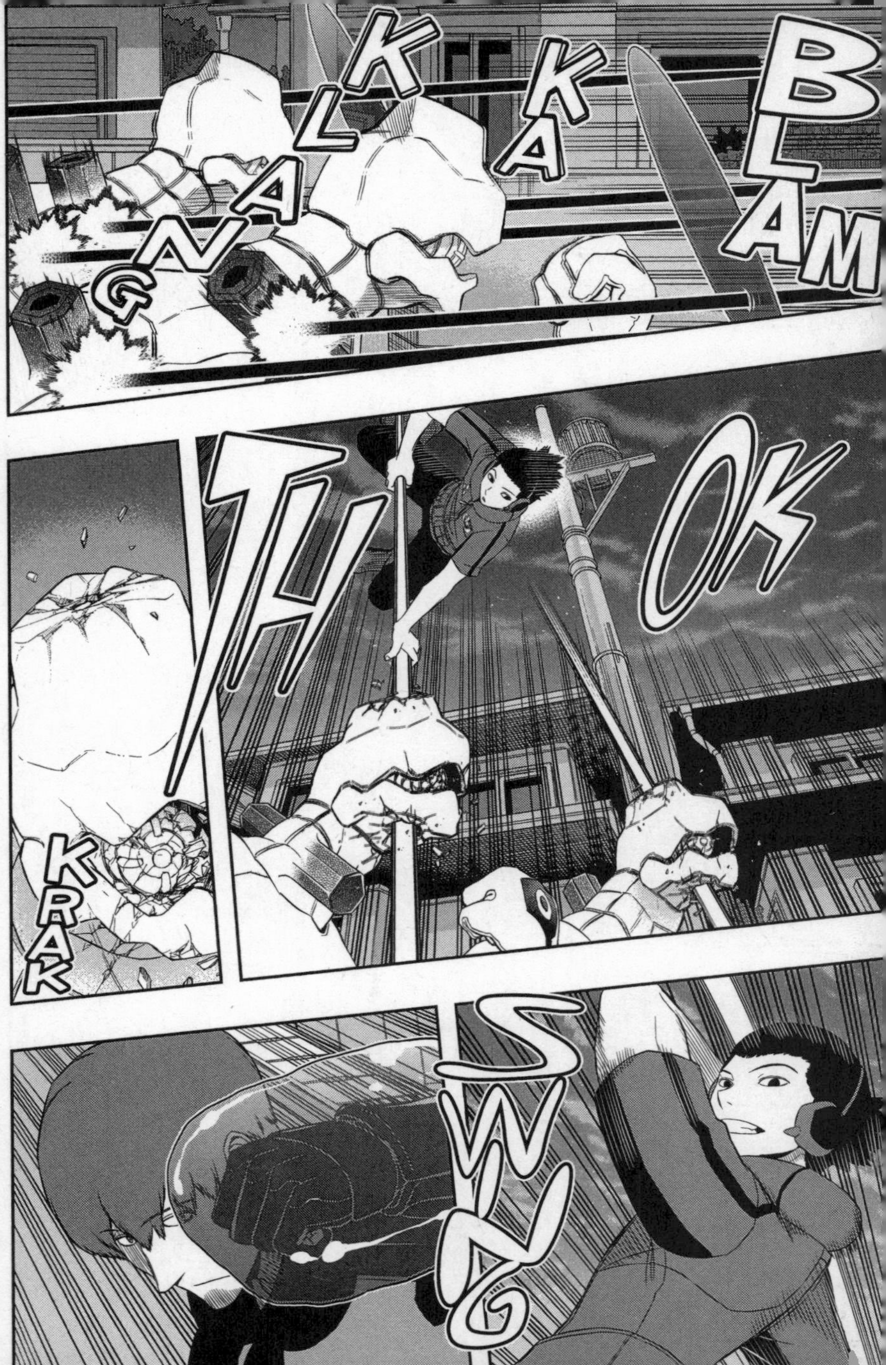

BLAM
KA
KLANG
THOK
KRAK
SWING

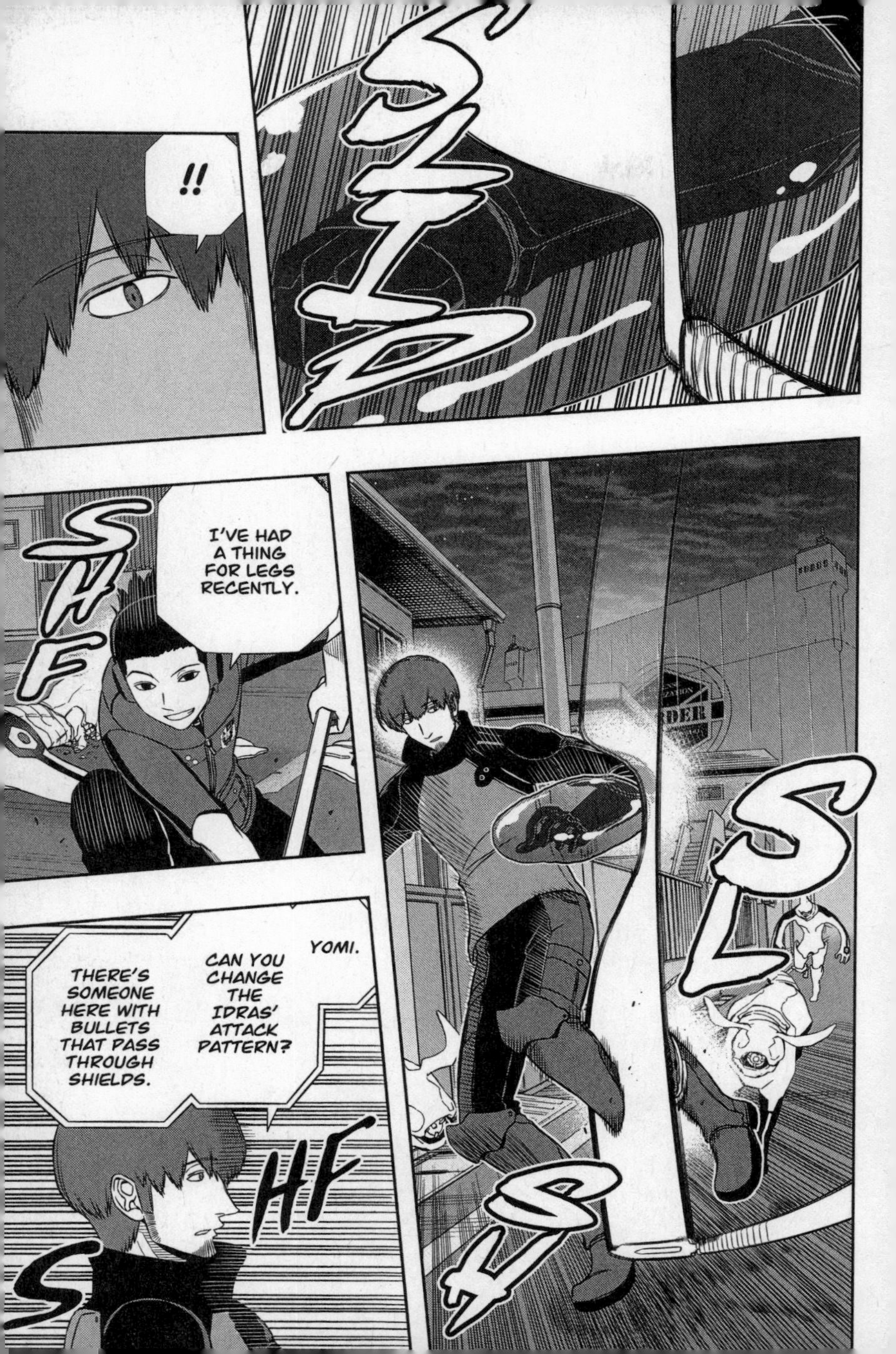
!!
SHF
I'VE HAD A THING FOR LEGS RECENTLY.
YOMI.
CAN YOU CHANGE THE IDRAS' ATTACK PATTERN?
THERE'S SOMEONE HERE WITH BULLETS THAT PASS THROUGH SHIELDS.
SHF

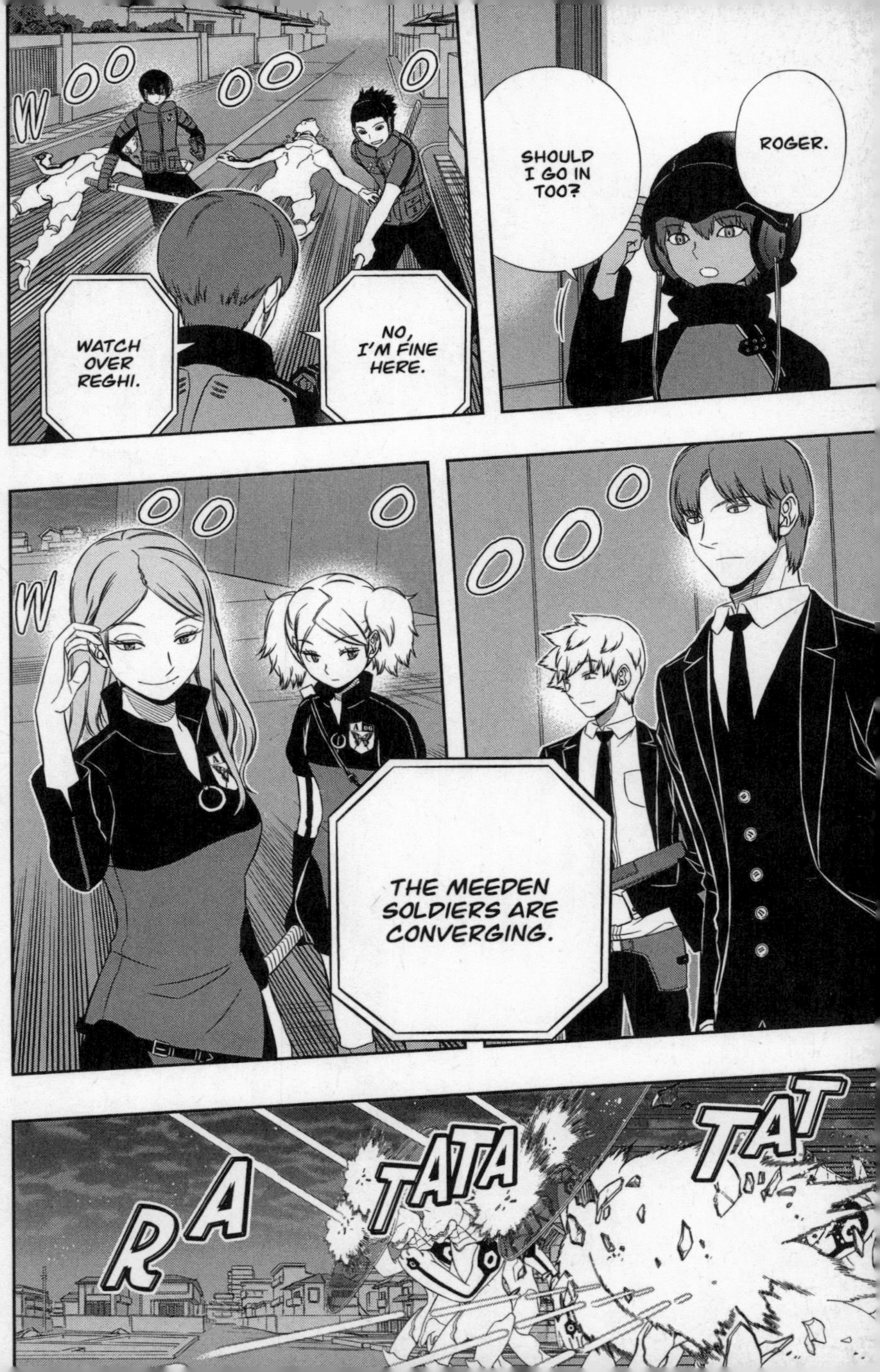

ROGER.
SHOULD I GO IN TOO?
WOOOOO
NO, I'M FINE HERE.
WATCH OVER REGHI.
OOOO
WOOO
THE MEEDEN SOLDIERS ARE CONVERGING.
RATATATAT

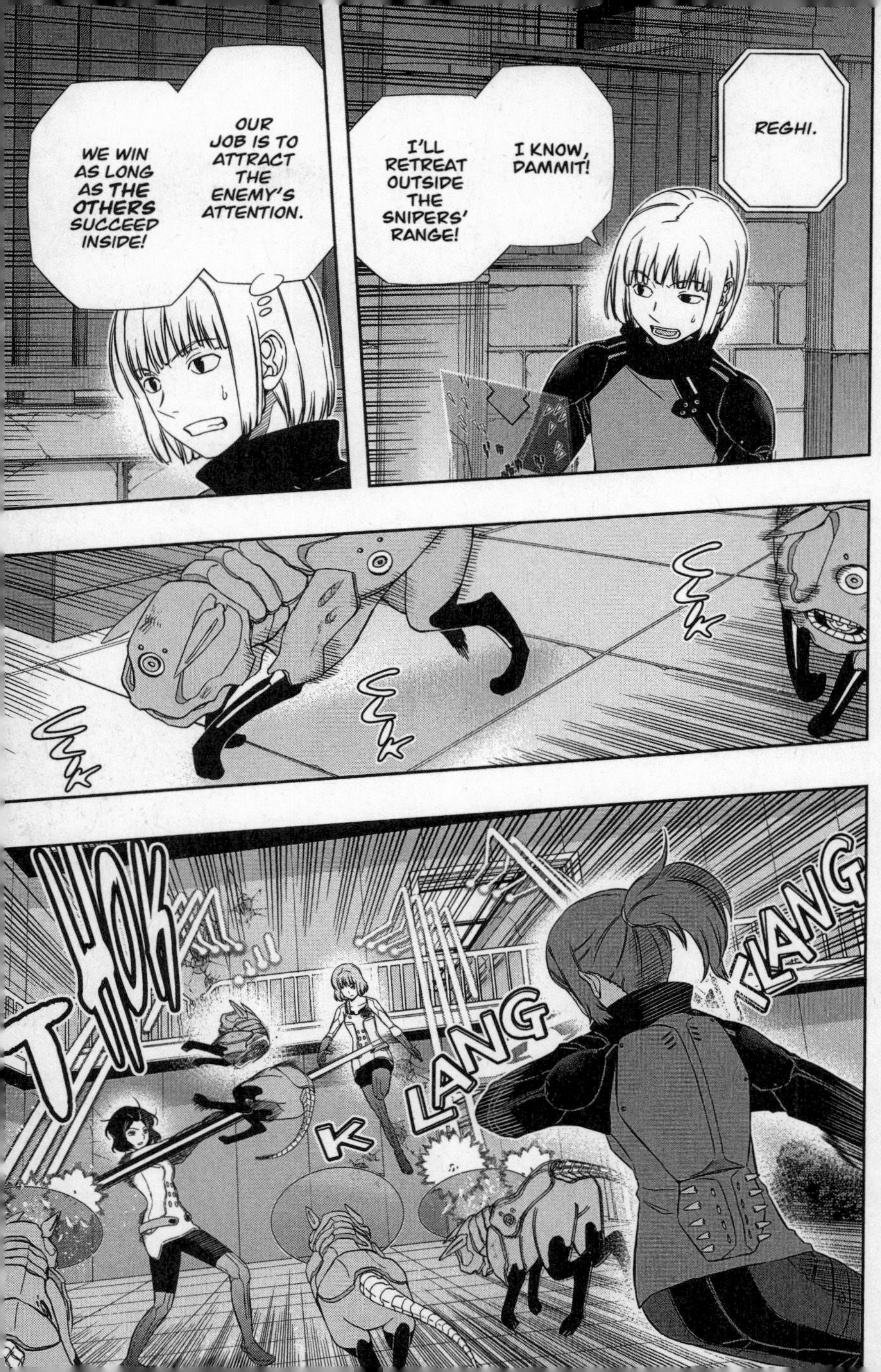
REGHI.
I KNOW, DAMMIT!
I'LL RETREAT OUTSIDE THE SNIPERS' RANGE!
OUR JOB IS TO ATTRACT THE ENEMY'S ATTENTION.
WE WIN AS LONG AS THE OTHERS SUCCEED INSIDE!
KLANG
K LANG
THOK

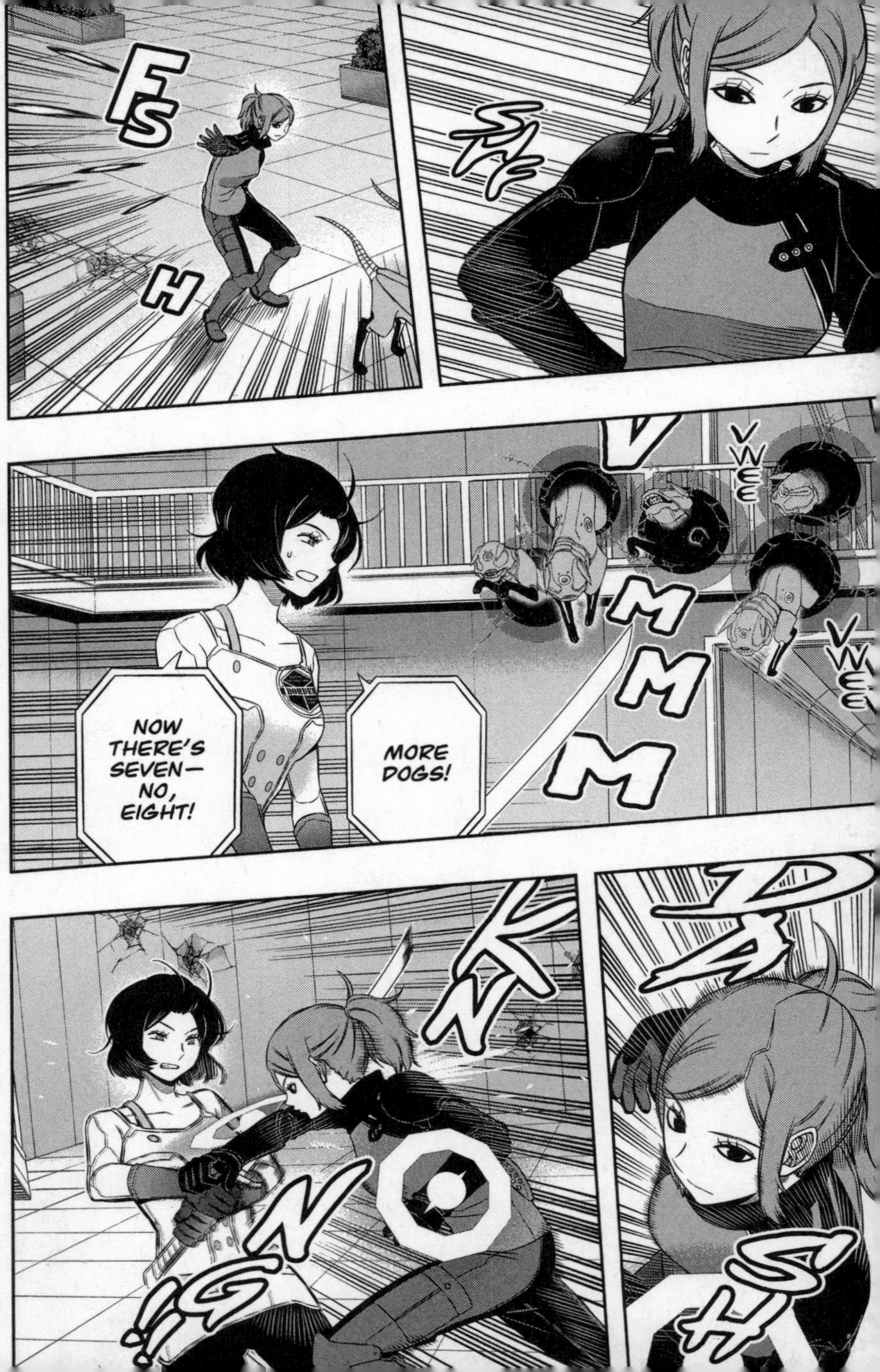
SHF
FS
H
VWEE
VWEE
VMMM
MORE DOGS!
NOW THERE'S SEVEN— NO, EIGHT!
SH
KN
NG!!

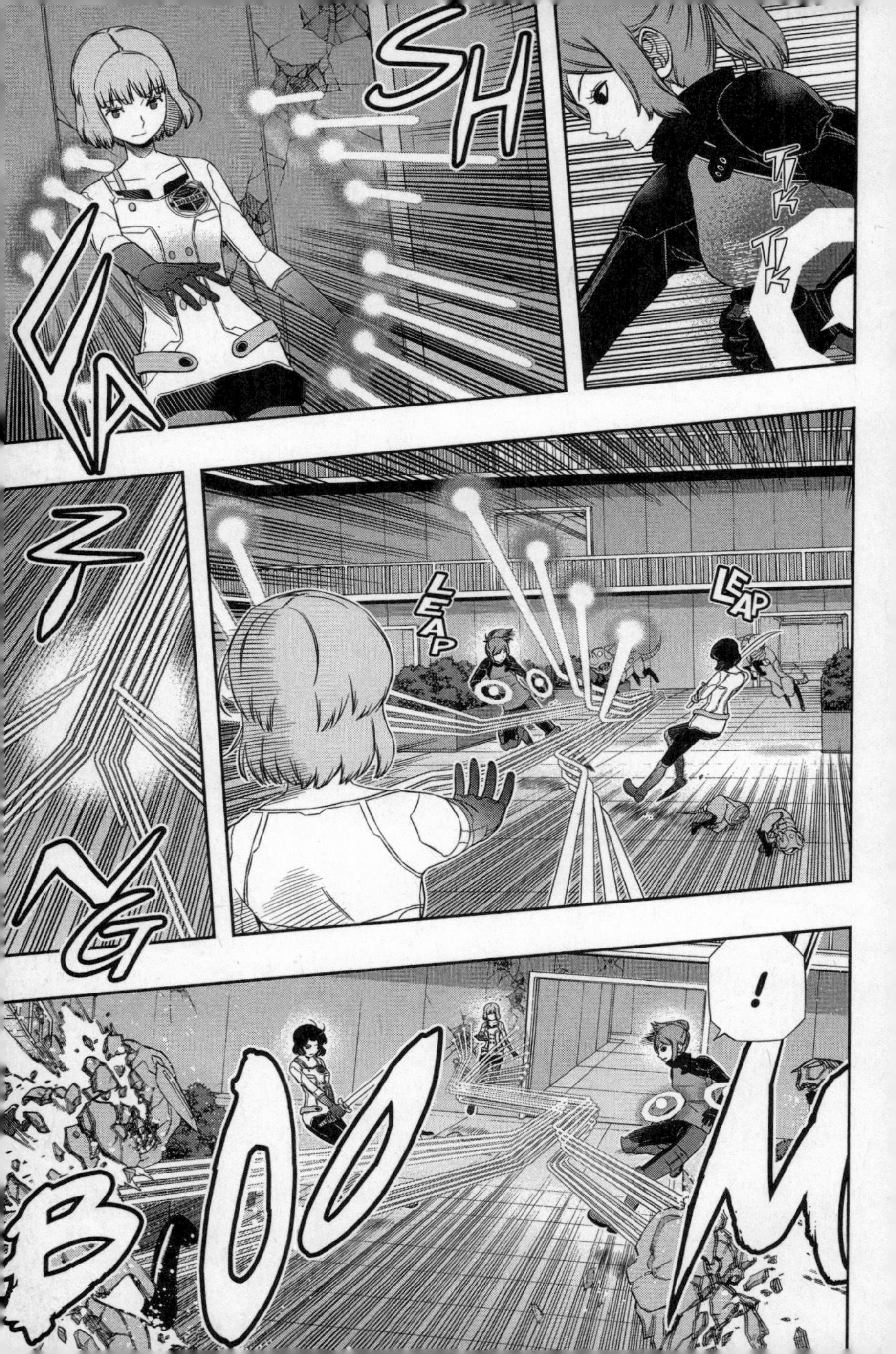

TIK
TIK
SH
KA
ZANG
LEAP
LEAP
!
BOOM

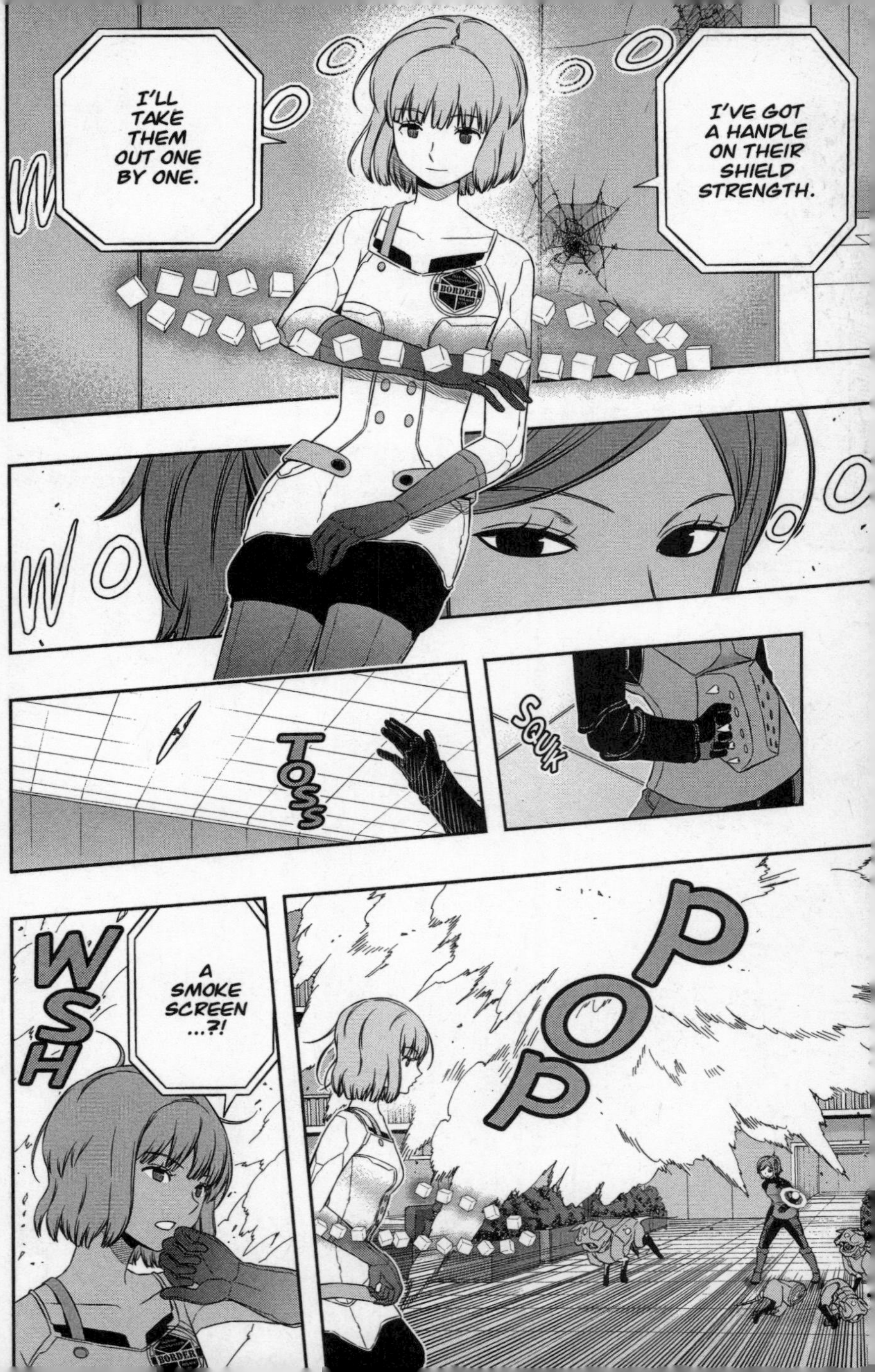
I'VE GOT A HANDLE ON THEIR SHIELD STRENGTH.
I'LL TAKE THEM OUT ONE BY ONE.
WOOOOO
WOOOO
SQUK
TOSS
POP
WSH
A SMOKE SCREEN ...?!

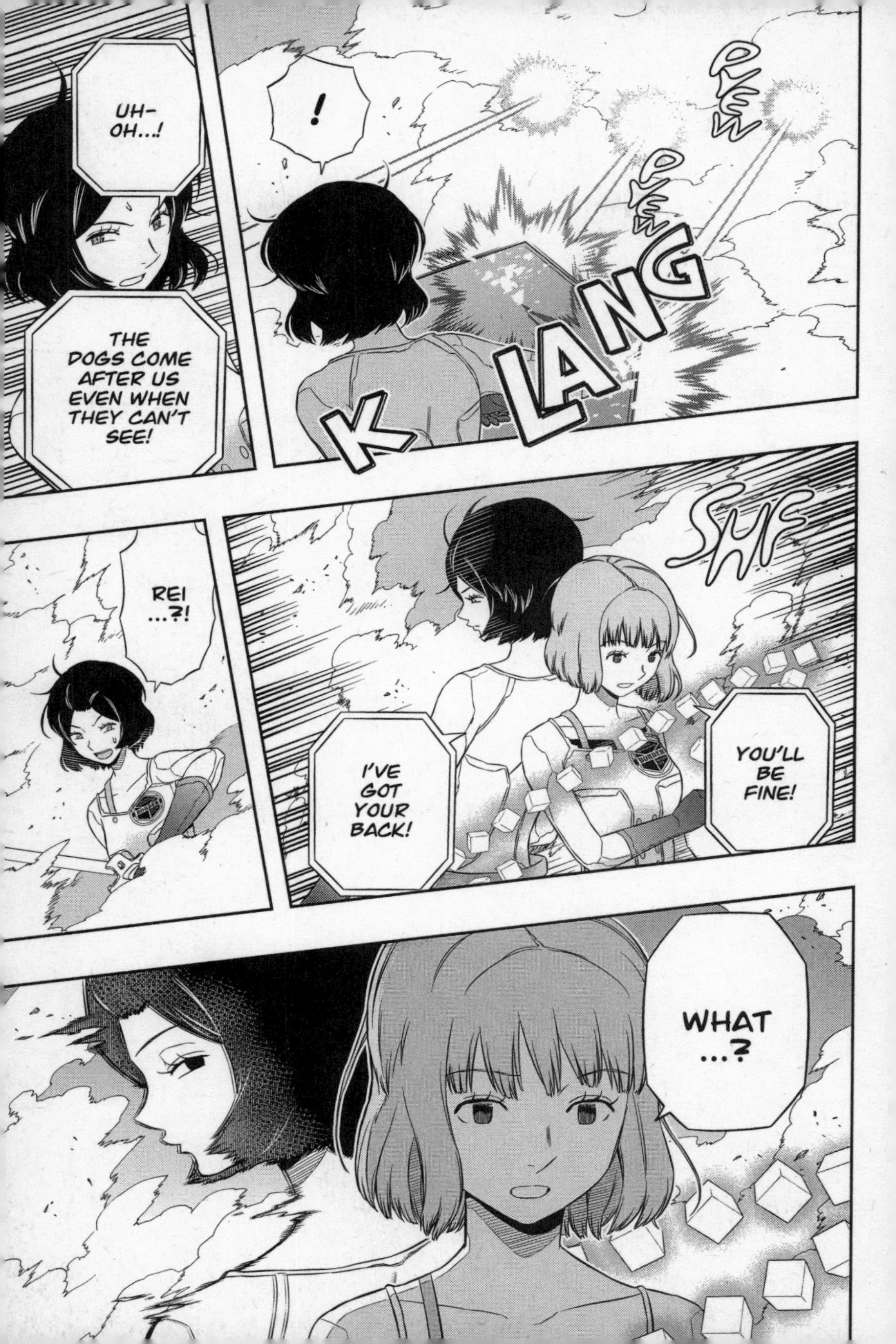
PYEW
PYEW
!
KLANG
UH-OH...!
THE DOGS COME AFTER US EVEN WHEN THEY CAN'T SEE!
SHF
YOU'LL BE FINE!
I'VE GOT YOUR BACK!
REI ...?!
WHAT ...?

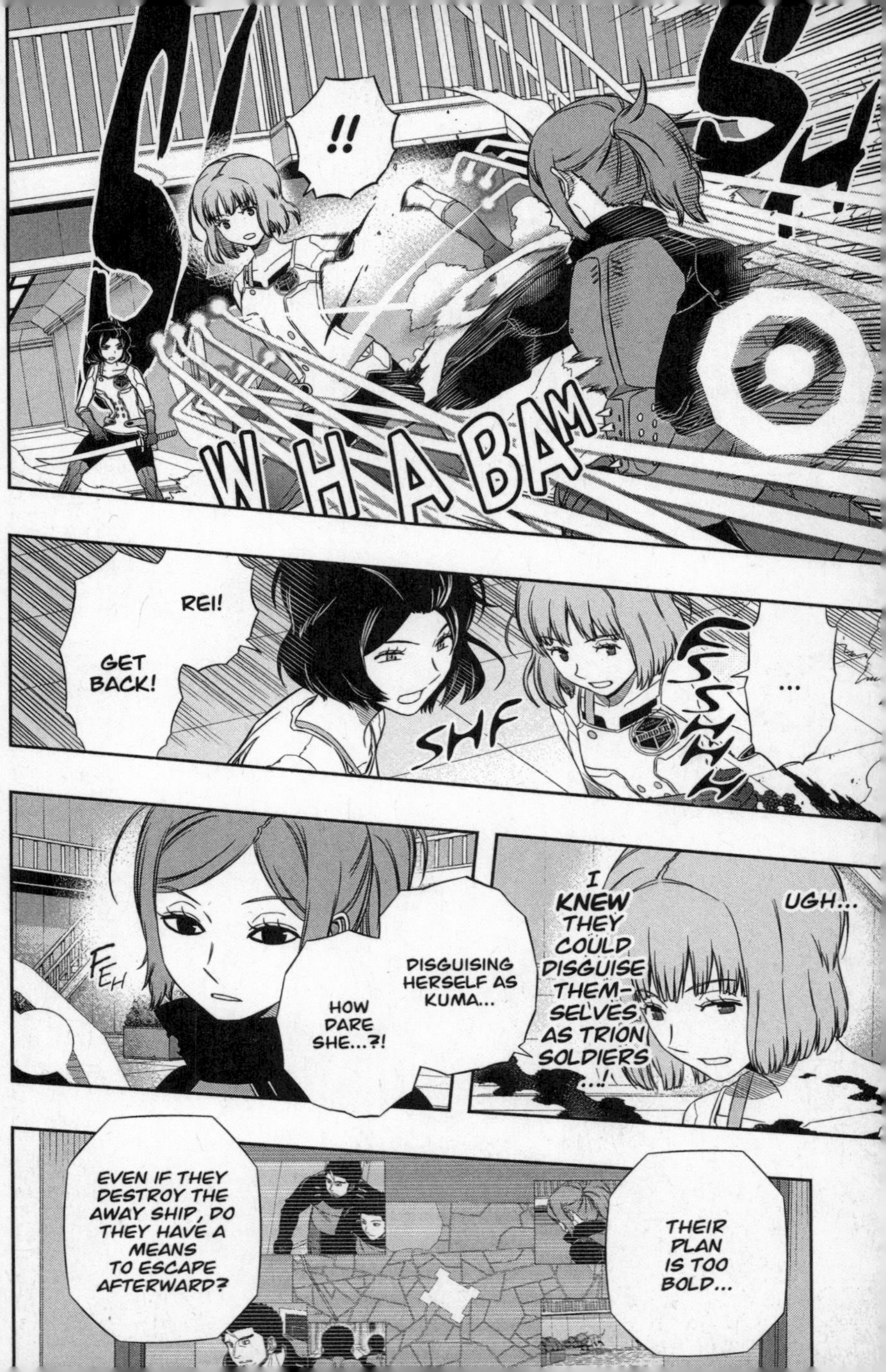
!!
WHABAM
...
FSSHH
SHF
REI!
GET BACK!
UGH...
I KNEW THEY COULD DISGUISE THEM-SELVES AS TRION SOLDIERS...!
DISGUISING HERSELF AS KUMA...
HOW DARE SHE...?!
FEH
THEIR PLAN IS TOO BOLD...
EVEN IF THEY DESTROY THE AWAY SHIP, DO THEY HAVE A MEANS TO ESCAPE AFTERWARD?

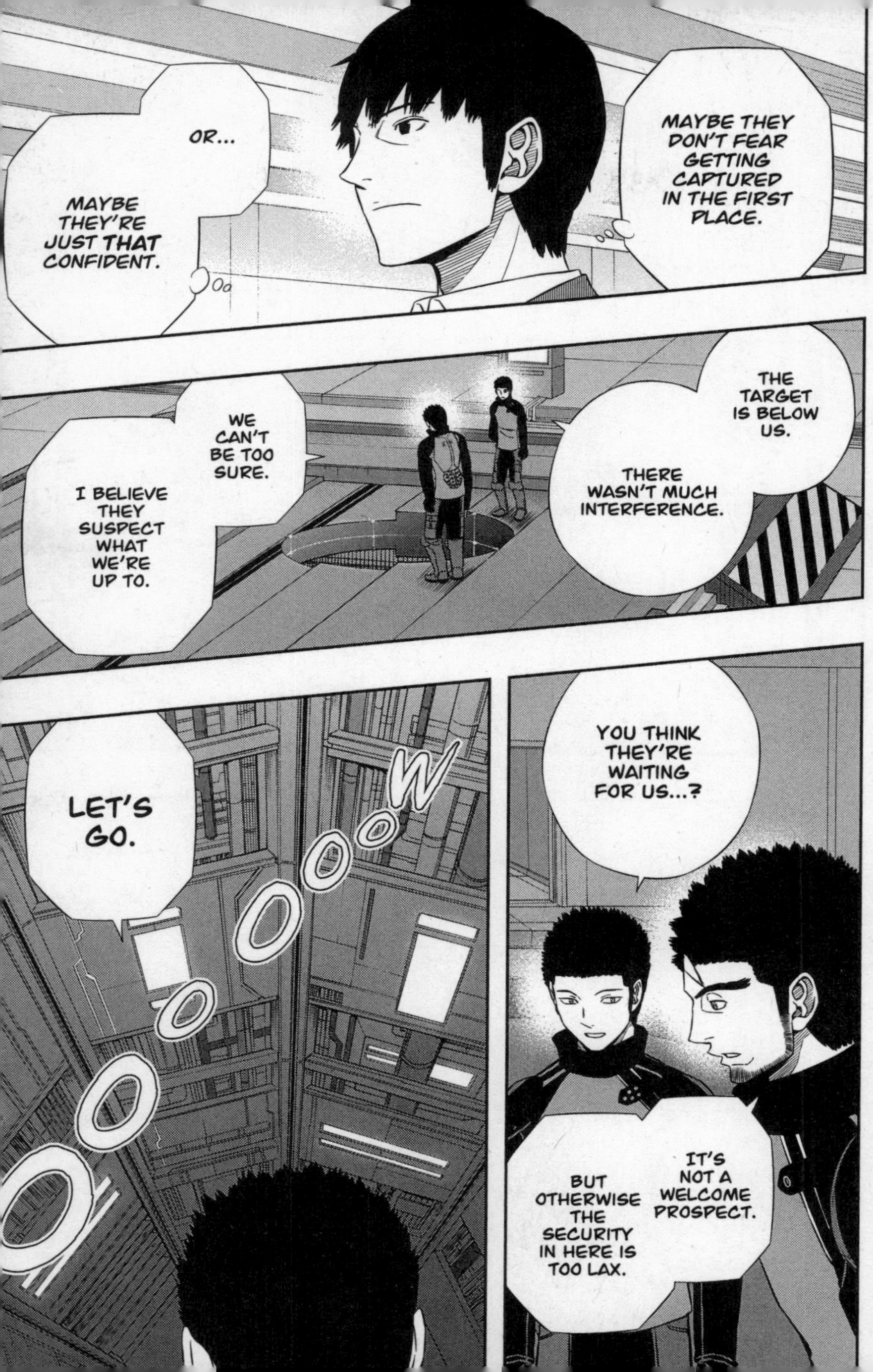

MAYBE THEY DON'T FEAR GETTING CAPTURED IN THE FIRST PLACE.
OR...
MAYBE THEY'RE JUST THAT CONFIDENT.
THE TARGET IS BELOW US.
THERE WASN'T MUCH INTERFERENCE.
WE CAN'T BE TOO SURE.
I BELIEVE THEY SUSPECT WHAT WE'RE UP TO.
YOU THINK THEY'RE WAITING FOR US...?
IT'S NOT A WELCOME PROSPECT.
BUT OTHERWISE THE SECURITY IN HERE IS TOO LAX.
LET'S GO.
WOOOOOO

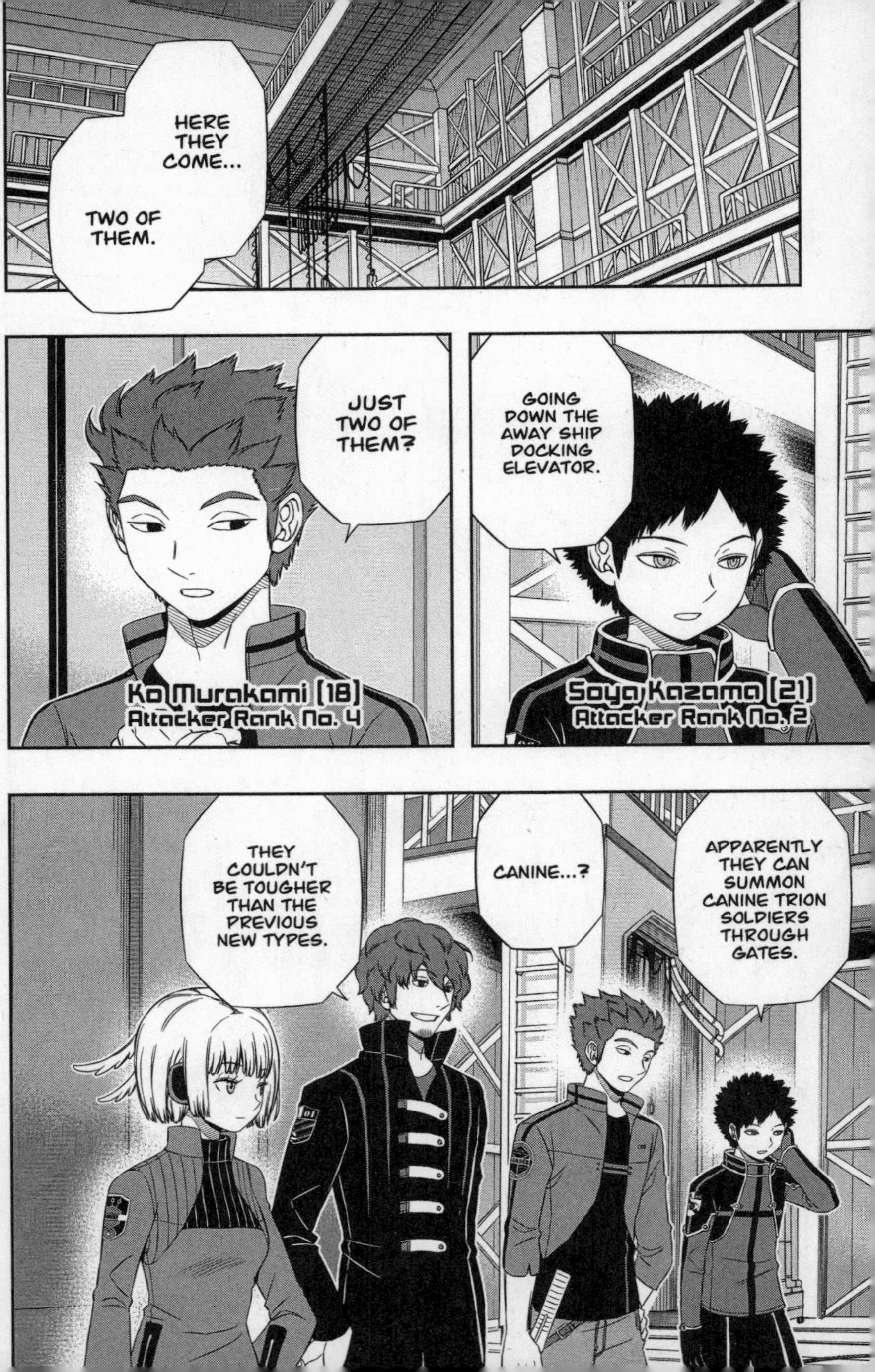
HERE THEY COME...
TWO OF THEM.
GOING DOWN THE AWAY SHIP DOCKING ELEVATOR.
Soya Kazama (21)
Attacker Rank No. 2
JUST TWO OF THEM?
Ko Murakami (18)
Attacker Rank No. 4
APPARENTLY THEY CAN SUMMON CANINE TRION SOLDIERS THROUGH GATES.
CANINE...?
THEY COULDN'T BE TOUGHER THAN THE PREVIOUS NEW TYPES.

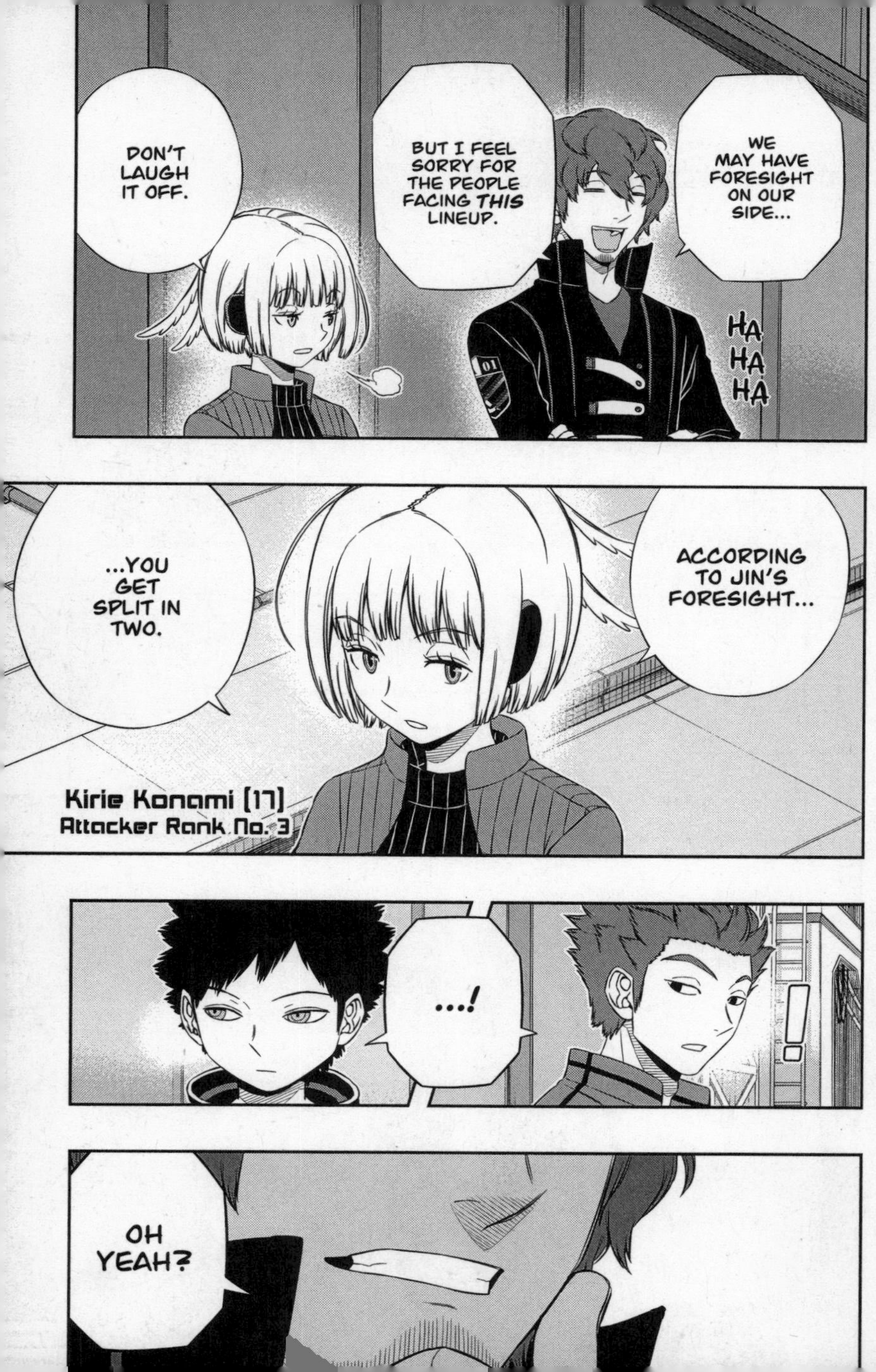
WE MAY HAVE FORESIGHT ON OUR SIDE...
BUT I FEEL SORRY FOR THE PEOPLE FACING THIS LINEUP.
HA HA HA
DON'T LAUGH IT OFF.
ACCORDING TO JIN'S FORESIGHT...
...YOU GET SPLIT IN TWO.
Kirie Konami (17)
Attacker Rank No. 3
!
...!
OH YEAH?

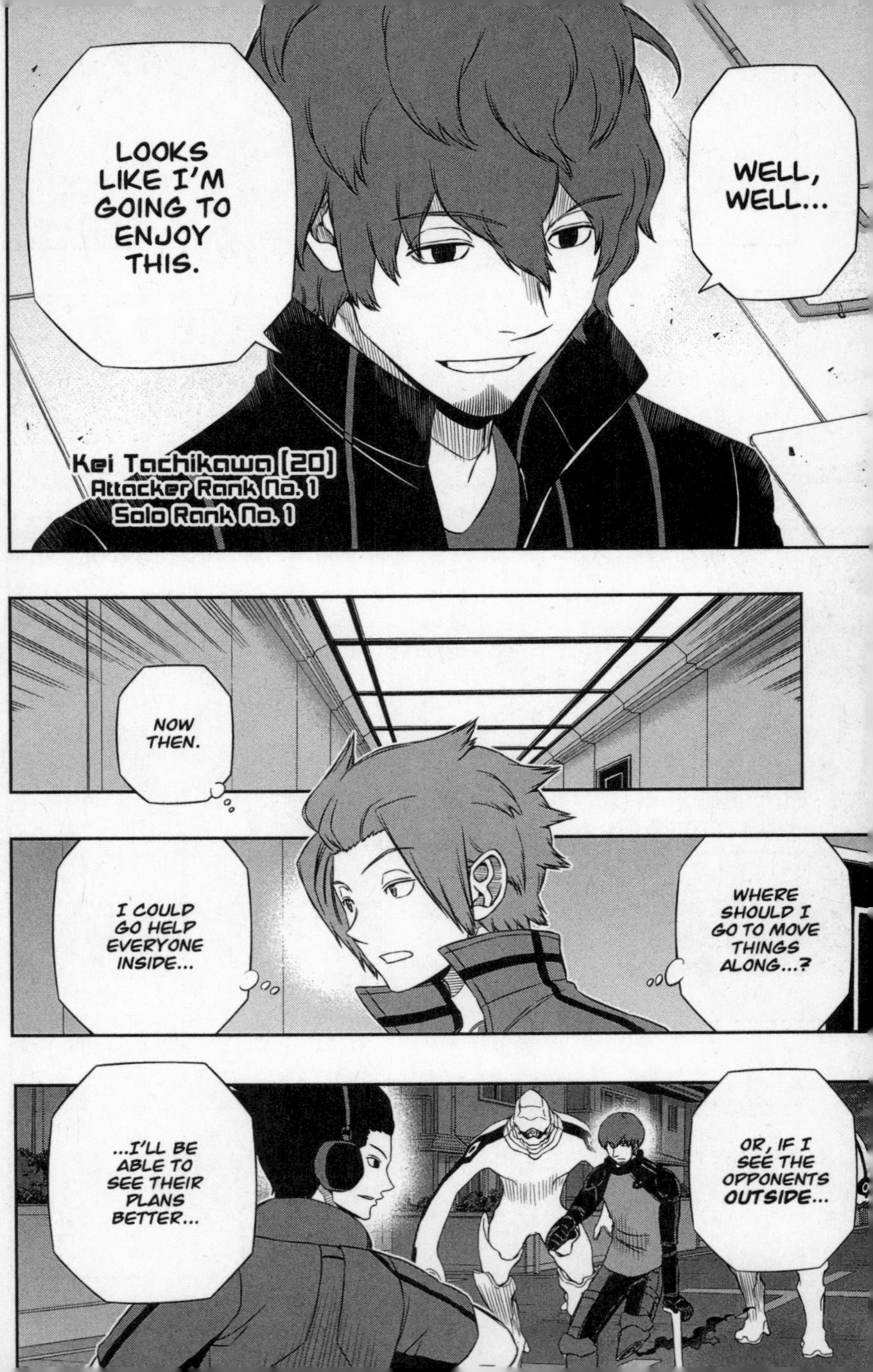
WELL, WELL...
LOOKS LIKE I'M GOING TO ENJOY THIS.
Kei Tachikawa [20]
Attacker Rank No. 1
Solo Rank No. 1
NOW THEN.
WHERE SHOULD I GO TO MOVE THINGS ALONG...?
I COULD GO HELP EVERYONE INSIDE...
OR, IF I SEE THE OPPONENTS OUTSIDE...
...I'LL BE ABLE TO SEE THEIR PLANS BETTER...

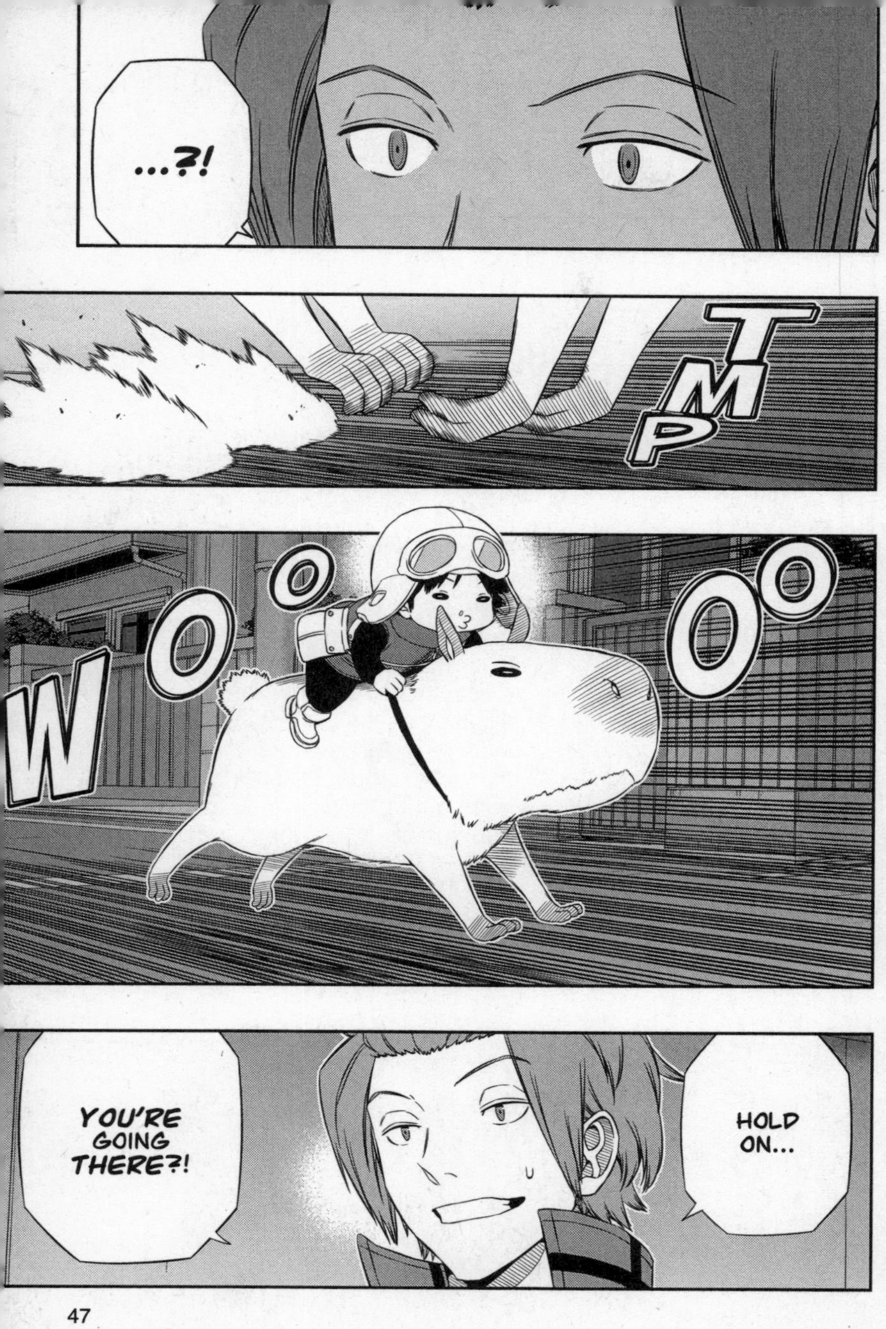
...?!
TMP
WOOOOO
HOLD ON...
YOU'RE GOING THERE?!

Trion Soldiers

Neighbor Minions

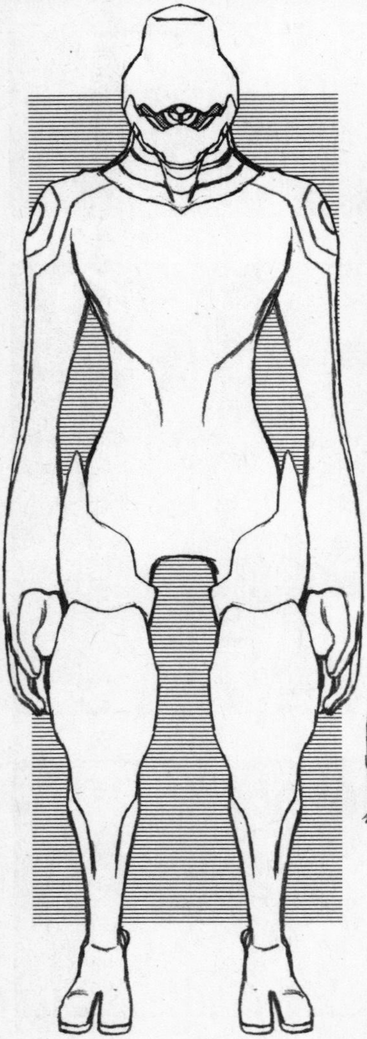

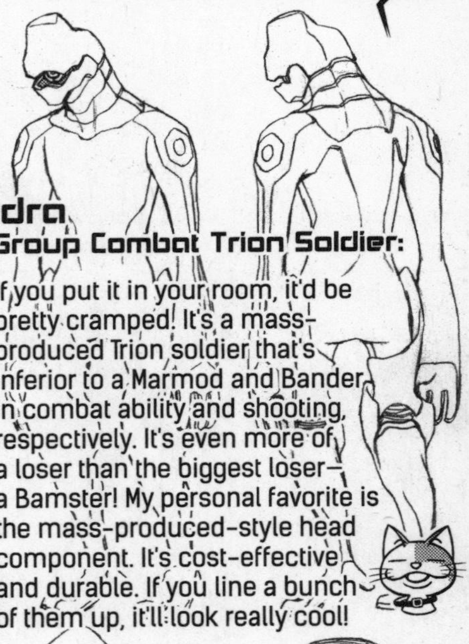

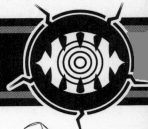

Idra
Group Combat Trion Soldier:

If you put it in your room, it'd be pretty cramped! It's a mass-produced Trion soldier that's inferior to a Marmod and Bander in combat ability and shooting, respectively. It's even more of a loser than the biggest loser—a Bamster! My personal favorite is the mass-produced-style head component. It's cost-effective and durable. If you line a bunch of them up, it'll look really cool!

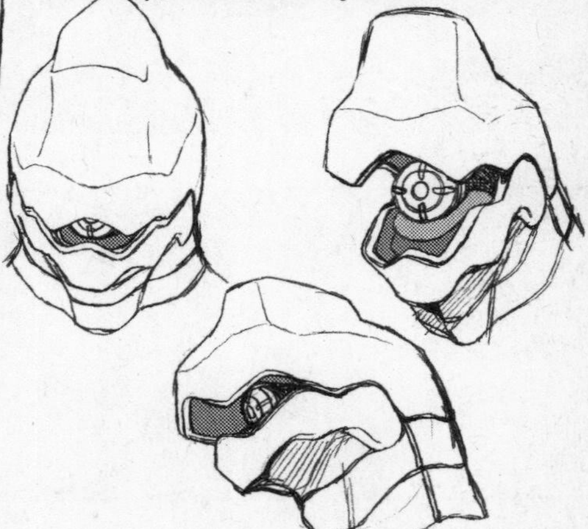

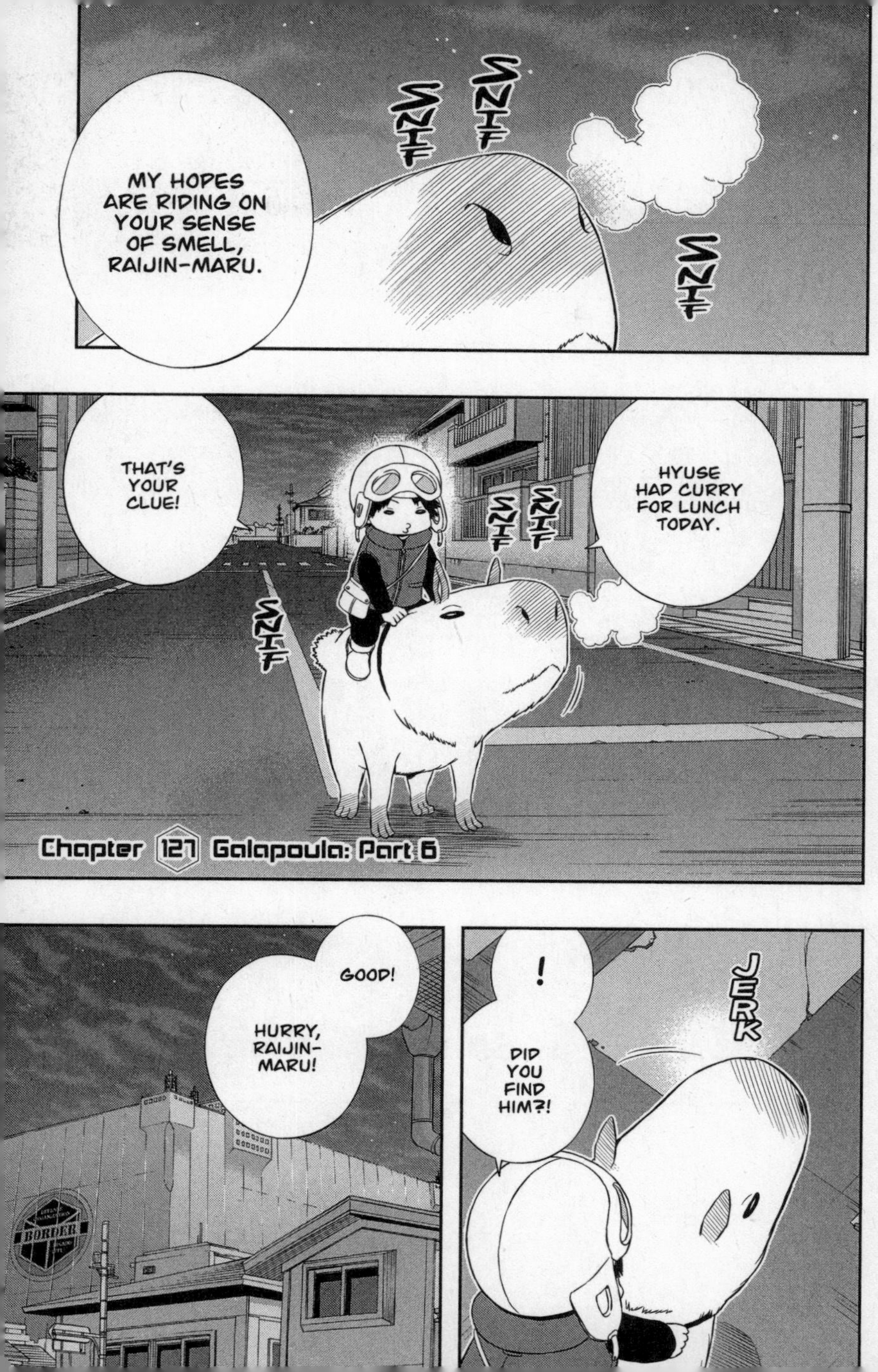
SNIF
SNIF
SNIF
MY HOPES ARE RIDING ON YOUR SENSE OF SMELL, RAIJIN-MARU.
HYUSE HAD CURRY FOR LUNCH TODAY.
SNIF
SNIF
THAT'S YOUR CLUE!
SNIF
Chapter 127 Galapoula: Part 6
JERK
!
DID YOU FIND HIM?!
GOOD!
HURRY, RAIJIN-MARU!
BORDER

Chapter 121 Galopoula: Part 6

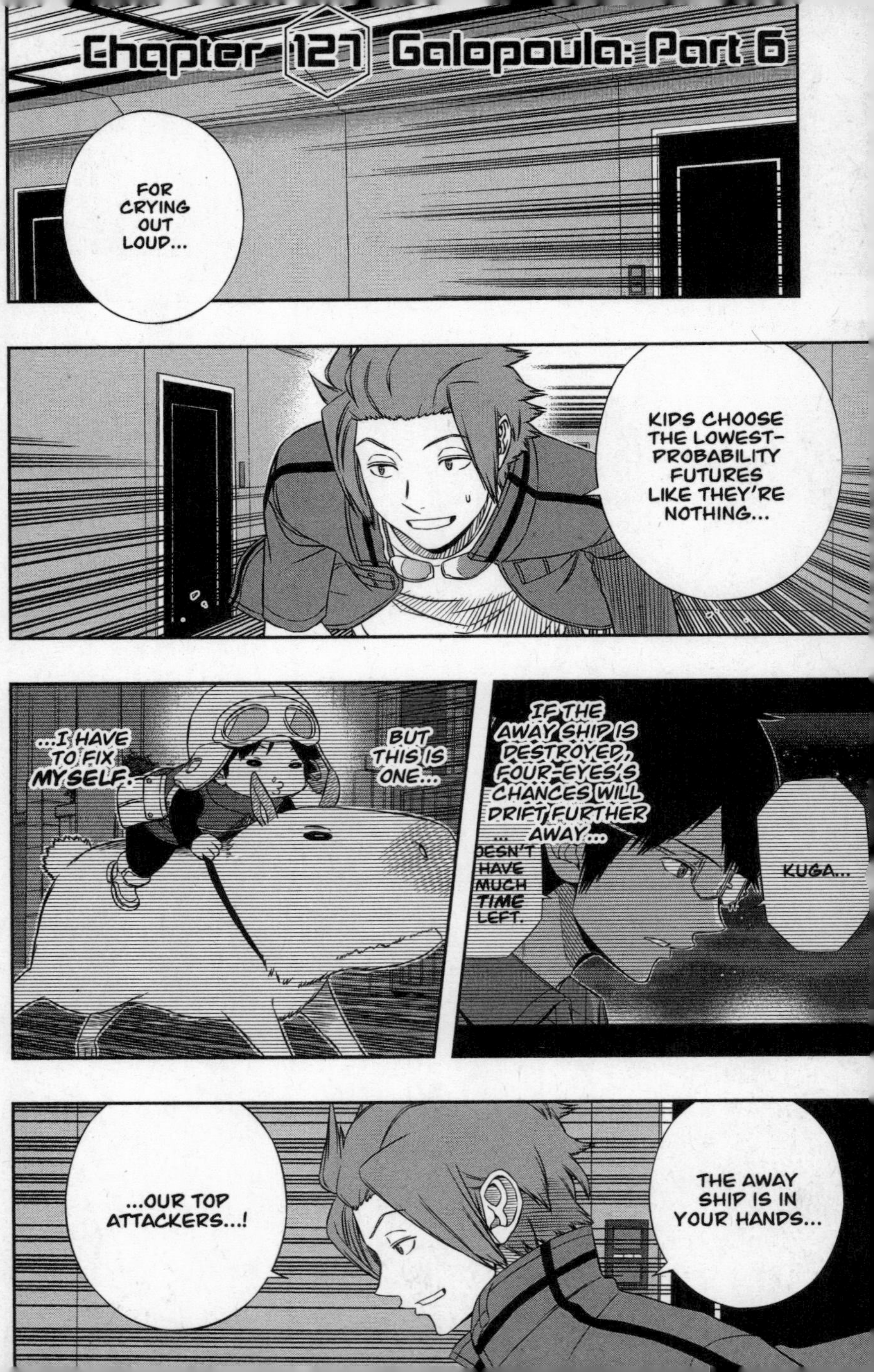
FOR CRYING OUT LOUD...
KIDS CHOOSE THE LOWEST-PROBABILITY FUTURES LIKE THEY'RE NOTHING...
IF THE AWAY SHIP IS DESTROYED, FOUR-EYES'S CHANCES WILL DRIFT FURTHER AWAY...
KUGA...
...DOESN'T HAVE MUCH TIME LEFT.
BUT THIS IS ONE...
...I HAVE TO FIX MYSELF.
THE AWAY SHIP IS IN YOUR HANDS...
...OUR TOP ATTACKERS...!

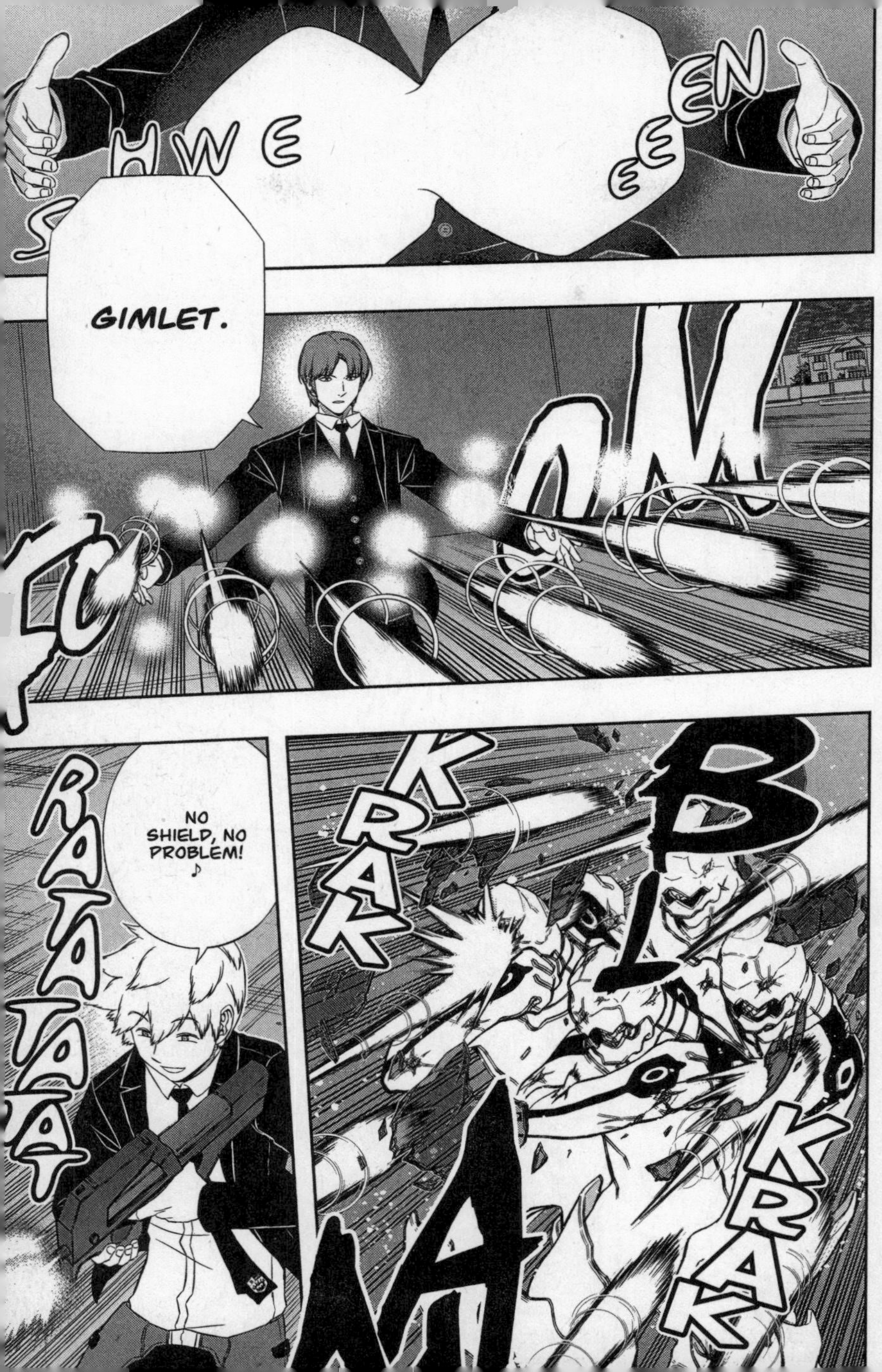
SHWEEEEN
GIMLET.
KRAK
KRAK
NO SHIELD, NO PROBLEM! ♪
RATATATAT

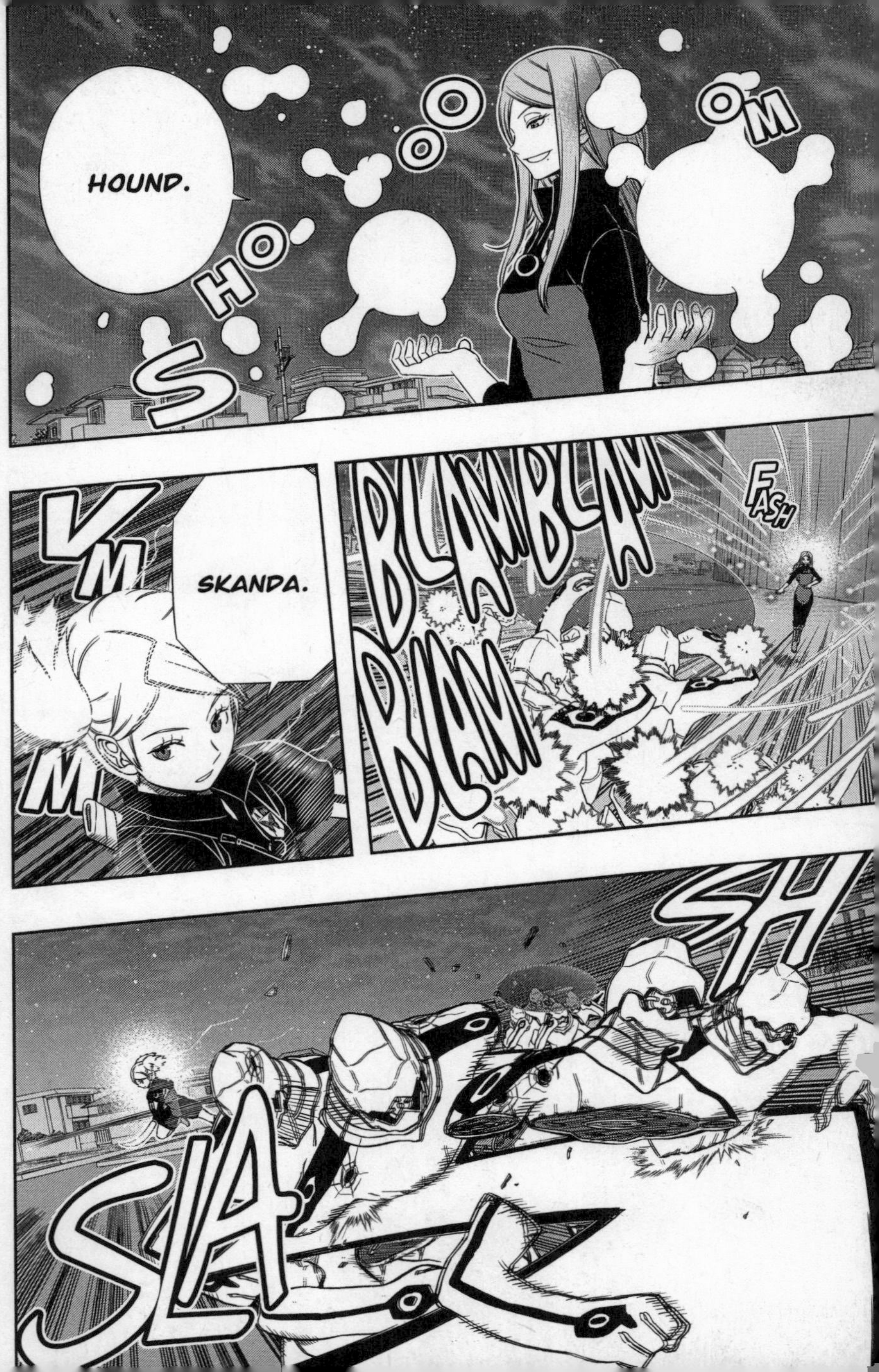
HOUND.
SHOOOOOOM
FASH
BLAMBLAM
BLAM
VMM
SKANDA.
SLASH

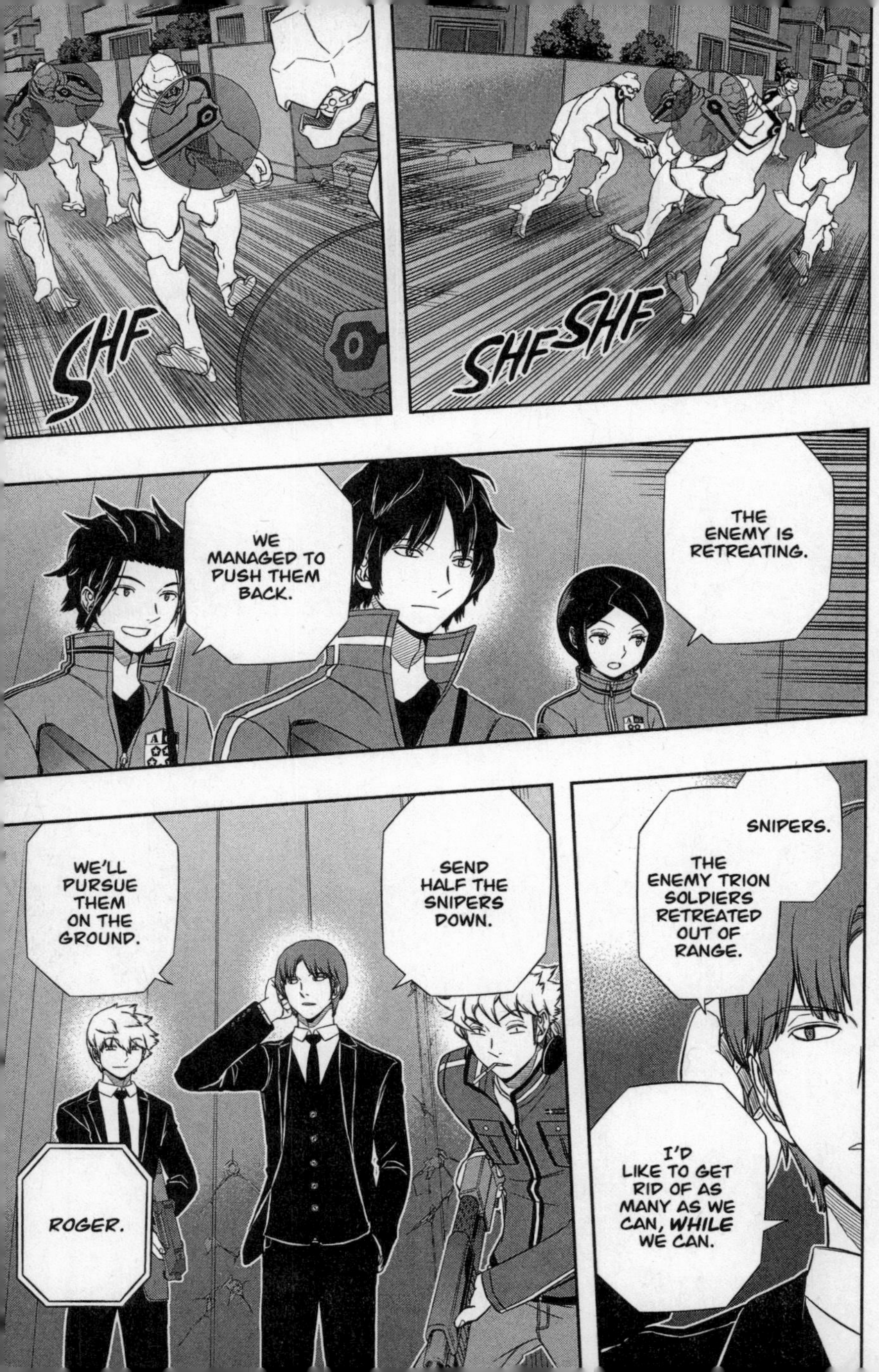
SHF SHF
SHF
THE ENEMY IS RETREATING.
WE MANAGED TO PUSH THEM BACK.
SNIPERS.
THE ENEMY TRION SOLDIERS RETREATED OUT OF RANGE.
I'D LIKE TO GET RID OF AS MANY AS WE CAN, WHILE WE CAN.
SEND HALF THE SNIPERS DOWN.
WE'LL PURSUE THEM ON THE GROUND.
ROGER.

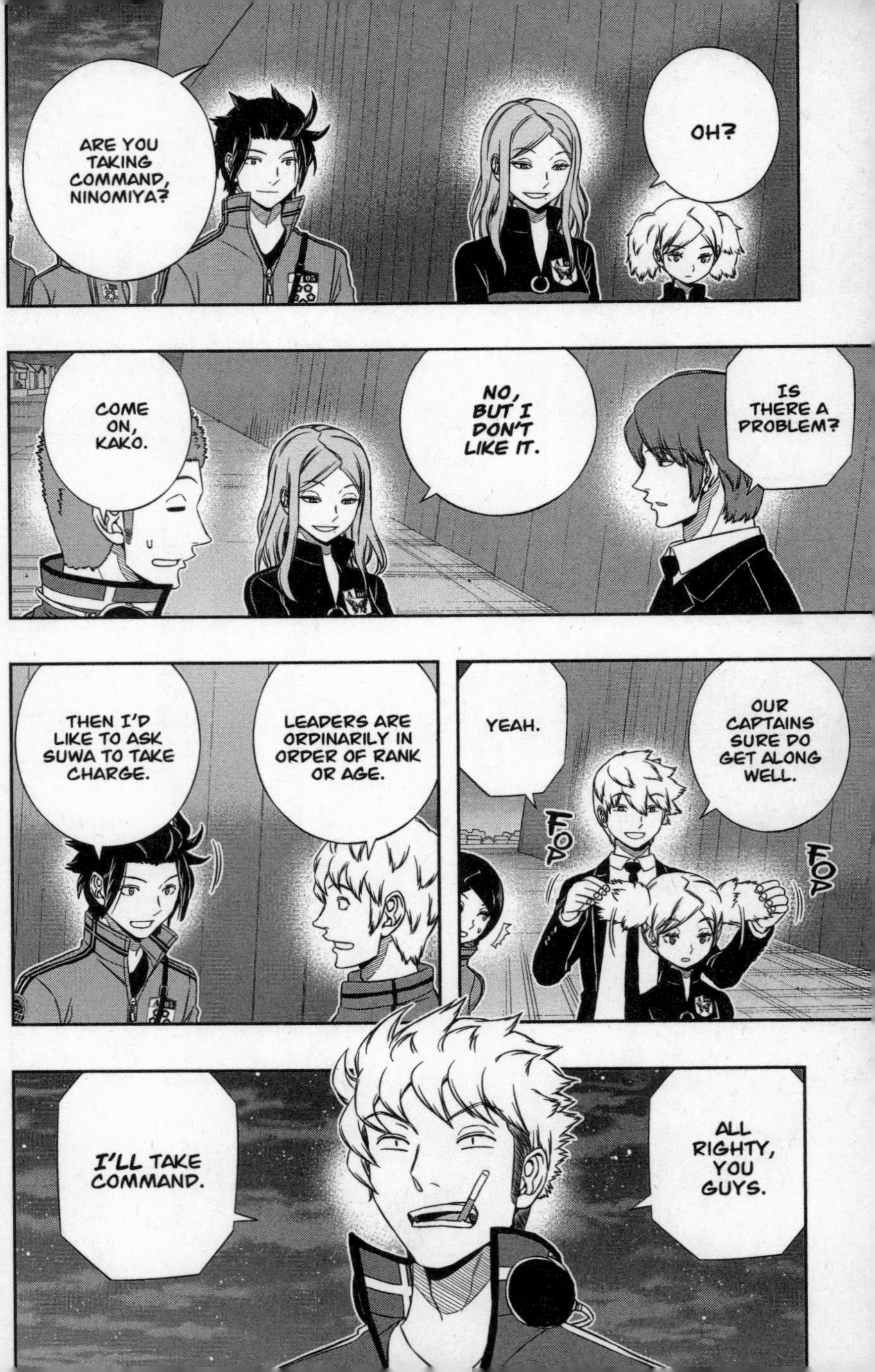
OH?
ARE YOU TAKING COMMAND, NINOMIYA?
IS THERE A PROBLEM?
NO, BUT I DON'T LIKE IT.
COME ON, KAKO.
OUR CAPTAINS SURE DO GET ALONG WELL.
FOP
FOP
YEAH.
LEADERS ARE ORDINARILY IN ORDER OF RANK OR AGE.
THEN I'D LIKE TO ASK SUWA TO TAKE CHARGE.
ALL RIGHTY, YOU GUYS.
I'LL TAKE COMMAND.

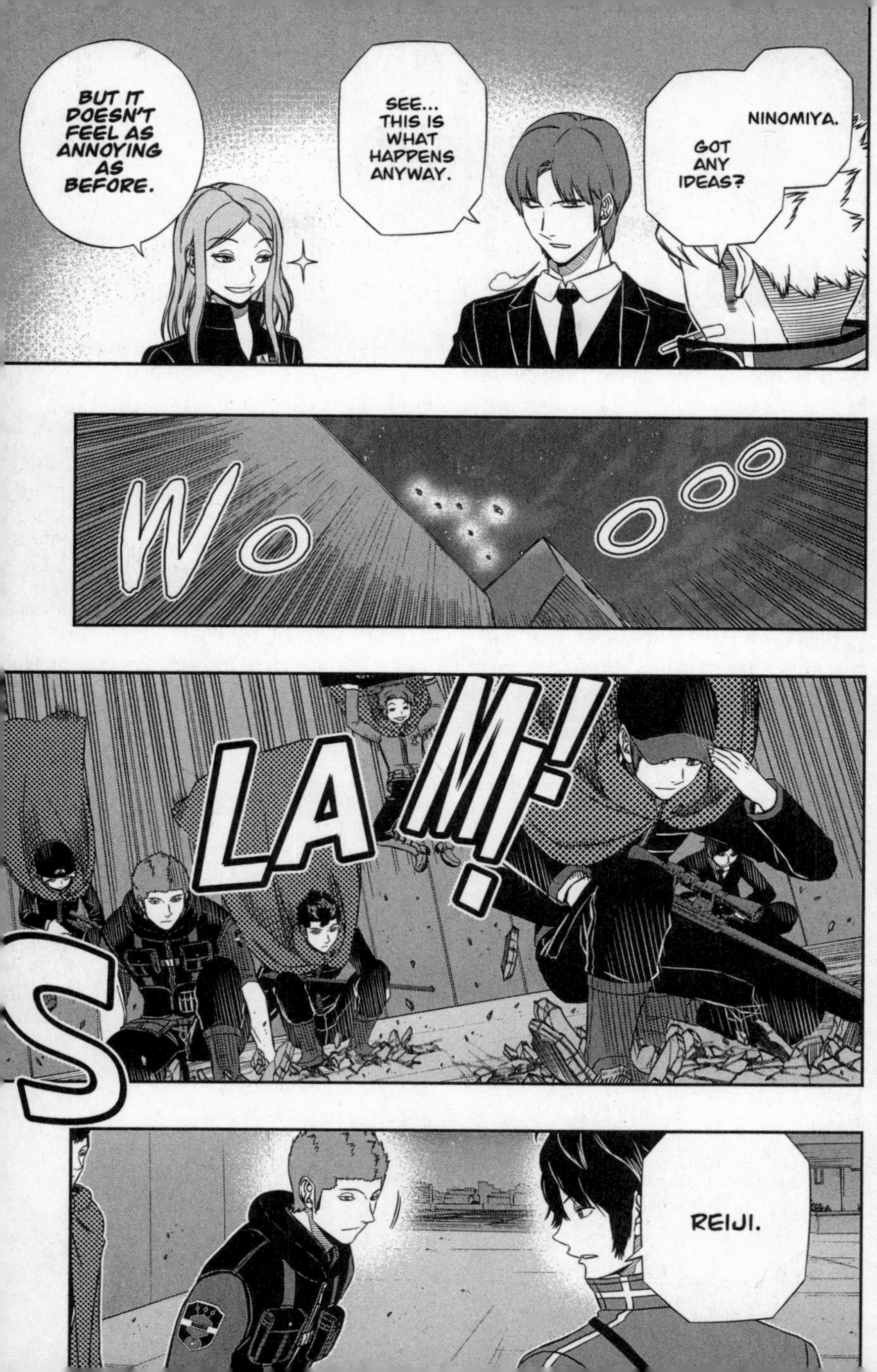
NINOMIYA.
GOT ANY IDEAS?
SEE... THIS IS WHAT HAPPENS ANYWAY.
BUT IT DOESN'T FEEL AS ANNOYING AS BEFORE.
WOOOO
SLAM!
REIJI.

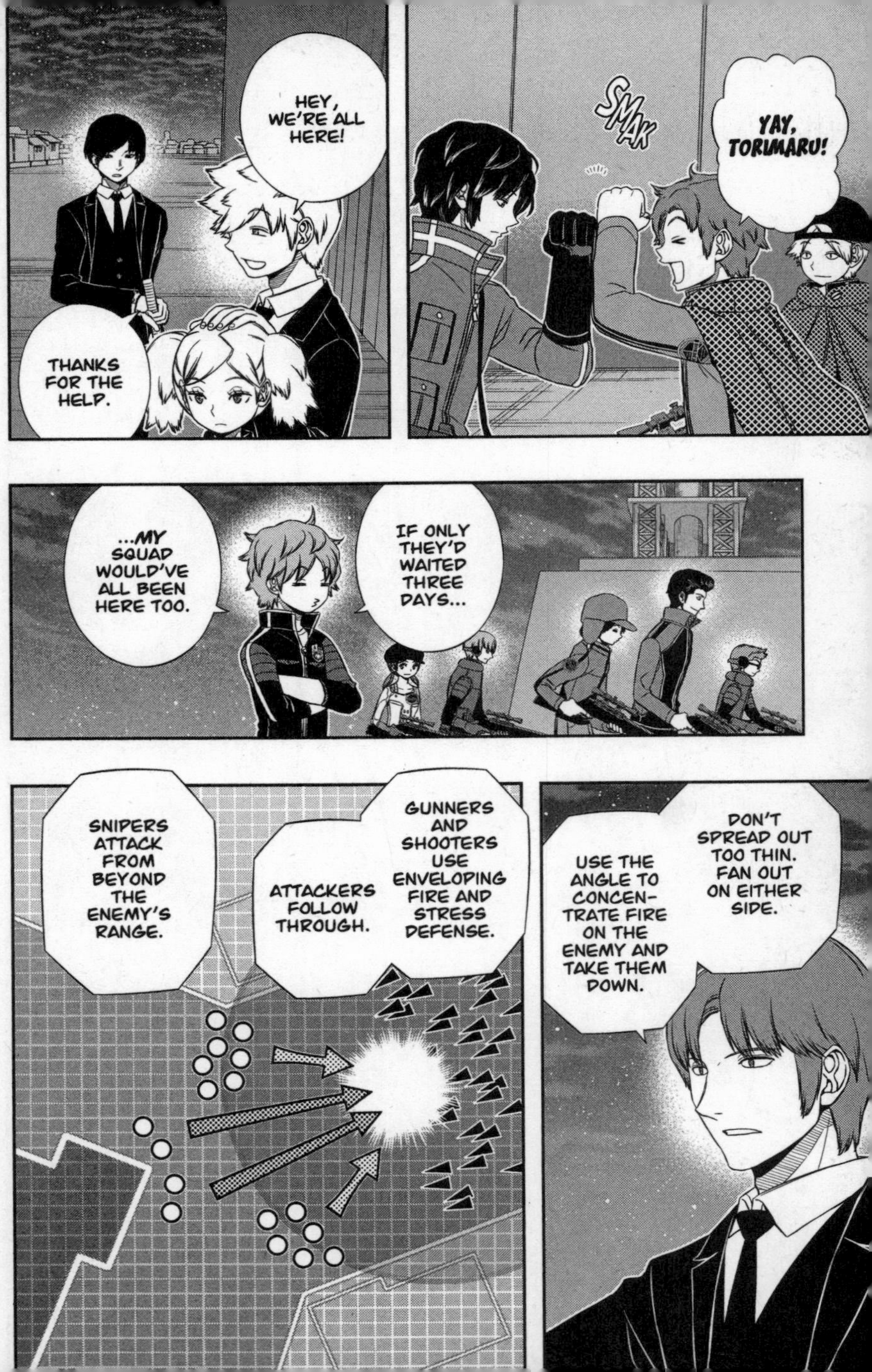
SMAK
YAY, TORIMARU!
HEY, WE'RE ALL HERE!
THANKS FOR THE HELP.
IF ONLY THEY'D WAITED THREE DAYS...
...MY SQUAD WOULD'VE ALL BEEN HERE TOO.
DON'T SPREAD OUT TOO THIN. FAN OUT ON EITHER SIDE.
USE THE ANGLE TO CONCEN-TRATE FIRE ON THE ENEMY AND TAKE THEM DOWN.
GUNNERS AND SHOOTERS USE ENVELOPING FIRE AND STRESS DEFENSE.
ATTACKERS FOLLOW THROUGH.
SNIPERS ATTACK FROM BEYOND THE ENEMY'S RANGE.

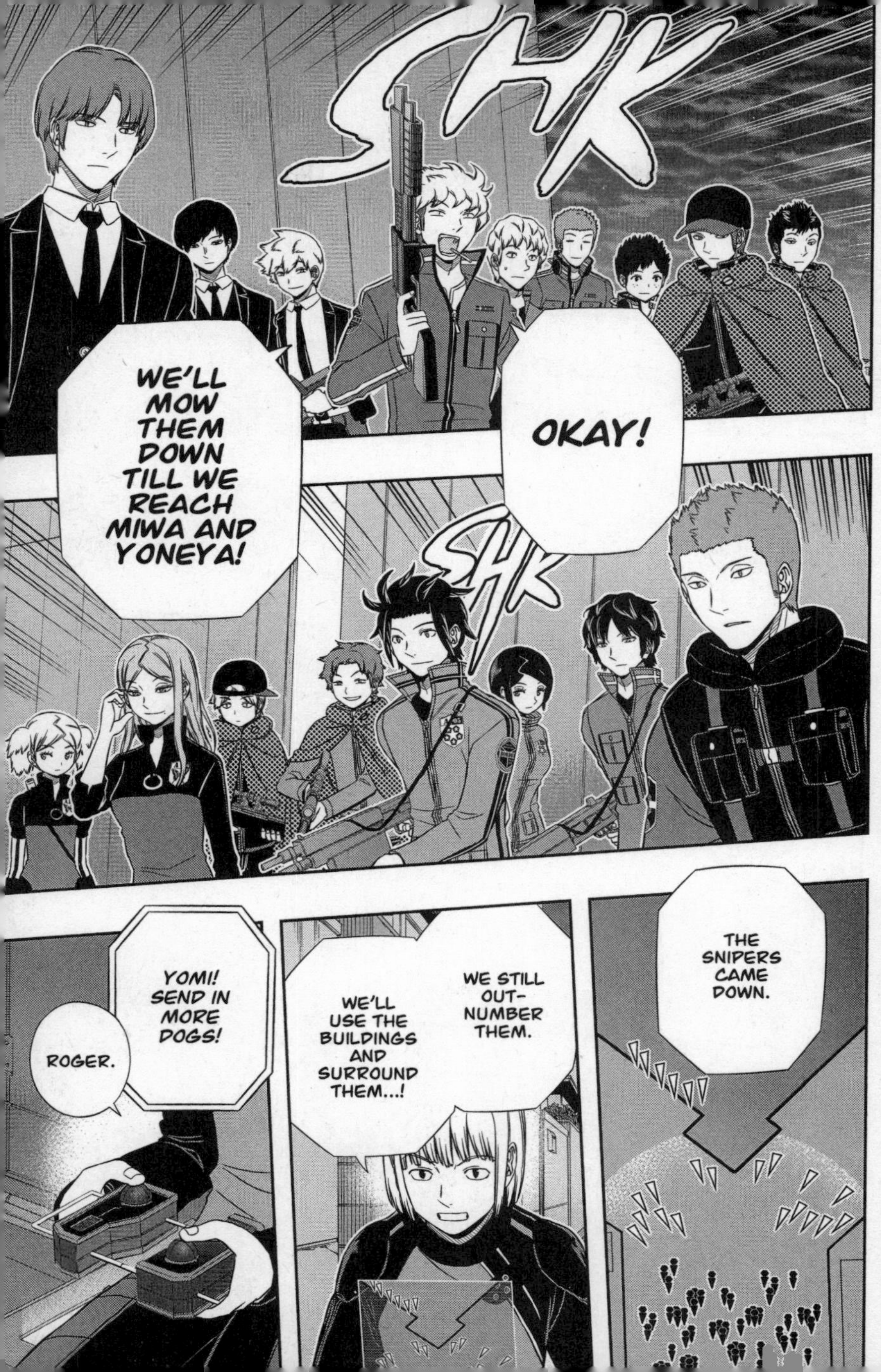
SHK
WE'LL MOW THEM DOWN TILL WE REACH MIWA AND YONEYA!
OKAY!
SHK
THE SNIPERS CAME DOWN.
WE STILL OUT-NUMBER THEM.
WE'LL USE THE BUILDINGS AND SURROUND THEM...!
YOMI! SEND IN MORE DOGS!
ROGER.

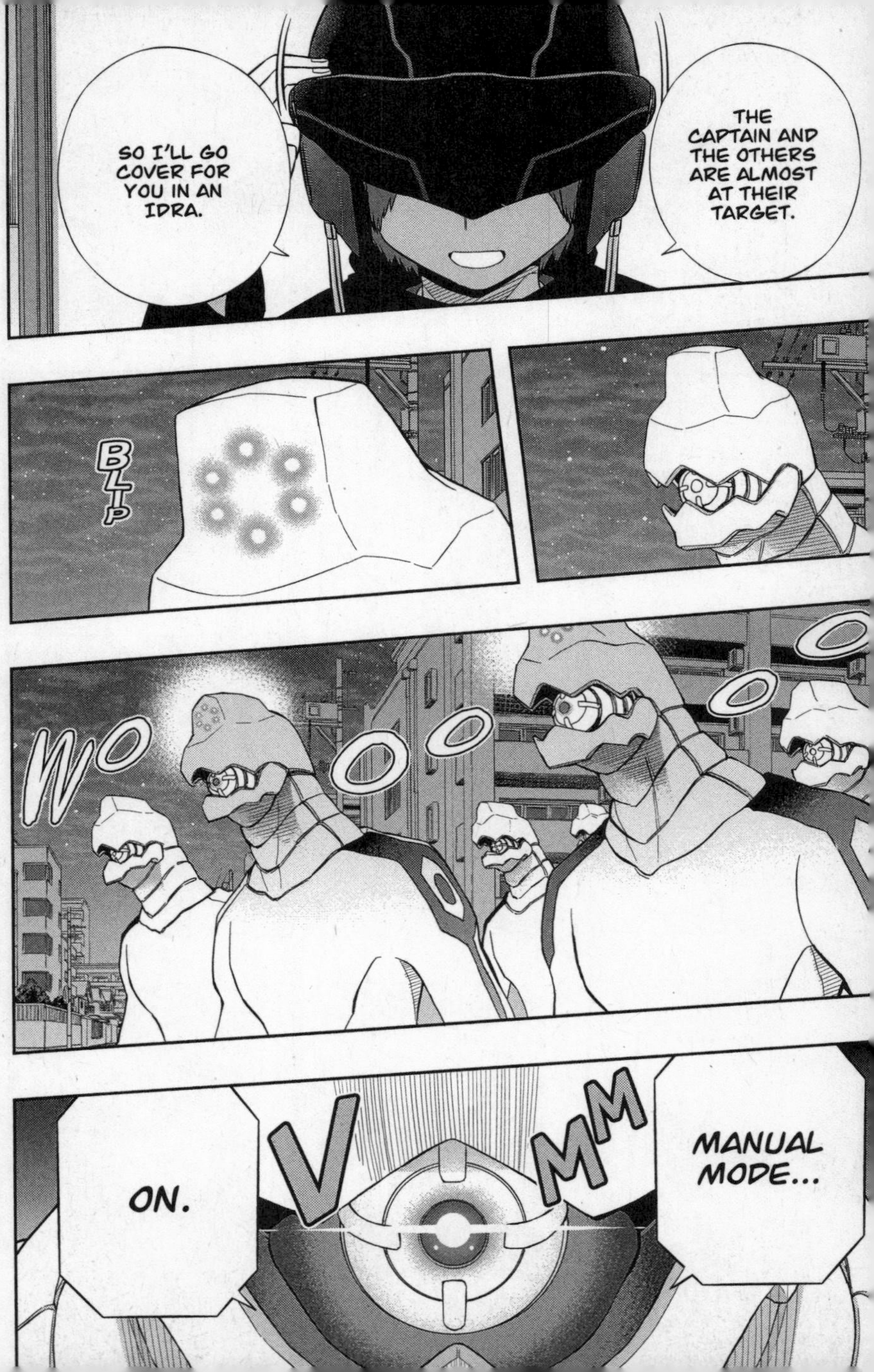
THE CAPTAIN AND THE OTHERS ARE ALMOST AT THEIR TARGET.
SO I'LL GO COVER FOR YOU IN AN IDRA.
BLIP
WOOOOOO
MANUAL MODE...
VMMM
ON.

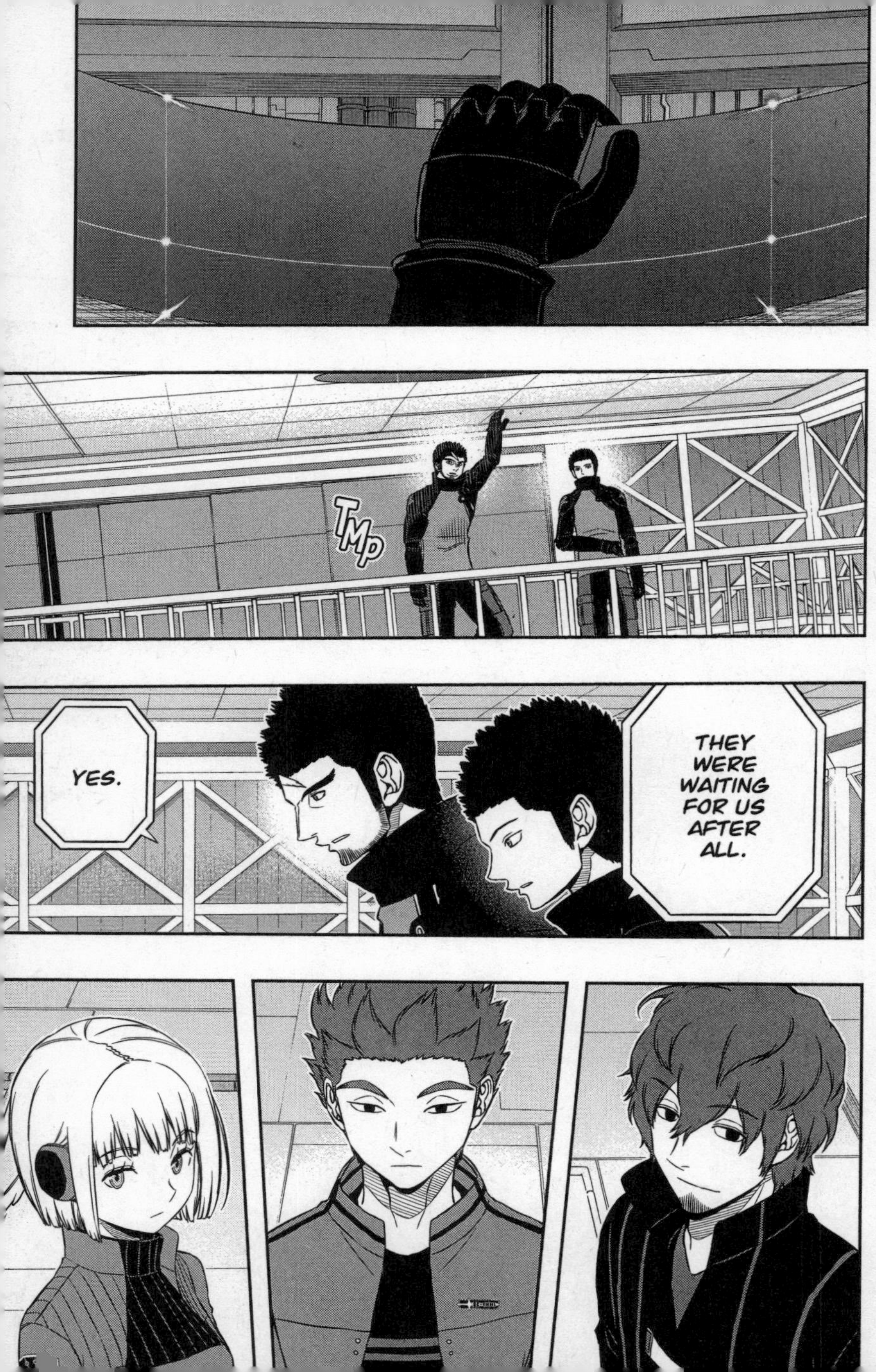
TMP
THEY WERE WAITING FOR US AFTER ALL.
YES.

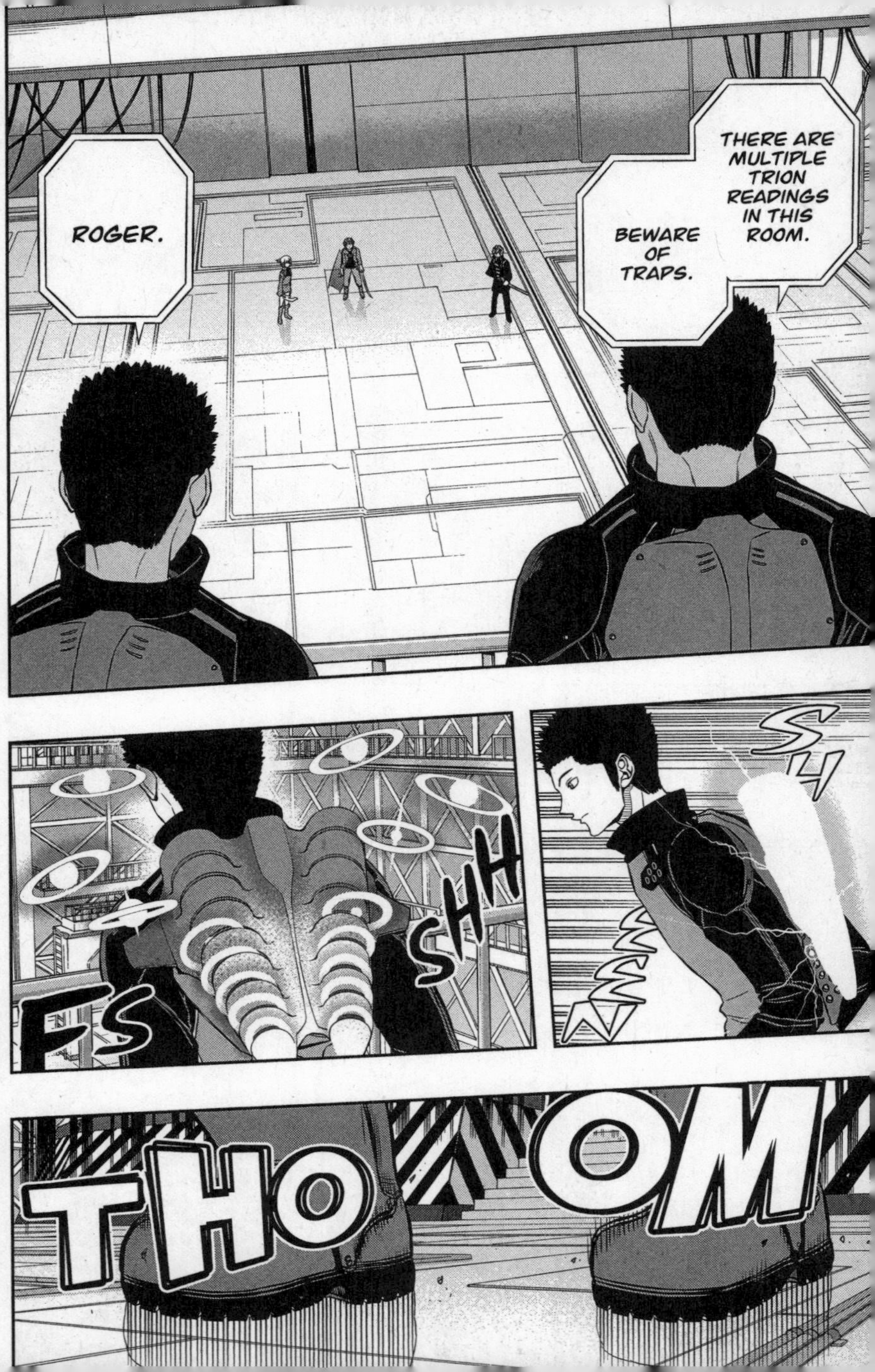
THERE ARE MULTIPLE TRION READINGS IN THIS ROOM.
BEWARE OF TRAPS.
ROGER.
SH
SHH
FS
THOOM

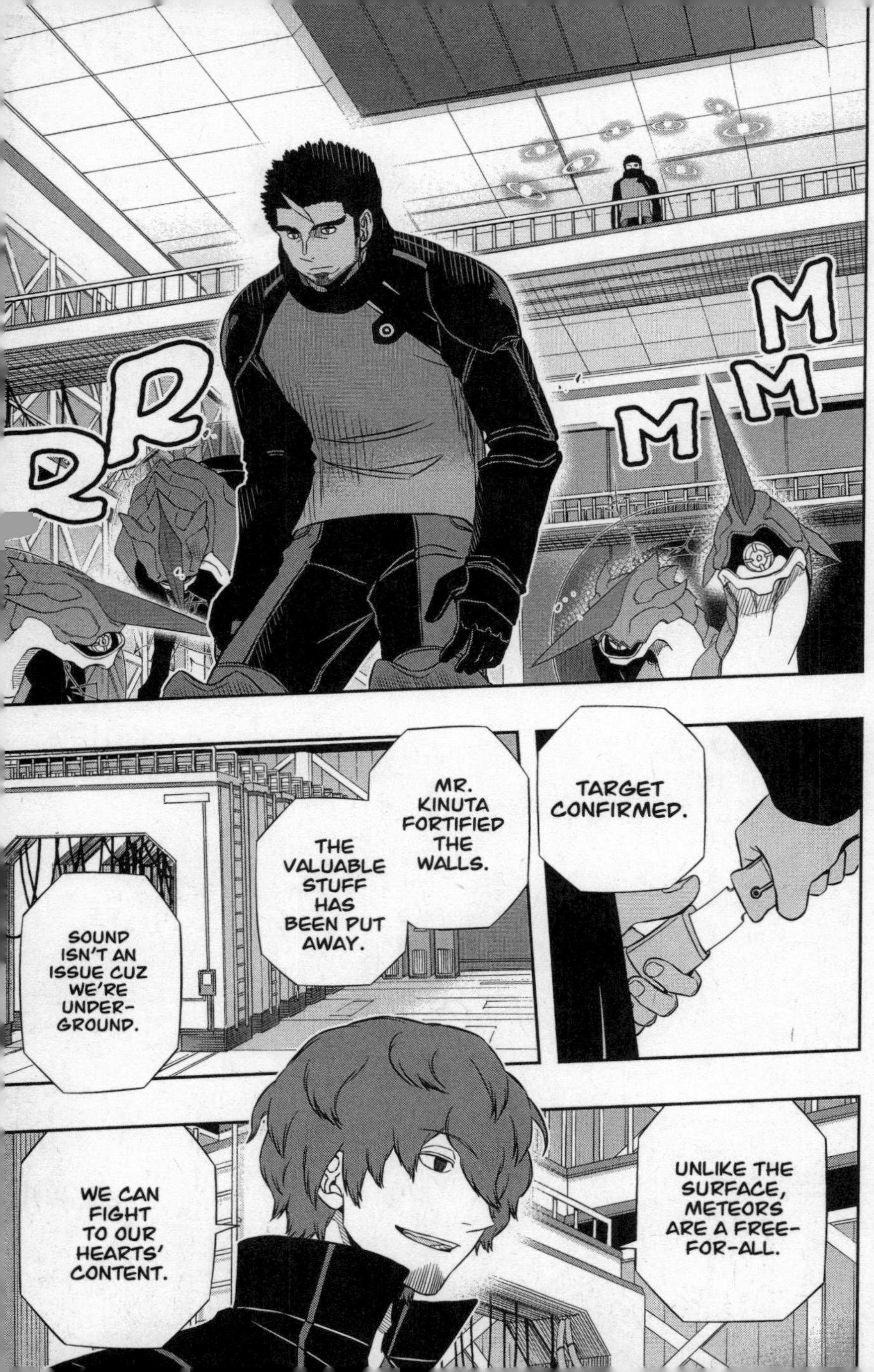
MMM
TARGET CONFIRMED.
MR. KINUTA FORTIFIED THE WALLS.
THE VALUABLE STUFF HAS BEEN PUT AWAY.
SOUND ISN'T AN ISSUE CUZ WE'RE UNDER-GROUND.
UNLIKE THE SURFACE, METEORS ARE A FREE-FOR-ALL.
WE CAN FIGHT TO OUR HEARTS' CONTENT.

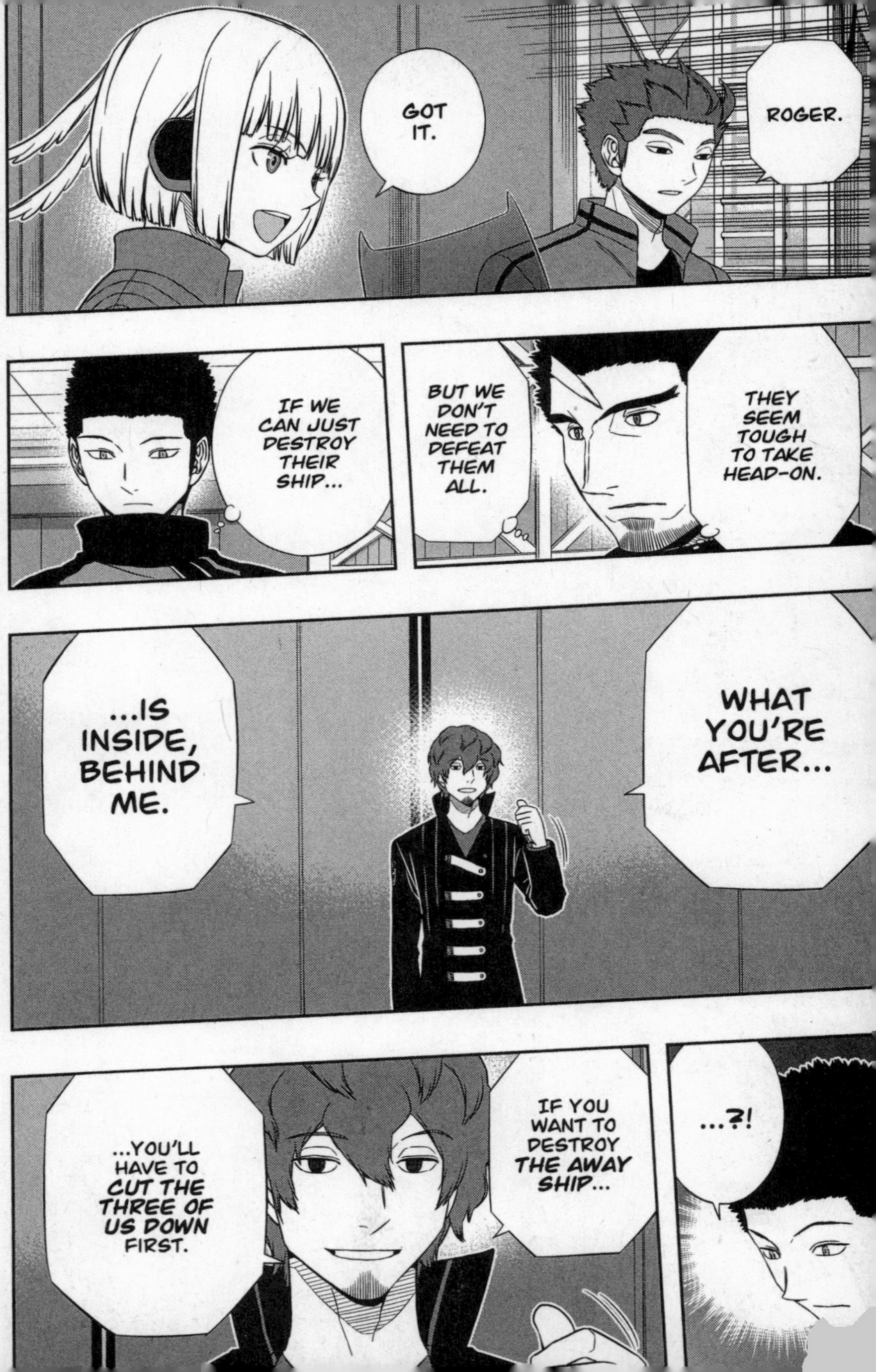
ROGER.
GOT IT.
THEY SEEM TOUGH TO TAKE HEAD-ON.
BUT WE DON'T NEED TO DEFEAT THEM ALL.
IF WE CAN JUST DESTROY THEIR SHIP...
WHAT YOU'RE AFTER...
...IS INSIDE, BEHIND ME.
...?!
IF YOU WANT TO DESTROY THE AWAY SHIP...
...YOU'LL HAVE TO CUT THE THREE OF US DOWN FIRST.

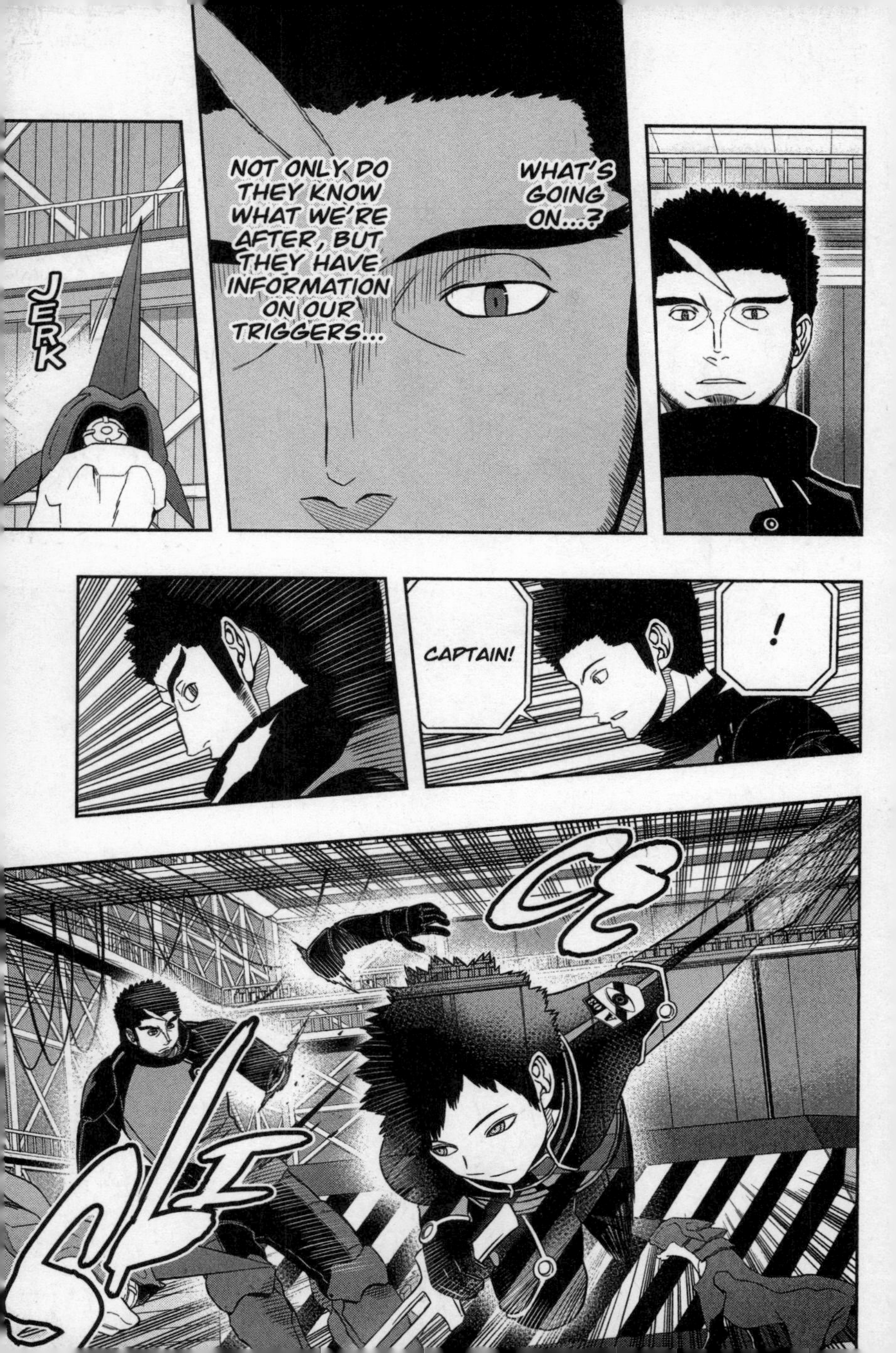
WHAT'S GOING ON...?
NOT ONLY DO THEY KNOW WHAT WE'RE AFTER, BUT THEY HAVE INFORMATION ON OUR TRIGGERS...
JERK
!
CAPTAIN!

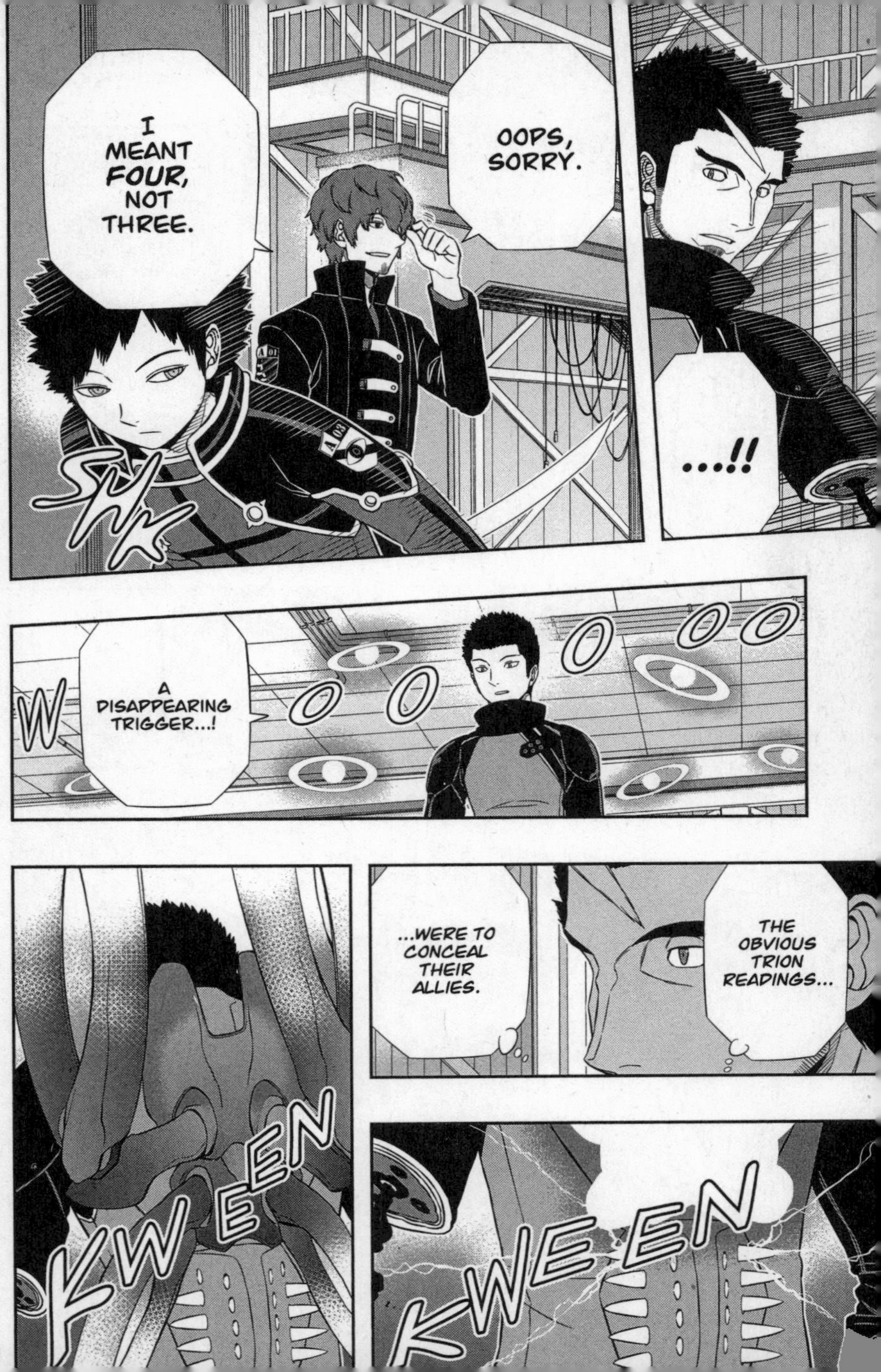
...!!
OOPS, SORRY.
I MEANT FOUR, NOT THREE.
SHK
A DISAPPEARING TRIGGER...!
WOOOOOO
THE OBVIOUS TRION READINGS...
...WERE TO CONCEAL THEIR ALLIES.
KWEEN
KWEEN

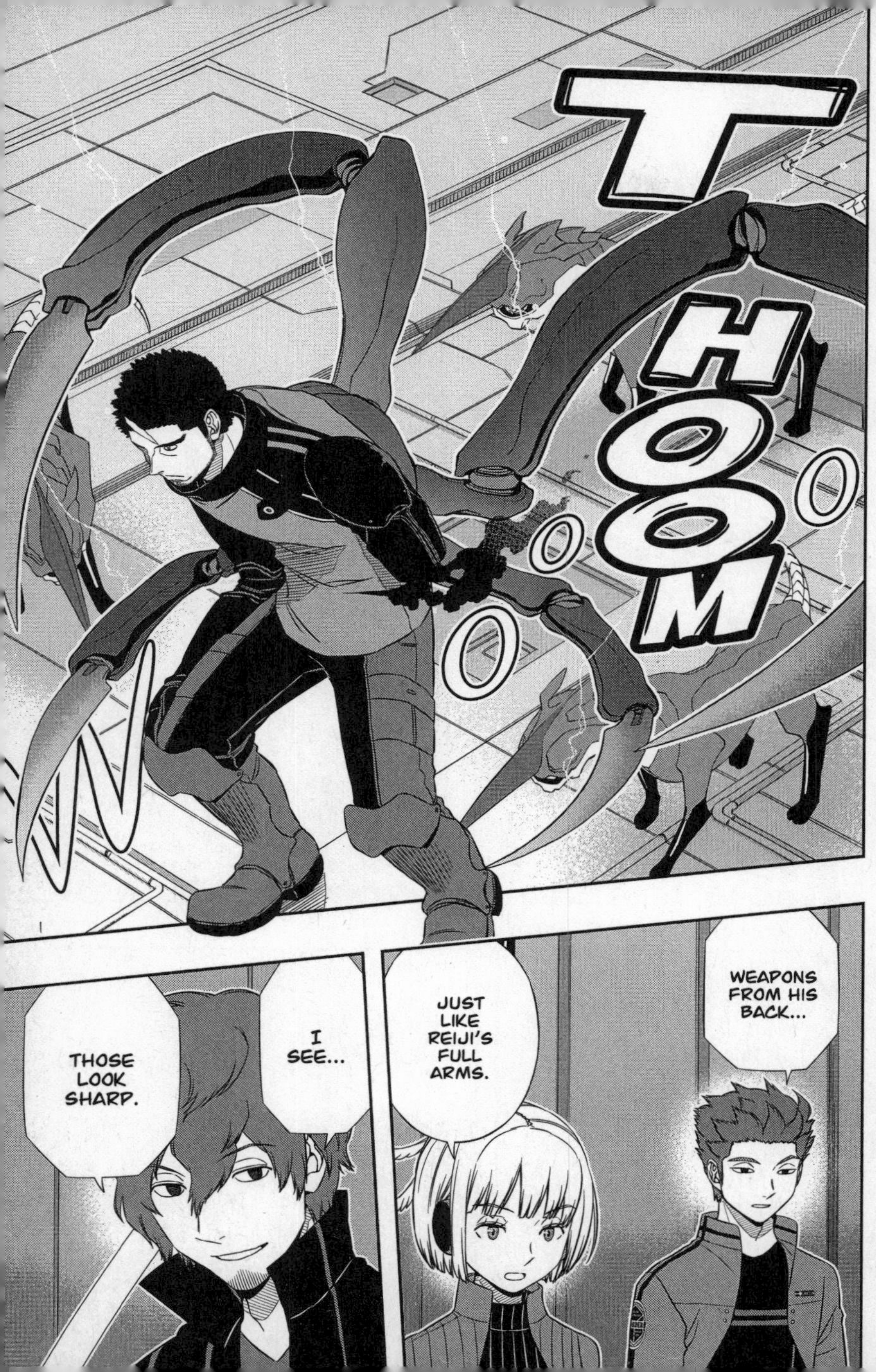
THOOOM
WEAPONS FROM HIS BACK...
JUST LIKE REIJI'S FULL ARMS.
I SEE...
THOSE LOOK SHARP.

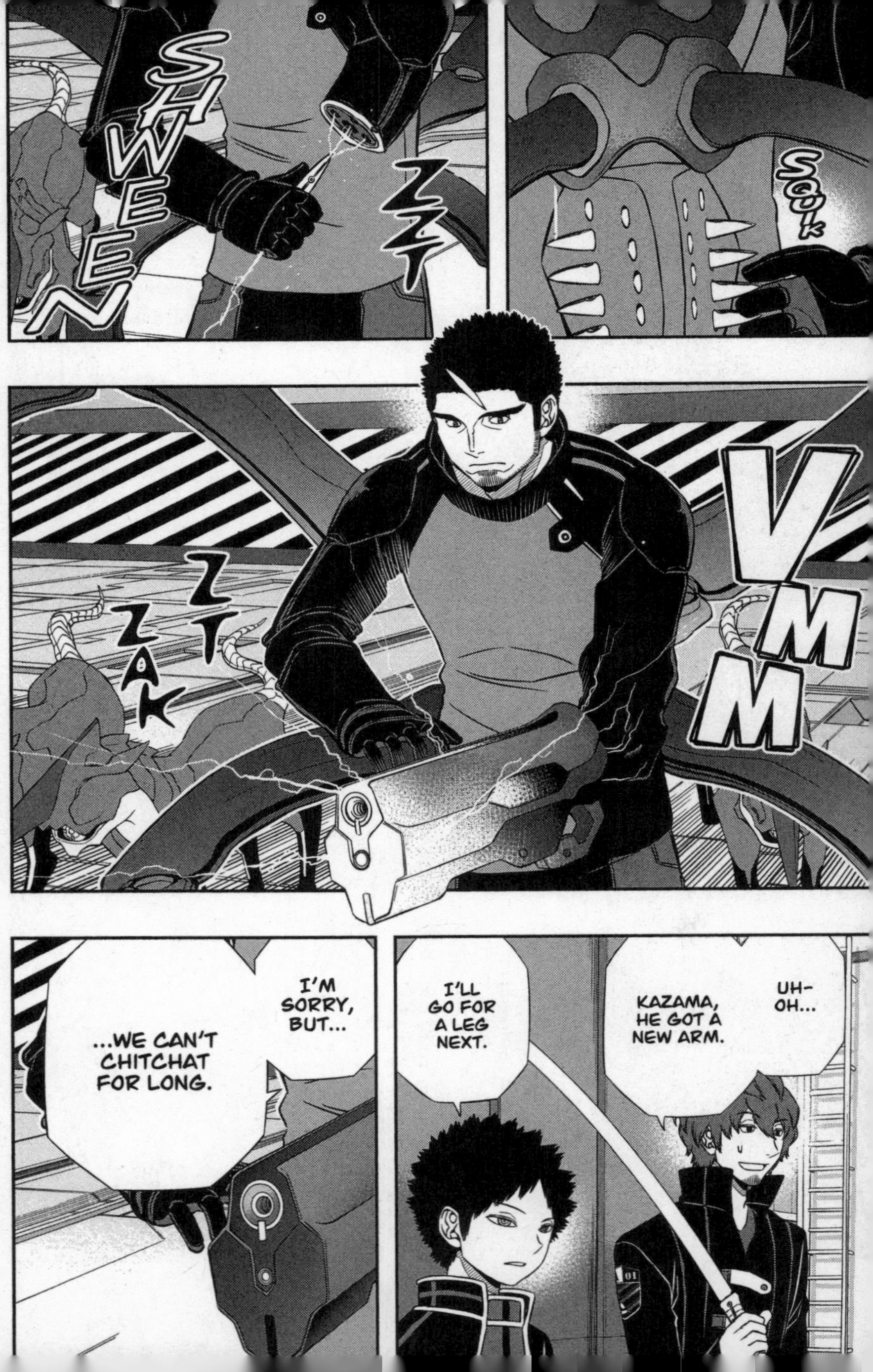
SQUK
ZZZT
SHWEEN
VMM
ZZT
ZAK
UH-OH...
KAZAMA, HE GOT A NEW ARM.
I'LL GO FOR A LEG NEXT.
I'M SORRY, BUT...
...WE CAN'T CHITCHAT FOR LONG.

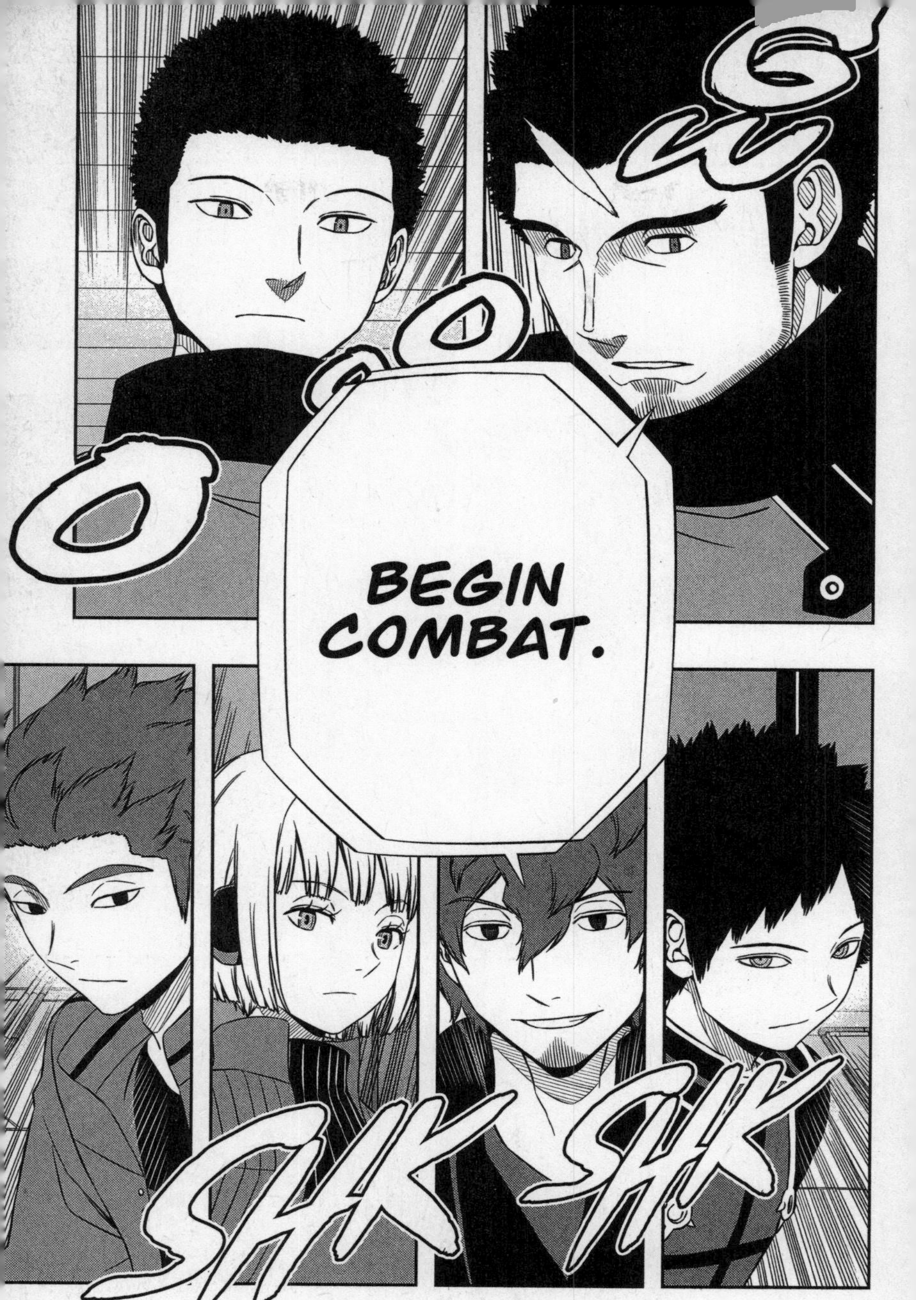
BEGIN COMBAT.
SHK
SHK

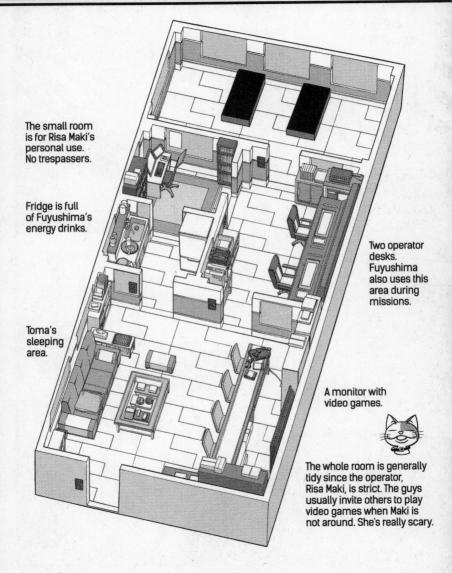

The small room is for Risa Maki's personal use. No trespassers.

Fridge is full of Fuyushima's energy drinks.

Toma's sleeping area.

Two operator desks. Fuyushima also uses this area during missions.

A monitor with video games.

The whole room is generally tidy since the operator, Risa Maki, is strict. The guys usually invite others to play video games when Maki is not around. She's really scary.

Chapter 128
Galopoula: Part 7

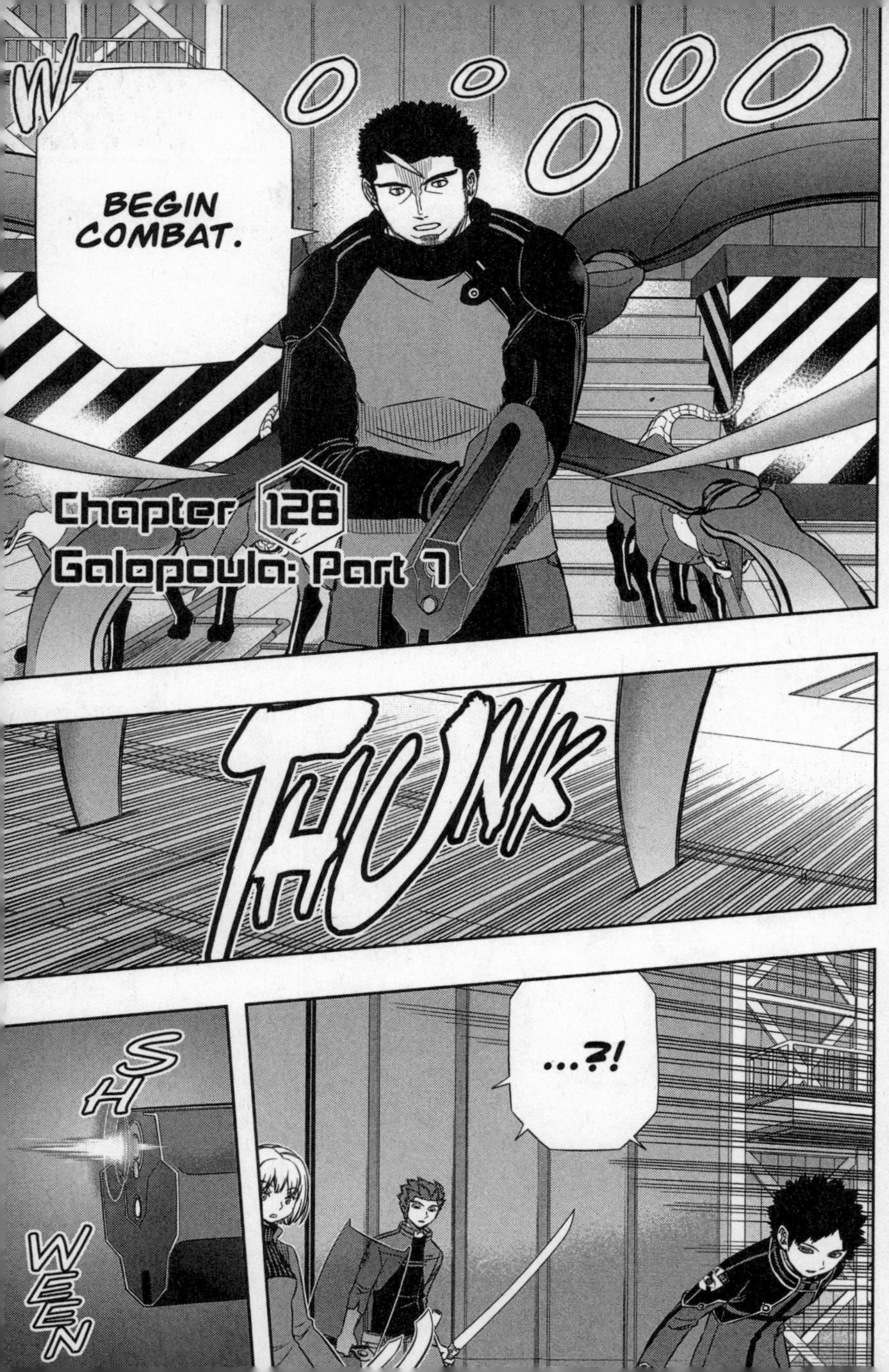
WOOOOOOO
BEGIN COMBAT.
THUNK
...?!
SH
WEEN

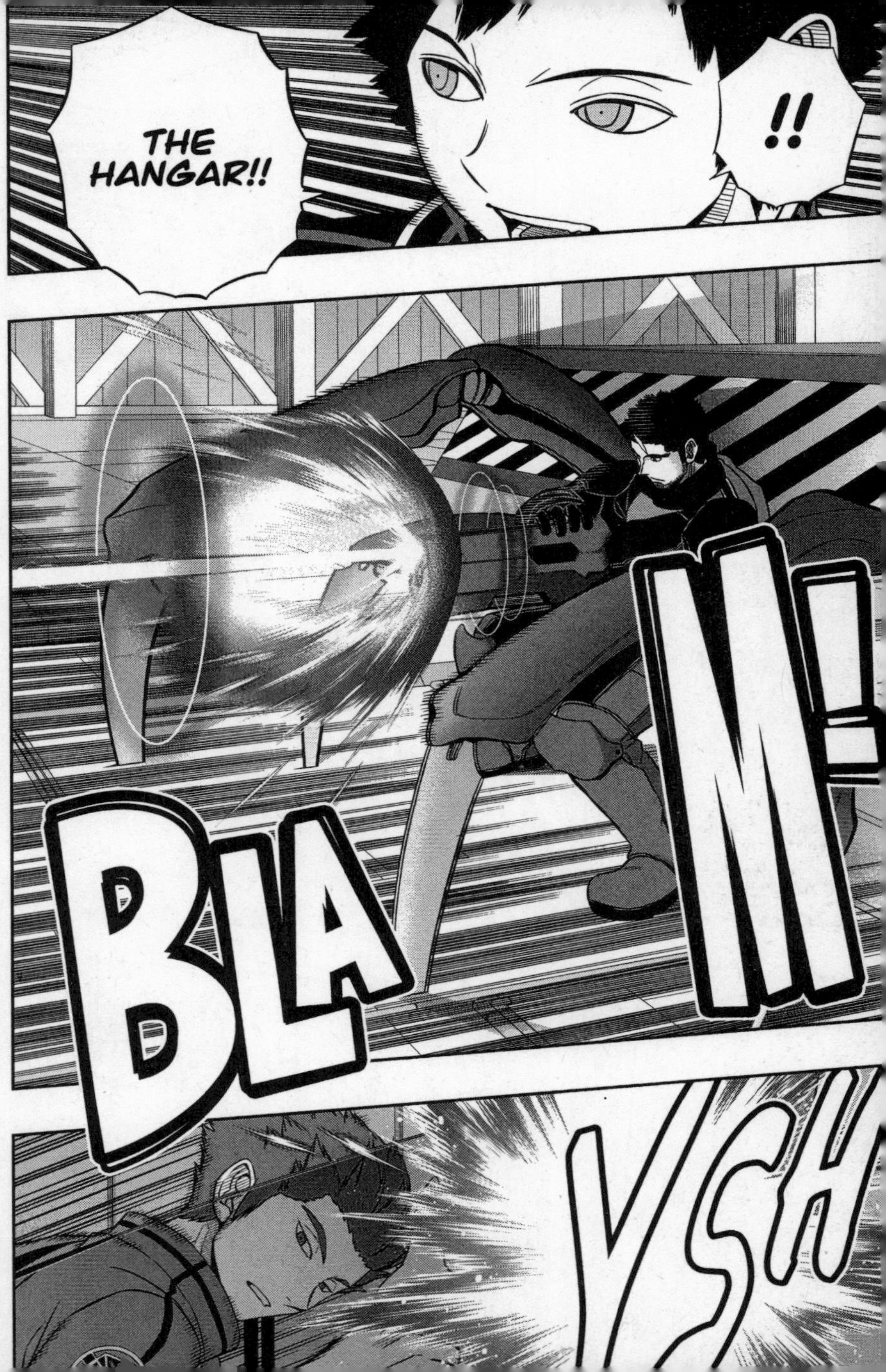
!!
THE HANGAR!!
BLAM!
VSH

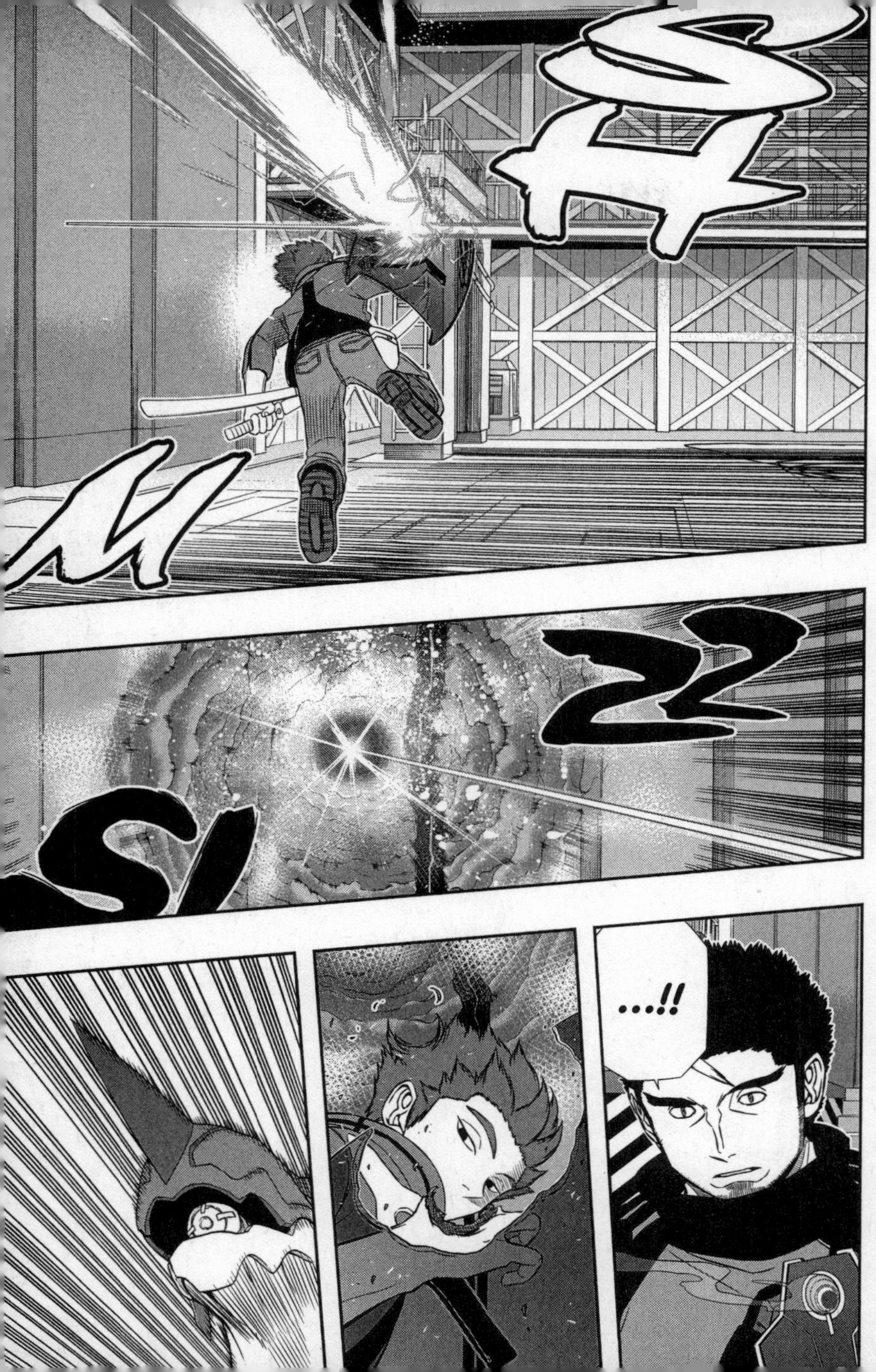
...!!

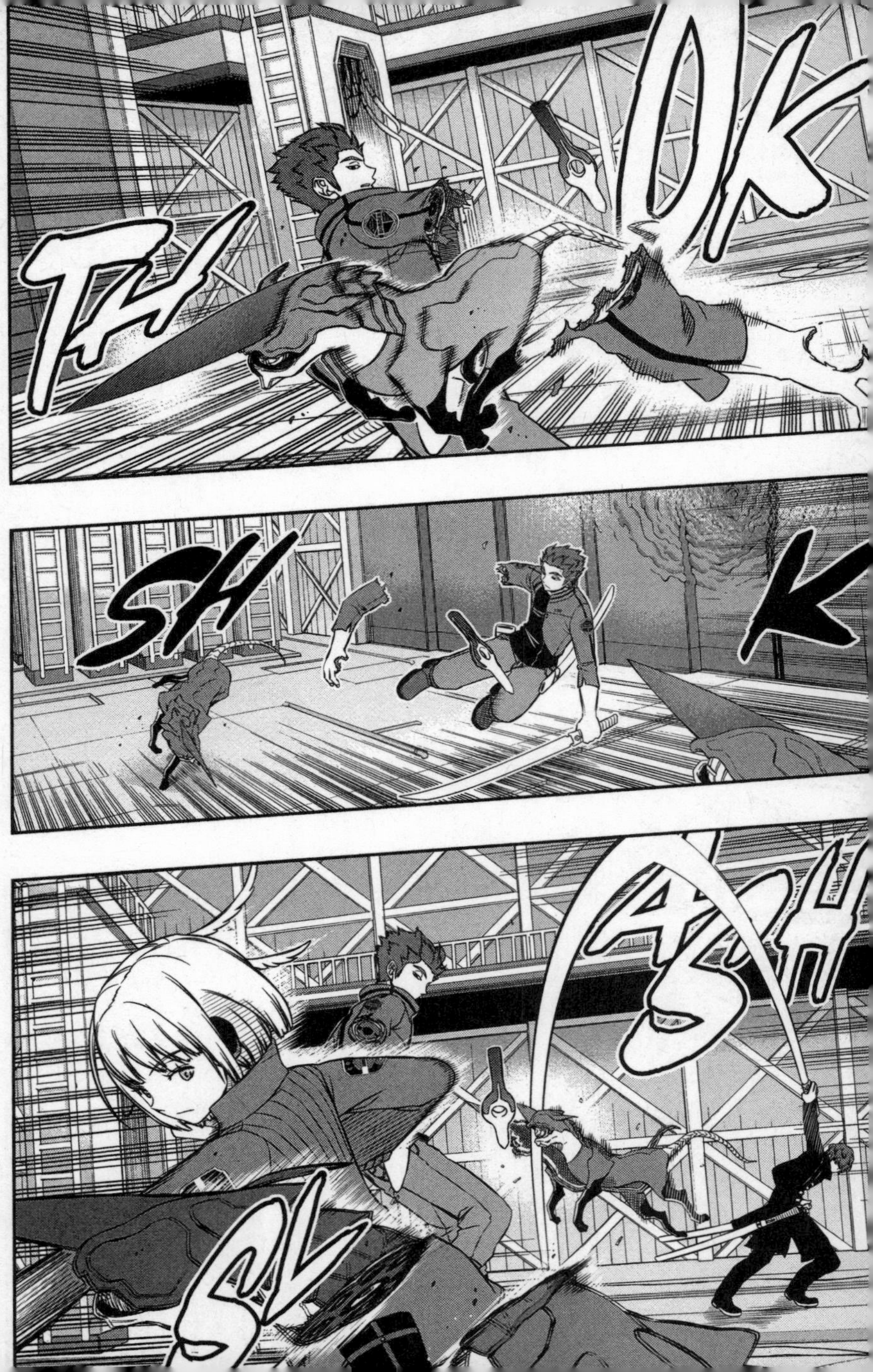
TH
UK
SH
K
ASH

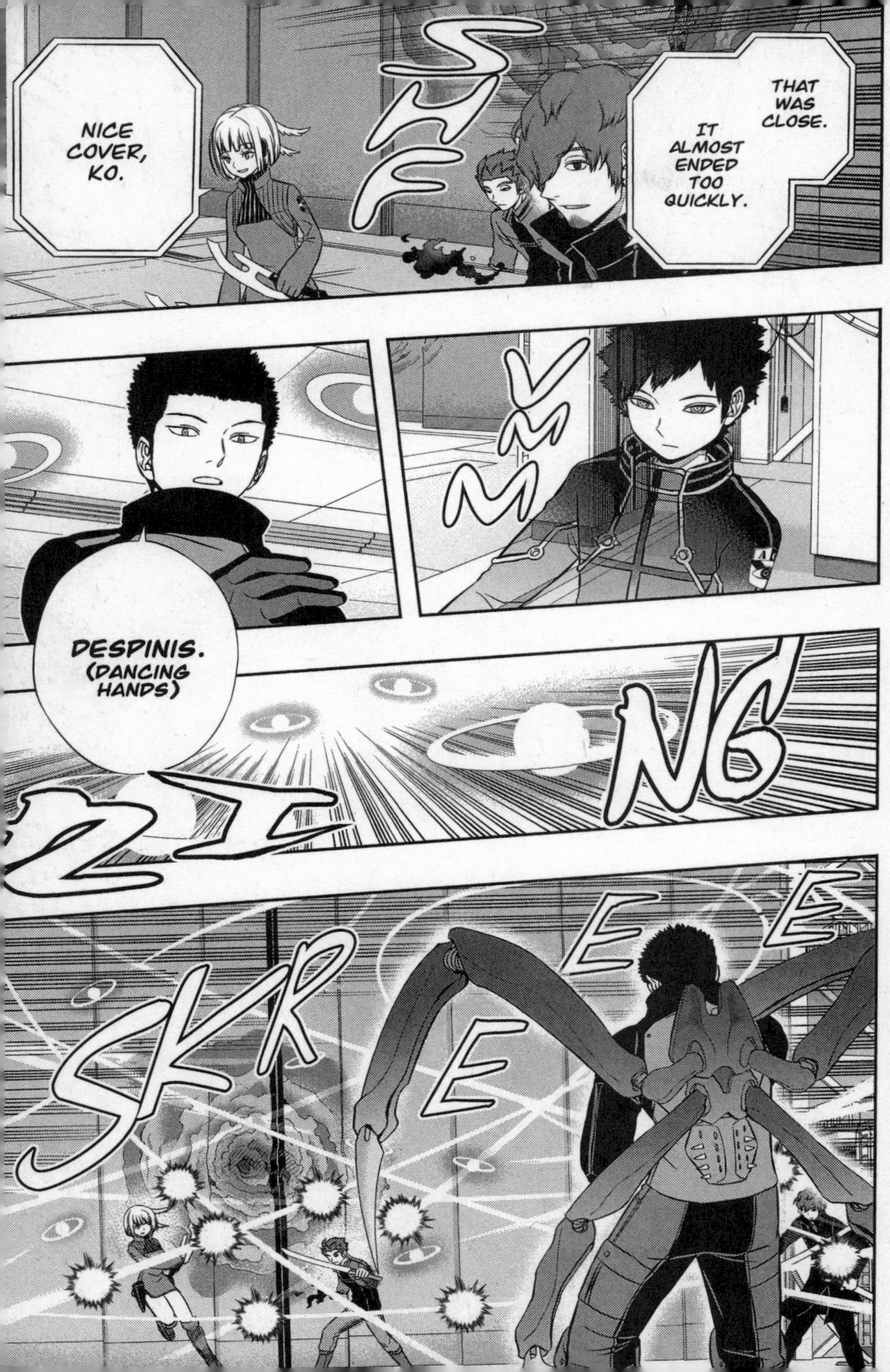
THAT WAS CLOSE.
IT ALMOST ENDED TOO QUICKLY.
SHF
NICE COVER, KO.
VMMM
DESPINIS. (DANCING HANDS)
ZING
SKREEEE

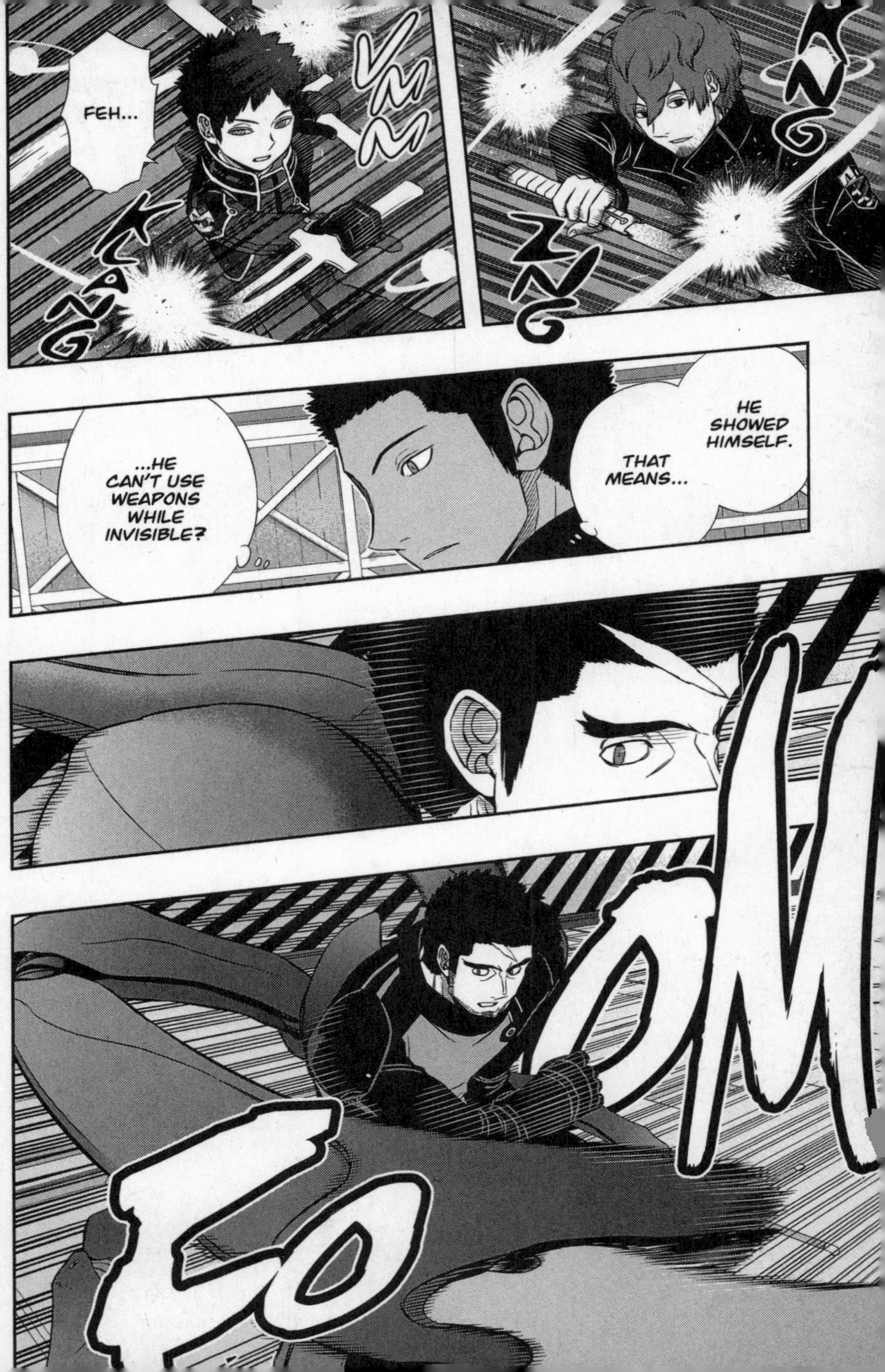
KNG
ZNG
VMM
FEH...
KLANG
HE SHOWED HIMSELF.
THAT MEANS...
...HE CAN'T USE WEAPONS WHILE INVISIBLE?

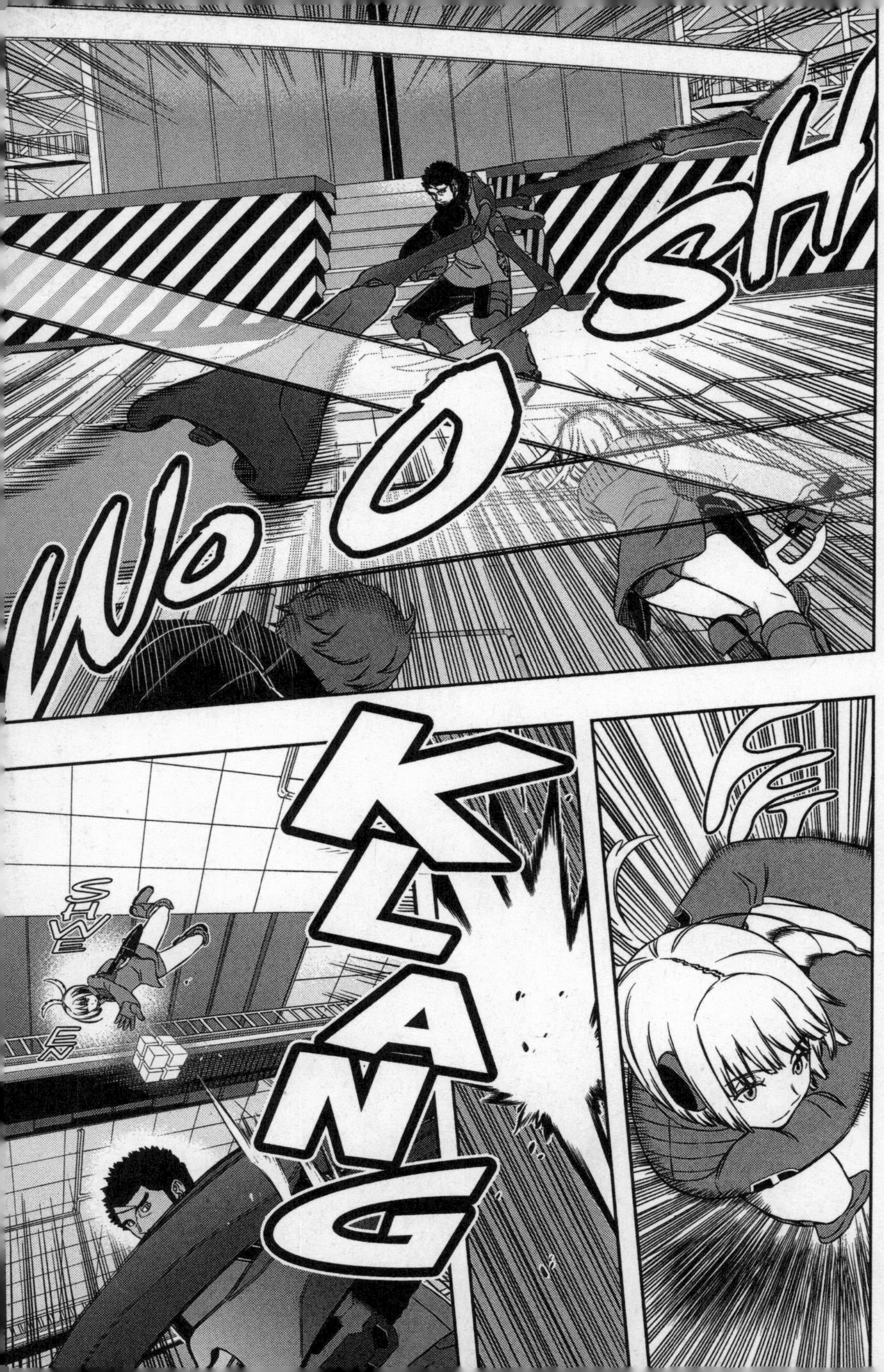
WOOSH
FF
KLANG
SHWEEN

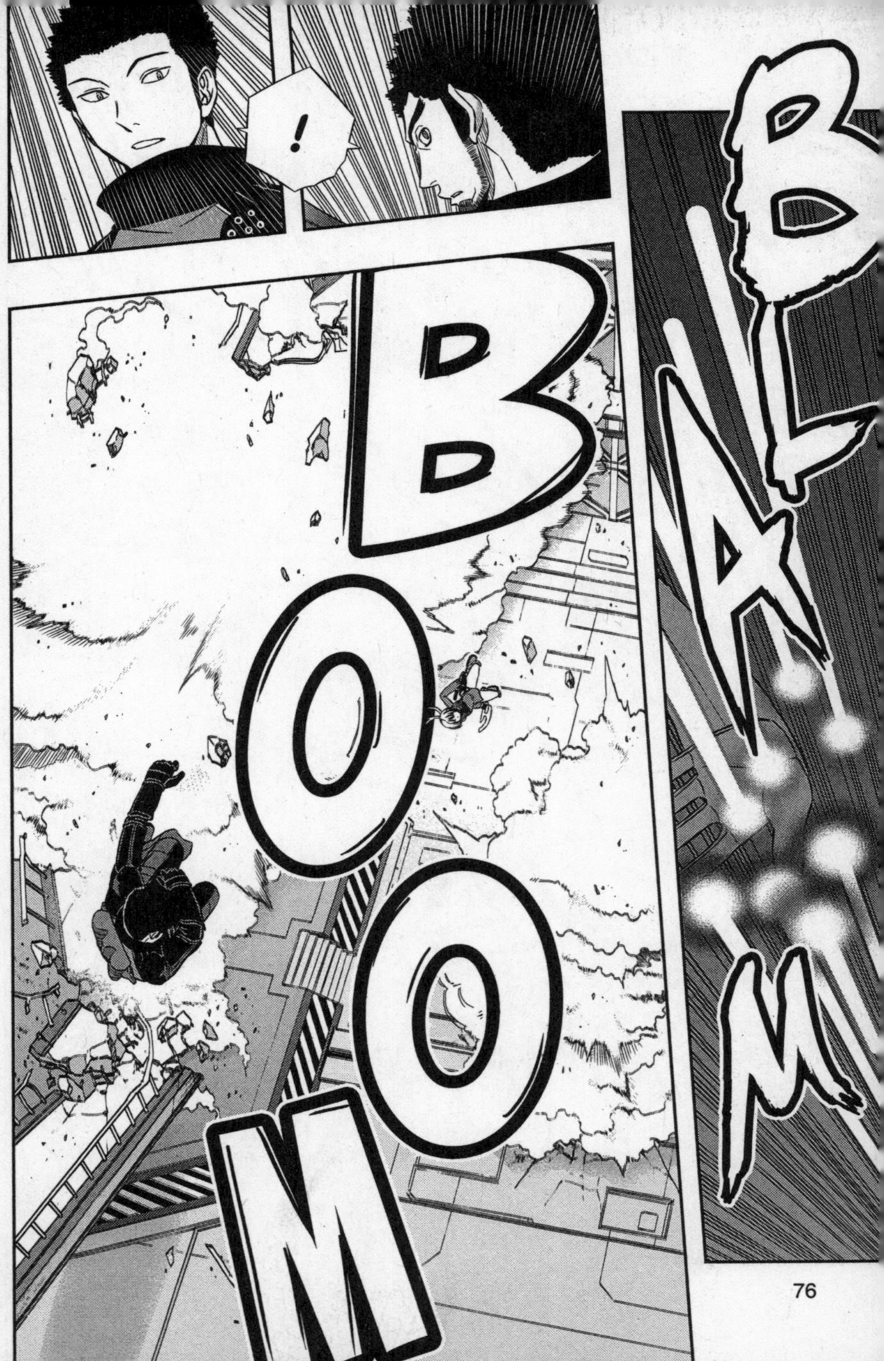
BAM
!
BOOOM

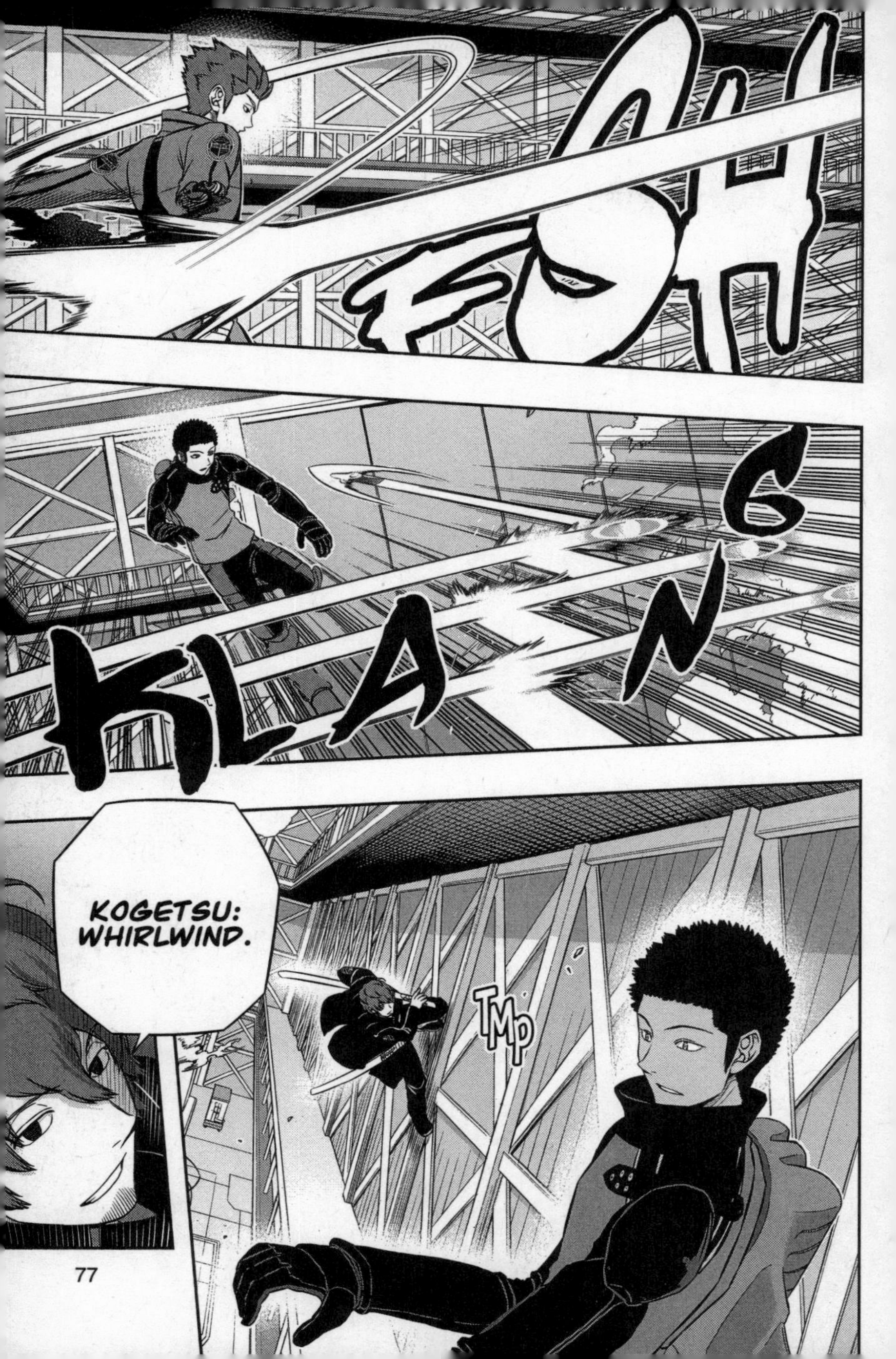
KLANG
KOGETSU: WHIRLWIND.
TMP

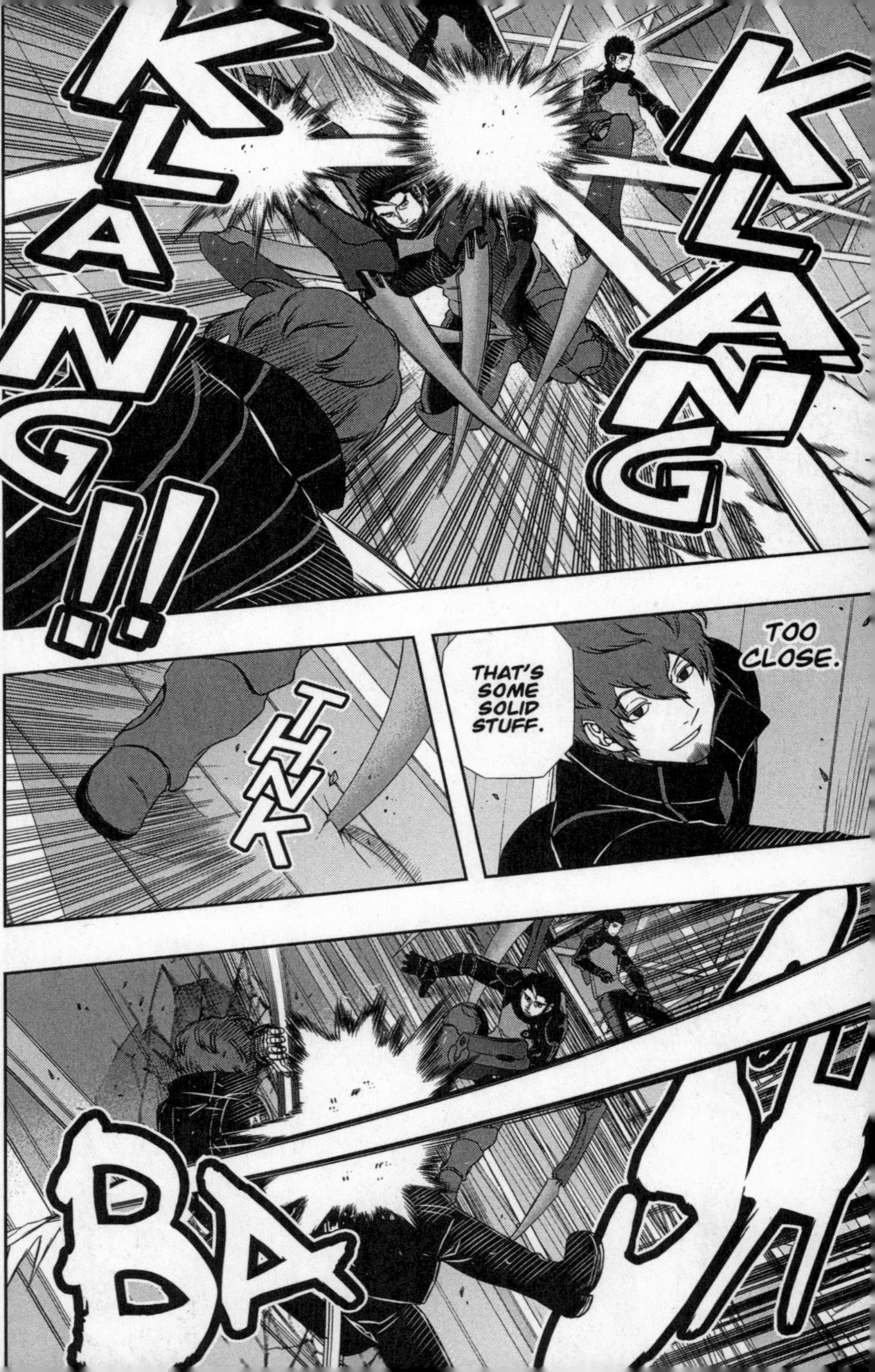
KLANG
KLANG!!
TOO CLOSE.
THAT'S SOME SOLID STUFF.
THNK
BA

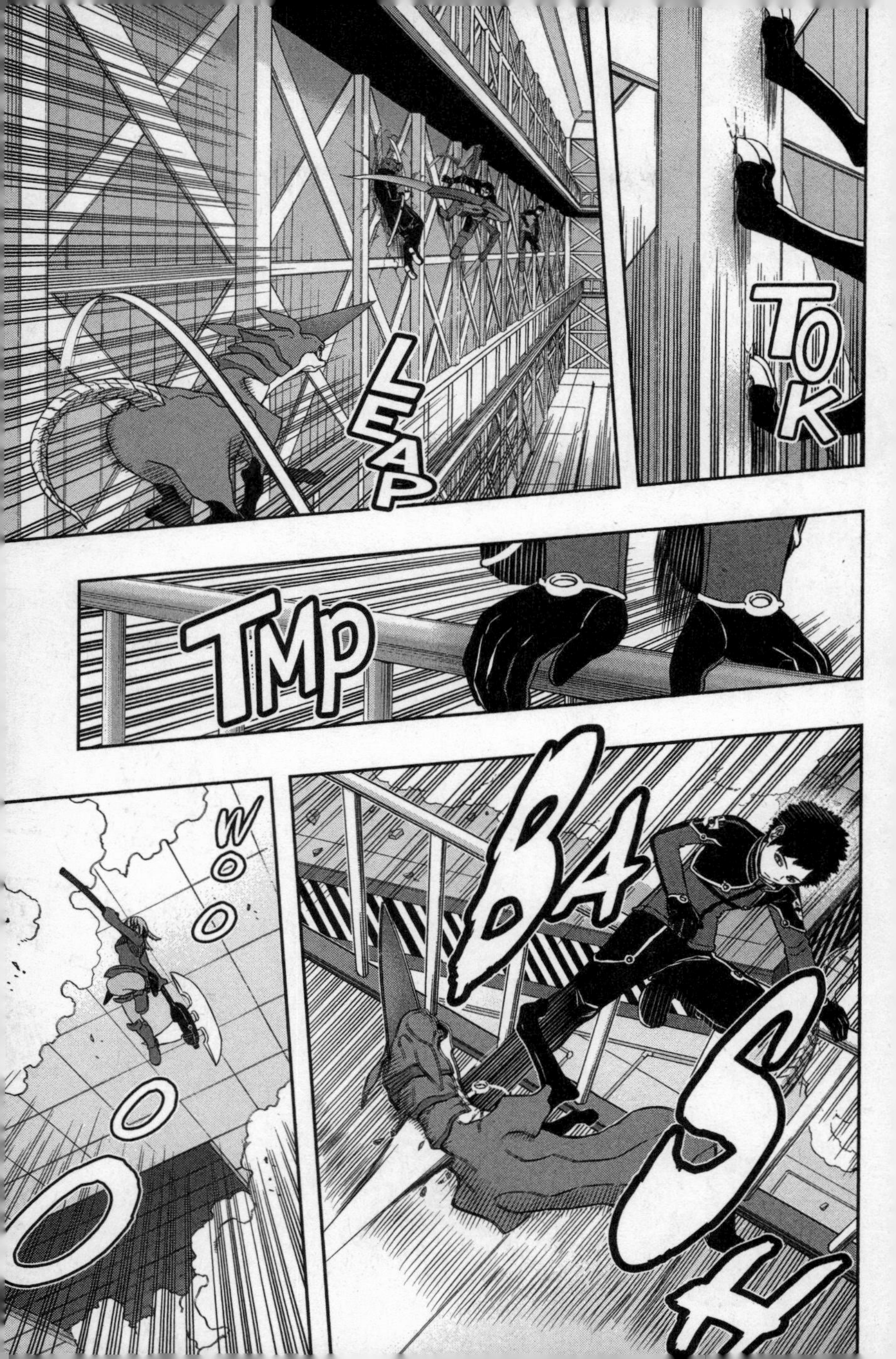
TOK
LEAP
TMP
BASH
WOOOO

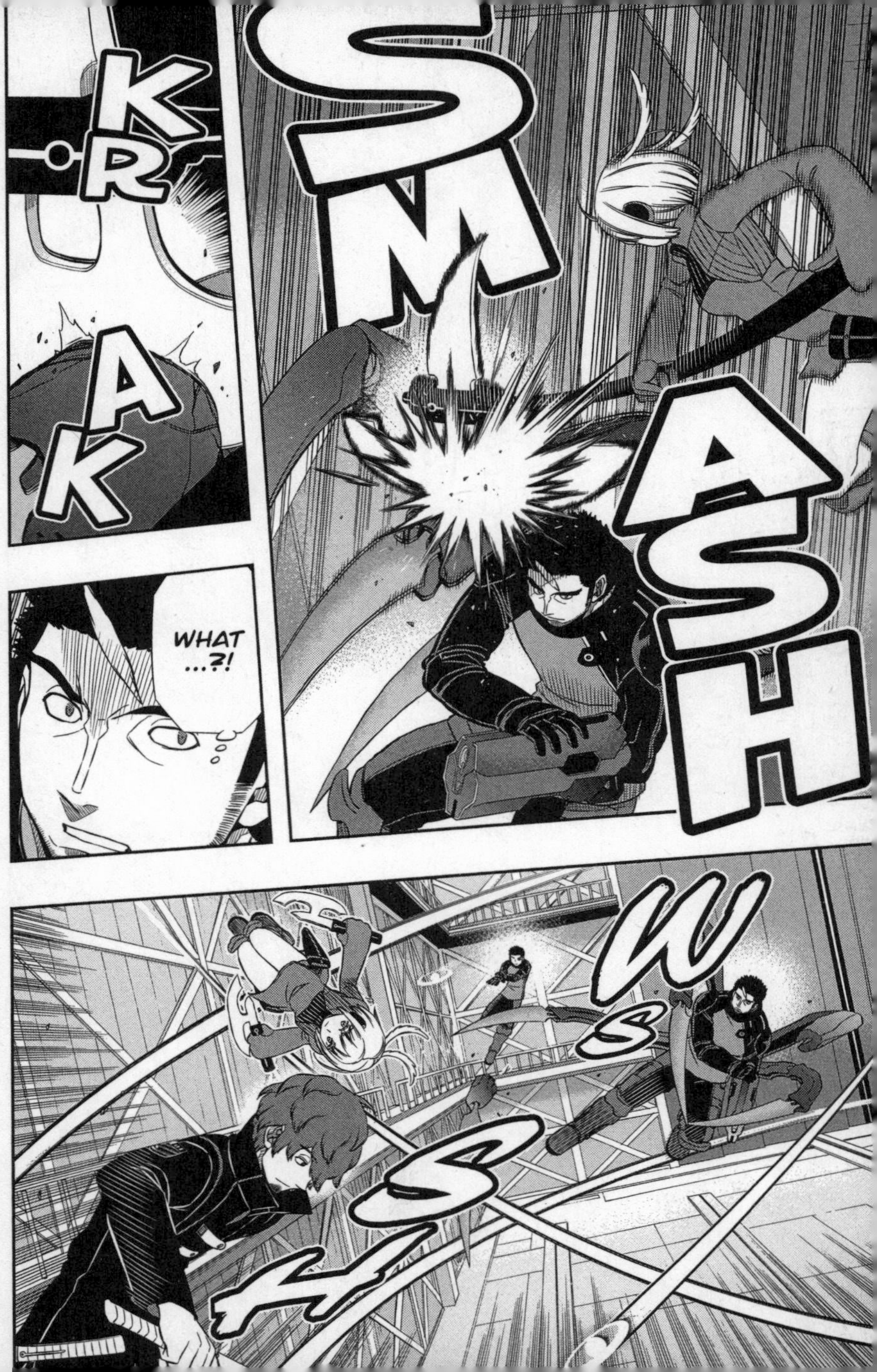
SMASH
KRAK
WHAT ...?!
WS
SH

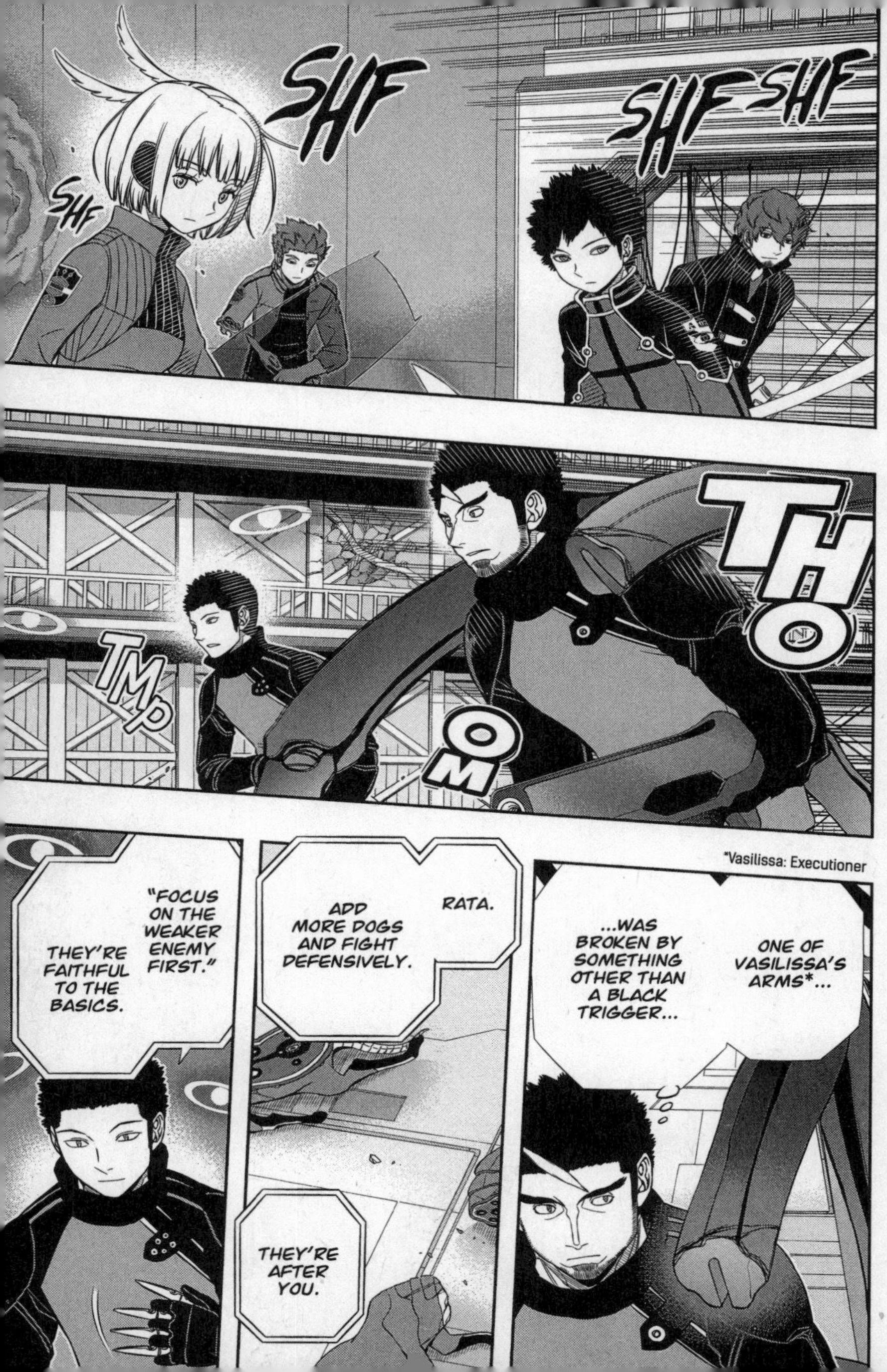
SHF SHF
SHF
SHF
THOOM
TMP
ONE OF VASILISSA'S ARMS*...
...WAS BROKEN BY SOMETHING OTHER THAN A BLACK TRIGGER...
*Vasilissa: Executioner
RATA.
ADD MORE DOGS AND FIGHT DEFENSIVELY.
THEY'RE AFTER YOU.
"FOCUS ON THE WEAKER ENEMY FIRST."
THEY'RE FAITHFUL TO THE BASICS.

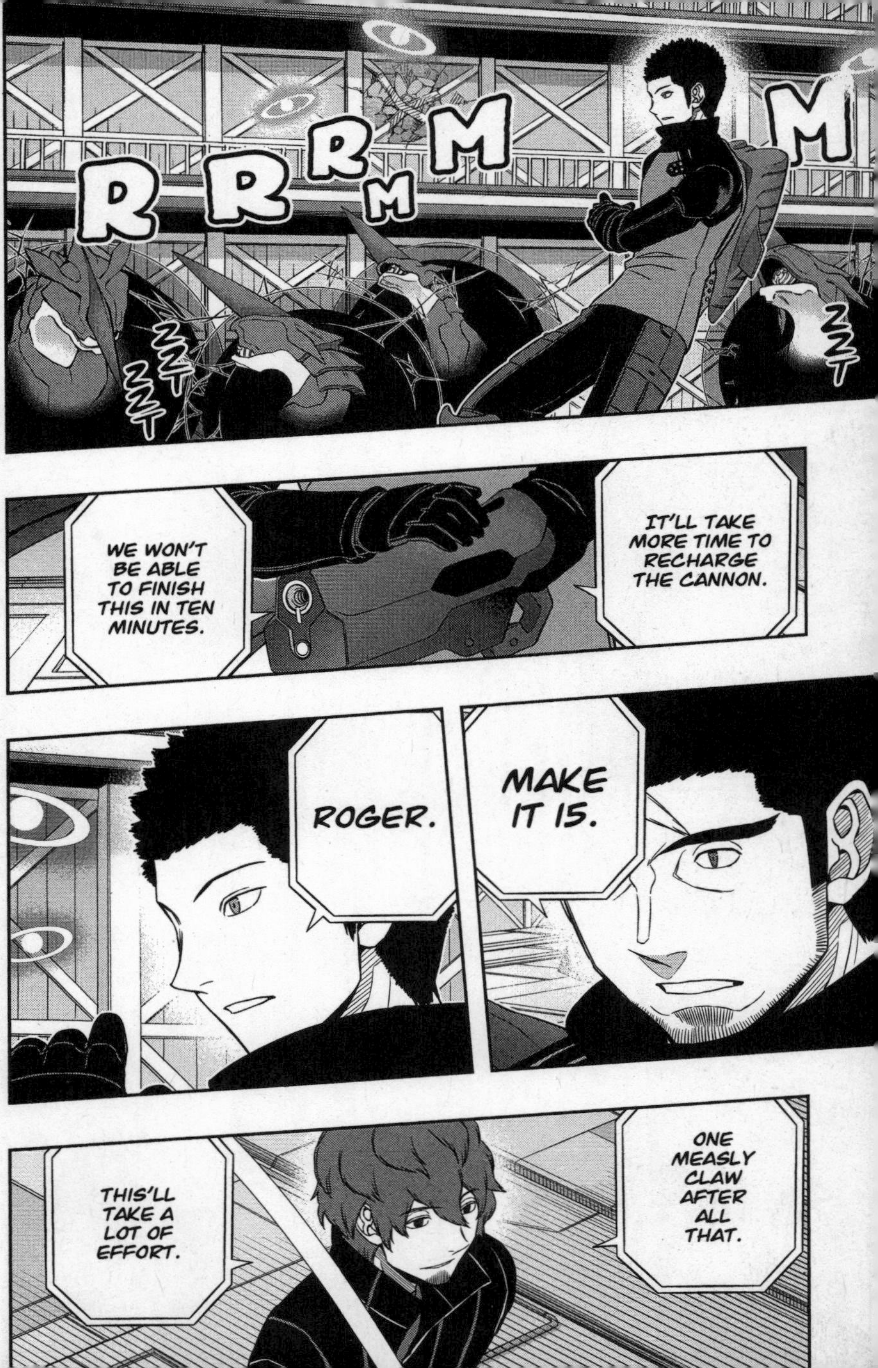
RRRMMM
ZZZT
ZZZT
ZZZT
IT'LL TAKE MORE TIME TO RECHARGE THE CANNON.
WE WON'T BE ABLE TO FINISH THIS IN TEN MINUTES.
MAKE IT 15.
ROGER.
ONE MEASLY CLAW AFTER ALL THAT.
THIS'LL TAKE A LOT OF EFFORT.

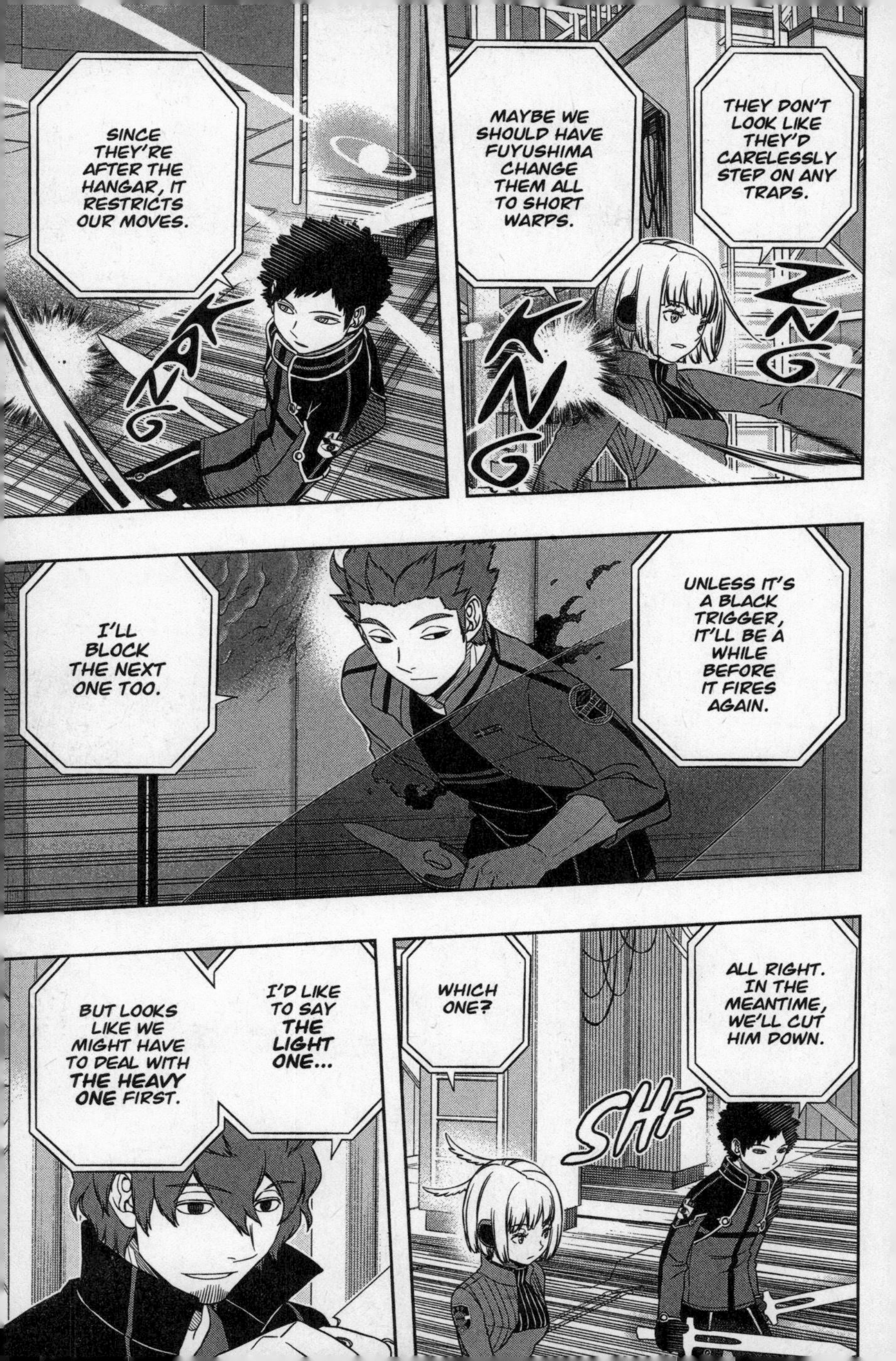
THEY DON'T LOOK LIKE THEY'D CARELESSLY STEP ON ANY TRAPS.
MAYBE WE SHOULD HAVE FUYUSHIMA CHANGE THEM ALL TO SHORT WARPS.
ZNG
KNG
SINCE THEY'RE AFTER THE HANGAR, IT RESTRICTS OUR MOVES.
KANG
UNLESS IT'S A BLACK TRIGGER, IT'LL BE A WHILE BEFORE IT FIRES AGAIN.
I'LL BLOCK THE NEXT ONE TOO.
ALL RIGHT. IN THE MEANTIME, WE'LL CUT HIM DOWN.
WHICH ONE?
SHF
I'D LIKE TO SAY THE LIGHT ONE...
BUT LOOKS LIKE WE MIGHT HAVE TO DEAL WITH THE HEAVY ONE FIRST.

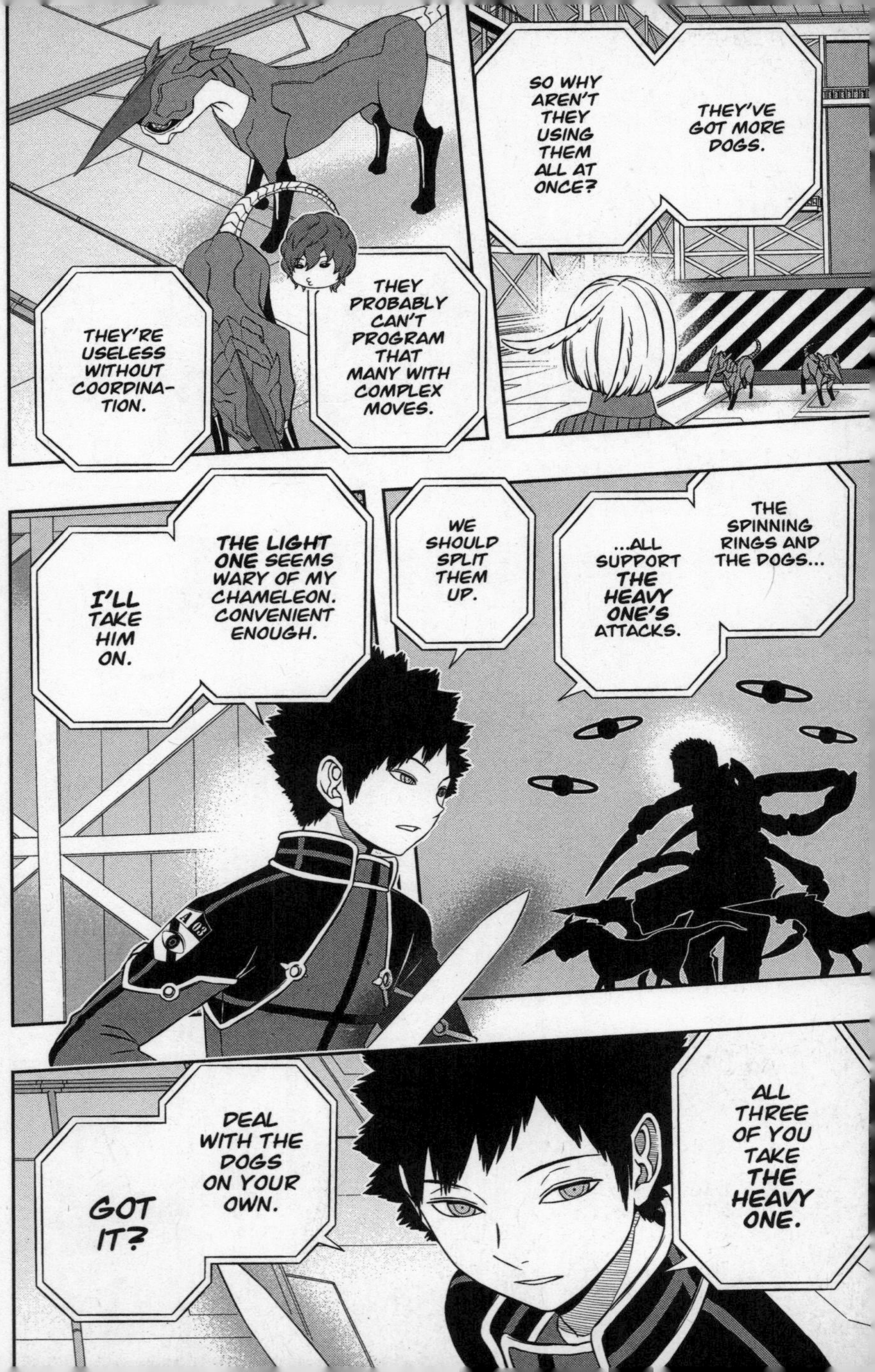
THEY'VE GOT MORE DOGS.
SO WHY AREN'T THEY USING THEM ALL AT ONCE?
THEY PROBABLY CAN'T PROGRAM THAT MANY WITH COMPLEX MOVES.
THEY'RE USELESS WITHOUT COORDINATION.
THE SPINNING RINGS AND THE DOGS...
...ALL SUPPORT THE HEAVY ONE'S ATTACKS.
WE SHOULD SPLIT THEM UP.
THE LIGHT ONE SEEMS WARY OF MY CHAMELEON. CONVENIENT ENOUGH.
I'LL TAKE HIM ON.
ALL THREE OF YOU TAKE THE HEAVY ONE.
DEAL WITH THE DOGS ON YOUR OWN.
GOT IT?

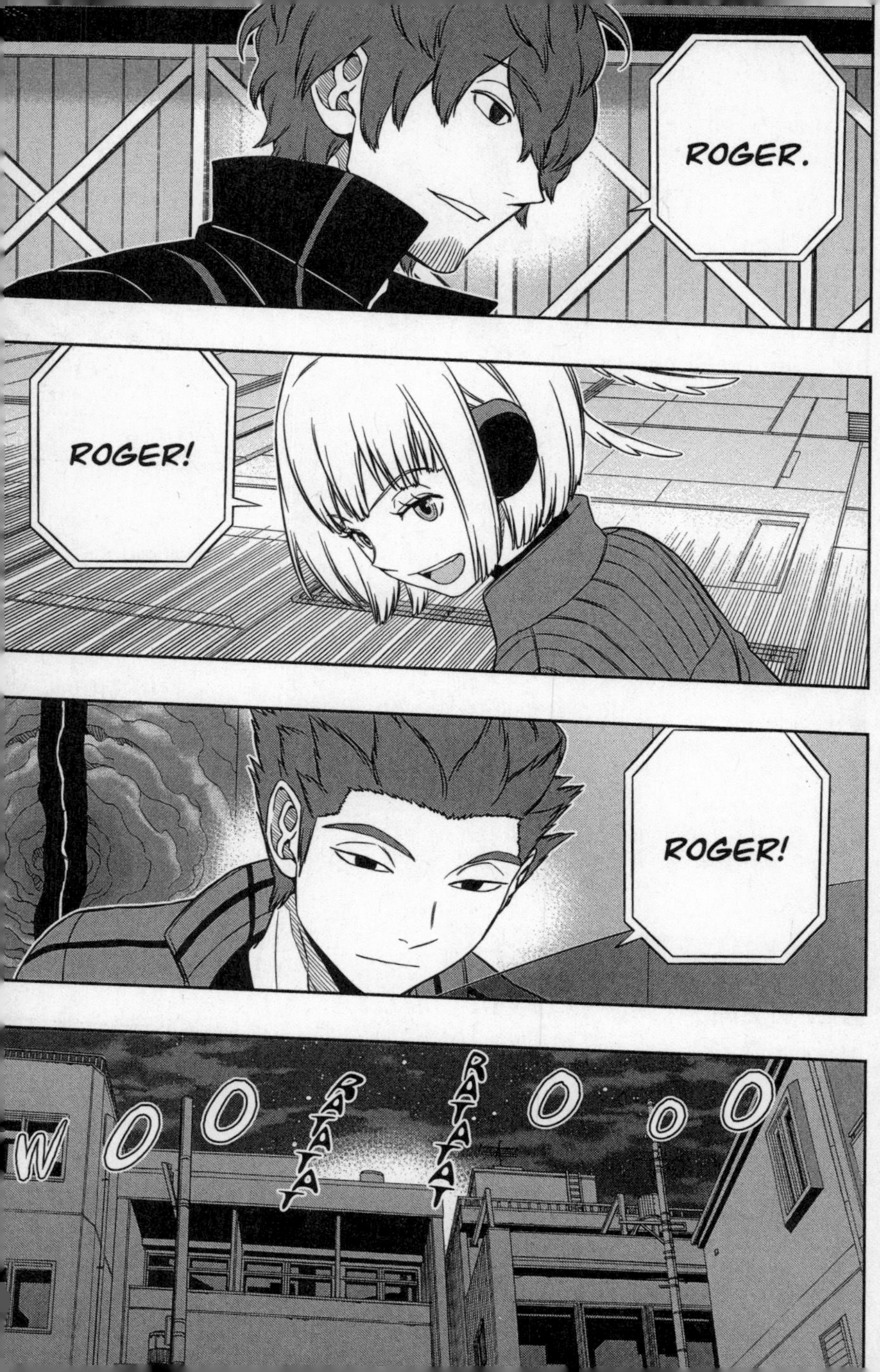
ROGER.
ROGER!
ROGER!
WOOOOO
RATATA
RATATA

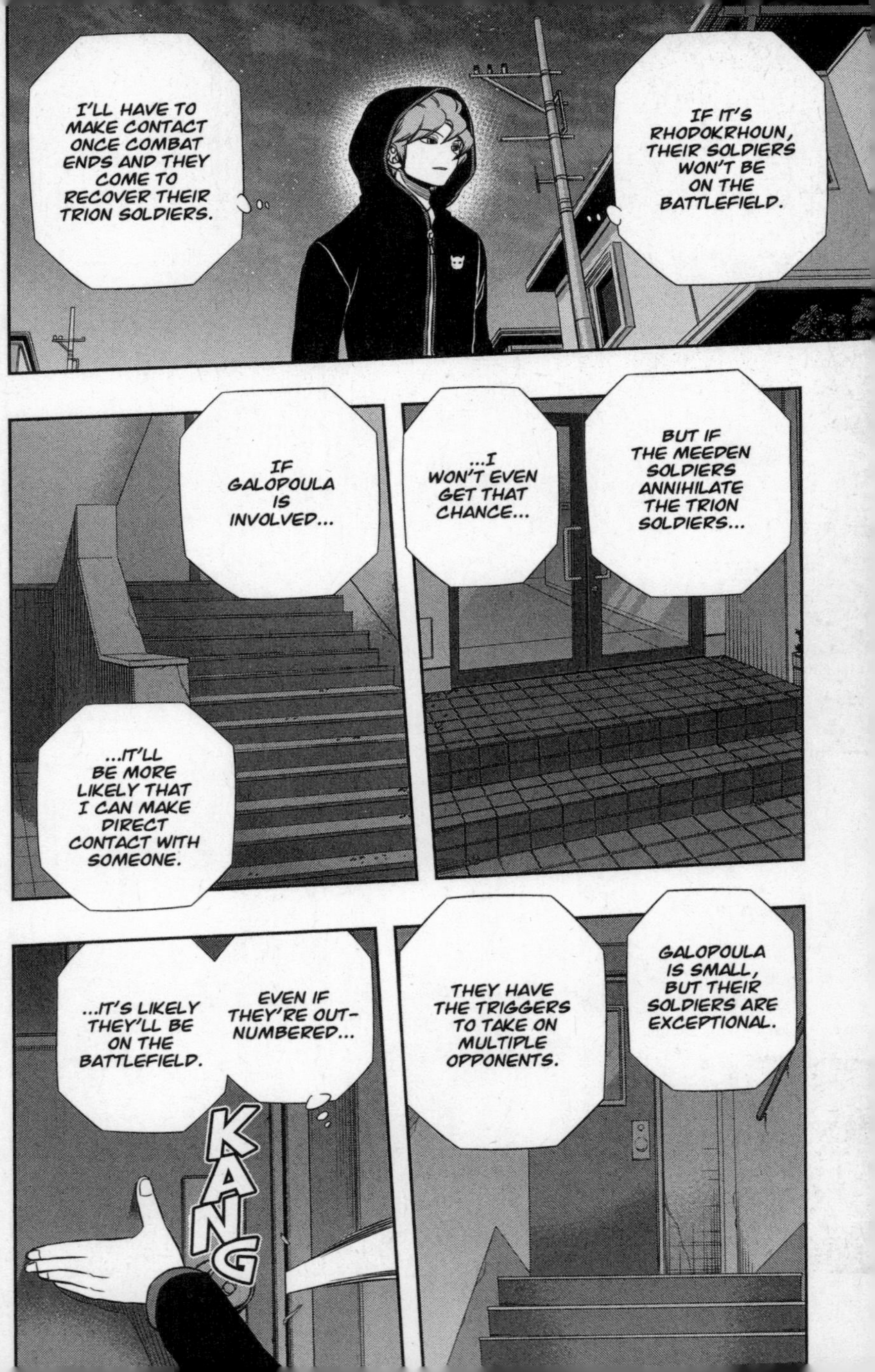
IF IT'S RHODOKRHOUN, THEIR SOLDIERS WON'T BE ON THE BATTLEFIELD.
I'LL HAVE TO MAKE CONTACT ONCE COMBAT ENDS AND THEY COME TO RECOVER THEIR TRION SOLDIERS.
BUT IF THE MEEDEN SOLDIERS ANNIHILATE THE TRION SOLDIERS...
...I WON'T EVEN GET THAT CHANCE...
IF GALOPOULA IS INVOLVED...
...IT'LL BE MORE LIKELY THAT I CAN MAKE DIRECT CONTACT WITH SOMEONE.
GALOPOULA IS SMALL, BUT THEIR SOLDIERS ARE EXCEPTIONAL.
THEY HAVE THE TRIGGERS TO TAKE ON MULTIPLE OPPONENTS.
EVEN IF THEY'RE OUT-NUMBERED...
...IT'S LIKELY THEY'LL BE ON THE BATTLEFIELD.
KANG

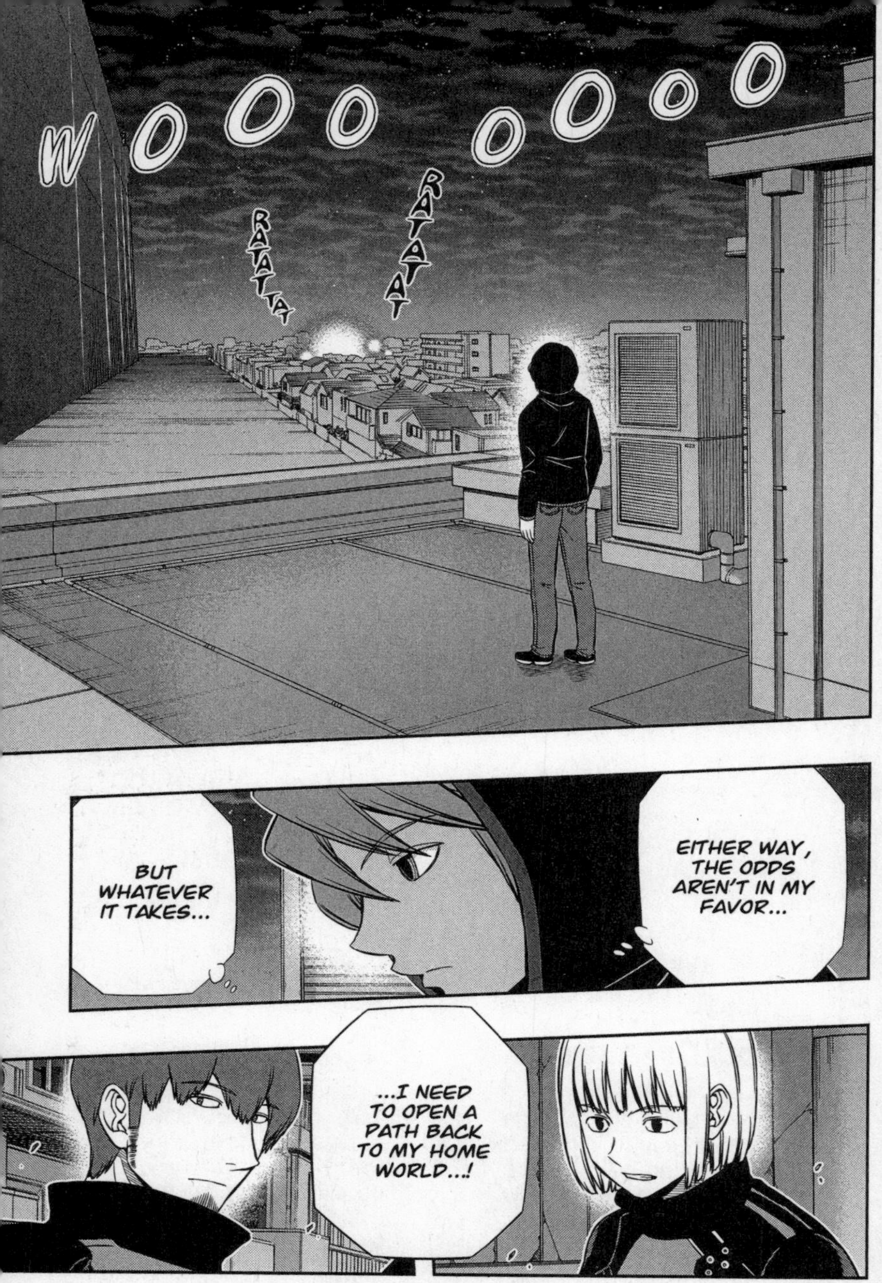
WOOOOOOO
RATATAT
RATATAT
EITHER WAY, THE ODDS AREN'T IN MY FAVOR...
BUT WHATEVER IT TAKES...
...I NEED TO OPEN A PATH BACK TO MY HOME WORLD...!

Trion soldier

Neighbor Troops

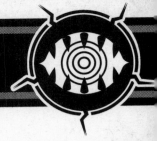

Dog Takia
Recon and Group Combat Trion Soldier

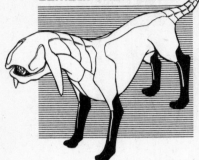

About the size of a medium-large dog, and it acts just like a dog. It can shoot beams from its eye. Fighting only one of these is a piece of cake, but fighting a pack can be an annoying piece of cake. This Dog Takia is the only model that can switch to reconnaissance mode and remain hidden from radar.

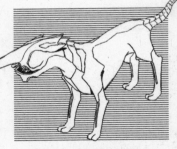

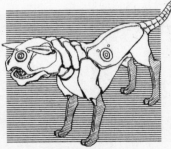

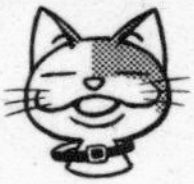

Dog Manverd

A combat-support dog equipped with a shield. It can also shoot beams from its eye. It's a great companion on the battlefield, but its face is ugly.

Dog Batelier

An assault-type dog with a blade on its head. It can't shoot beams from its eye, but it is relatively stronger than other dogs. It's a handsome dog with a strong fighting spirit. Just an overall cool dog.

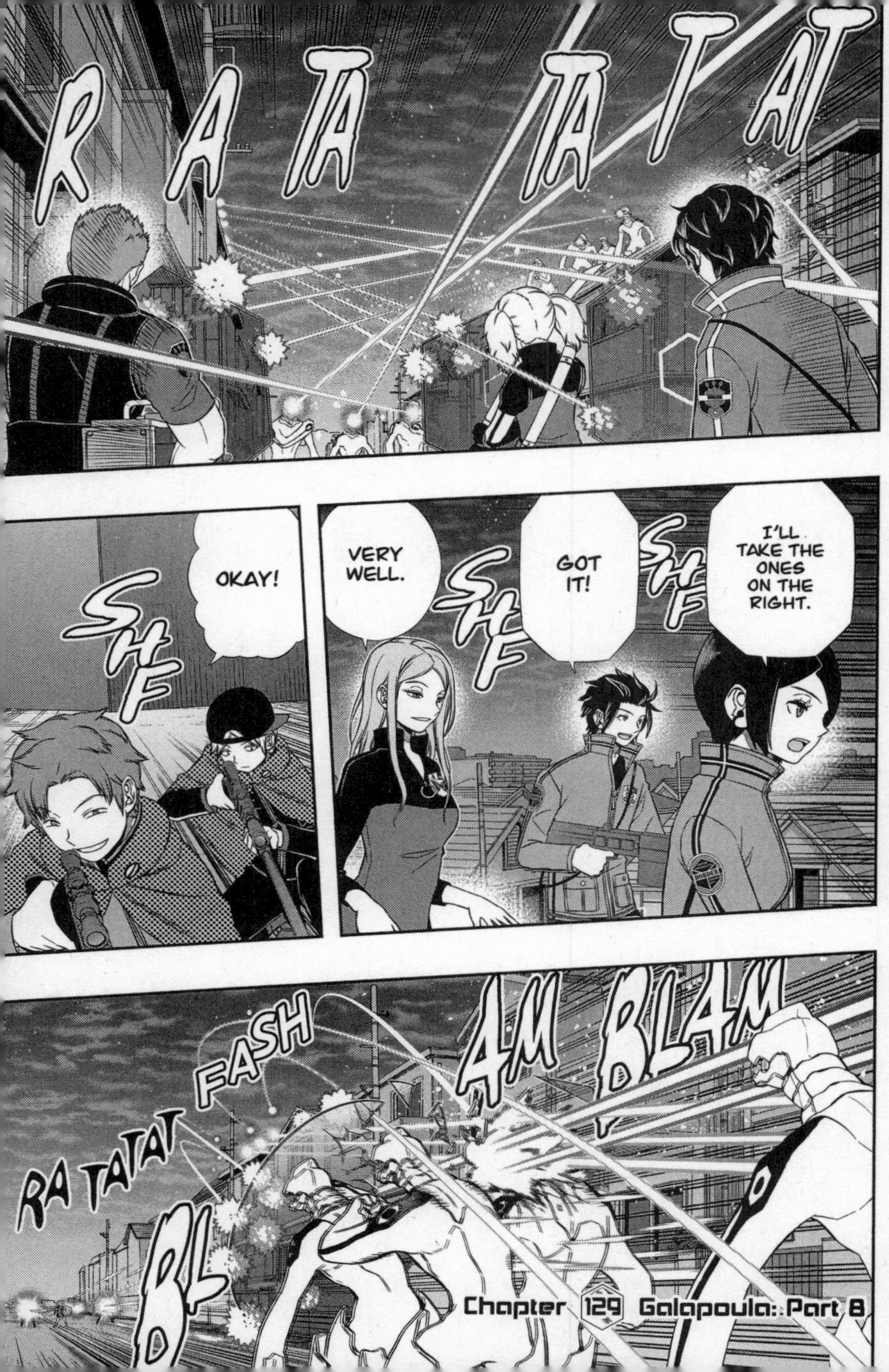
RATATATAT
I'LL TAKE THE ONES ON THE RIGHT.
SHF
GOT IT!
SHF
VERY WELL.
OKAY!
SHF
BLAM BLAM
FASH
RA TATAT
BL
Chapter 129 Galapoula: Part 8

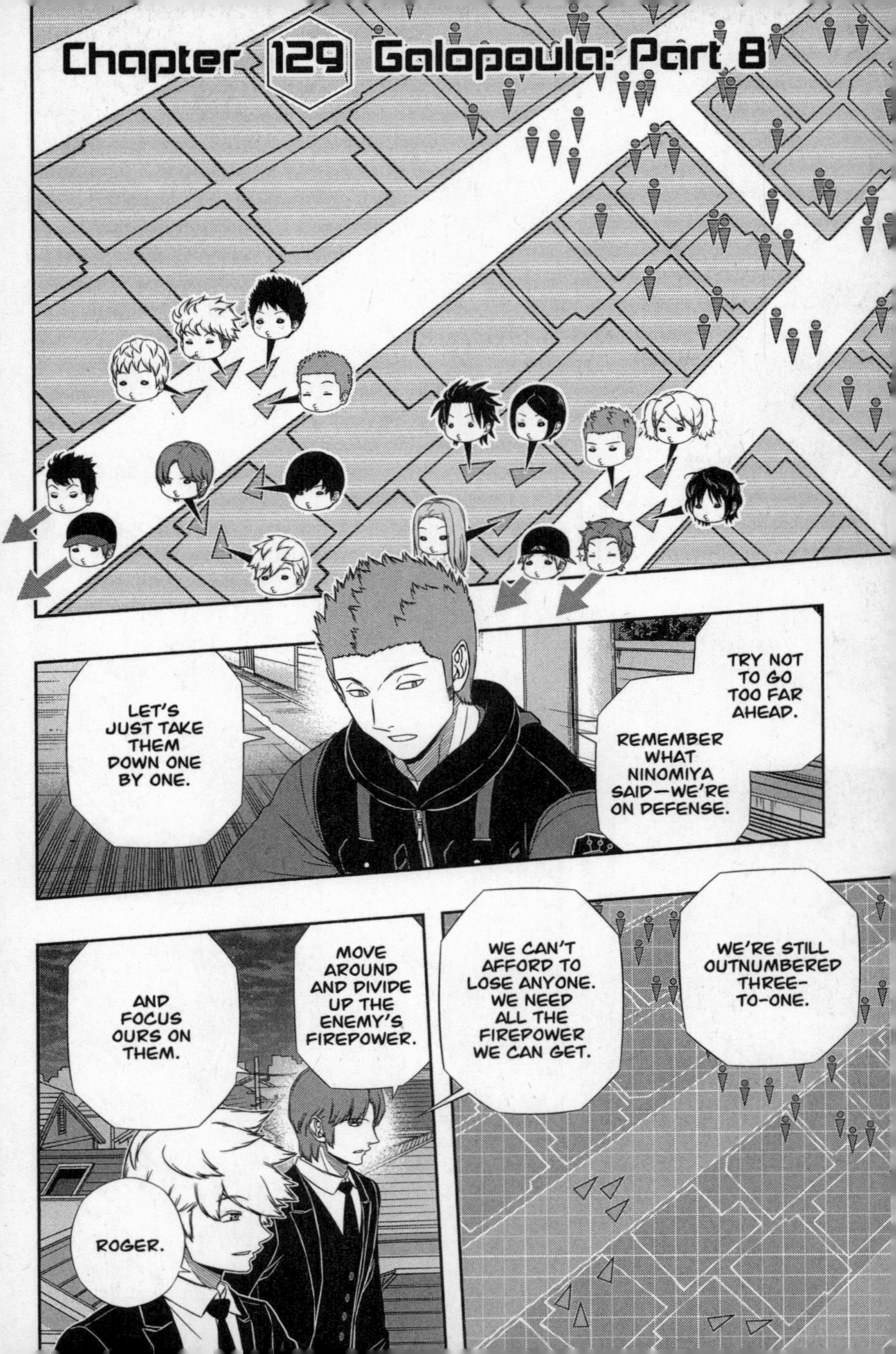
Chapter 129 Galopoula: Part 8
TRY NOT TO GO TOO FAR AHEAD.
REMEMBER WHAT NINOMIYA SAID—WE'RE ON DEFENSE.
LET'S JUST TAKE THEM DOWN ONE BY ONE.
WE'RE STILL OUTNUMBERED THREE-TO-ONE.
WE CAN'T AFFORD TO LOSE ANYONE. WE NEED ALL THE FIREPOWER WE CAN GET.
MOVE AROUND AND DIVIDE UP THE ENEMY'S FIREPOWER.
AND FOCUS OURS ON THEM.
ROGER.

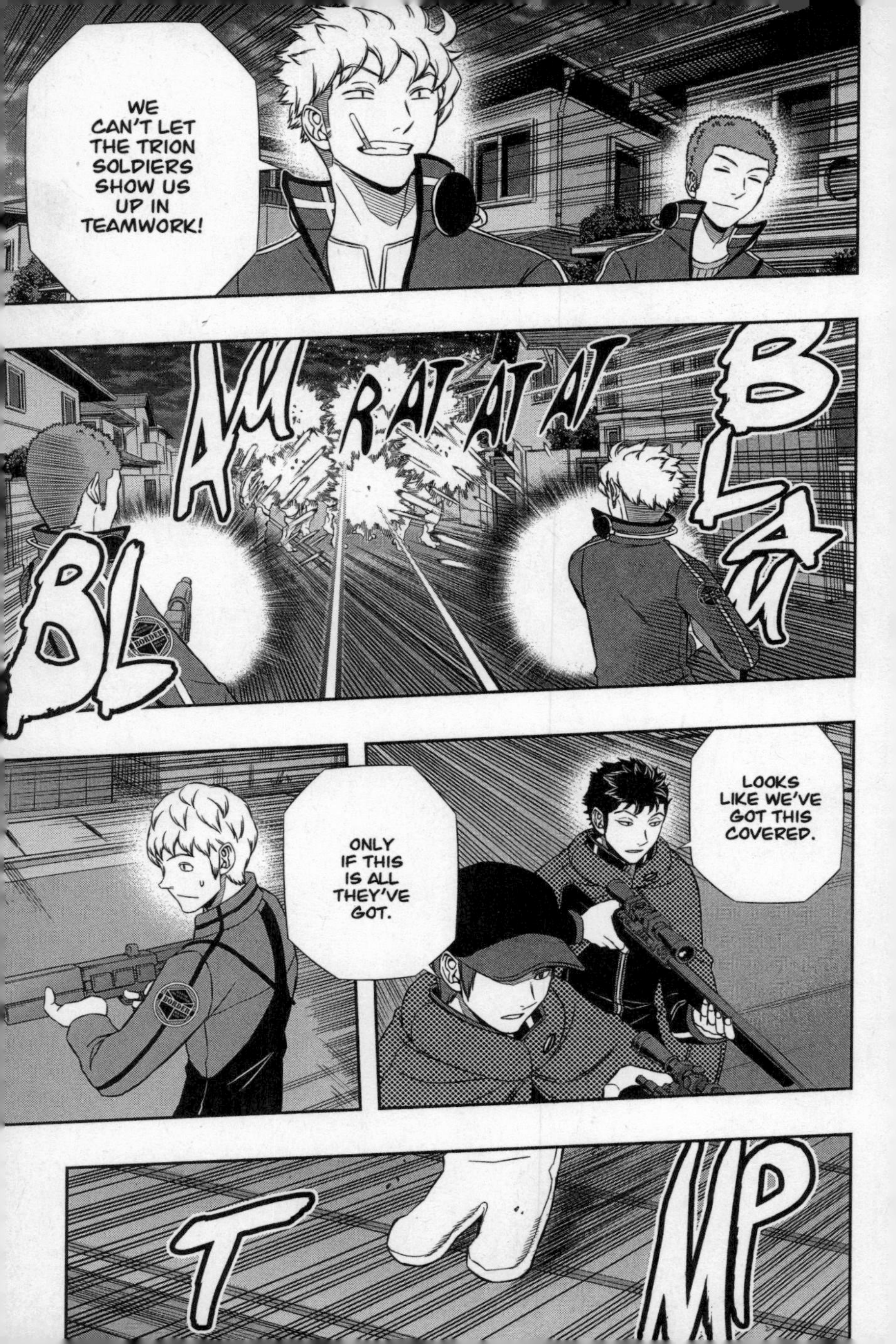
WE CAN'T LET THE TRION SOLDIERS SHOW US UP IN TEAMWORK!
BLAM
RATATAT
BLAM
LOOKS LIKE WE'VE GOT THIS COVERED.
ONLY IF THIS IS ALL THEY'VE GOT.
MP
T

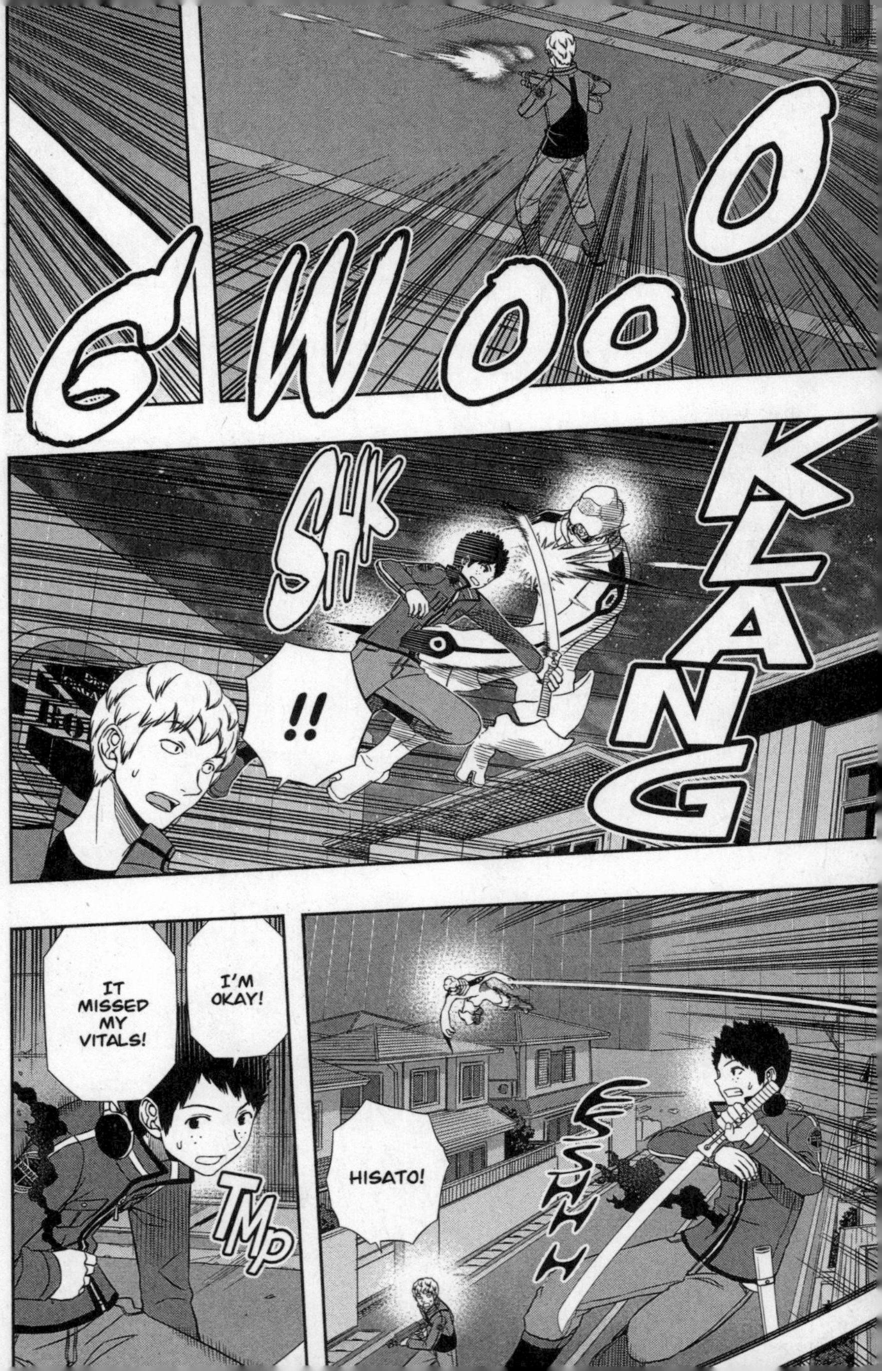
GWOOO
KLANG
SHK
!!
SSHHH
HISATO!
I'M OKAY!
IT MISSED MY VITALS!
TMP

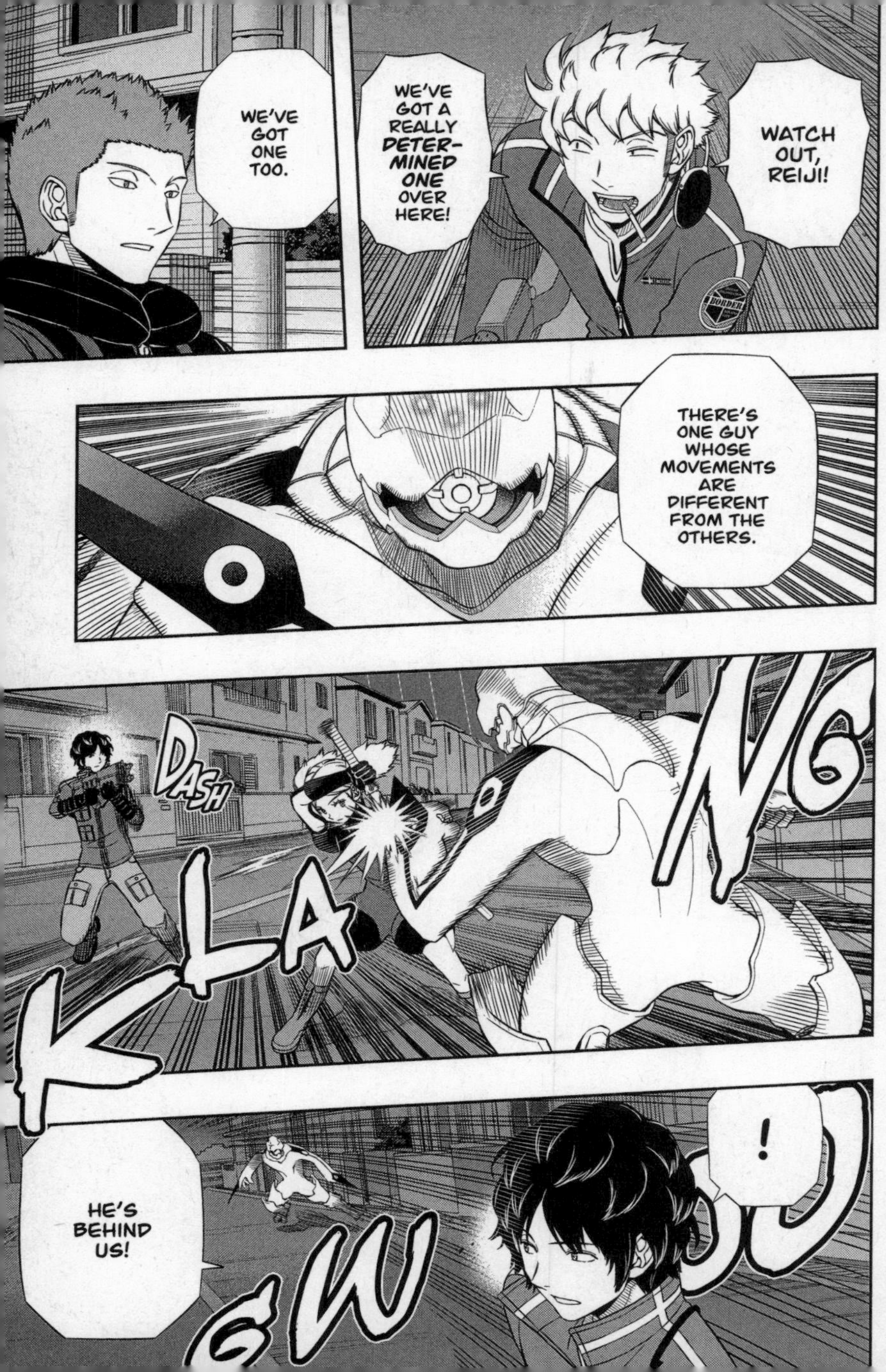
WATCH OUT, REIJI!
WE'VE GOT A REALLY DETERMINED ONE OVER HERE!
WE'VE GOT ONE TOO.
THERE'S ONE GUY WHOSE MOVEMENTS ARE DIFFERENT FROM THE OTHERS.
KLANG
DASH
!
HE'S BEHIND US!

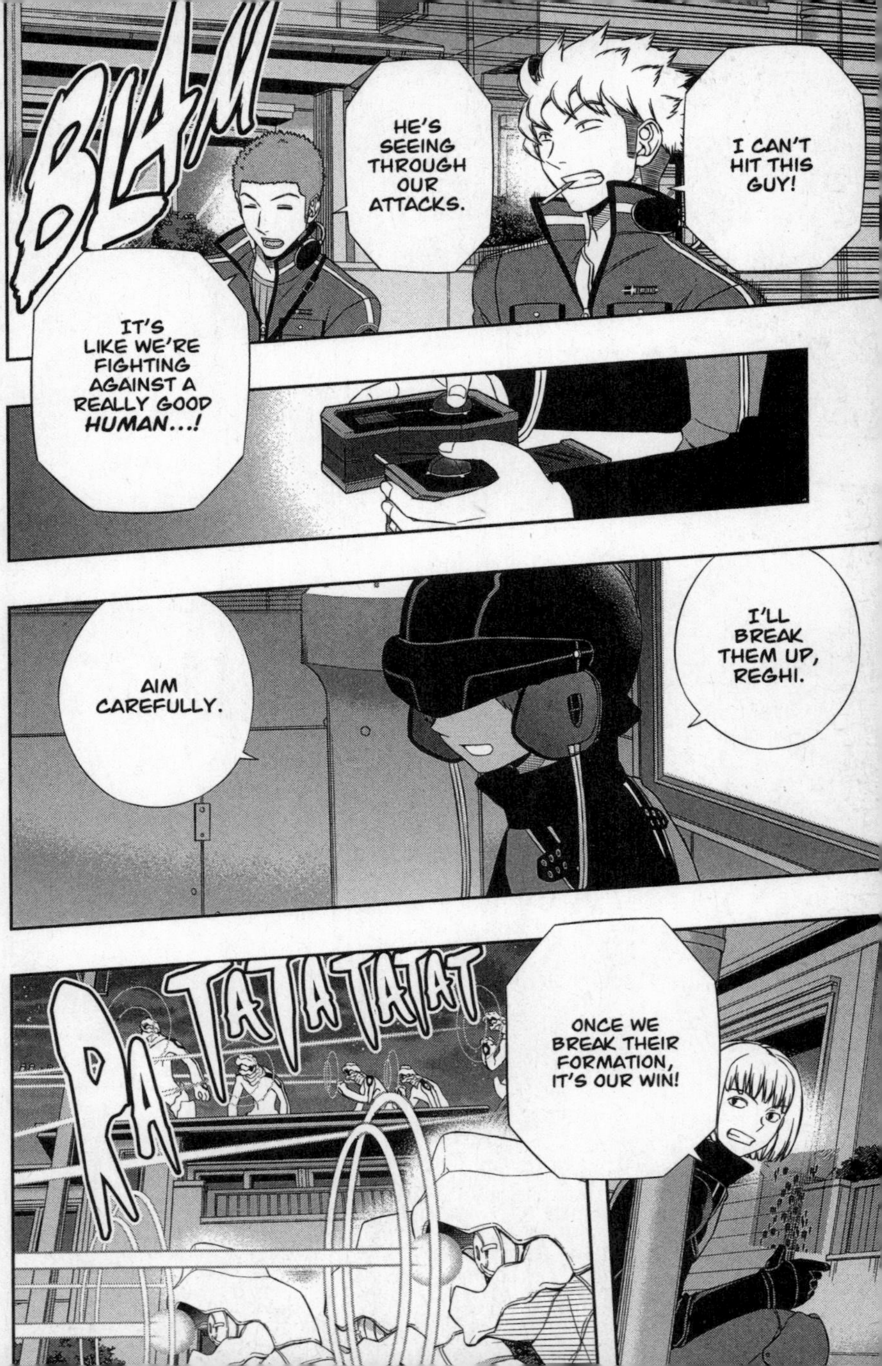
I CAN'T HIT THIS GUY!
HE'S SEEING THROUGH OUR ATTACKS.
BLAM
IT'S LIKE WE'RE FIGHTING AGAINST A REALLY GOOD HUMAN...!
I'LL BREAK THEM UP, REGHI.
AIM CAREFULLY.
ONCE WE BREAK THEIR FORMATION, IT'S OUR WIN!
RATATATATAT

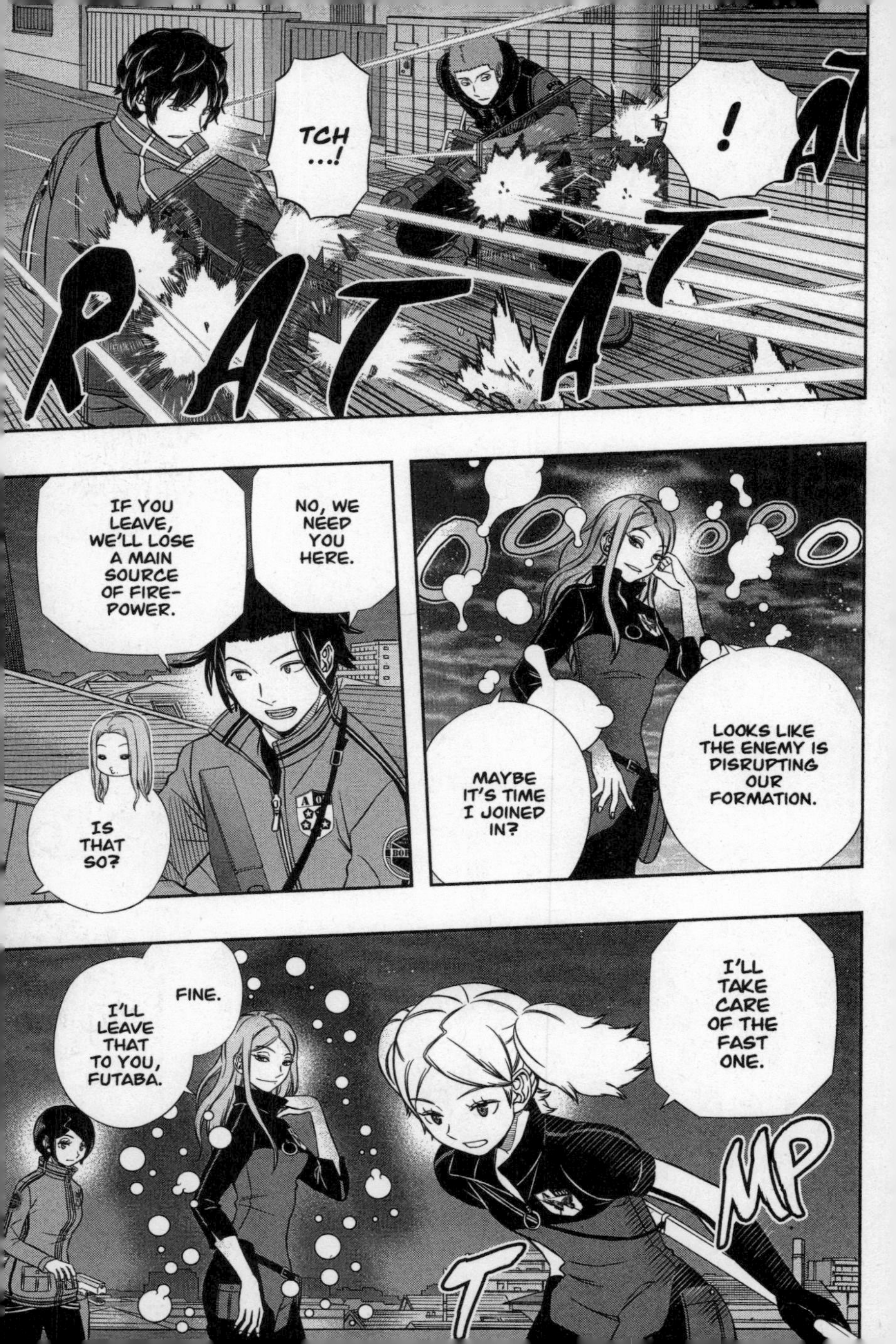
!
TCH...!
RATATAT
LOOKS LIKE THE ENEMY IS DISRUPTING OUR FORMATION.
MAYBE IT'S TIME I JOINED IN?
NO, WE NEED YOU HERE.
IF YOU LEAVE, WE'LL LOSE A MAIN SOURCE OF FIRE-POWER.
IS THAT SO?
I'LL TAKE CARE OF THE FAST ONE.
FINE.
I'LL LEAVE THAT TO YOU, FUTABA.
TMP

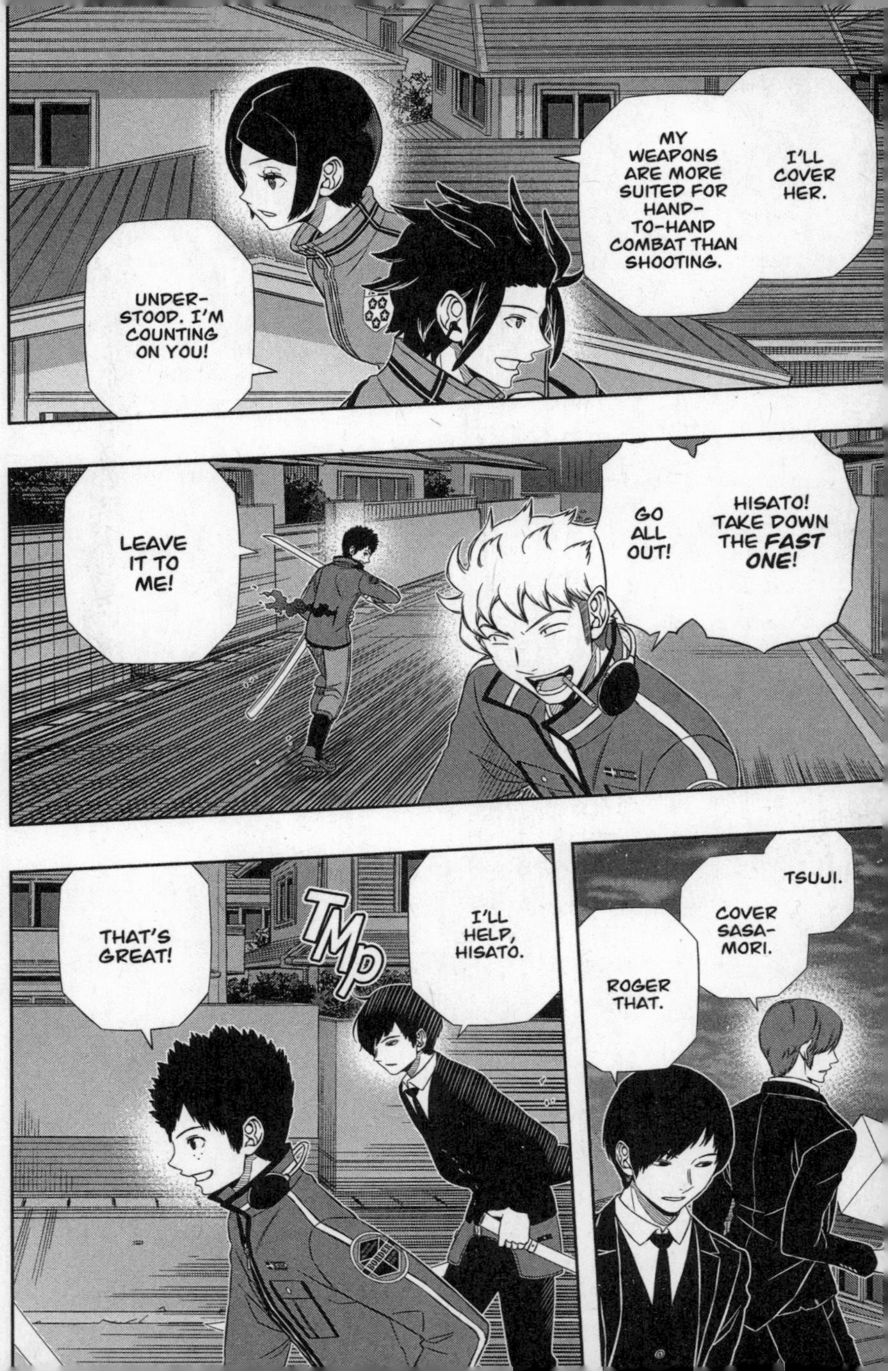
I'LL COVER HER.
MY WEAPONS ARE MORE SUITED FOR HAND-TO-HAND COMBAT THAN SHOOTING.
UNDER-STOOD. I'M COUNTING ON YOU!
HISATO! TAKE DOWN THE FAST ONE!
GO ALL OUT!
LEAVE IT TO ME!
TSUJI.
COVER SASA-MORI.
ROGER THAT.
I'LL HELP, HISATO.
TMP
THAT'S GREAT!

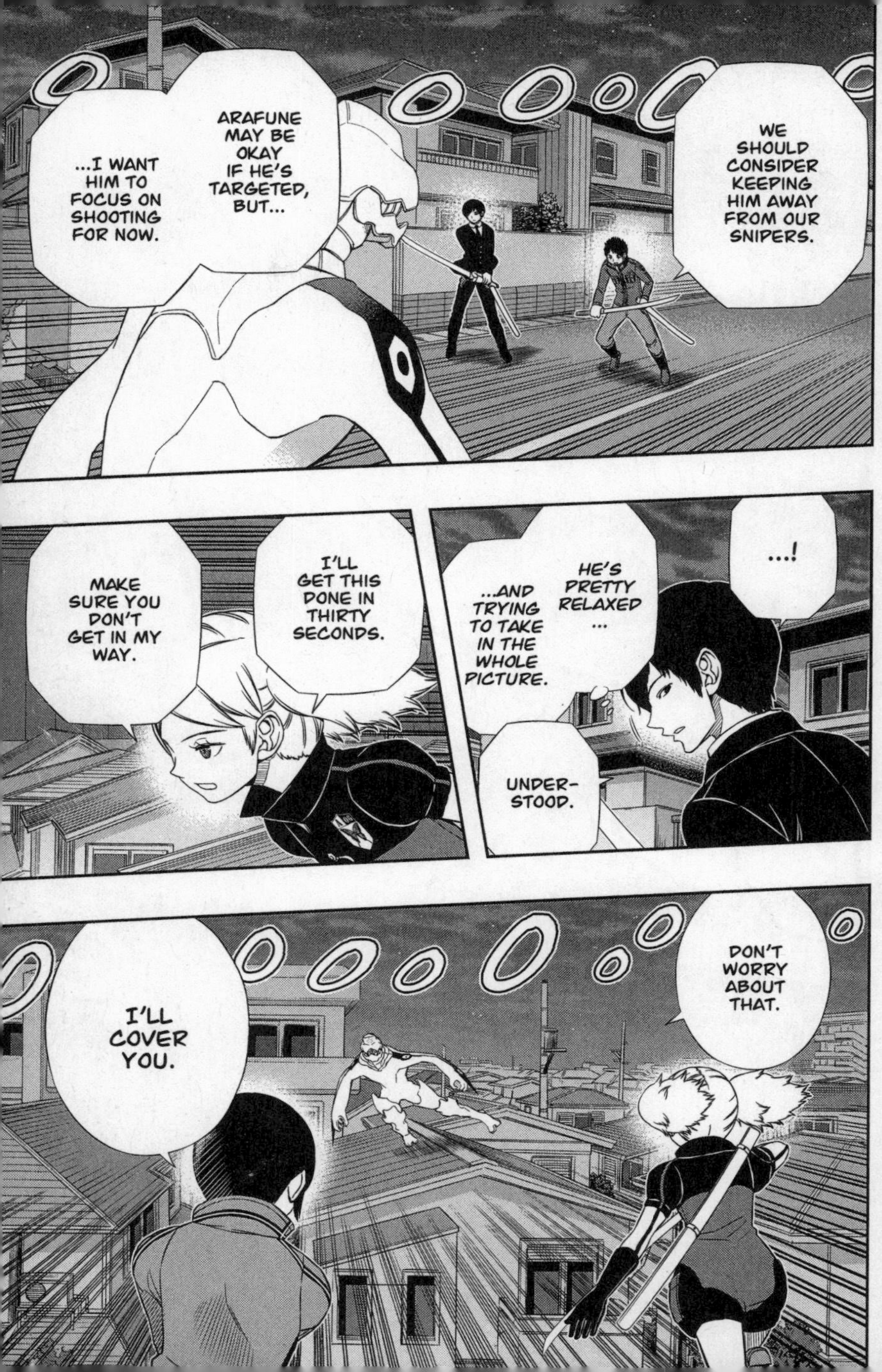
WE SHOULD CONSIDER KEEPING HIM AWAY FROM OUR SNIPERS.
ARAFUNE MAY BE OKAY IF HE'S TARGETED, BUT...
...I WANT HIM TO FOCUS ON SHOOTING FOR NOW.
...!
HE'S PRETTY RELAXED ...
...AND TRYING TO TAKE IN THE WHOLE PICTURE.
UNDER-STOOD.
I'LL GET THIS DONE IN THIRTY SECONDS.
MAKE SURE YOU DON'T GET IN MY WAY.
DON'T WORRY ABOUT THAT.
I'LL COVER YOU.

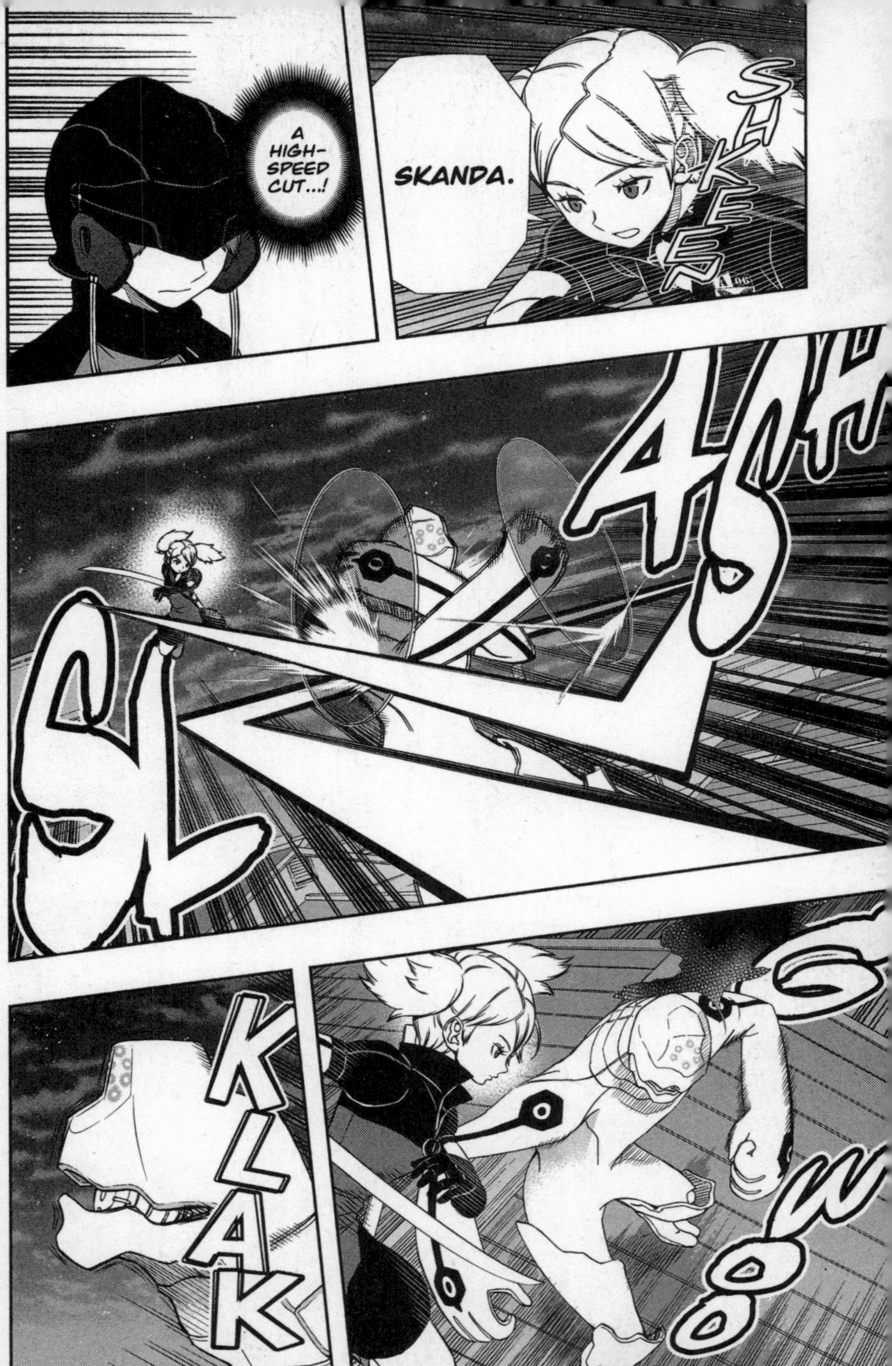
SKANDA.
SHKEER
A HIGH-SPEED CUT...!
KLAK

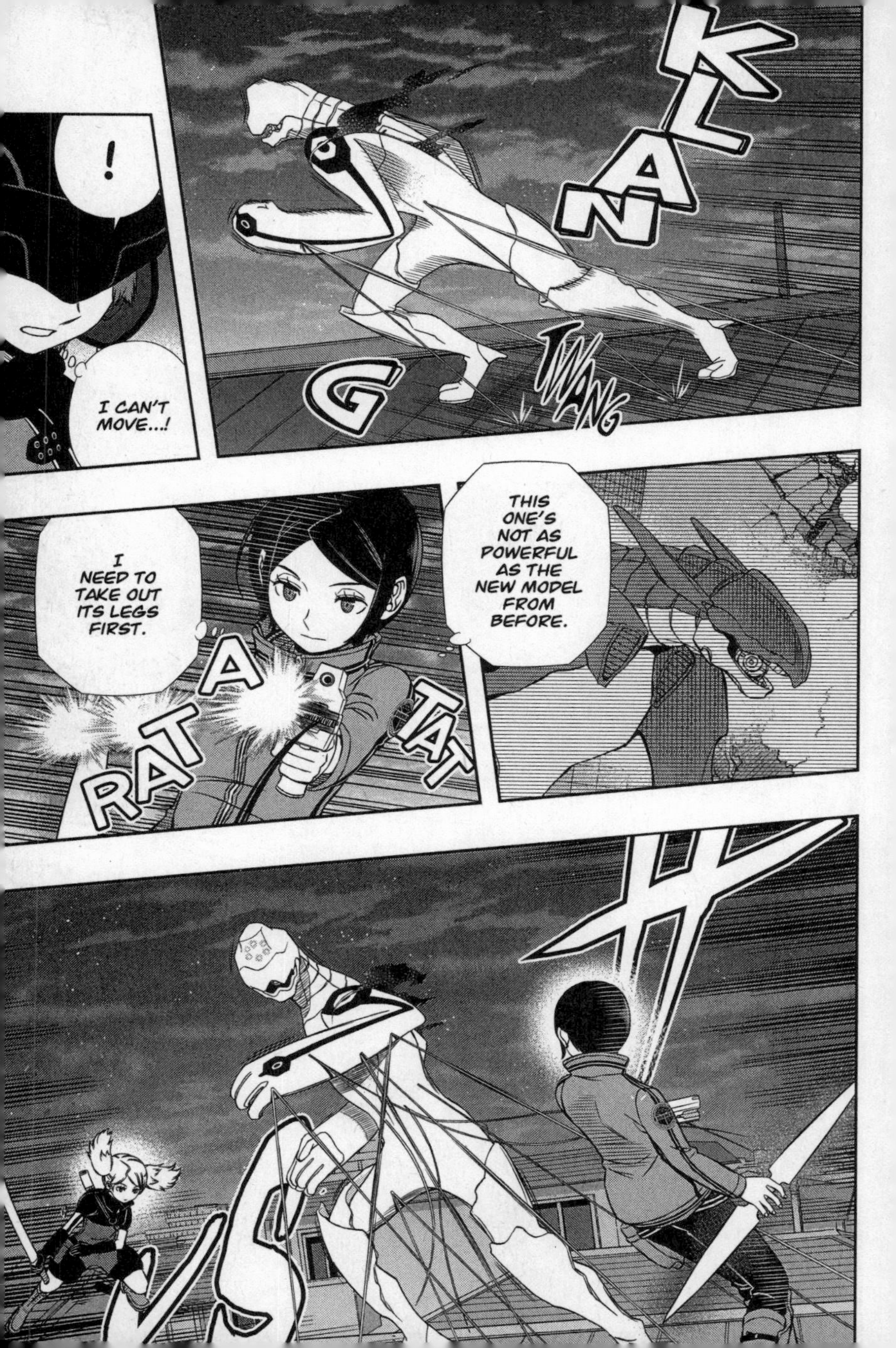
KLANG
TWANG
!
I CAN'T MOVE...!
THIS ONE'S NOT AS POWERFUL AS THE NEW MODEL FROM BEFORE.
I NEED TO TAKE OUT ITS LEGS FIRST.
RAT A TAT TAT

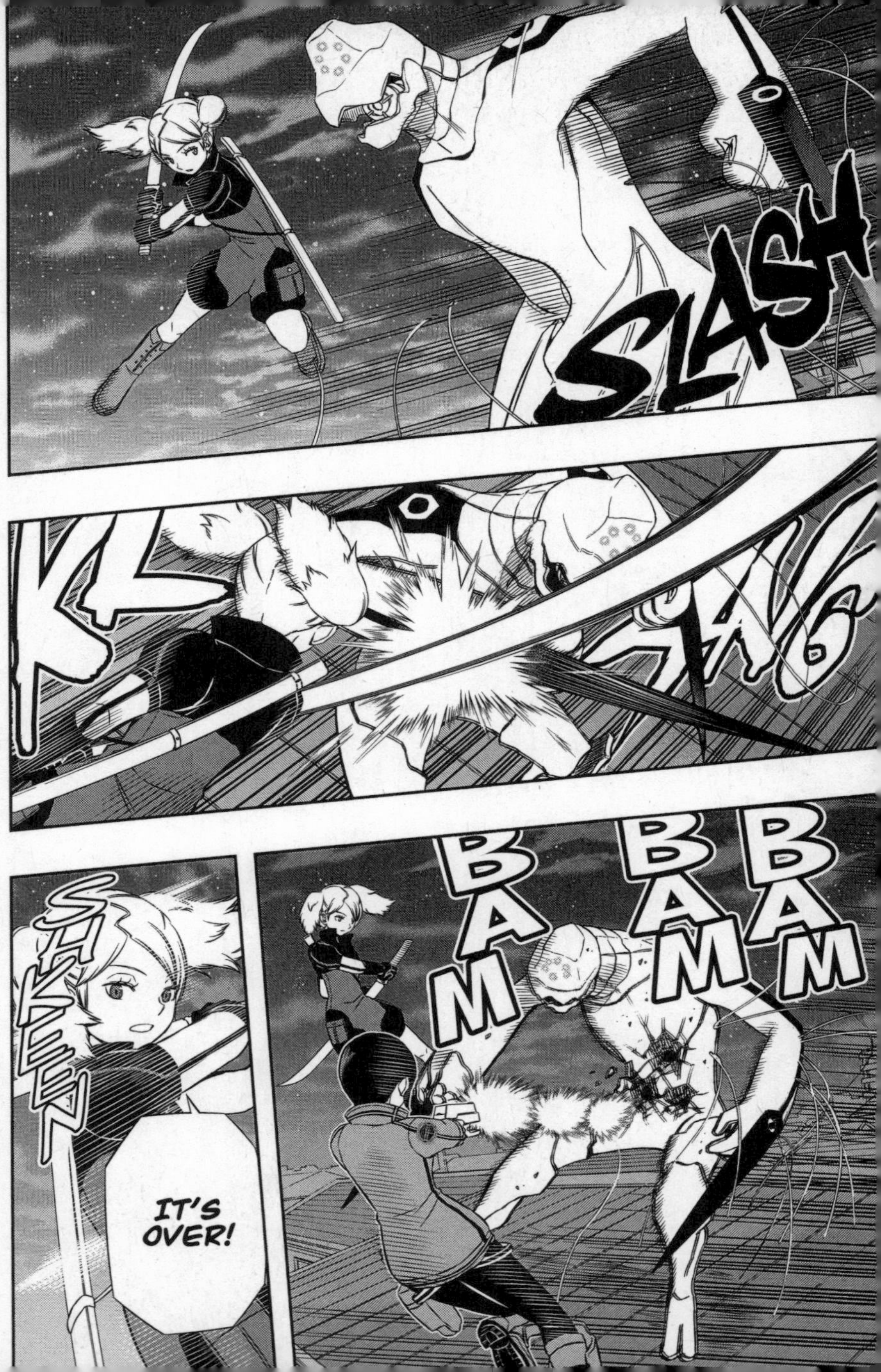
SLASH
KLANG
BAM BAM BAM
SHKEEN
IT'S OVER!

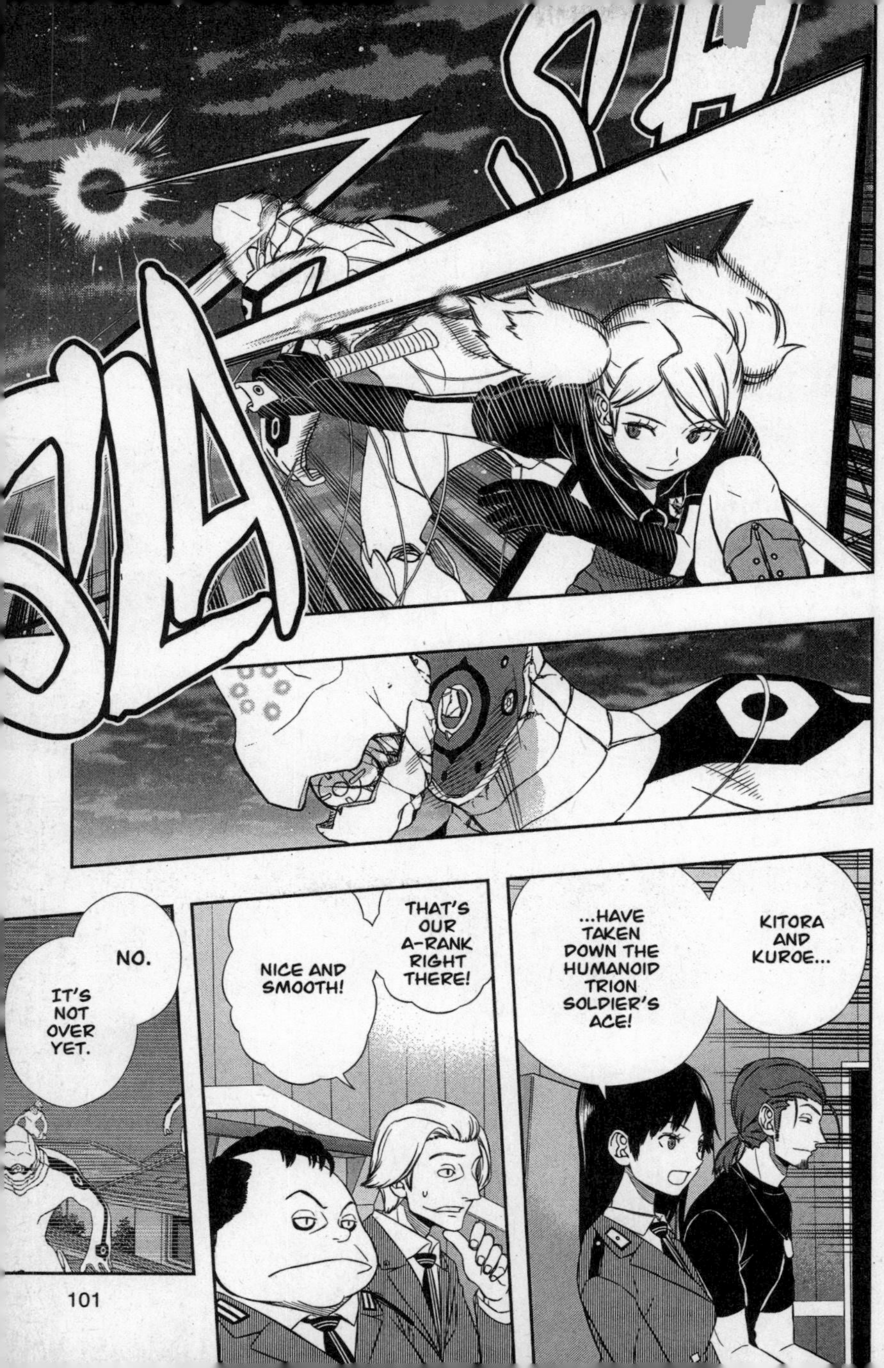
KITORA AND KUROE...
...HAVE TAKEN DOWN THE HUMANOID TRION SOLDIER'S ACE!
THAT'S OUR A-RANK RIGHT THERE!
NICE AND SMOOTH!
NO.
IT'S NOT OVER YET.

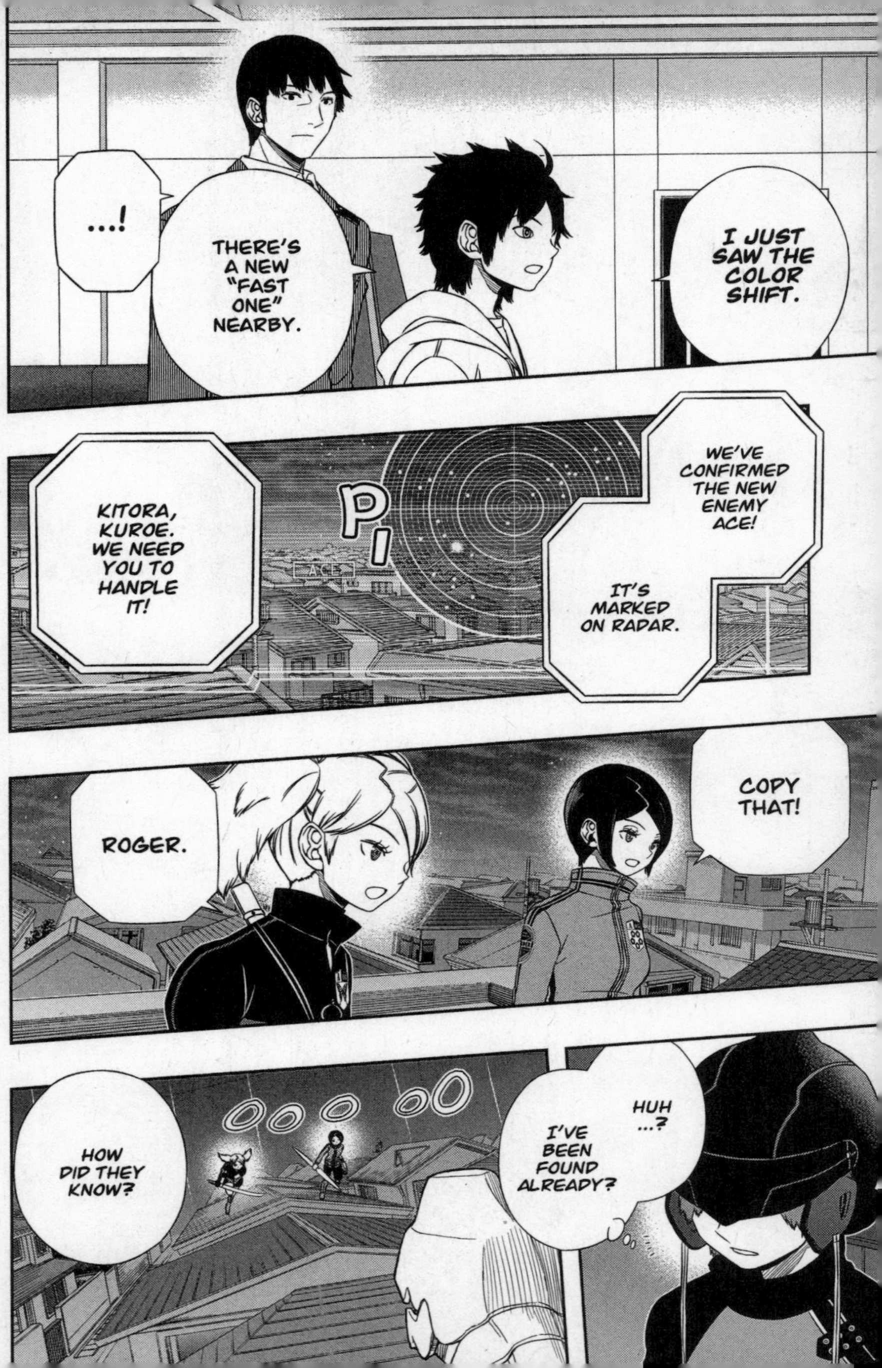
I JUST SAW THE COLOR SHIFT.
THERE'S A NEW "FAST ONE" NEARBY.
...!
WE'VE CONFIRMED THE NEW ENEMY ACE!
IT'S MARKED ON RADAR.
PI
ACE
KITORA, KUROE. WE NEED YOU TO HANDLE IT!
COPY THAT!
ROGER.
HUH ...?
I'VE BEEN FOUND ALREADY?
HOW DID THEY KNOW?

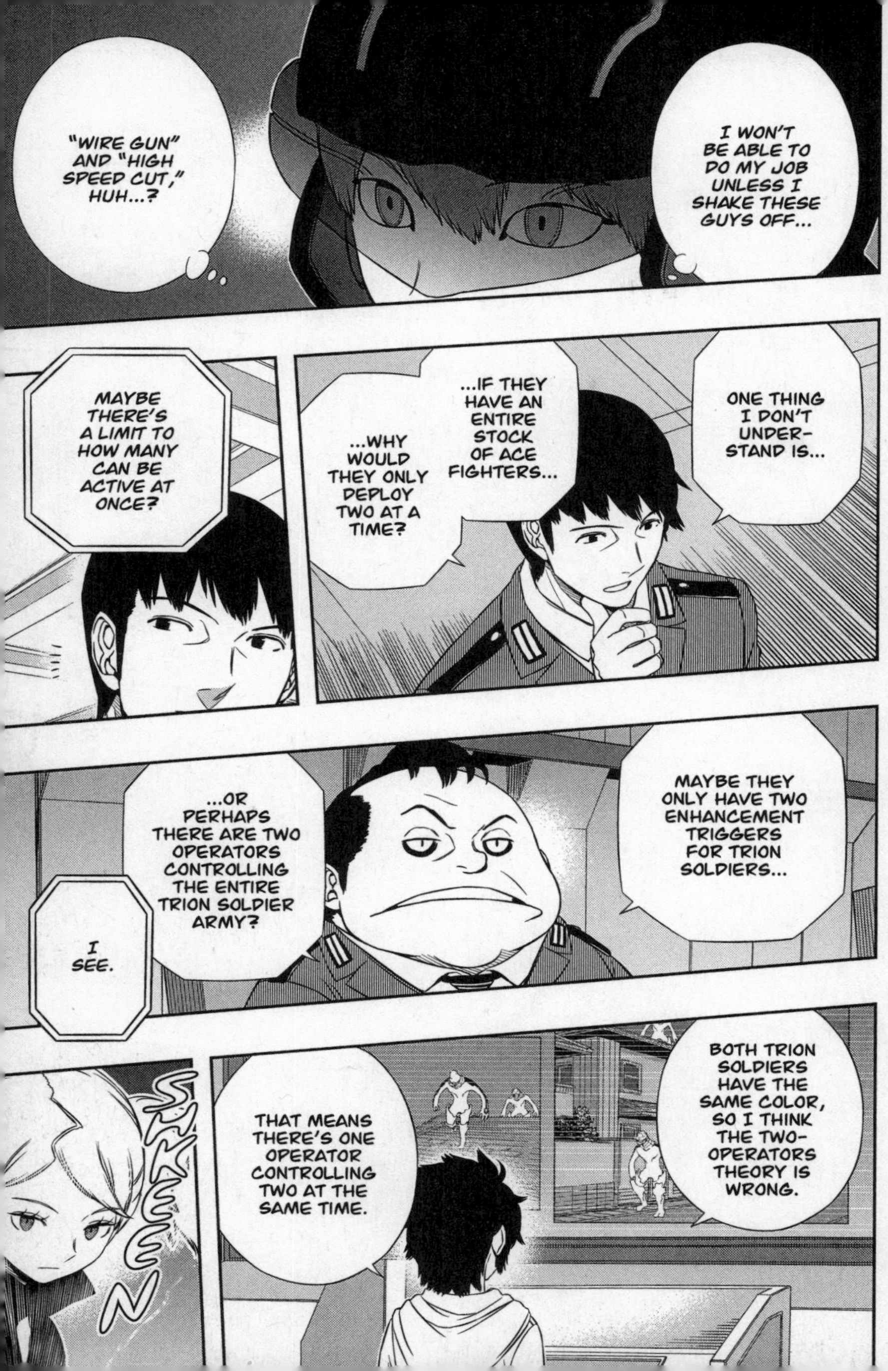

I WON'T BE ABLE TO DO MY JOB UNLESS I SHAKE THESE GUYS OFF...
"WIRE GUN" AND "HIGH SPEED CUT," HUH...?
ONE THING I DON'T UNDER-STAND IS...
...IF THEY HAVE AN ENTIRE STOCK OF ACE FIGHTERS...
...WHY WOULD THEY ONLY DEPLOY TWO AT A TIME?
MAYBE THERE'S A LIMIT TO HOW MANY CAN BE ACTIVE AT ONCE?
MAYBE THEY ONLY HAVE TWO ENHANCEMENT TRIGGERS FOR TRION SOLDIERS...
...OR PERHAPS THERE ARE TWO OPERATORS CONTROLLING THE ENTIRE TRION SOLDIER ARMY?
I SEE.
BOTH TRION SOLDIERS HAVE THE SAME COLOR, SO I THINK THE TWO-OPERATORS THEORY IS WRONG.
THAT MEANS THERE'S ONE OPERATOR CONTROLLING TWO AT THE SAME TIME.
SHKEEEN

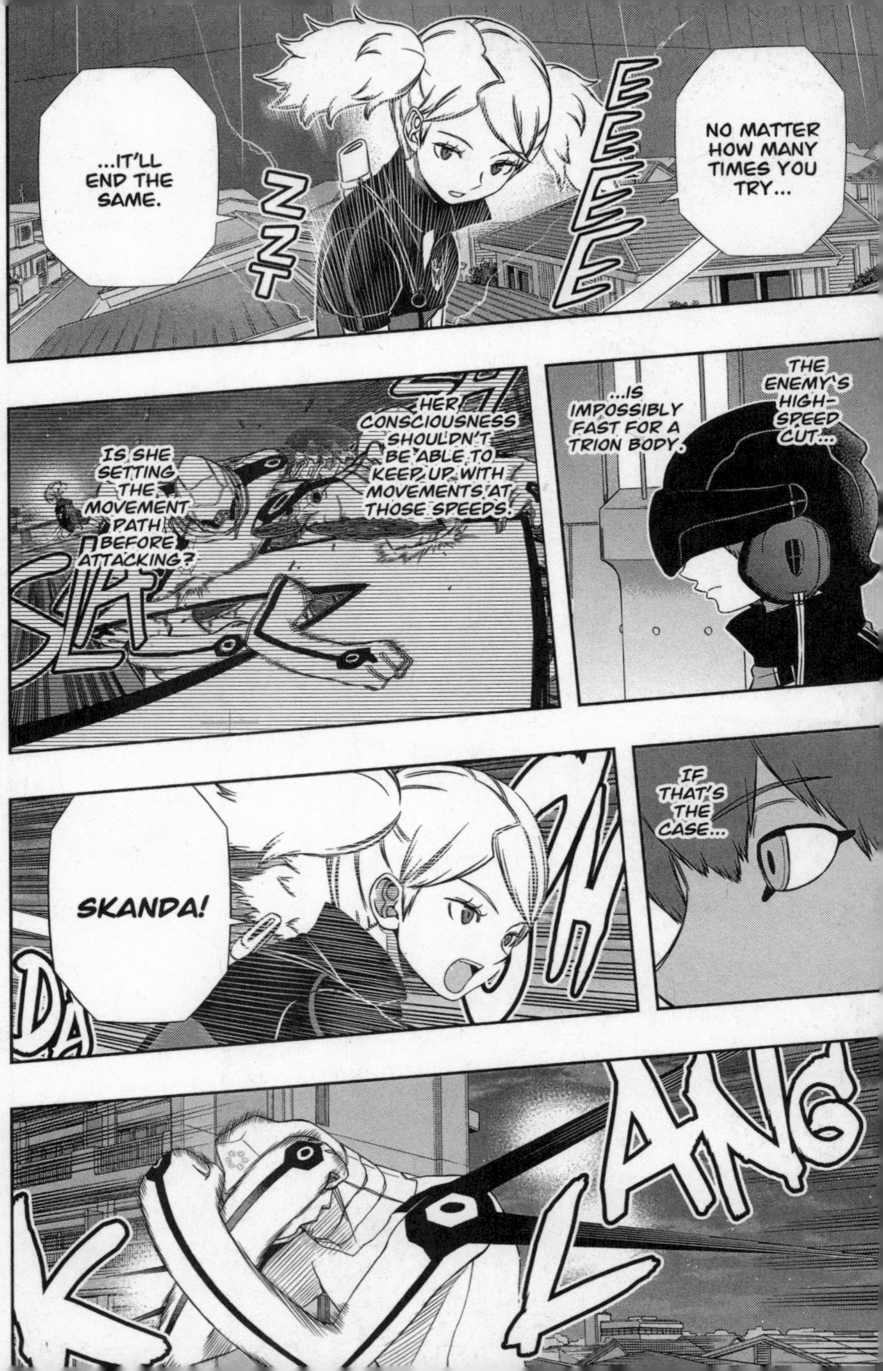
NO MATTER HOW MANY TIMES YOU TRY...
ZZZT
...IT'LL END THE SAME.
THE ENEMY'S HIGH-SPEED CUT...
...IS IMPOSSIBLY FAST FOR A TRION BODY.
HER CONSCIOUSNESS SHOULDN'T BE ABLE TO KEEP UP WITH MOVEMENTS AT THOSE SPEEDS.
IS SHE SETTING THE MOVEMENT PATH BEFORE ATTACKING?
IF THAT'S THE CASE...
SKANDA!

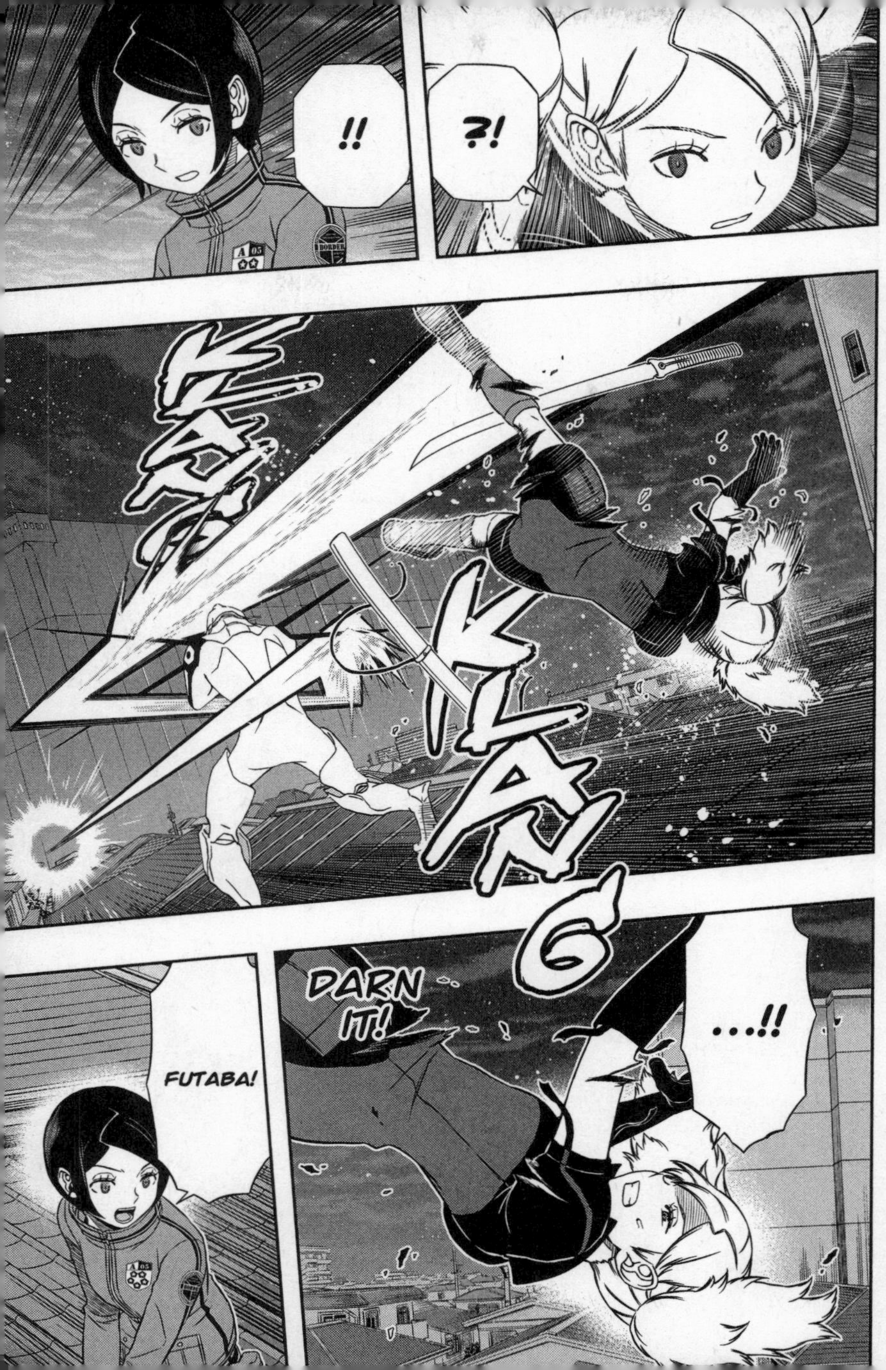
?!
!!
KLANG
...!!
DARN IT!
FUTABA!

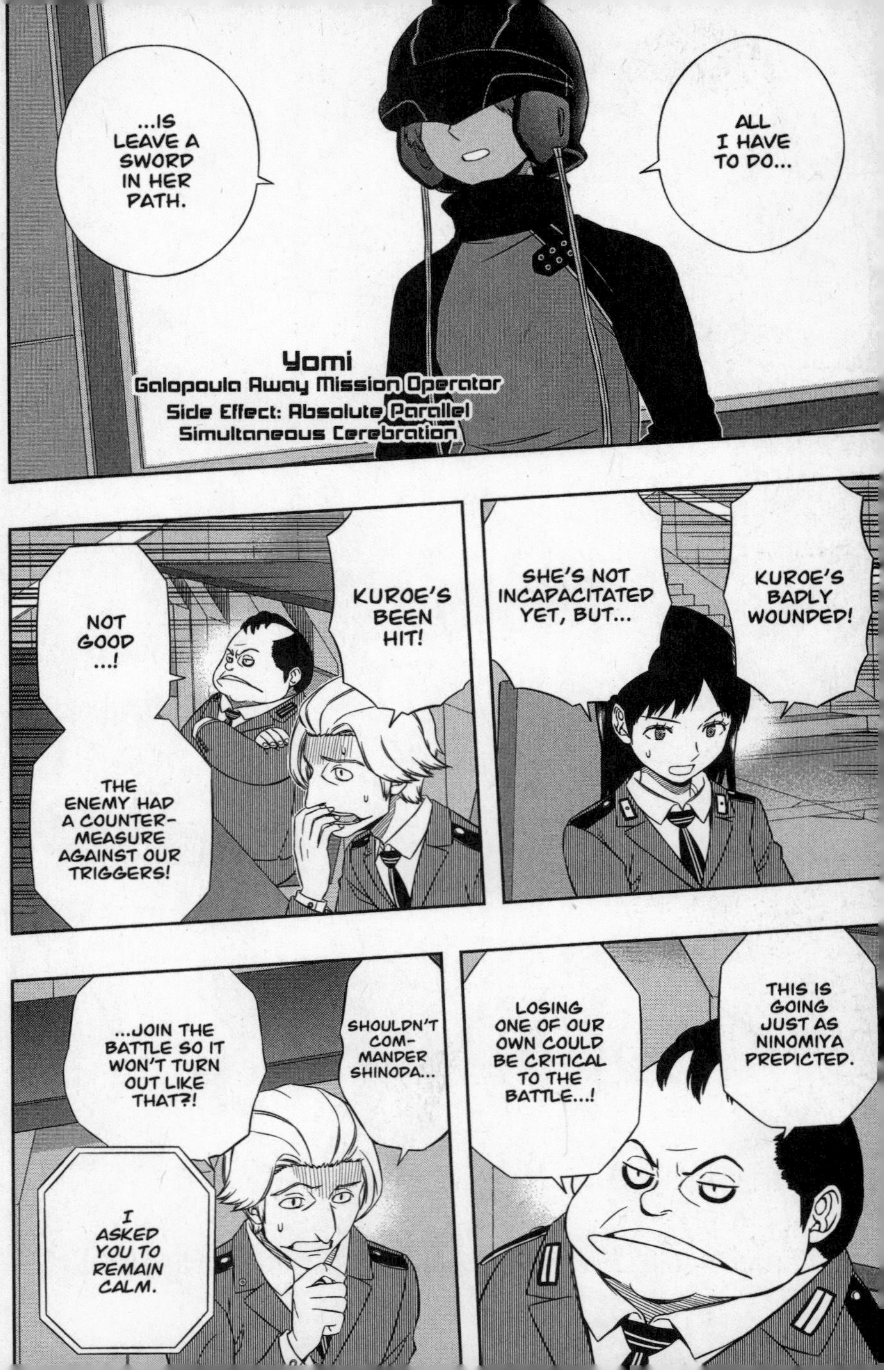
ALL I HAVE TO DO...
...IS LEAVE A SWORD IN HER PATH.
Yomi
Galopoula Away Mission Operator
Side Effect: Absolute Parallel Simultaneous Cerebration
KUROE'S BADLY WOUNDED!
SHE'S NOT INCAPACITATED YET, BUT...
KUROE'S BEEN HIT!
NOT GOOD ...!
THE ENEMY HAD A COUNTER-MEASURE AGAINST OUR TRIGGERS!
THIS IS GOING JUST AS NINOMIYA PREDICTED.
LOSING ONE OF OUR OWN COULD BE CRITICAL TO THE BATTLE...!
SHOULDN'T COMMANDER SHINODA...
...JOIN THE BATTLE SO IT WON'T TURN OUT LIKE THAT?!
I ASKED YOU TO REMAIN CALM.

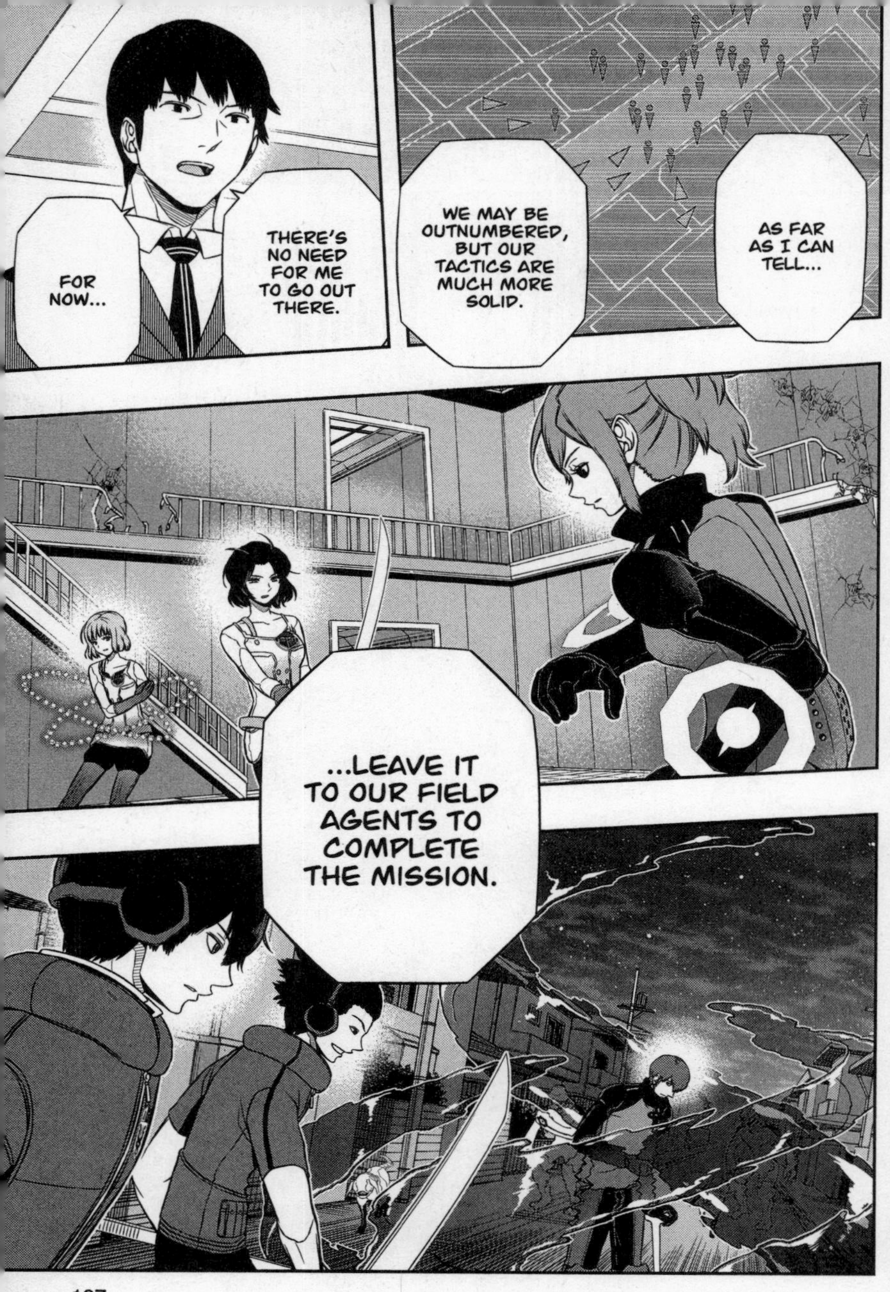
AS FAR AS I CAN TELL...
WE MAY BE OUTNUMBERED, BUT OUR TACTICS ARE MUCH MORE SOLID.
THERE'S NO NEED FOR ME TO GO OUT THERE.
FOR NOW...
...LEAVE IT TO OUR FIELD AGENTS TO COMPLETE THE MISSION.

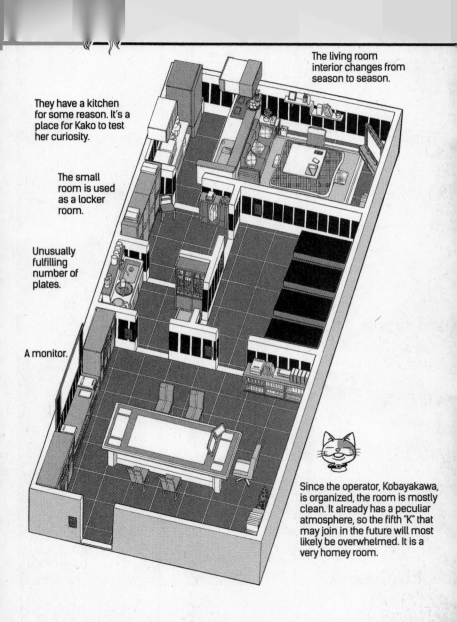

The living room interior changes from season to season.

They have a kitchen for some reason. It's a place for Kako to test her curiosity.

The small room is used as a locker room.

Unusually fulfilling number of plates.

A monitor.

Since the operator, Kobayakawa, is organized, the room is mostly clean. It already has a peculiar atmosphere, so the fifth "K" that may join in the future will most likely be overwhelmed. It is a very homey room.

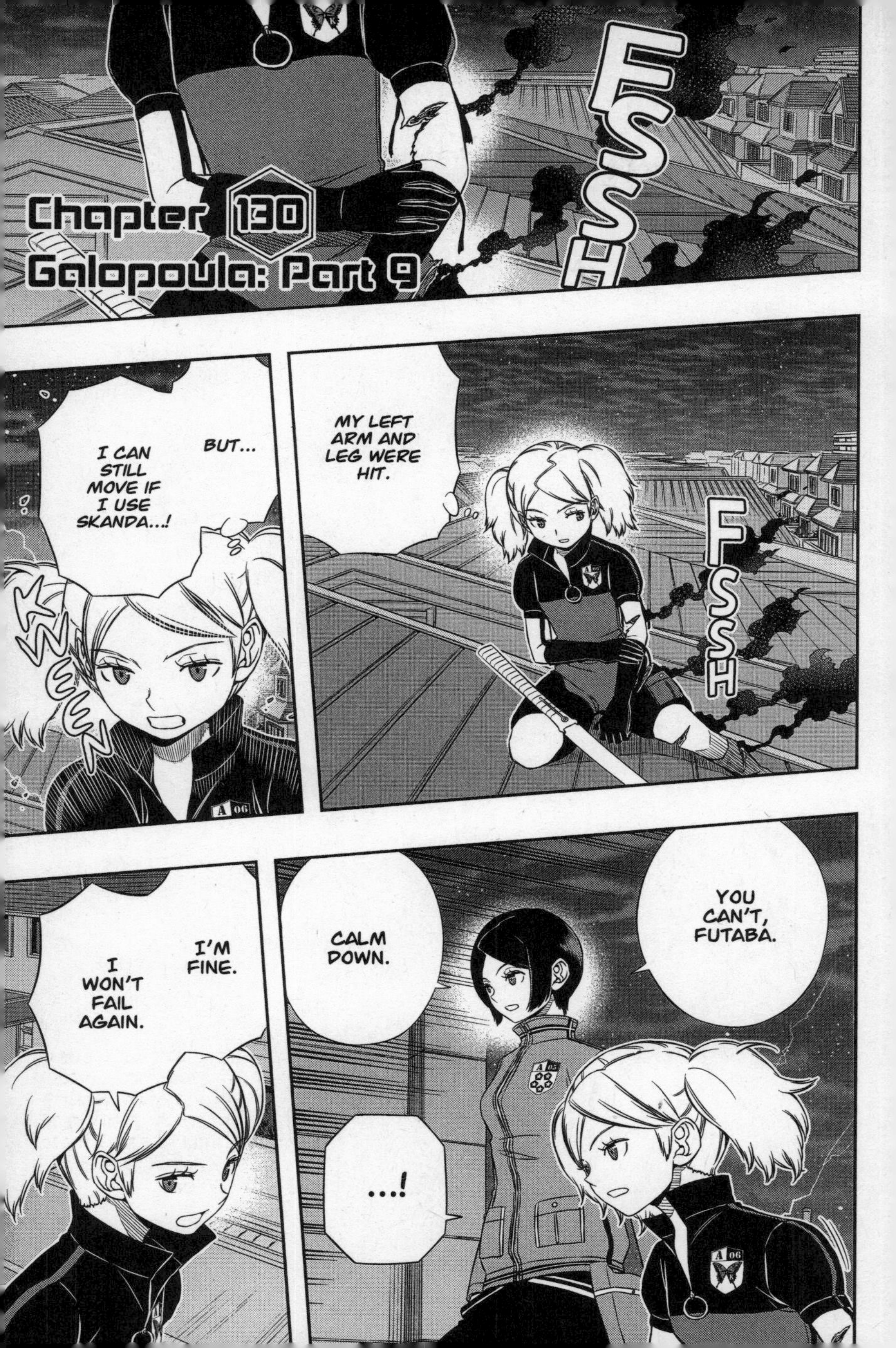
Chapter 130
Galopoula: Part 9
FSSH
MY LEFT ARM AND LEG WERE HIT.
FSSH
BUT...
I CAN STILL MOVE IF I USE SKANDA...!
KWEEN
YOU CAN'T, FUTABA.
CALM DOWN.
...!
I'M FINE.
I WON'T FAIL AGAIN.

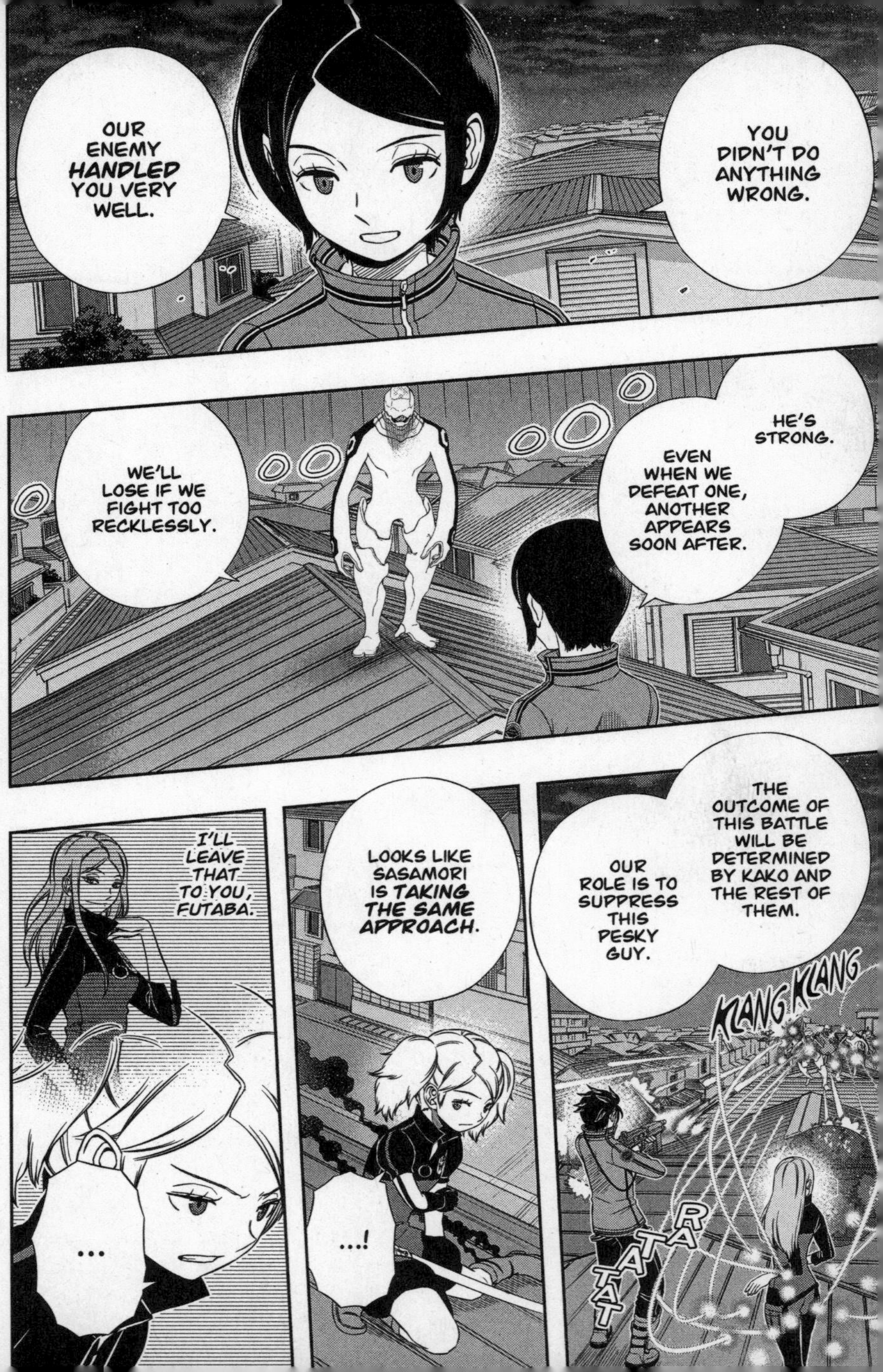
YOU DIDN'T DO ANYTHING WRONG.
OUR ENEMY *HANDLED* YOU VERY WELL.
HE'S STRONG.
EVEN WHEN WE DEFEAT ONE, ANOTHER APPEARS SOON AFTER.
WE'LL LOSE IF WE FIGHT TOO RECKLESSLY.
THE OUTCOME OF THIS BATTLE WILL BE DETERMINED BY KAKO AND THE REST OF THEM.
OUR ROLE IS TO SUPPRESS THIS PESKY GUY.
KLANG KLANG
RATATAT
LOOKS LIKE SASAMORI IS *TAKING THE SAME APPROACH.*
...!
I'LL LEAVE THAT TO YOU, FUTABA.
...

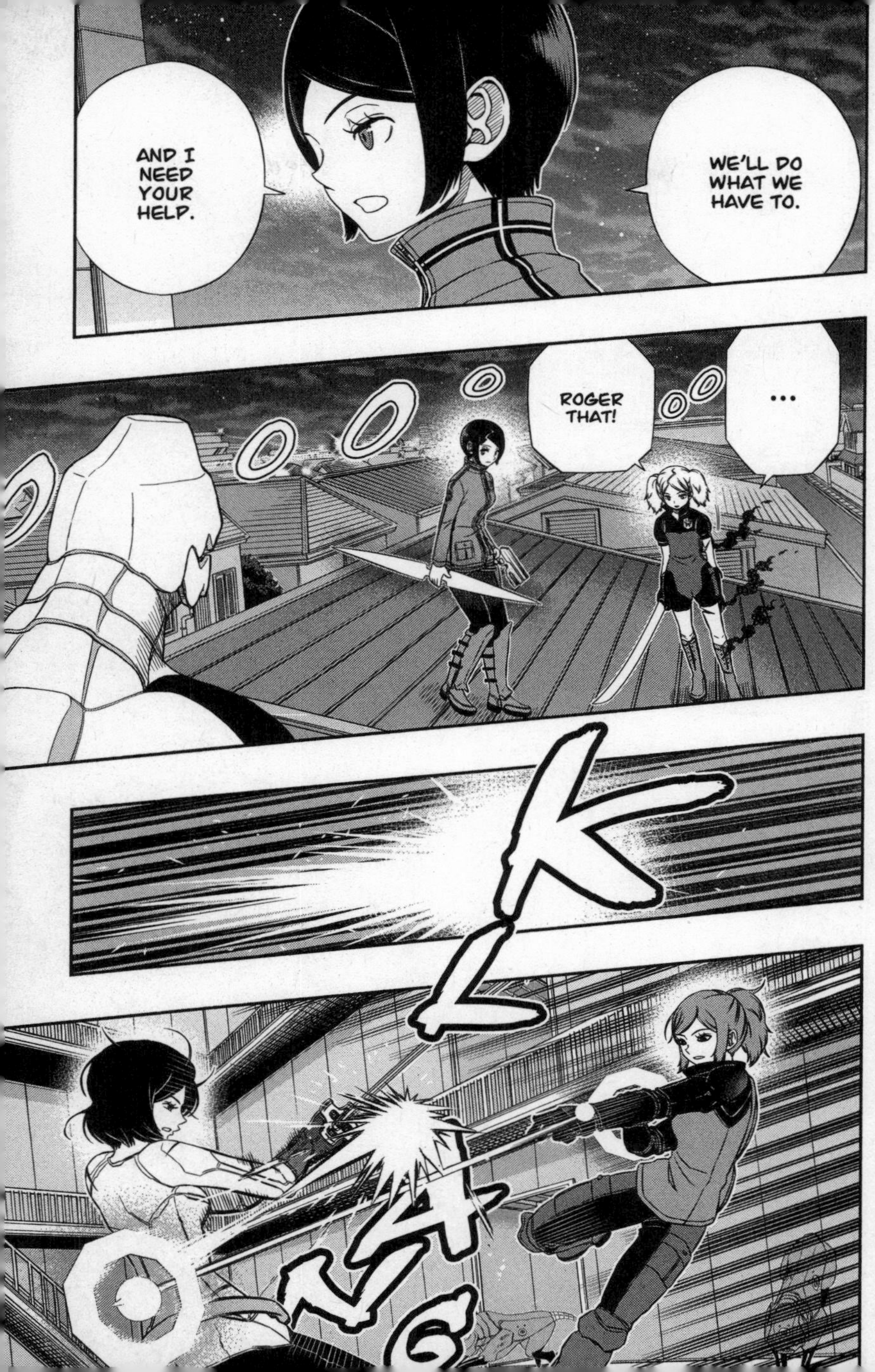
WE'LL DO WHAT WE HAVE TO.
AND I NEED YOUR HELP.
...
ROGER THAT!

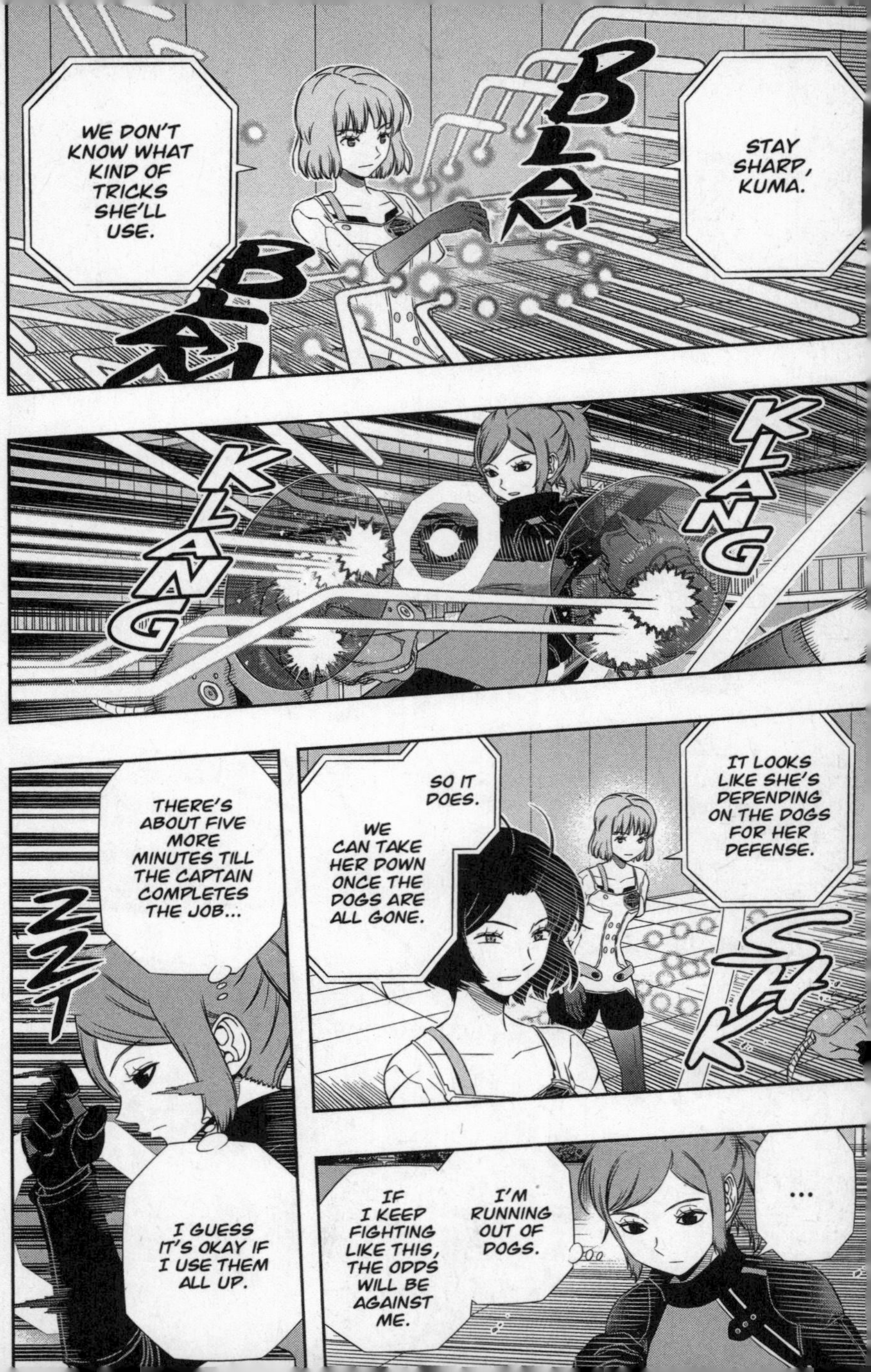
STAY SHARP, KUMA.
BLAM
WE DON'T KNOW WHAT KIND OF TRICKS SHE'LL USE.
KLANG
KLANG
IT LOOKS LIKE SHE'S DEPENDING ON THE DOGS FOR HER DEFENSE.
SHK
SO IT DOES.
WE CAN TAKE HER DOWN ONCE THE DOGS ARE ALL GONE.
...
I'M RUNNING OUT OF DOGS.
IF I KEEP FIGHTING LIKE THIS, THE ODDS WILL BE AGAINST ME.
THERE'S ABOUT FIVE MORE MINUTES TILL THE CAPTAIN COMPLETES THE JOB...
I GUESS IT'S OKAY IF I USE THEM ALL UP.

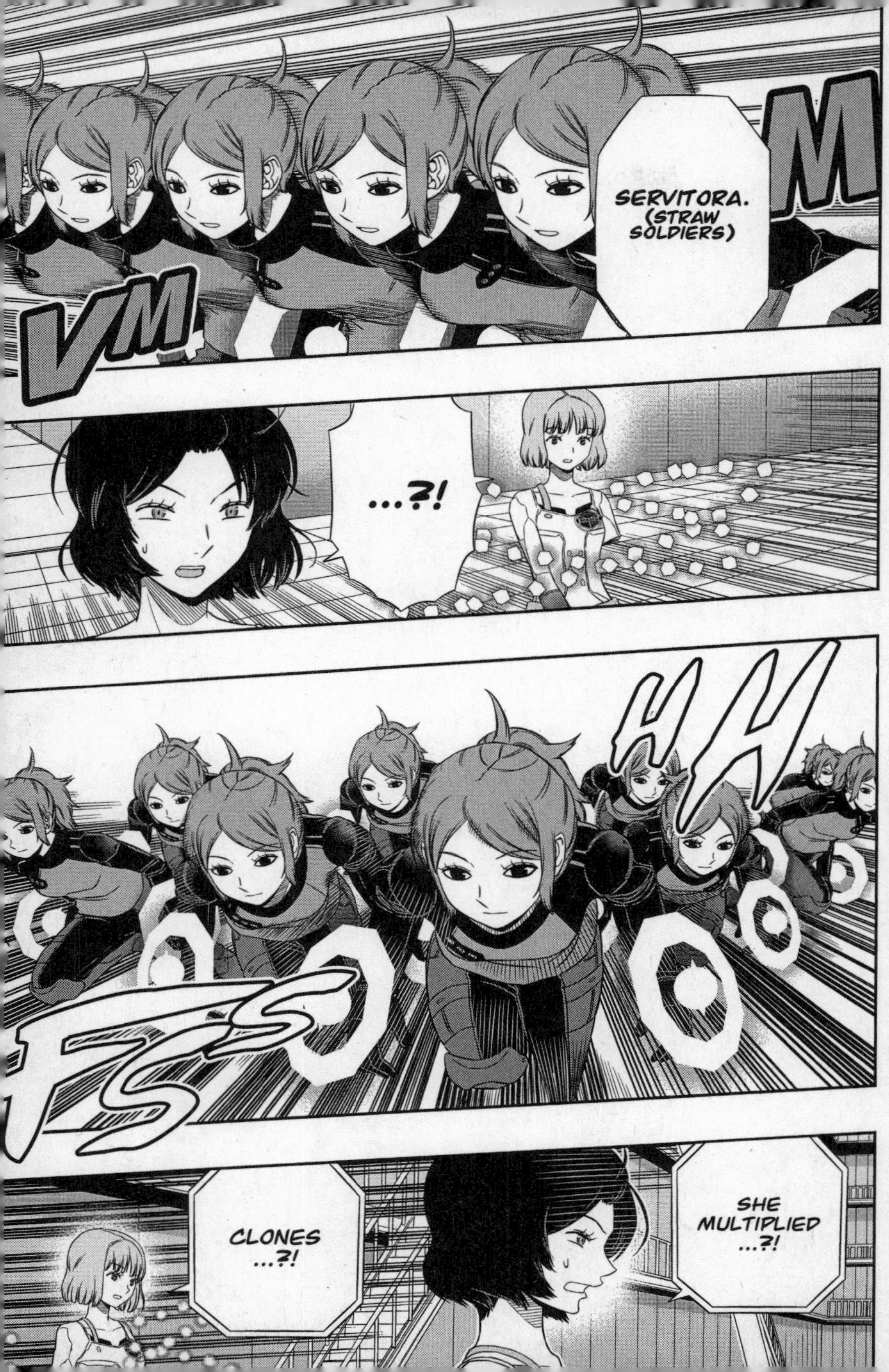
M
SERVITORA. (STRAW SOLDIERS)
VM
...?!
WH
FSS
SHE MULTIPLIED ...?!
CLONES ...?!

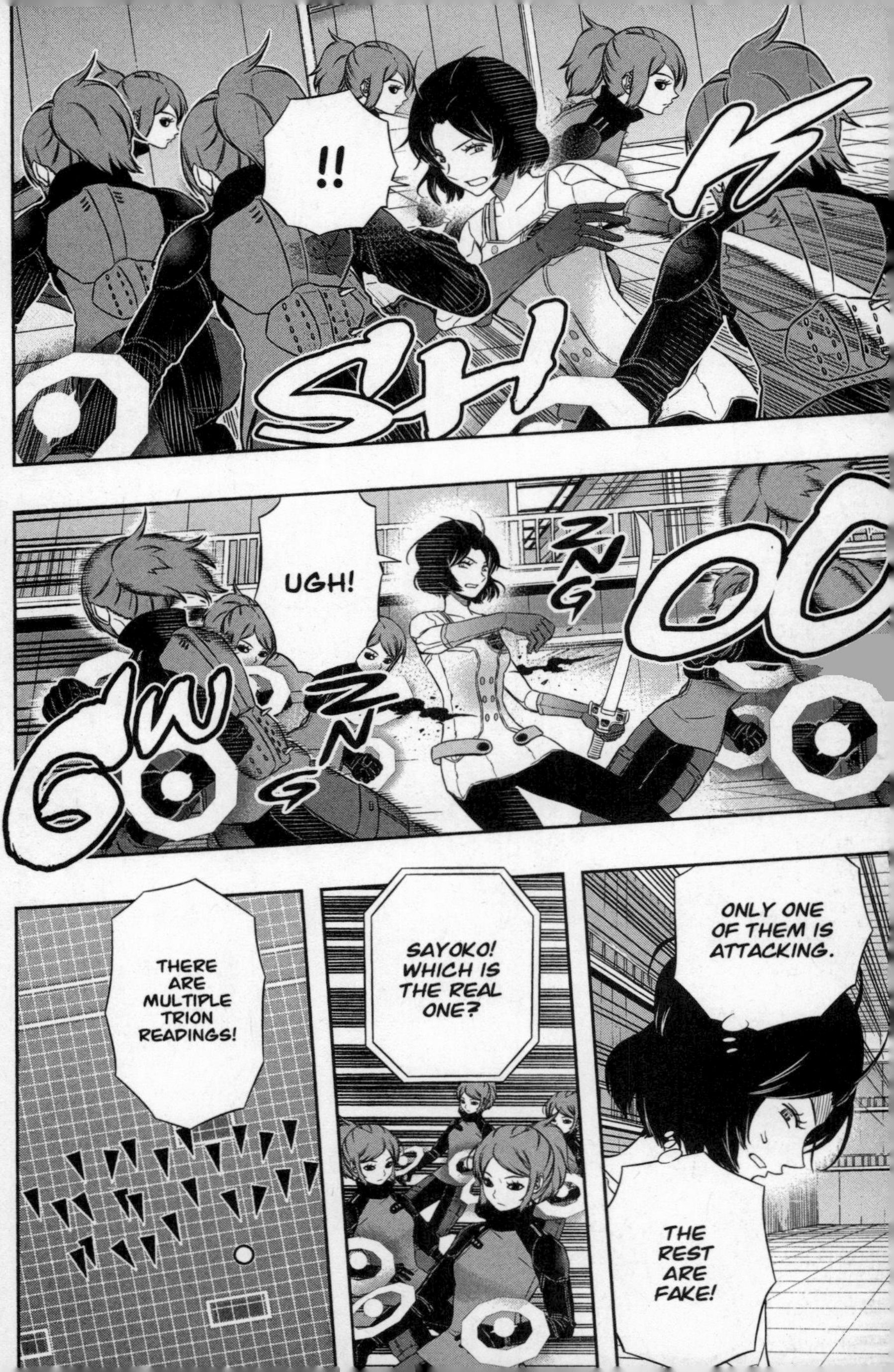
!!
SHK
UGH!
ZNG
ZNG
GWOO
ONLY ONE OF THEM IS ATTACKING.
THE REST ARE FAKE!
SAYOKO! WHICH IS THE REAL ONE?
THERE ARE MULTIPLE TRION READINGS!

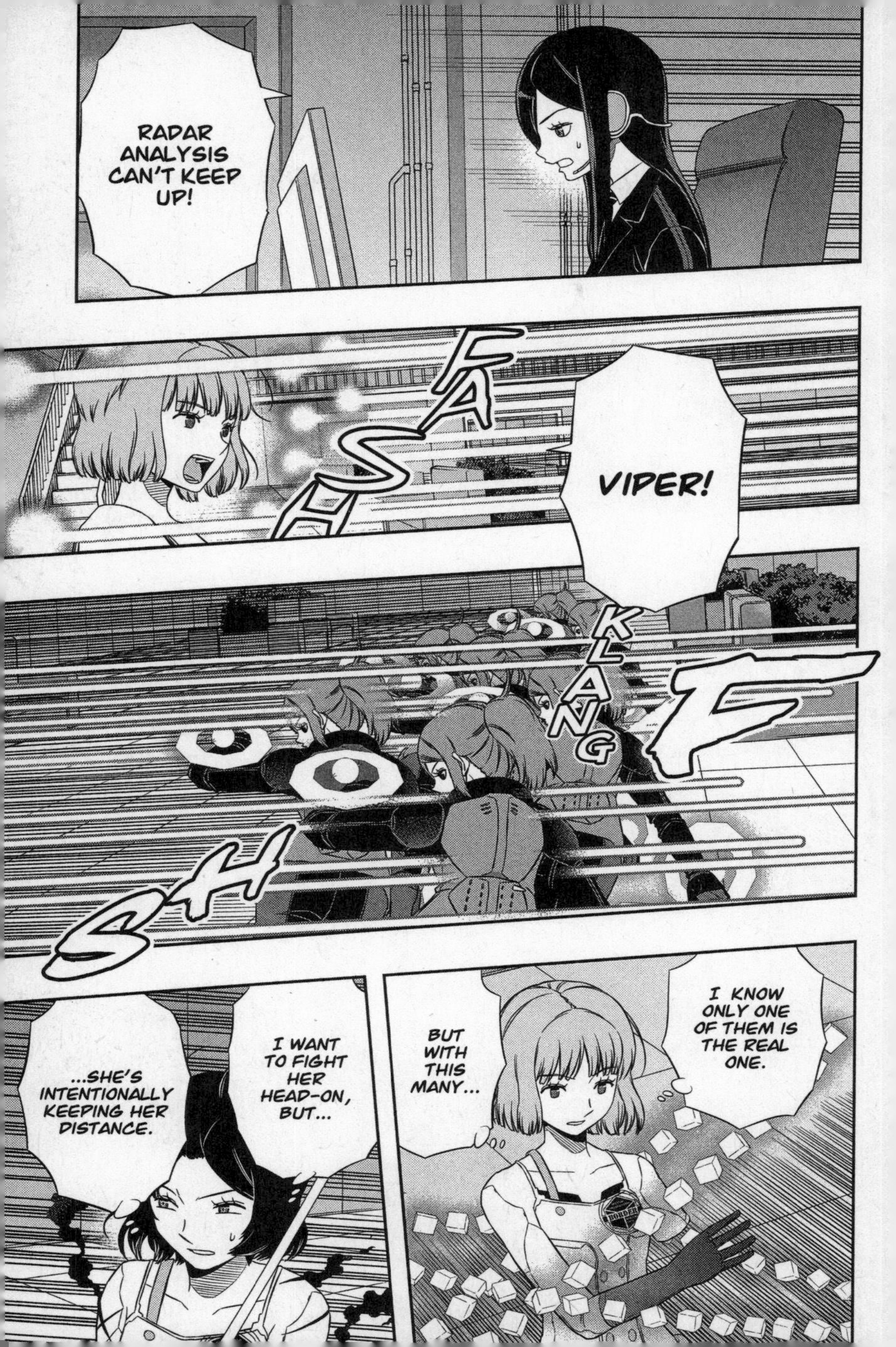
RADAR ANALYSIS CAN'T KEEP UP!
VIPER!
FASH
KLANG
F
SH
I KNOW ONLY ONE OF THEM IS THE REAL ONE.
BUT WITH THIS MANY...
I WANT TO FIGHT HER HEAD-ON, BUT...
...SHE'S INTENTIONALLY KEEPING HER DISTANCE.

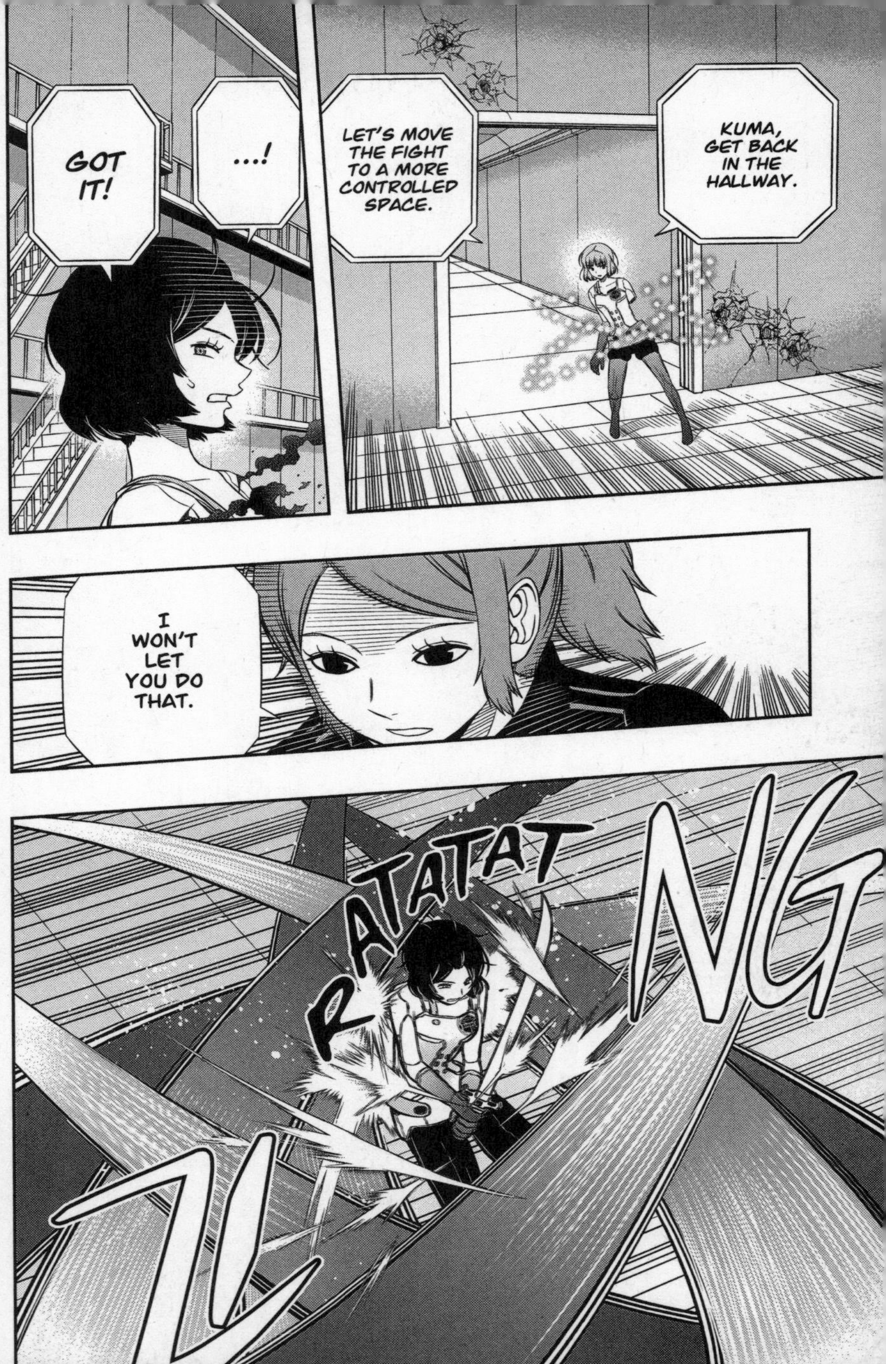
KUMA, GET BACK IN THE HALLWAY.
LET'S MOVE THE FIGHT TO A MORE CONTROLLED SPACE.
...!
GOT IT!
I WON'T LET YOU DO THAT.
RATATAT
NG

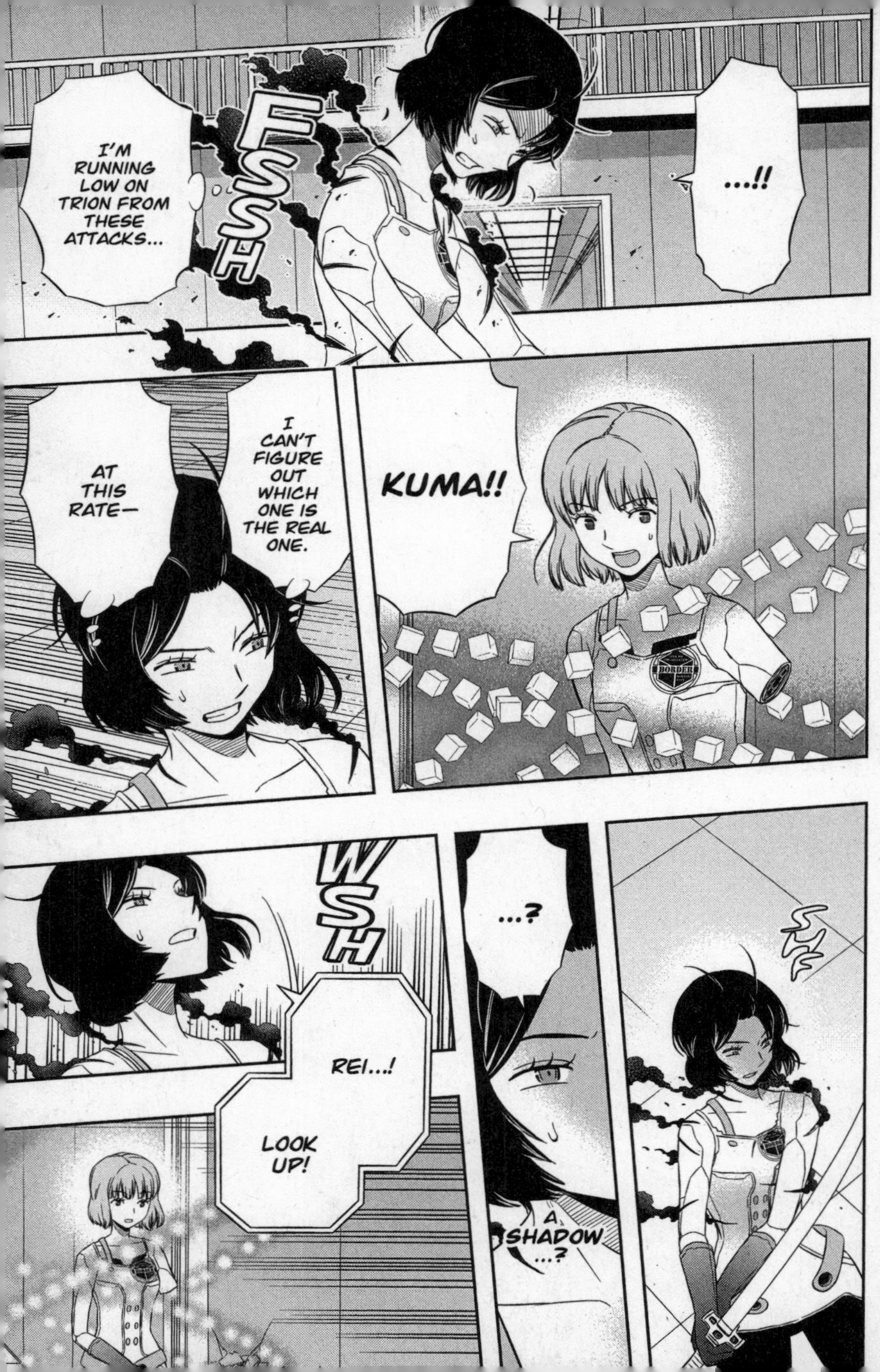
...!!
FSSH
I'M RUNNING LOW ON TRION FROM THESE ATTACKS...
KUMA!!
I CAN'T FIGURE OUT WHICH ONE IS THE REAL ONE.
AT THIS RATE—
...?
A SHADOW ...?
WSH
REI...!
LOOK UP!

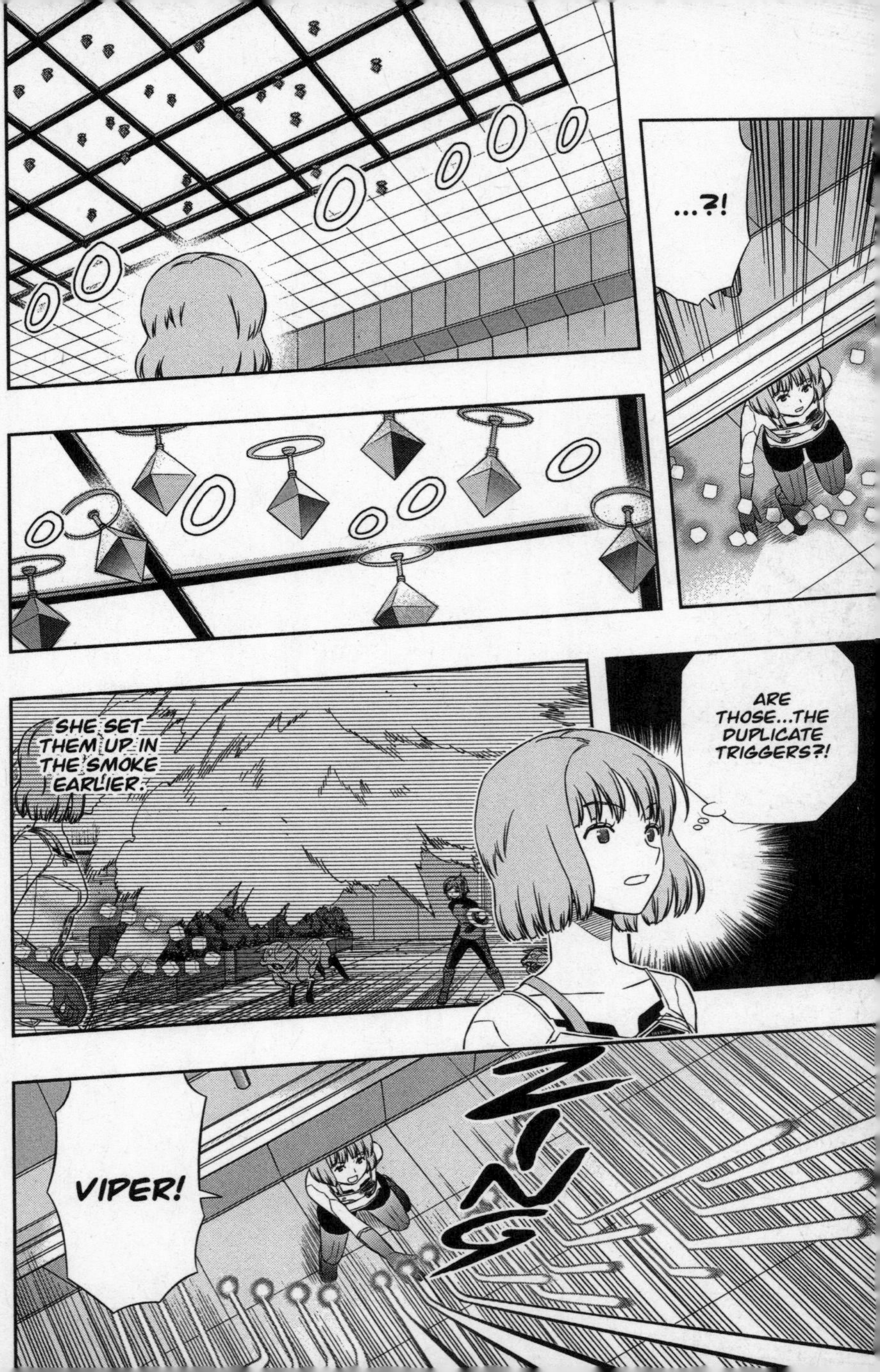
...?!
ARE THOSE...THE DUPLICATE TRIGGERS?!
SHE SET THEM UP IN THE SMOKE EARLIER.
ZING
VIPER!

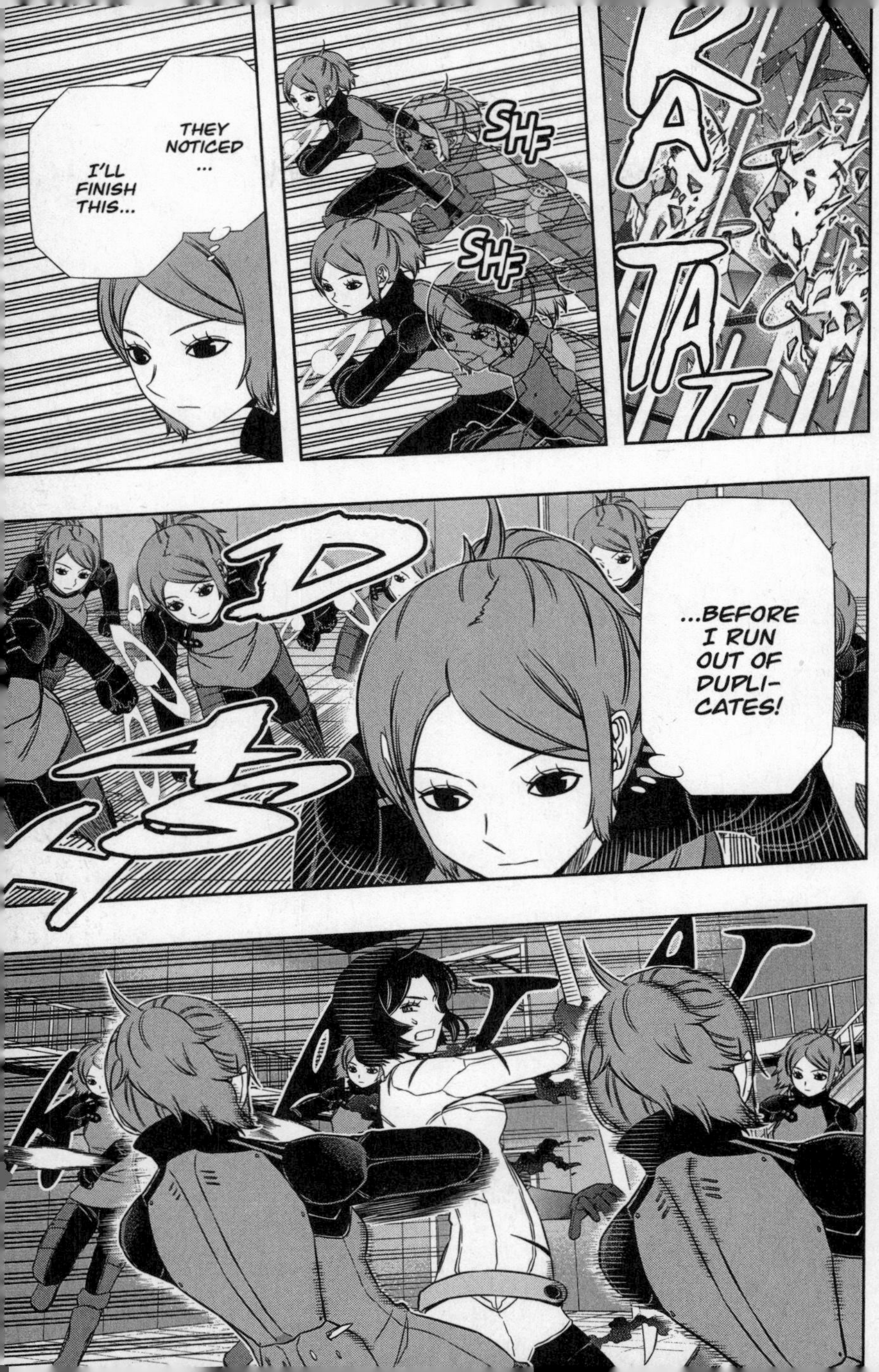

SHF
SHF
THEY NOTICED ...
I'LL FINISH THIS...
...BEFORE I RUN OUT OF DUPLI- CATES!

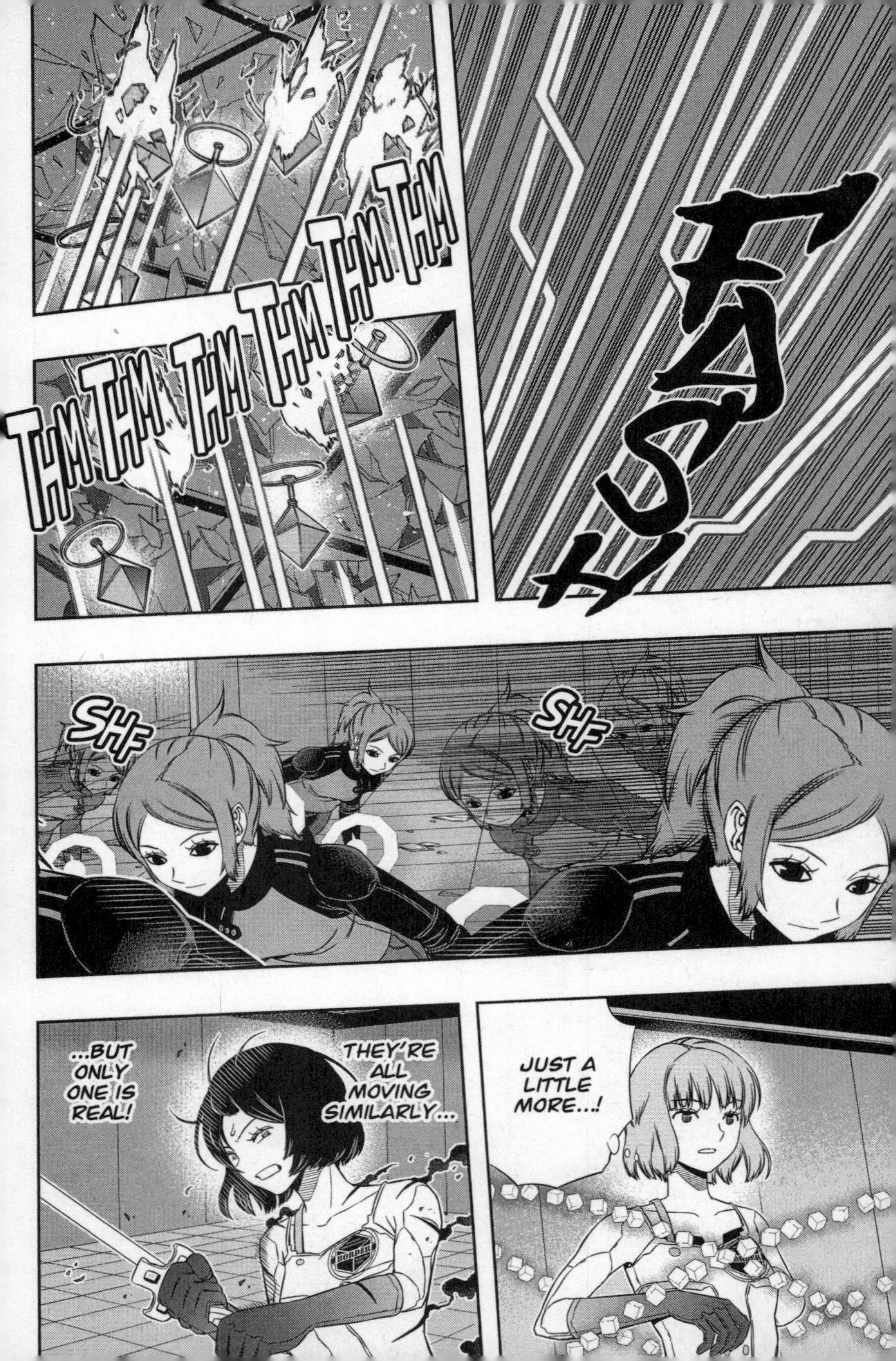
FASH
THM THM THM THM THM THM THM
SHF
SHF
JUST A LITTLE MORE...!
THEY'RE ALL MOVING SIMILARLY...
...BUT ONLY ONE IS REAL!

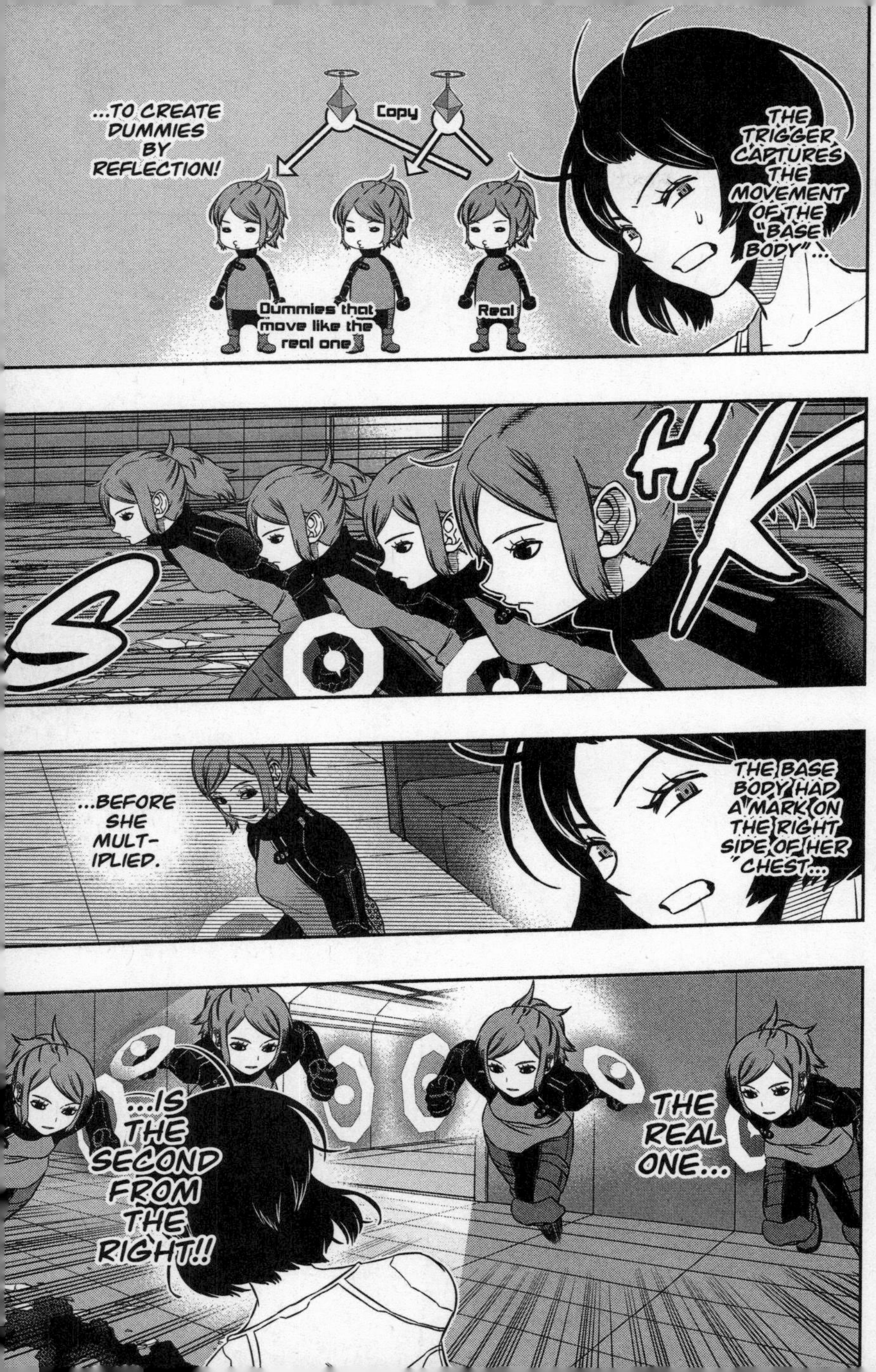

THE TRIGGER CAPTURES THE MOVEMENT OF THE "BASE BODY"...
...TO CREATE DUMMIES BY REFLECTION!
Copy
Real
Dummies that move like the real one
S
HK
THE BASE BODY HAD A MARK ON THE RIGHT SIDE OF HER CHEST...
...BEFORE SHE MULT-IPLIED.
THE REAL ONE...
...IS THE SECOND FROM THE RIGHT!!

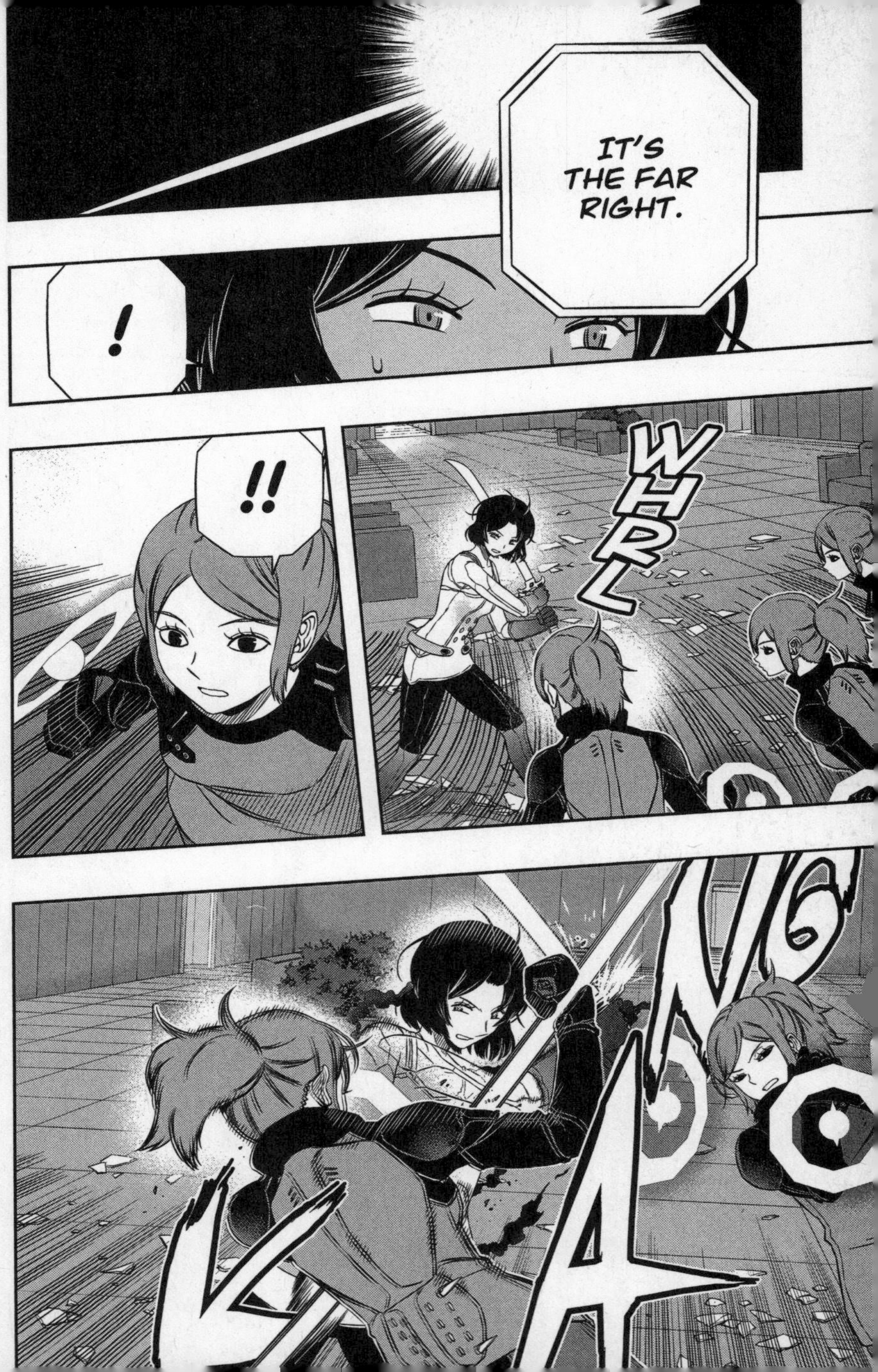
IT'S THE FAR RIGHT.
!
WHRL
!!

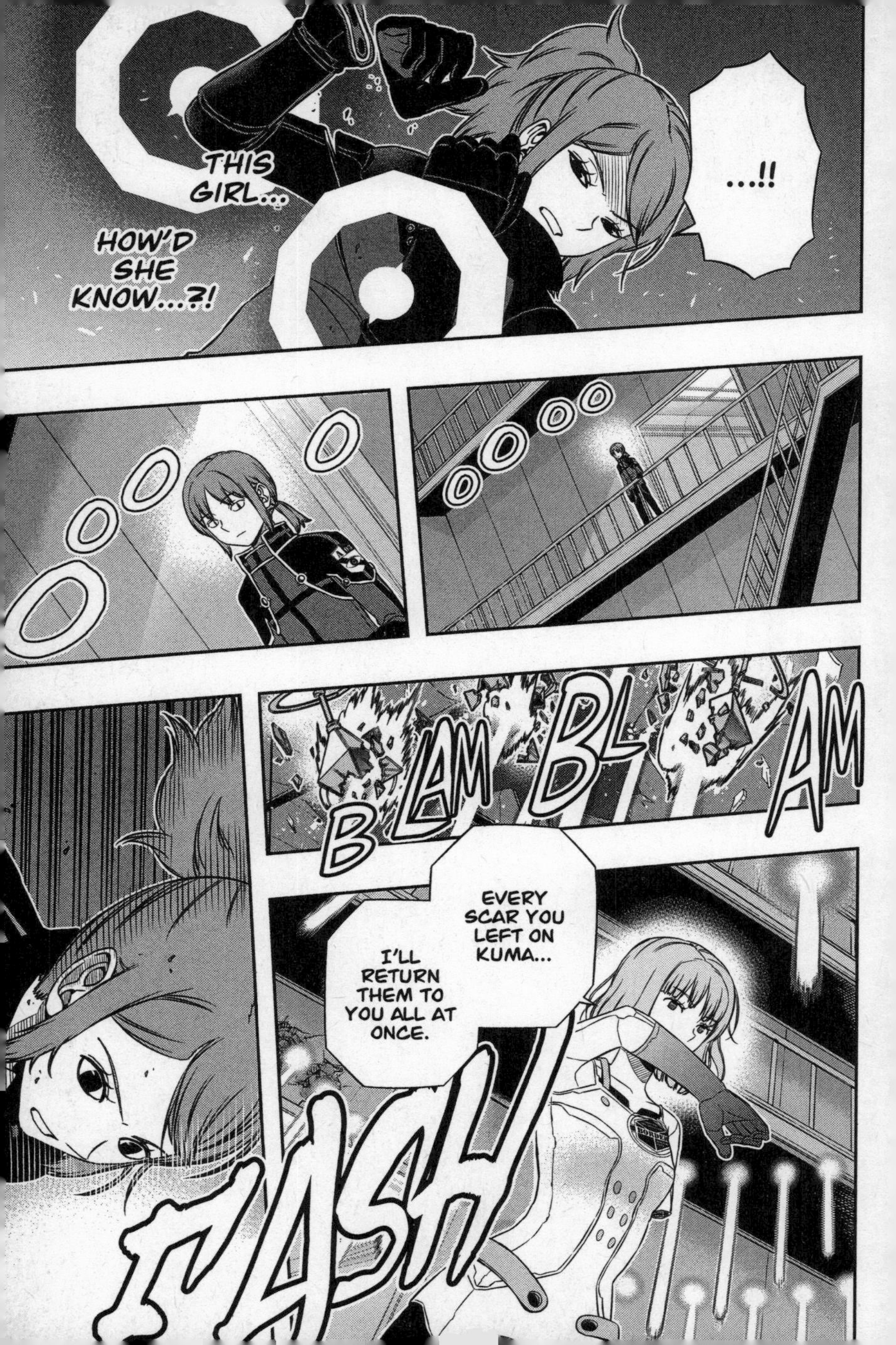

...!!
THIS GIRL...
HOW'D SHE KNOW...?!
BLAM BLAM
EVERY SCAR YOU LEFT ON KUMA...
I'LL RETURN THEM TO YOU ALL AT ONCE.
TASH

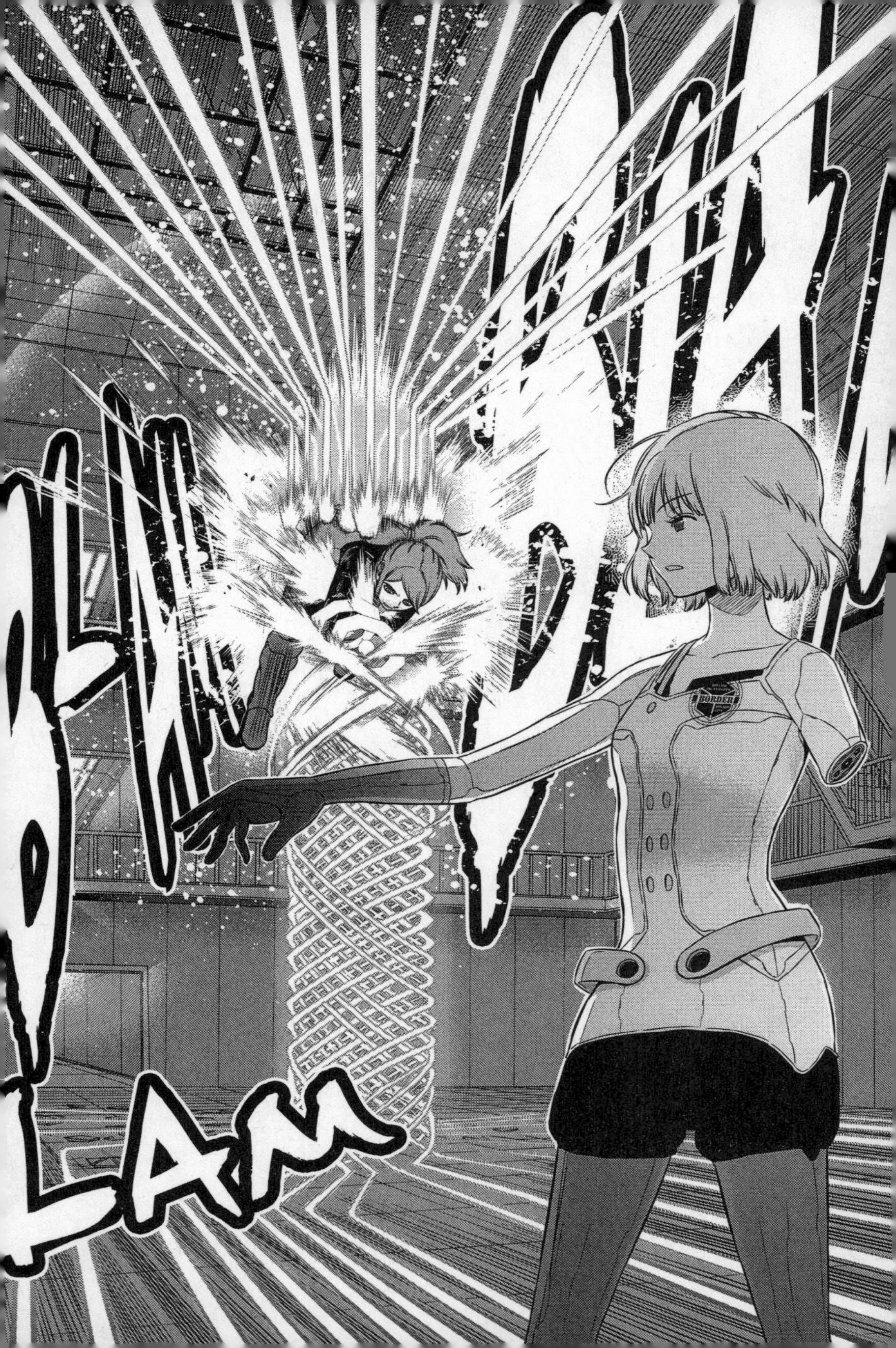
SLAM
BORDER

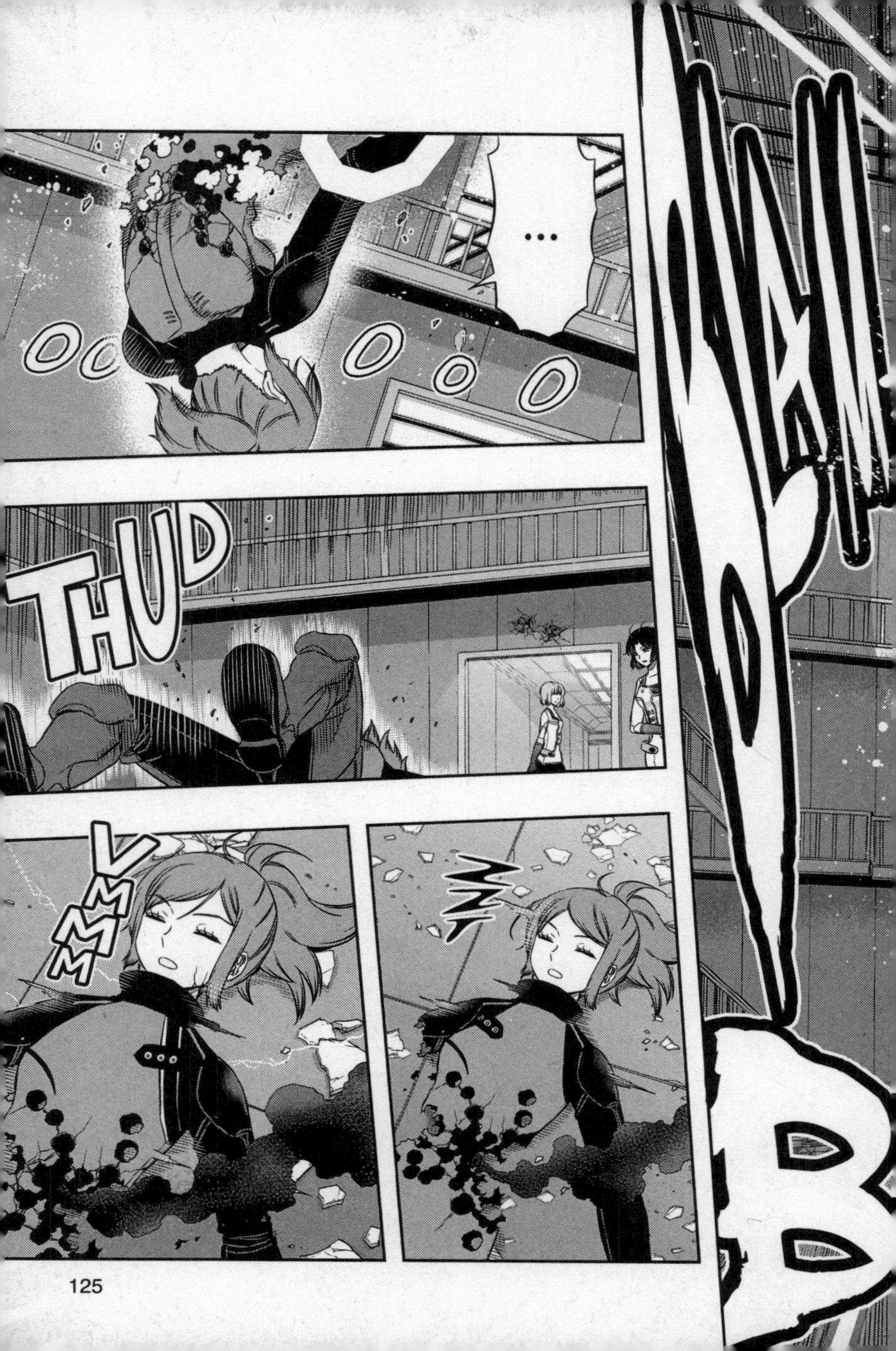
...
THUD
VMMMM

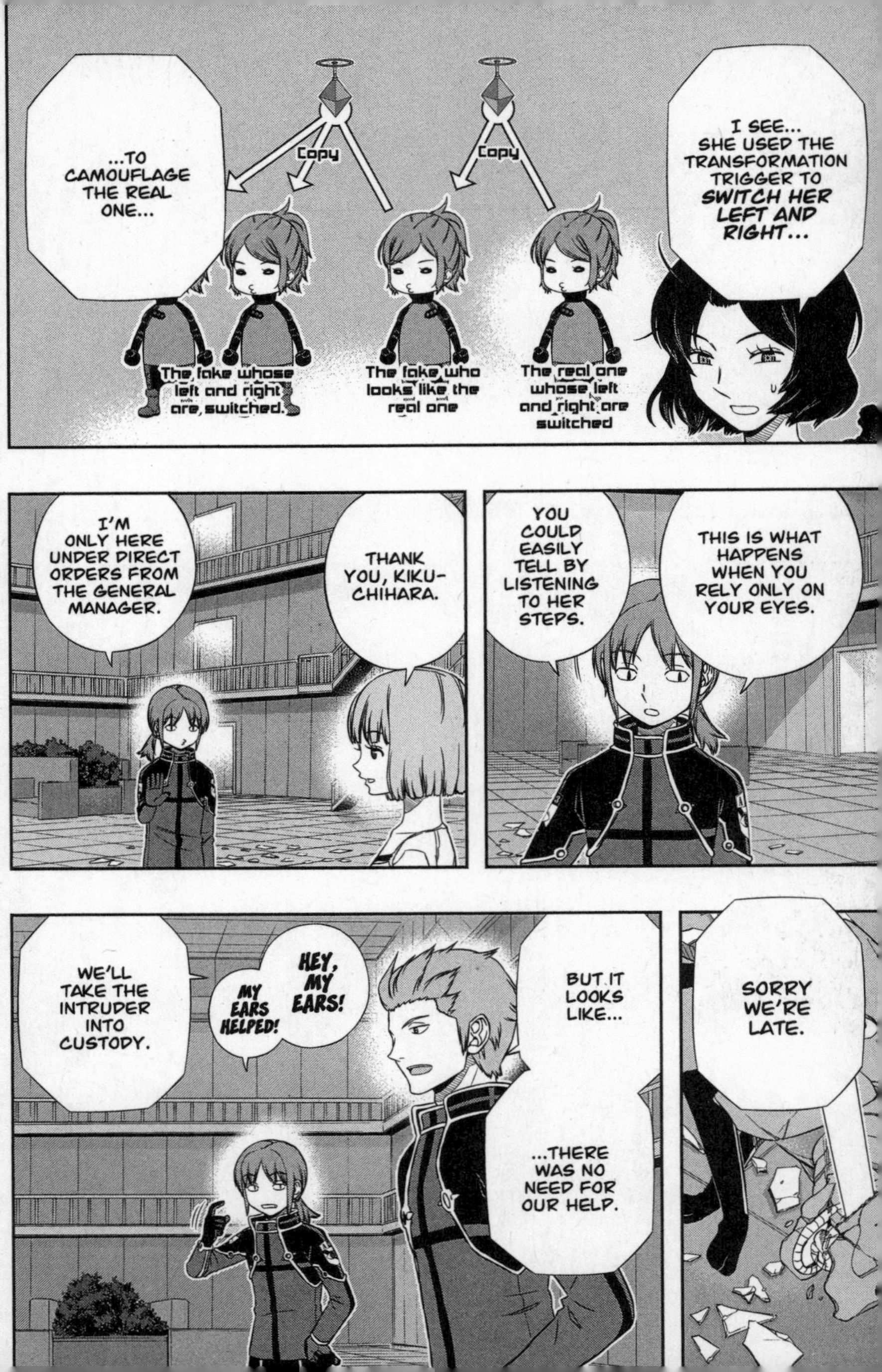
I SEE... SHE USED THE TRANSFORMATION TRIGGER TO SWITCH HER LEFT AND RIGHT...
...TO CAMOUFLAGE THE REAL ONE...
Copy
Copy
The real one whose left and right are switched
The fake who looks like the real one
The fake whose left and right are switched.
THIS IS WHAT HAPPENS WHEN YOU RELY ONLY ON YOUR EYES.
YOU COULD EASILY TELL BY LISTENING TO HER STEPS.
THANK YOU, KIKU-CHIHARA.
I'M ONLY HERE UNDER DIRECT ORDERS FROM THE GENERAL MANAGER.
SORRY WE'RE LATE.
BUT IT LOOKS LIKE...
...THERE WAS NO NEED FOR OUR HELP.
HEY, MY EARS!
MY EARS HELPED!
WE'LL TAKE THE INTRUDER INTO CUSTODY.

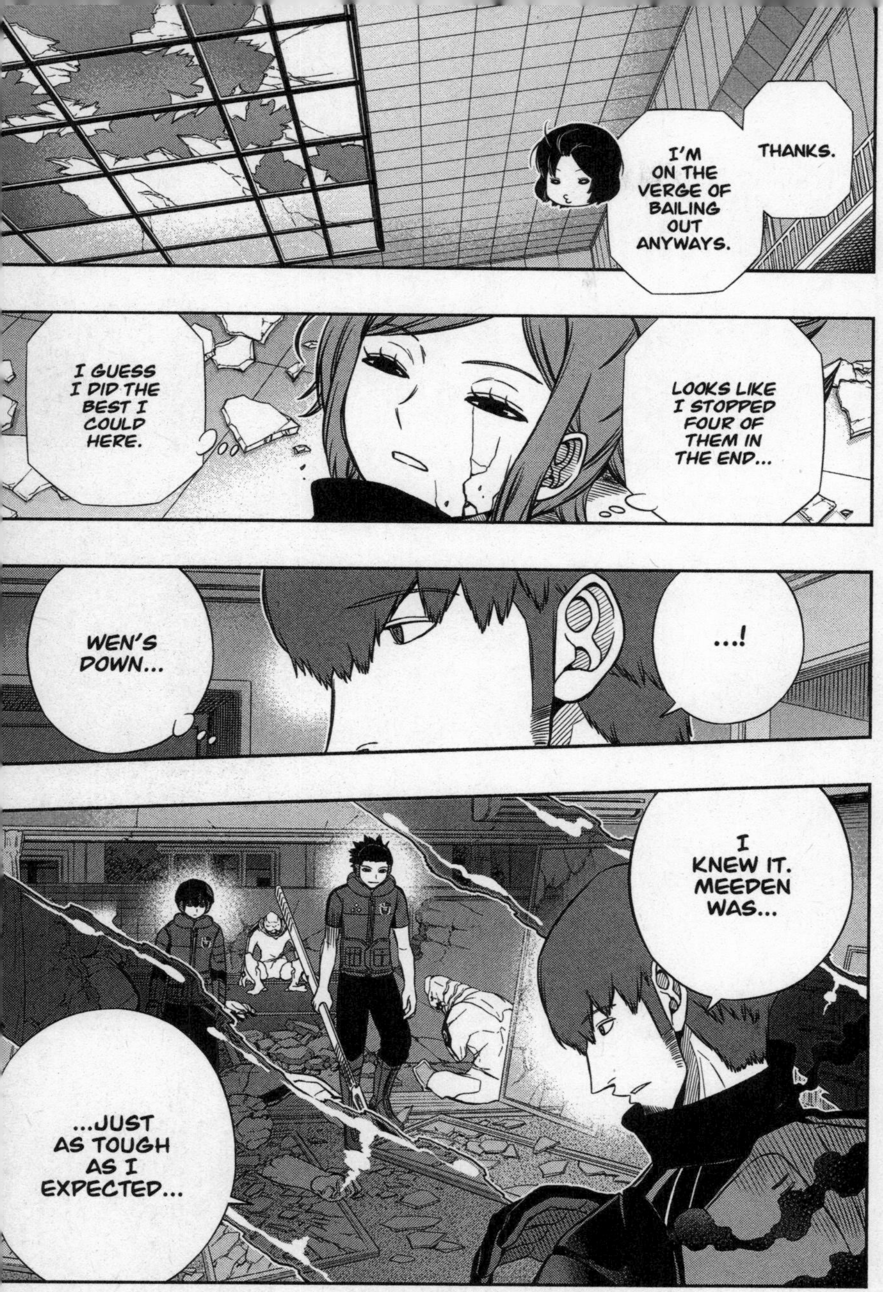
THANKS.
I'M ON THE VERGE OF BAILING OUT ANYWAYS.
LOOKS LIKE I STOPPED FOUR OF THEM IN THE END...
I GUESS I DID THE BEST I COULD HERE.
...!
WEN'S DOWN...
I KNEW IT. MEEDEN WAS...
...JUST AS TOUGH AS I EXPECTED...

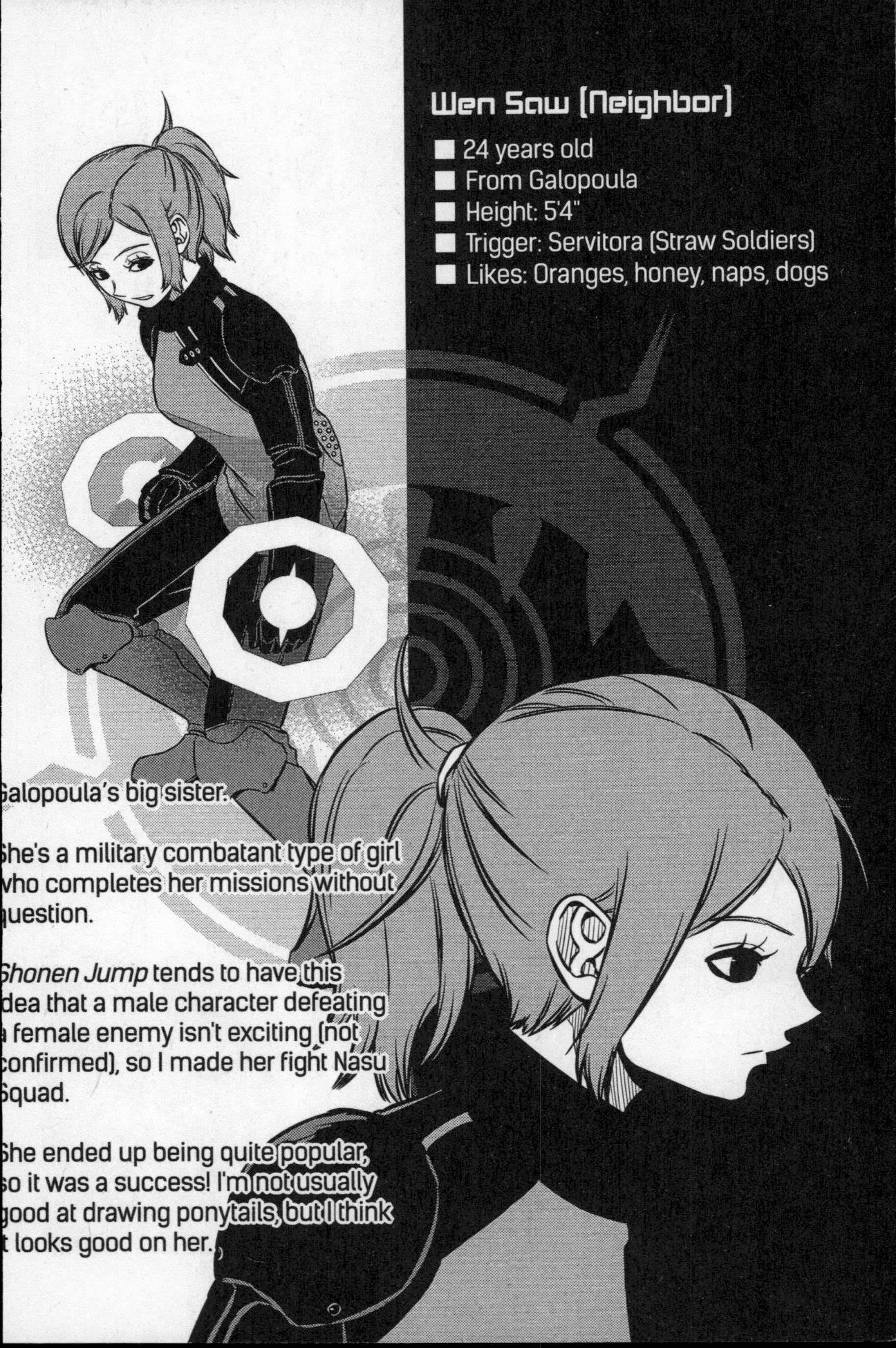

Wen Saw [Neighbor]

- 24 years old
- From Galopoula
- Height: 5'4"
- Trigger: Servitora (Straw Soldiers)
- Likes: Oranges, honey, naps, dogs

Galopoula's big sister.

She's a military combatant type of girl who completes her missions without question.

Shonen Jump tends to have this idea that a male character defeating a female enemy isn't exciting (not confirmed), so I made her fight Nasu Squad.

She ended up being quite popular, so it was a success! I'm not usually good at drawing ponytails, but I think it looks good on her.

Chapter 129 - Galapoula: Part 10

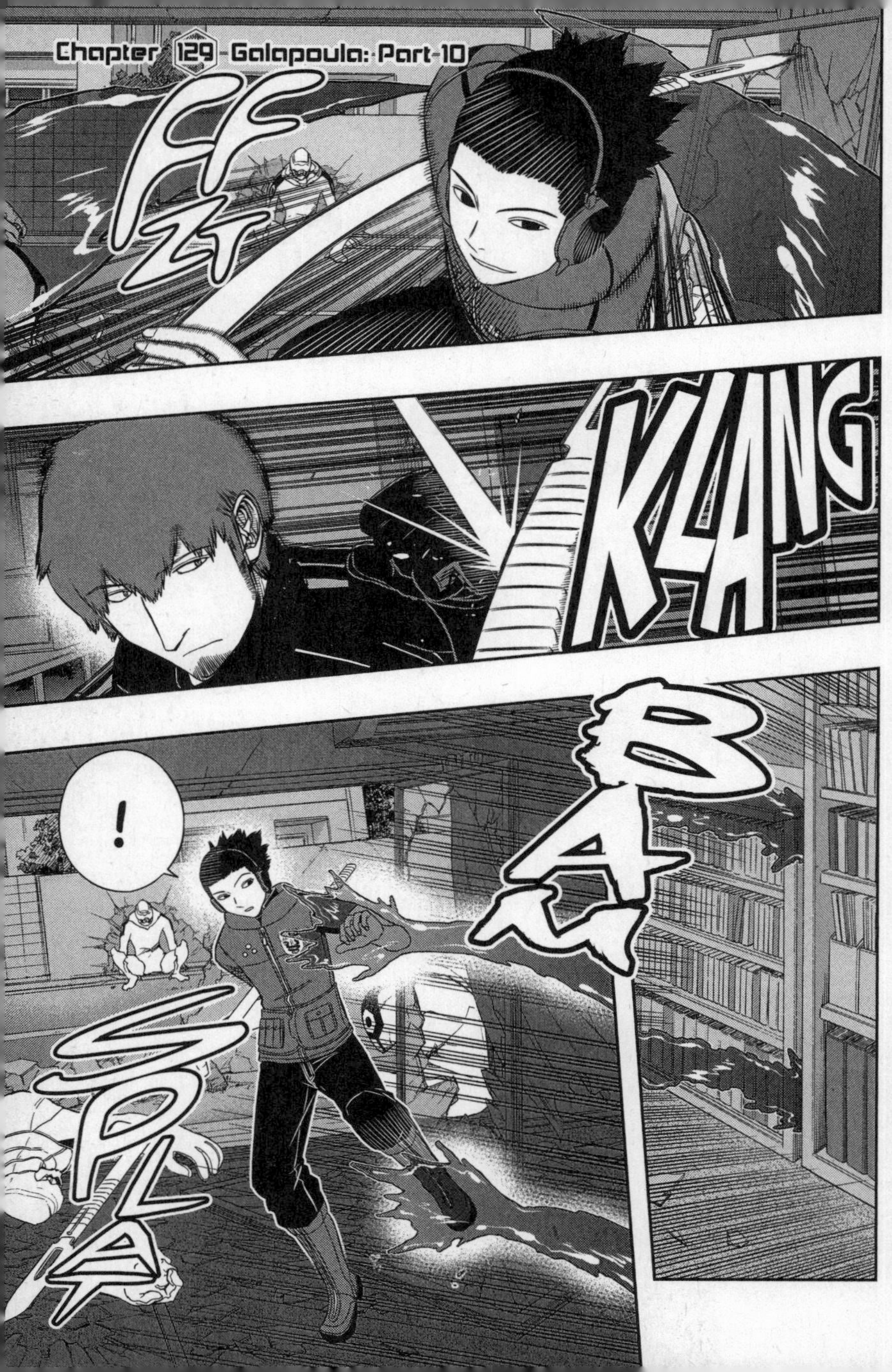
FFZZ
KLANG
BAM
!
SPLA

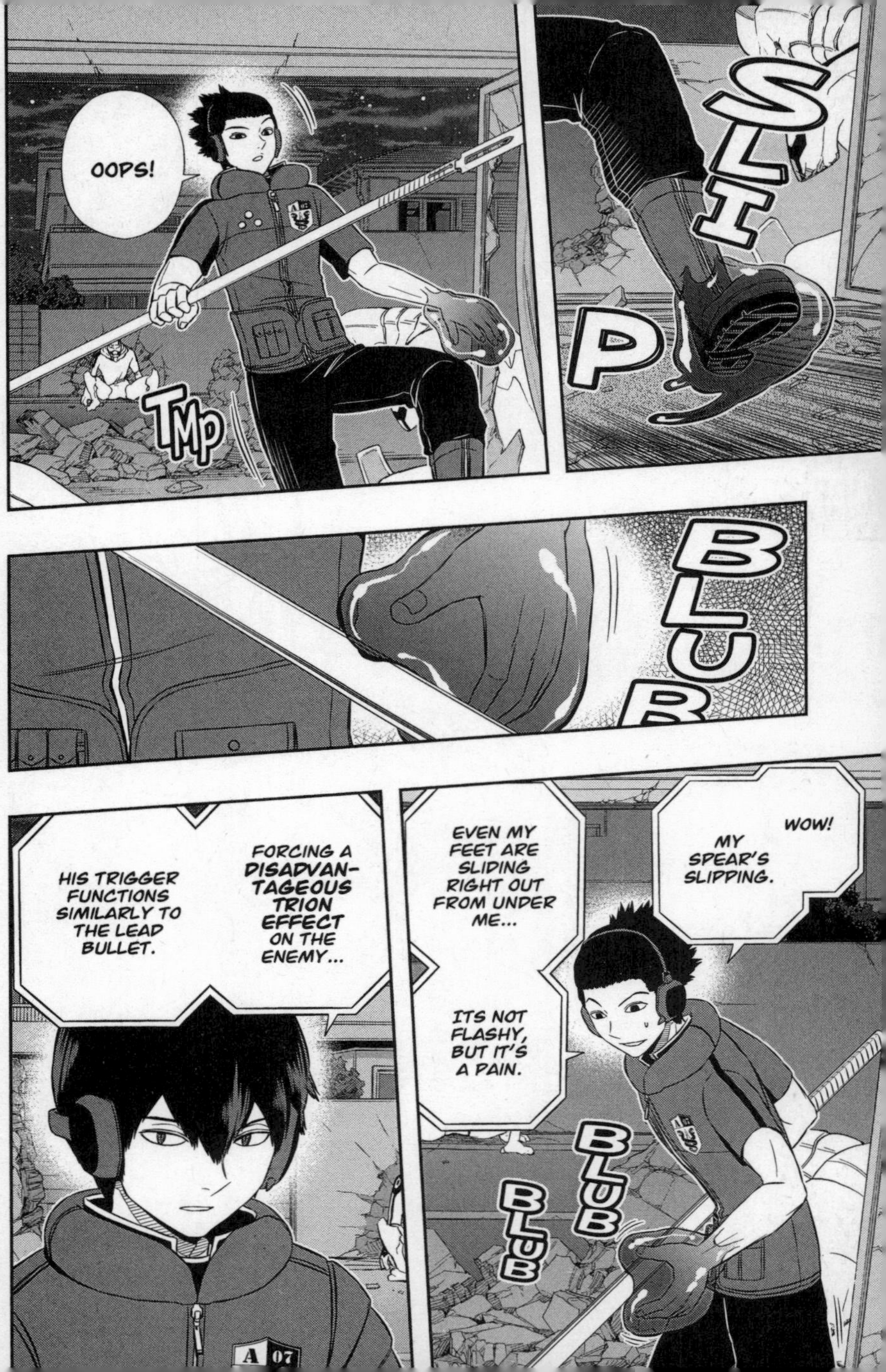
SLIP
P
OOPS!
TMp
BLUB
WOW! MY SPEAR'S SLIPPING.
EVEN MY FEET ARE SLIDING RIGHT OUT FROM UNDER ME...
ITS NOT FLASHY, BUT IT'S A PAIN.
BLUB
BLUB
FORCING A DISADVANTAGEOUS TRION EFFECT ON THE ENEMY...
HIS TRIGGER FUNCTIONS SIMILARLY TO THE LEAD BULLET.
A 07

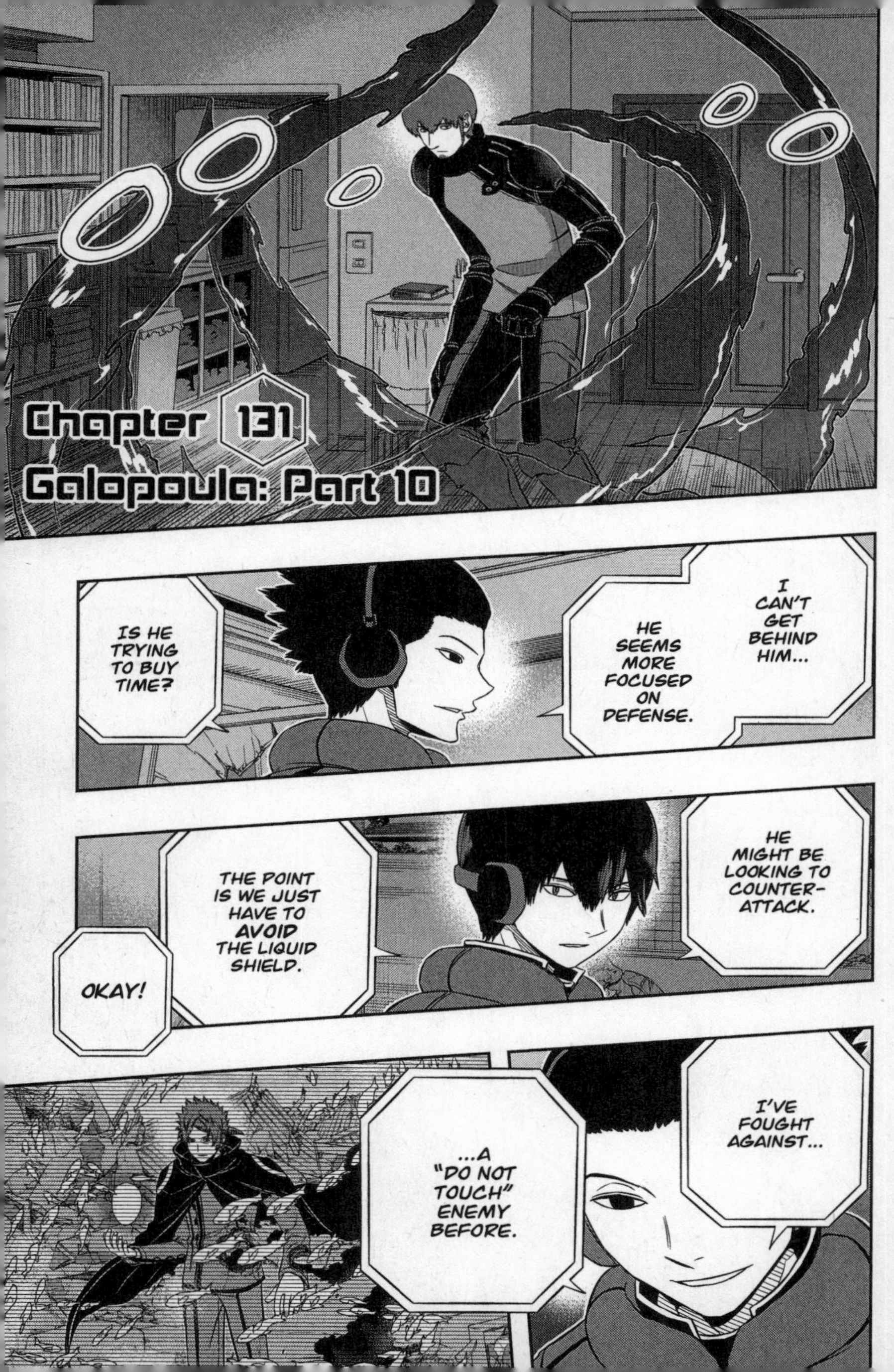
Chapter 131
Galopoula: Part 10
I CAN'T GET BEHIND HIM...
HE SEEMS MORE FOCUSED ON DEFENSE.
IS HE TRYING TO BUY TIME?
HE MIGHT BE LOOKING TO COUNTER-ATTACK.
THE POINT IS WE JUST HAVE TO AVOID THE LIQUID SHIELD.
OKAY!
I'VE FOUGHT AGAINST...
...A "DO NOT TOUCH" ENEMY BEFORE.

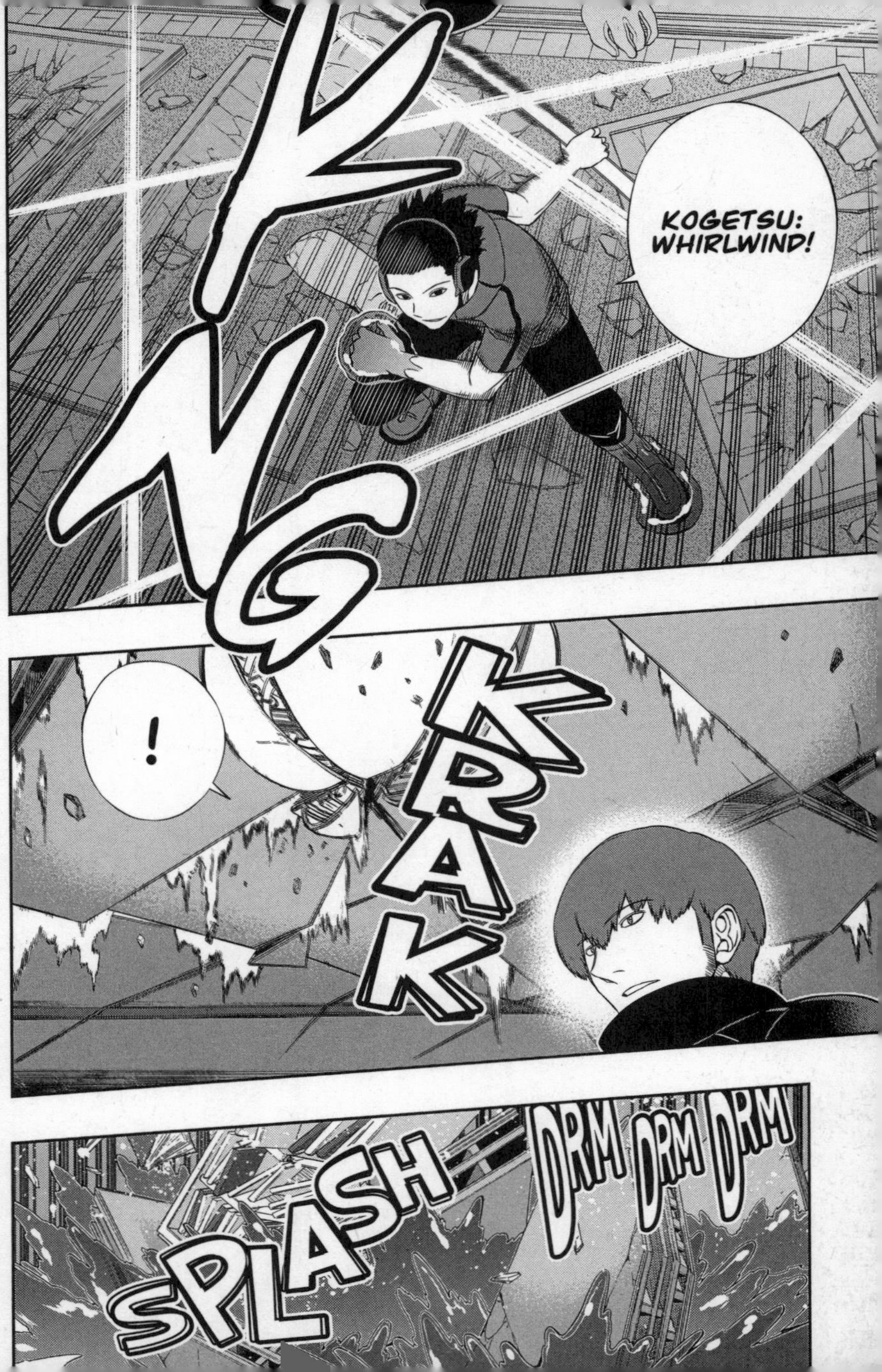
KOGETSU: WHIRLWIND!
VNG
KRAK
!
DRM DRM DRM
SPLASH

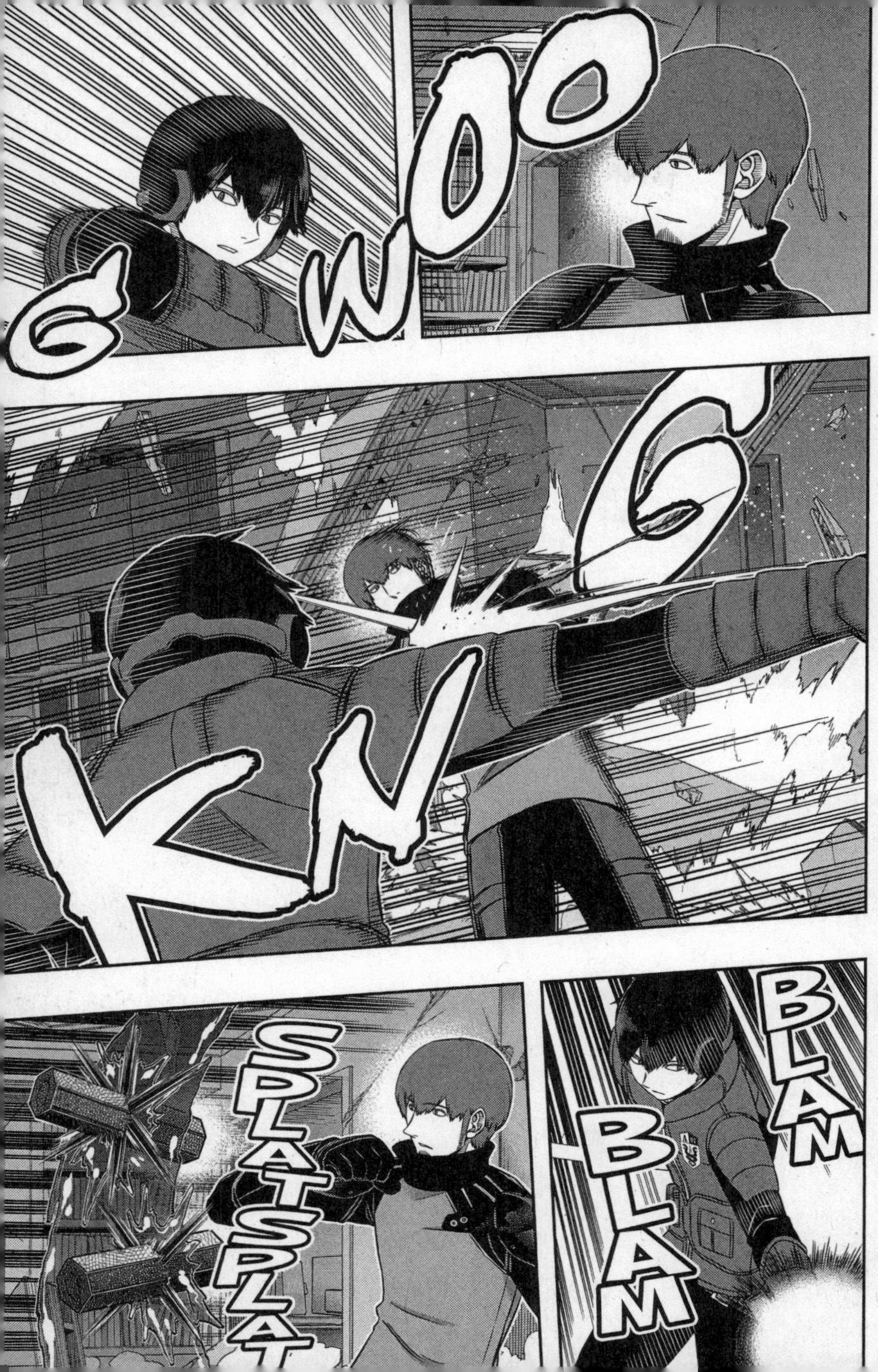
GWOO
KNG
BLAM
BLAM
SPLAT
SPLAT

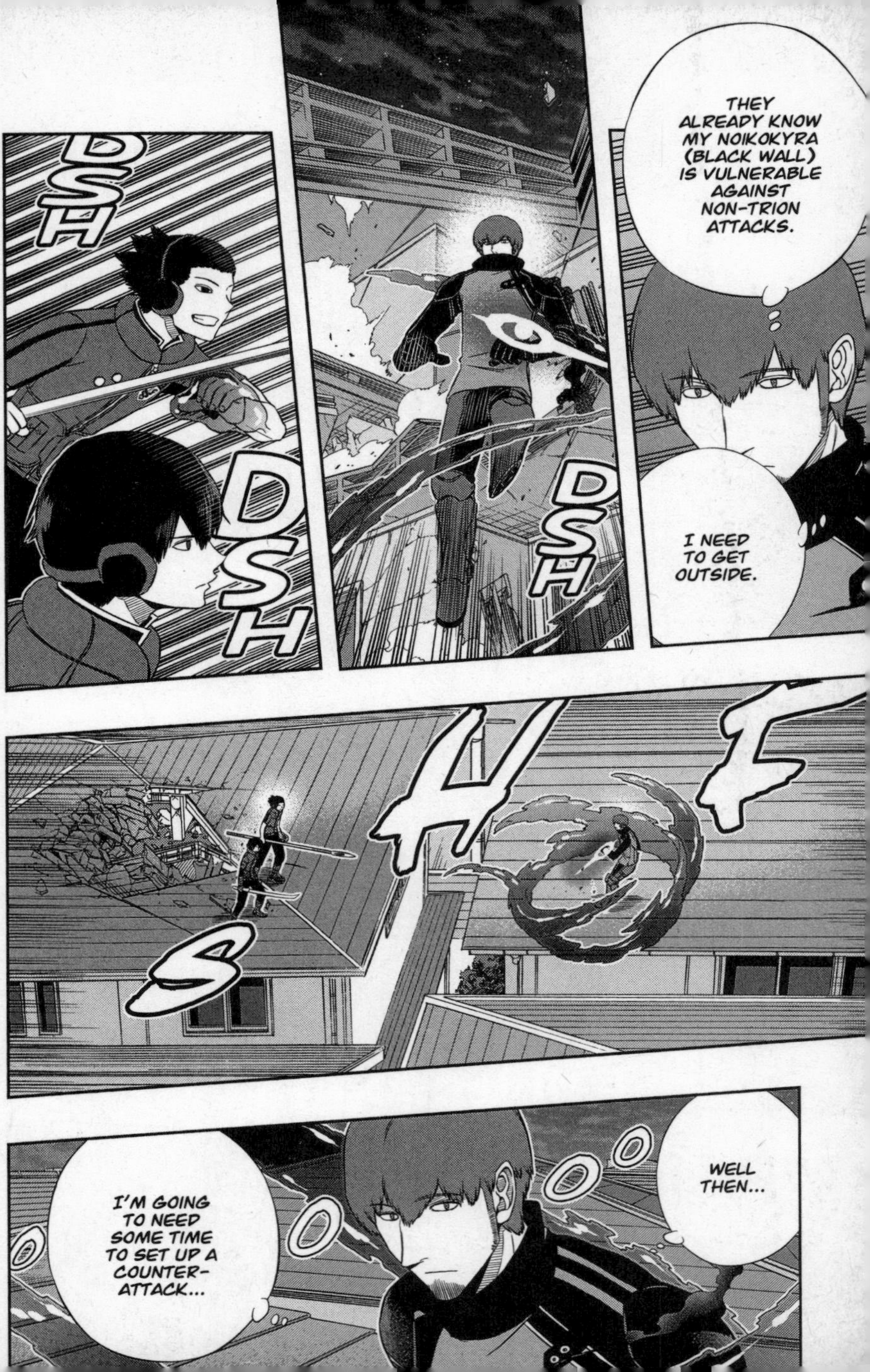
THEY ALREADY KNOW MY NOIKOKYRA (BLACK WALL) IS VULNERABLE AGAINST NON-TRION ATTACKS.
I NEED TO GET OUTSIDE.
DSH
DSH
DSH
H
S
WELL THEN...
I'M GOING TO NEED SOME TIME TO SET UP A COUNTER-ATTACK...

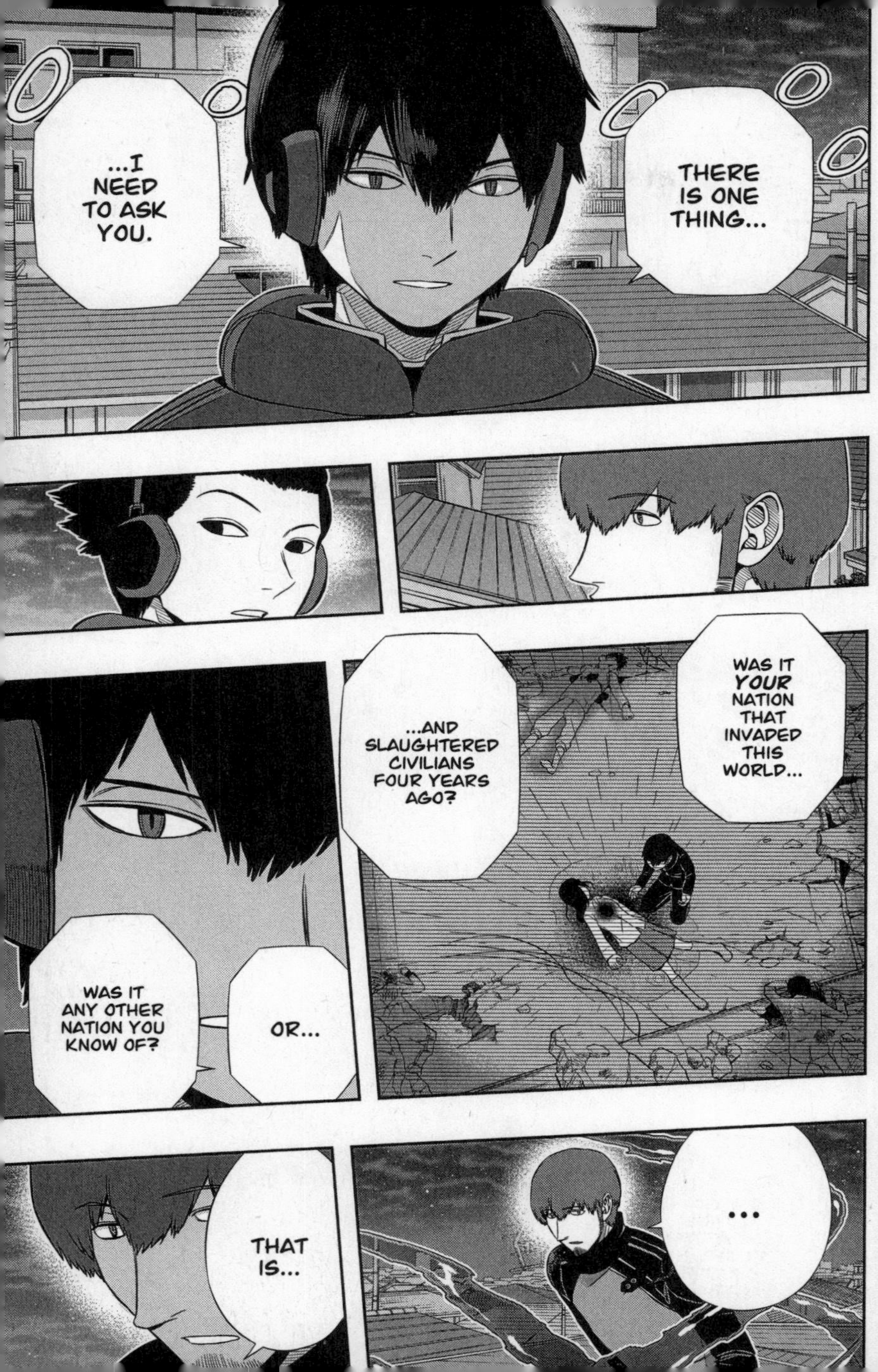
THERE IS ONE THING...
...I NEED TO ASK YOU.
WAS IT *YOUR* NATION THAT INVADED THIS WORLD...
...AND SLAUGHTERED CIVILIANS FOUR YEARS AGO?
OR...
WAS IT ANY OTHER NATION YOU KNOW OF?
...
THAT IS...

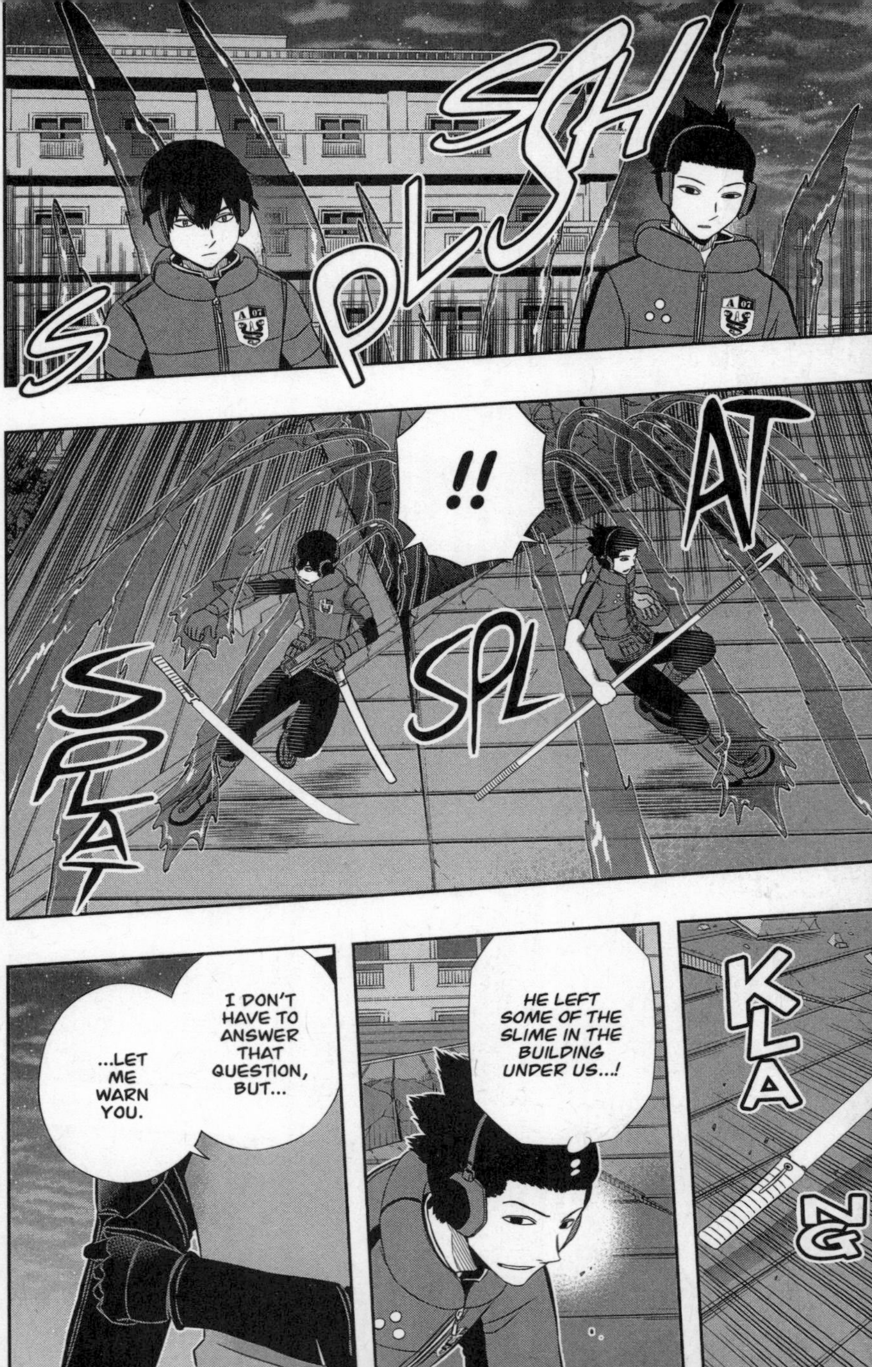
SPLSH
!!
SPLAT
SPLAT
KLANG
HE LEFT SOME OF THE SLIME IN THE BUILDING UNDER US...!
I DON'T HAVE TO ANSWER THAT QUESTION, BUT...
...LET ME WARN YOU.

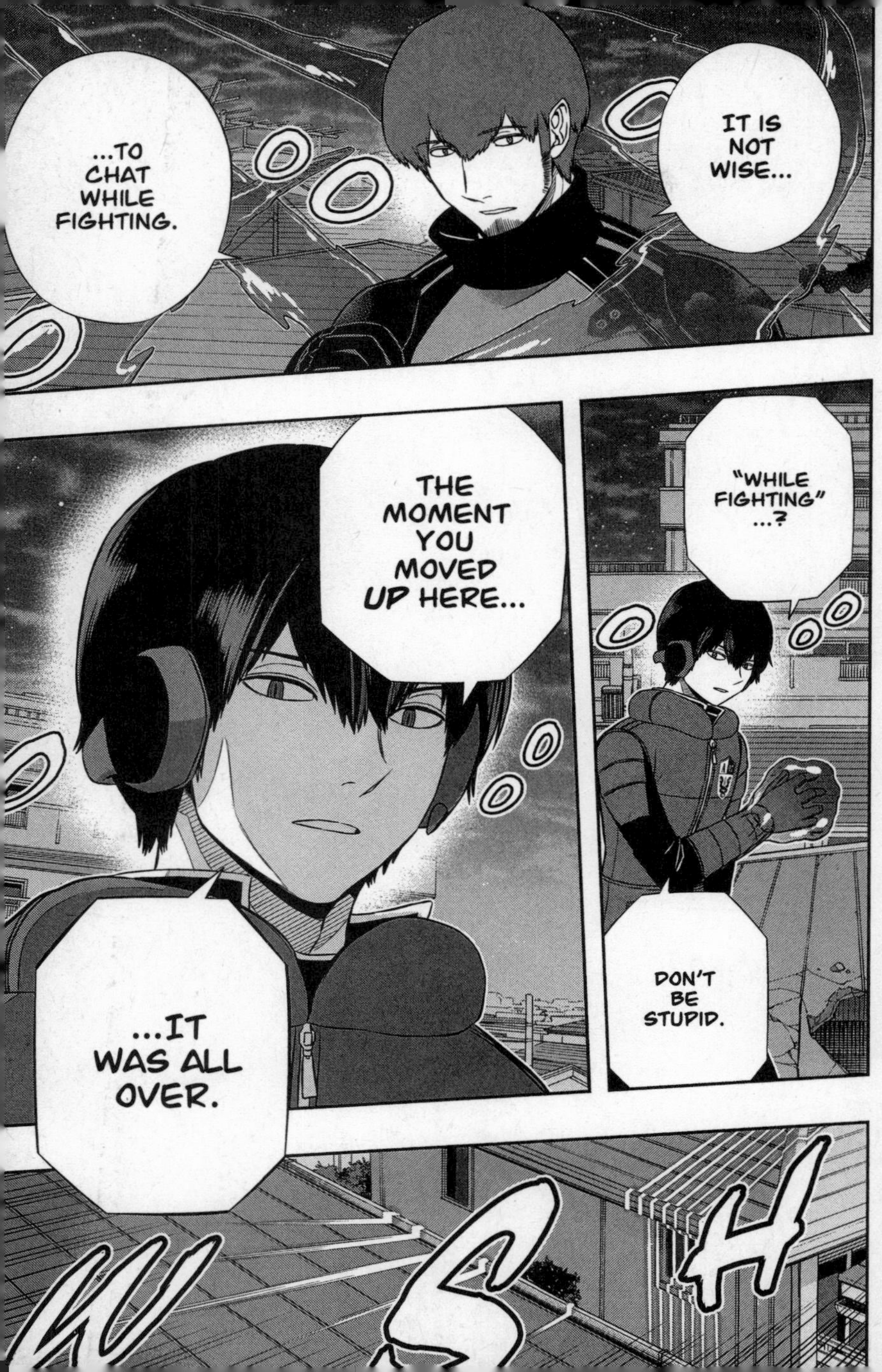
IT IS NOT WISE...
...TO CHAT WHILE FIGHTING.
"WHILE FIGHTING" ...?
DON'T BE STUPID.
THE MOMENT YOU MOVED UP HERE...
...IT WAS ALL OVER.
WSH

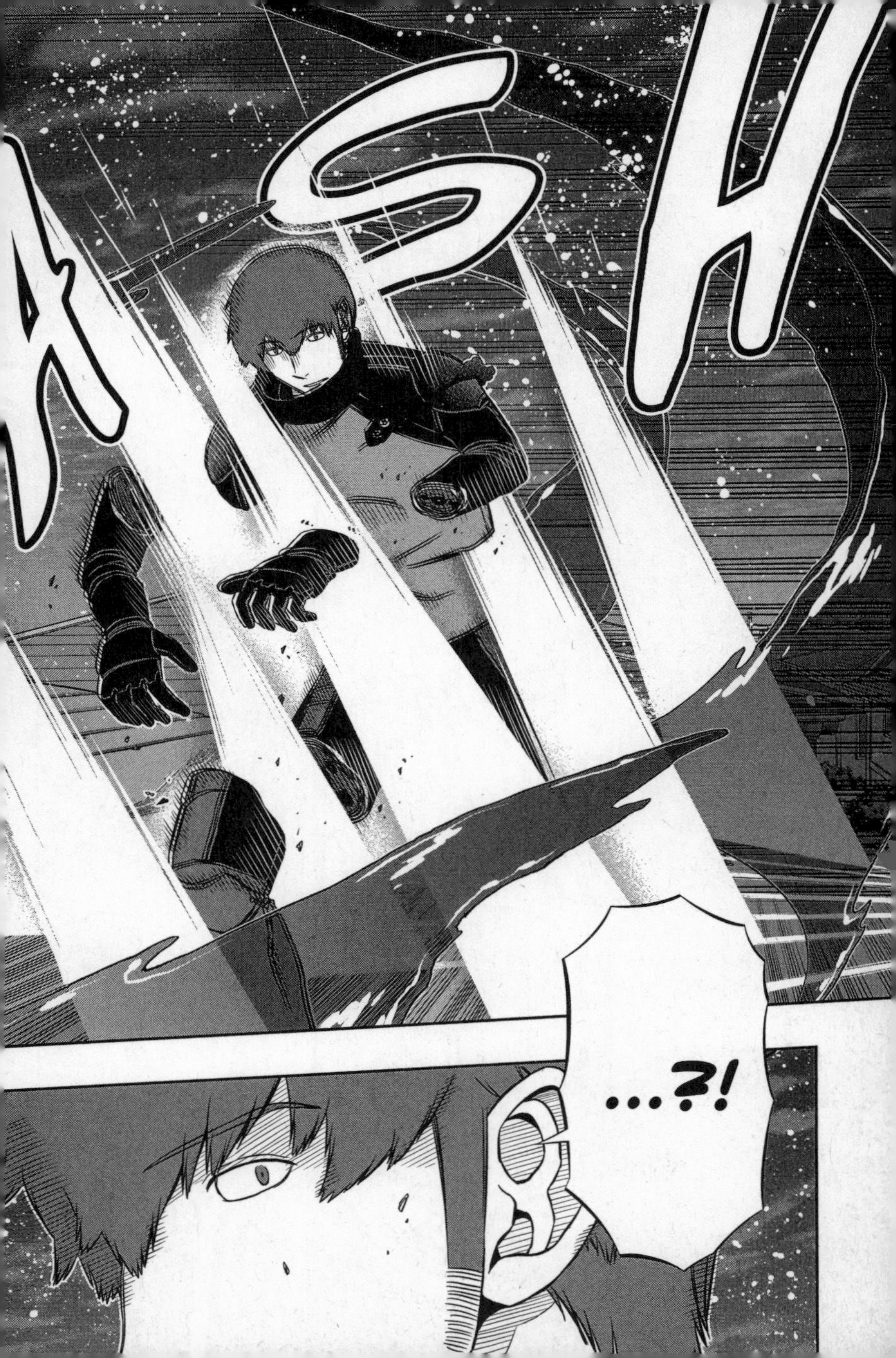
ASH
...?!

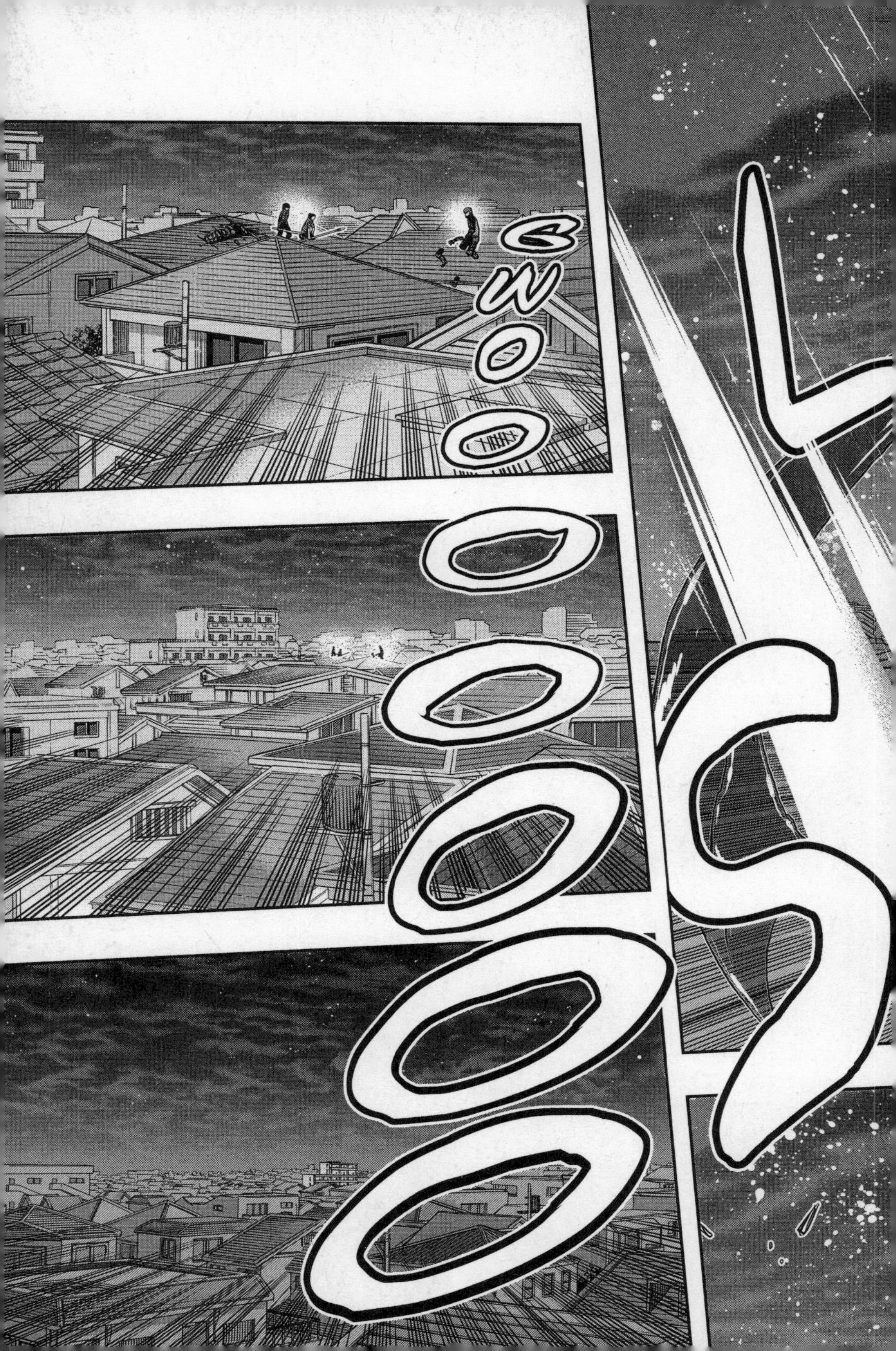
GWOOOOOOOSH

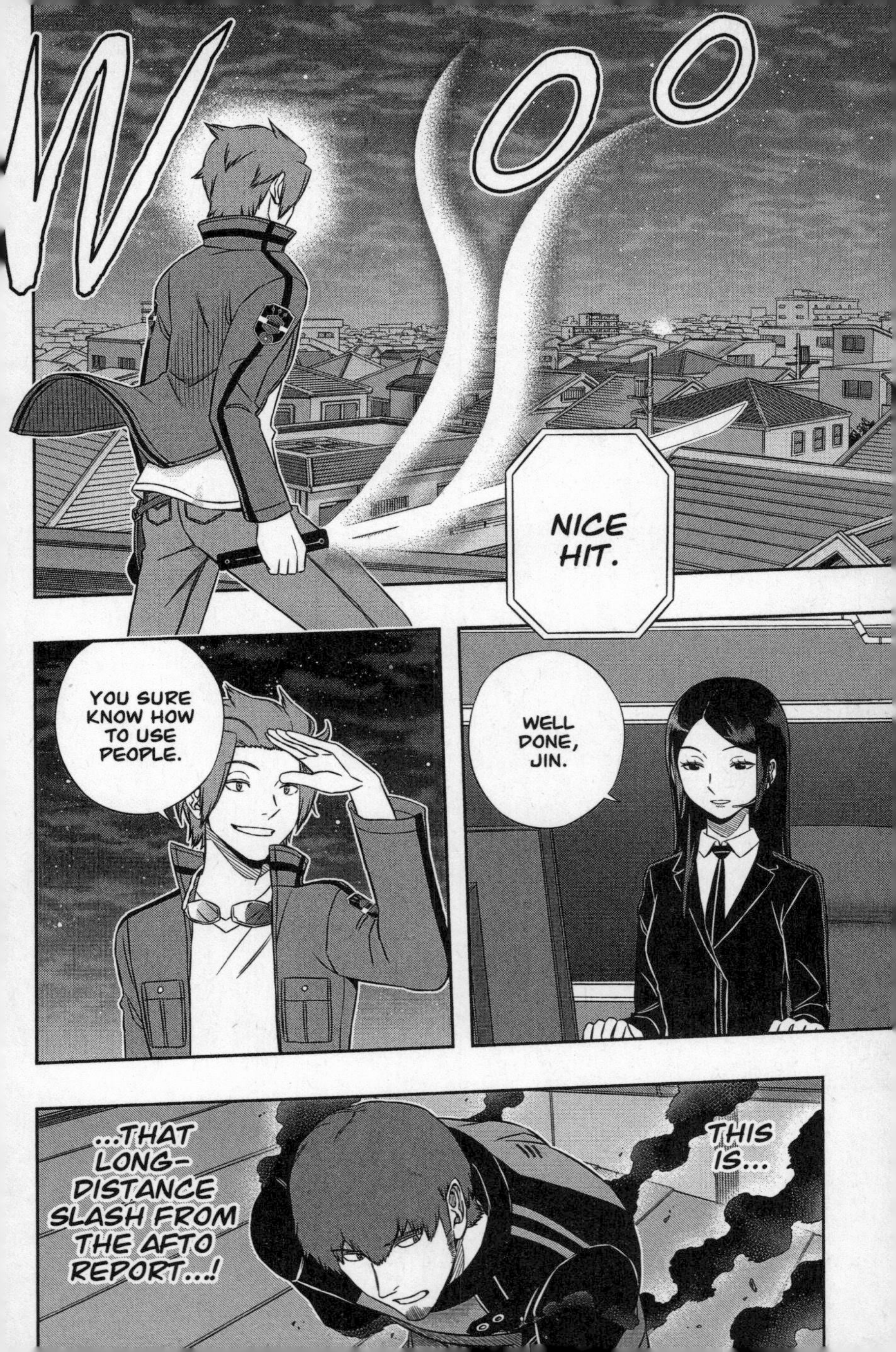
WOOO
NICE HIT.
WELL DONE, JIN.
YOU SURE KNOW HOW TO USE PEOPLE.
THIS IS...
...THAT LONG-DISTANCE SLASH FROM THE AFTO REPORT...!

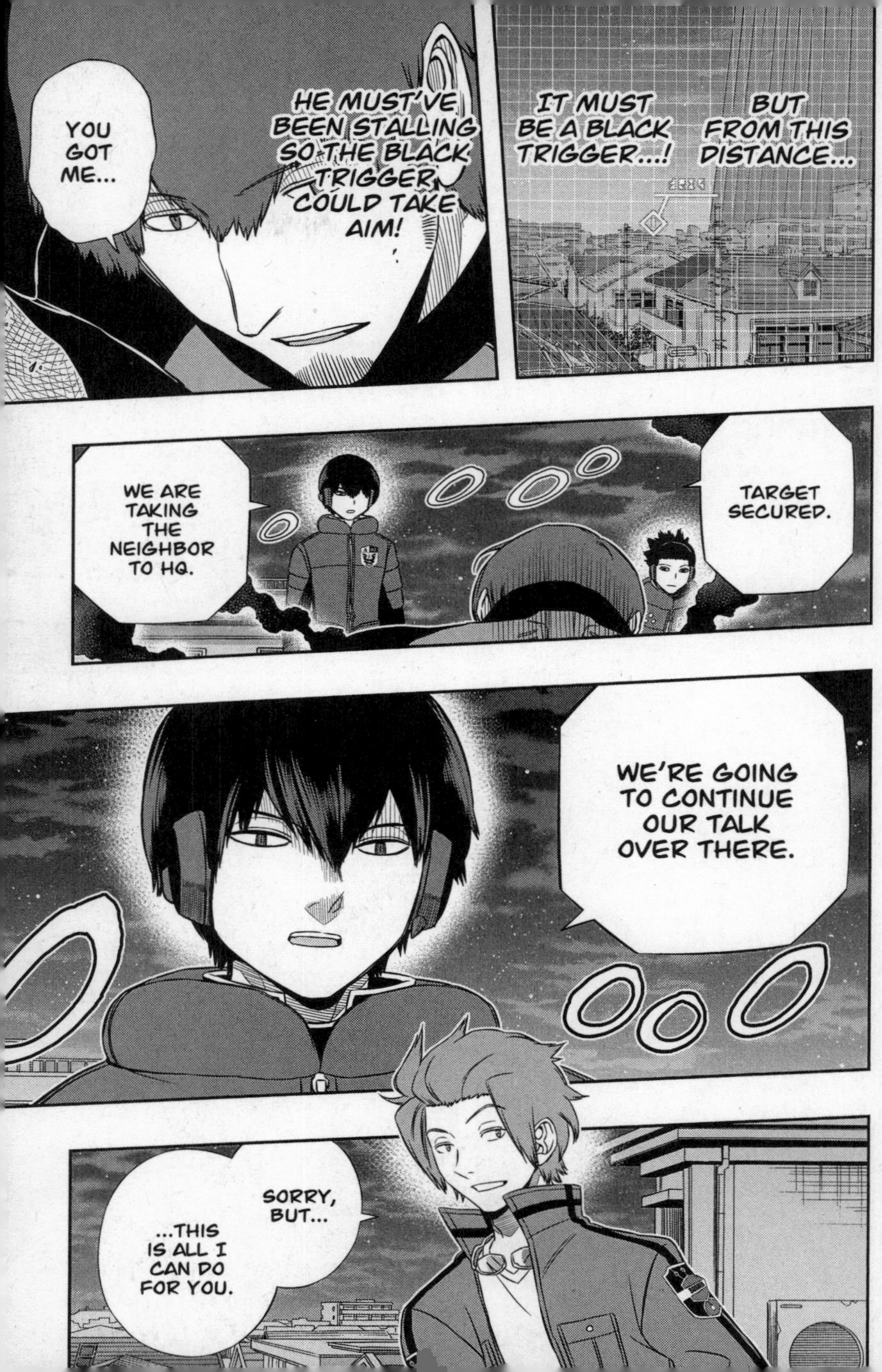
IT MUST BE A BLACK TRIGGER...!
BUT FROM THIS DISTANCE...
HE MUST'VE BEEN STALLING SO THE BLACK TRIGGER COULD TAKE AIM!
YOU GOT ME...
TARGET SECURED.
WE ARE TAKING THE NEIGHBOR TO HQ.
WE'RE GOING TO CONTINUE OUR TALK OVER THERE.
SORRY, BUT...
...THIS IS ALL I CAN DO FOR YOU.

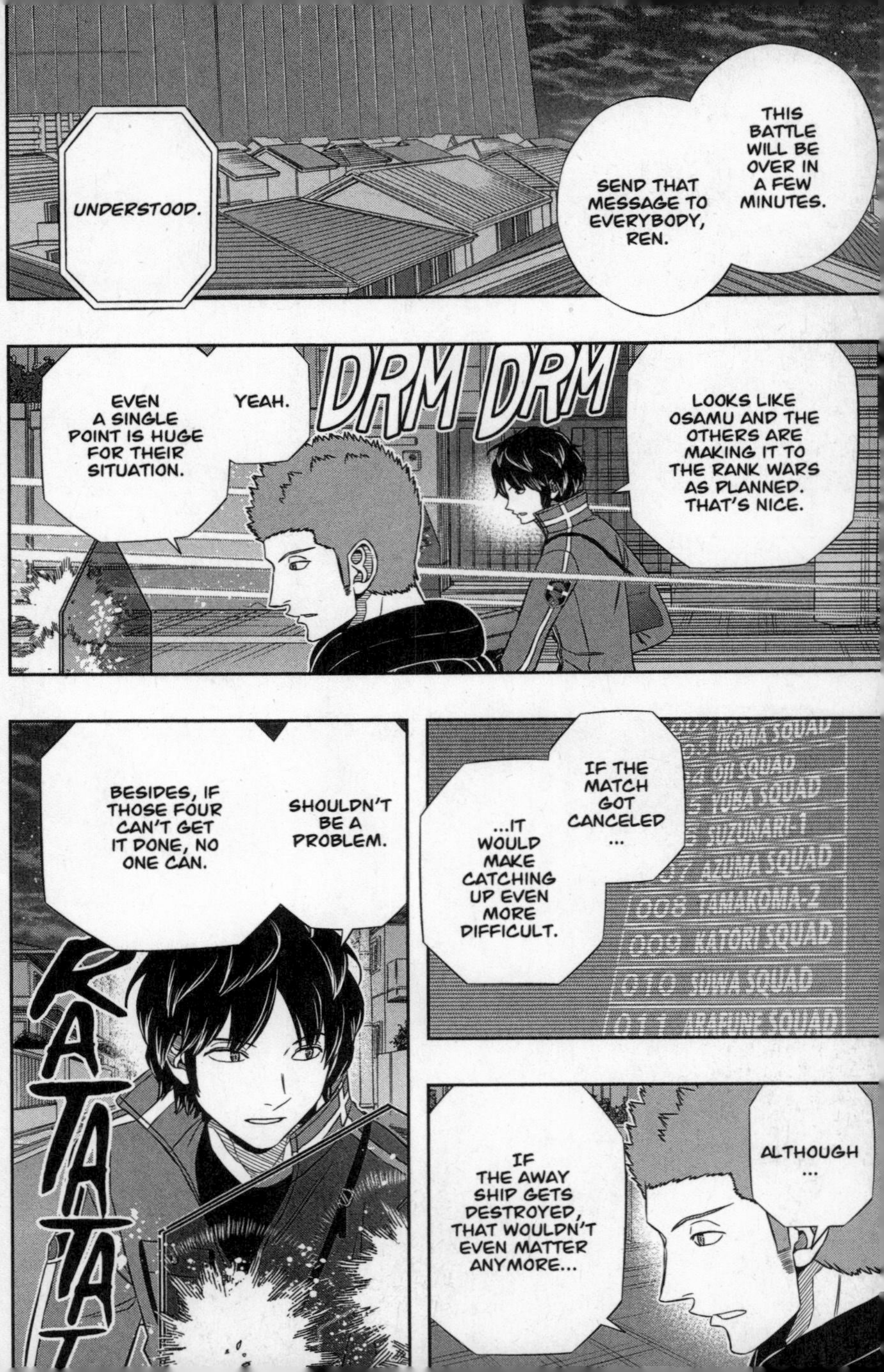
THIS BATTLE WILL BE OVER IN A FEW MINUTES.
SEND THAT MESSAGE TO EVERYBODY, REN.
UNDERSTOOD.
LOOKS LIKE OSAMU AND THE OTHERS ARE MAKING IT TO THE RANK WARS AS PLANNED. THAT'S NICE.
DRM DRM
YEAH.
EVEN A SINGLE POINT IS HUGE FOR THEIR SITUATION.
IF THE MATCH GOT CANCELED ...
...IT WOULD MAKE CATCHING UP EVEN MORE DIFFICULT.
IKOMA SQUAD
OJI SQUAD
YUBA SQUAD
SUZUNARI-1
AZUMA SQUAD
008 TAMAKOMA-2
009 KATORI SQUAD
010 SUWA SQUAD
011 ARAFUNE SQUAD
ALTHOUGH ...
IF THE AWAY SHIP GETS DESTROYED, THAT WOULDN'T EVEN MATTER ANYMORE...
SHOULDN'T BE A PROBLEM.
BESIDES, IF THOSE FOUR CAN'T GET IT DONE, NO ONE CAN.
RATATAT

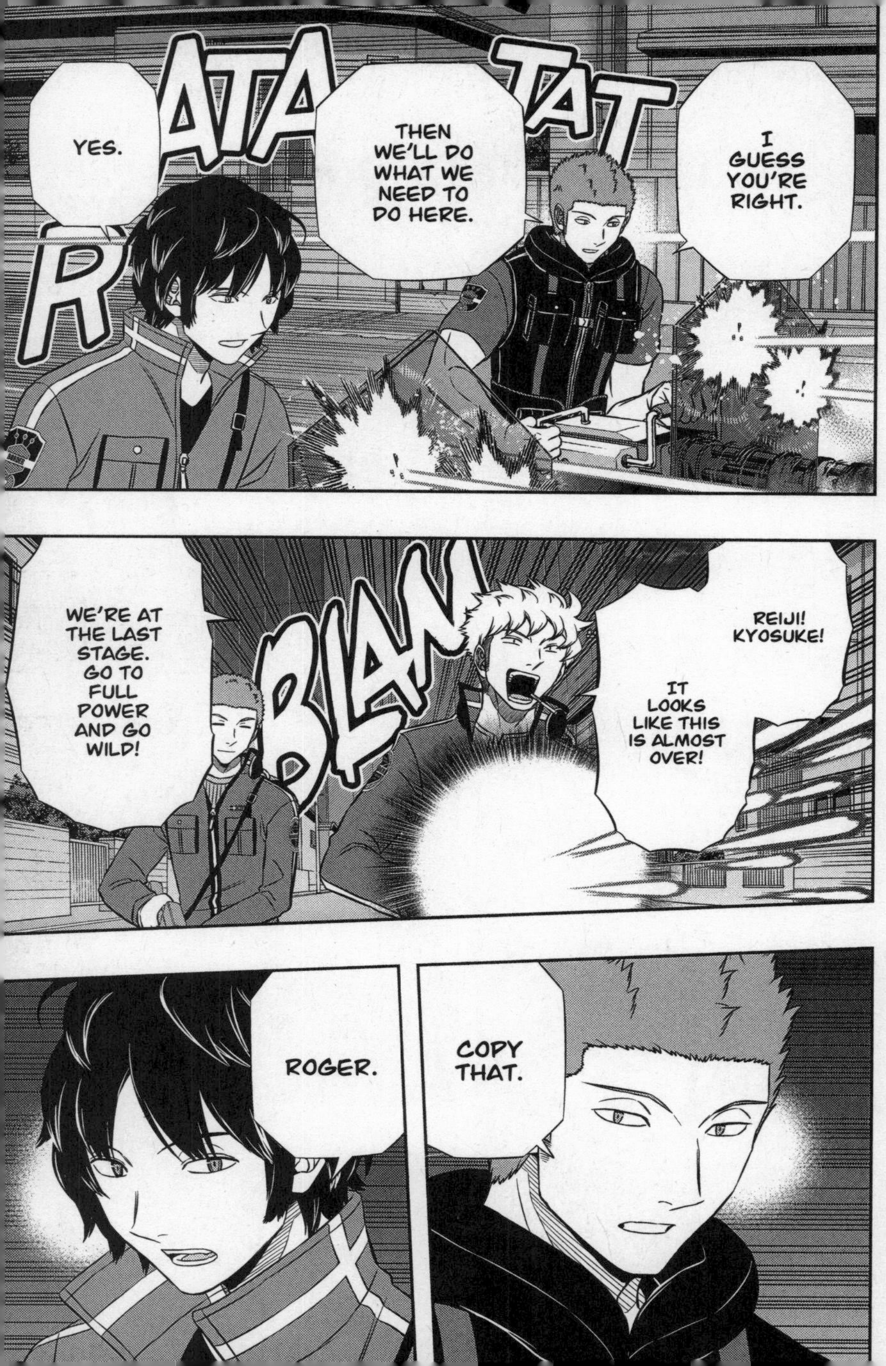
I GUESS YOU'RE RIGHT.
TAT
THEN WE'LL DO WHAT WE NEED TO DO HERE.
ATA
YES.
R
REIJI! KYOSUKE!
IT LOOKS LIKE THIS IS ALMOST OVER!
BLAM
WE'RE AT THE LAST STAGE. GO TO FULL POWER AND GO WILD!
COPY THAT.
ROGER.

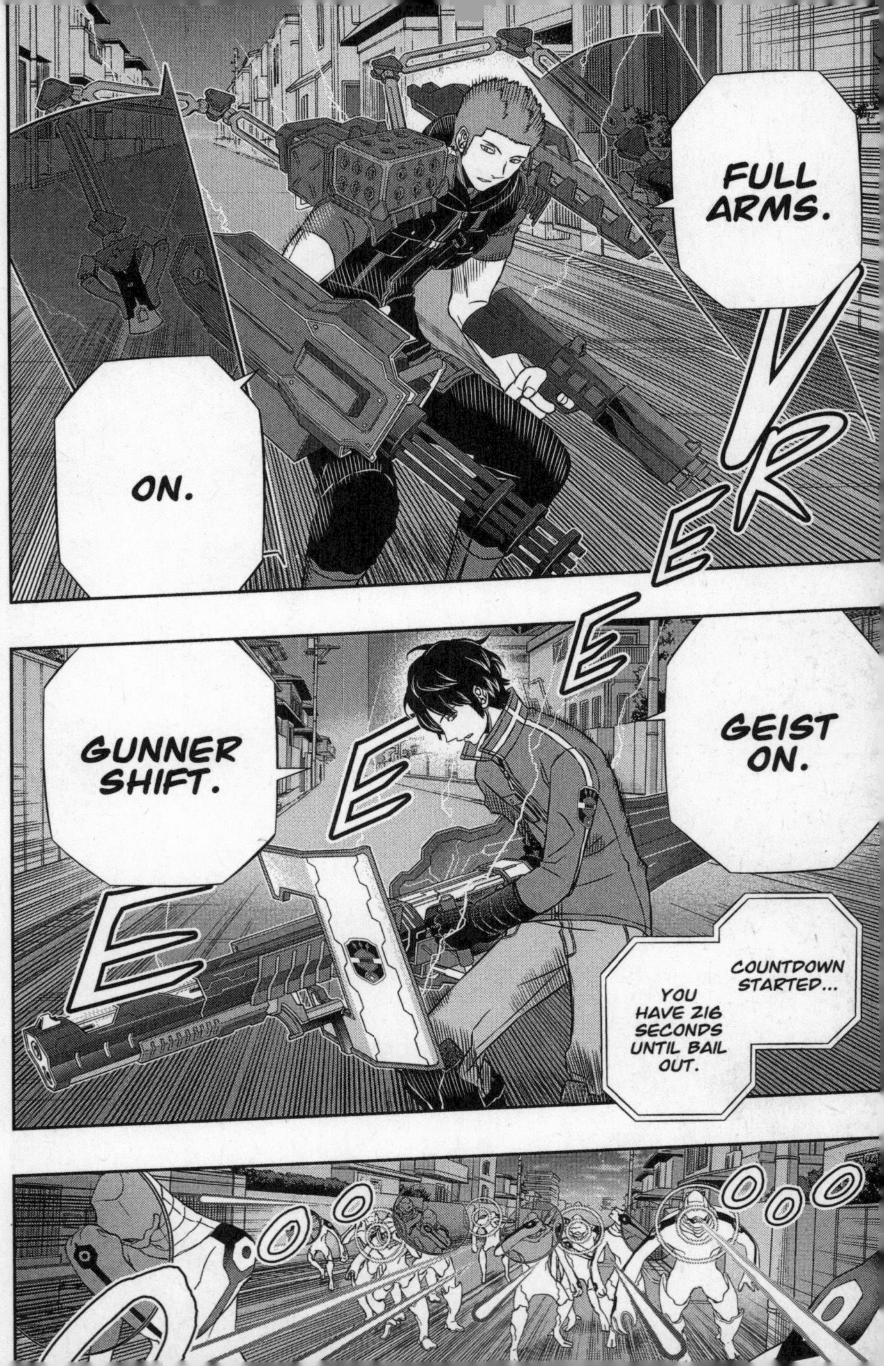
FULL ARMS.
ON.
VREEEE
GEIST ON.
GUNNER SHIFT.
COUNTDOWN STARTED... YOU HAVE 216 SECONDS UNTIL BAIL OUT.
OOO
OOO

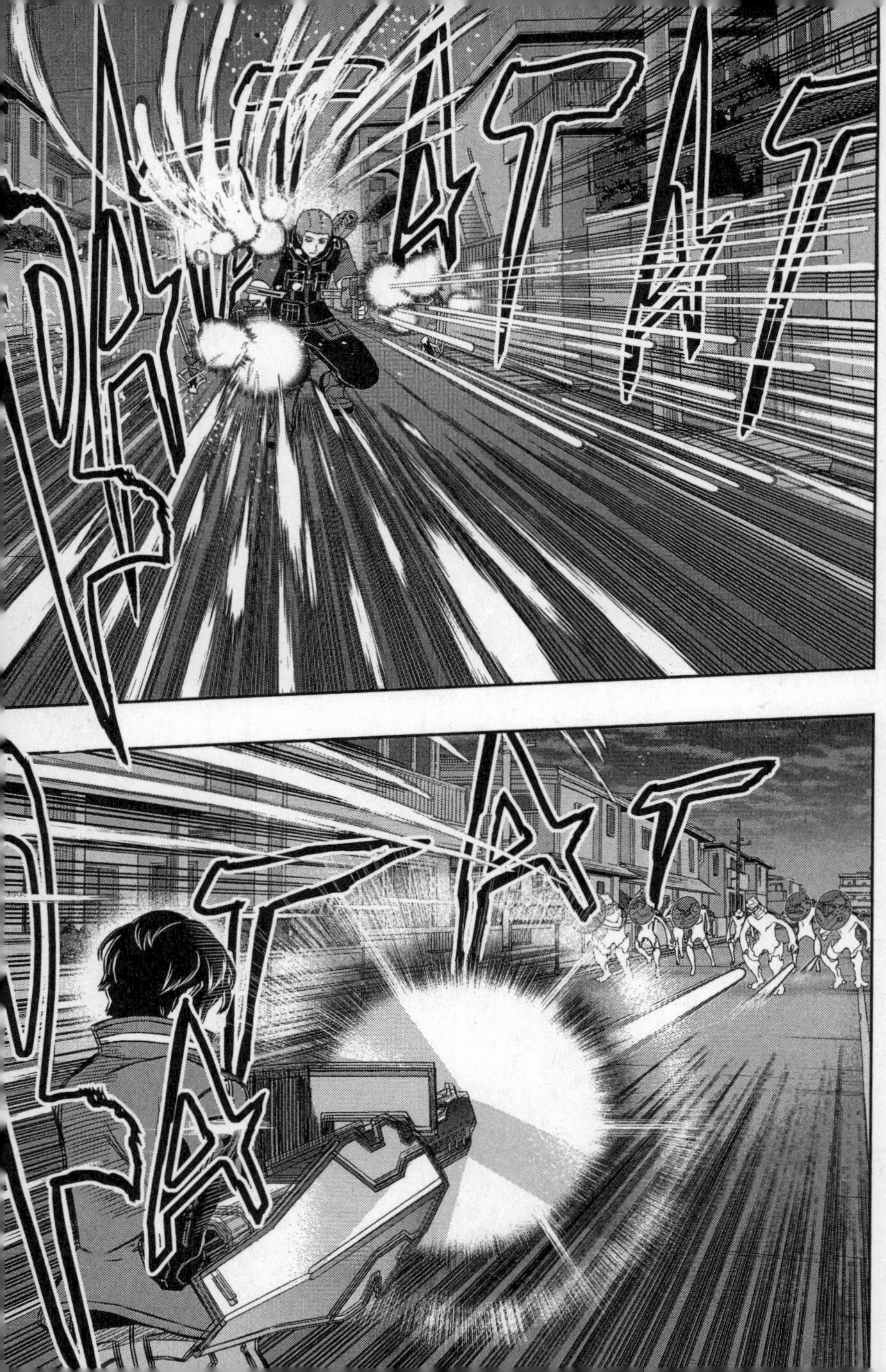

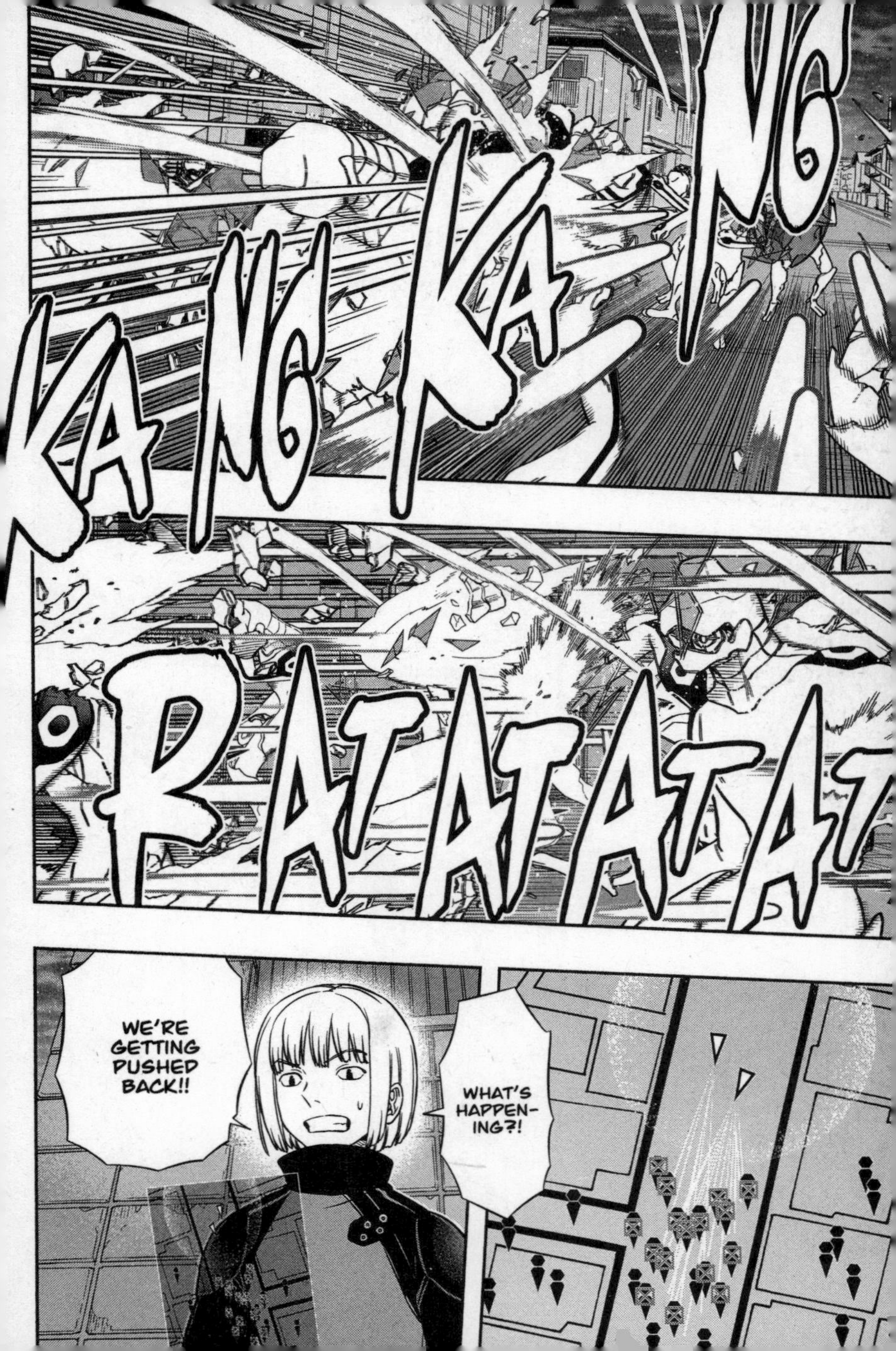
KANG KANG
PATATATA
WHAT'S HAPPEN-ING?!
WE'RE GETTING PUSHED BACK!!

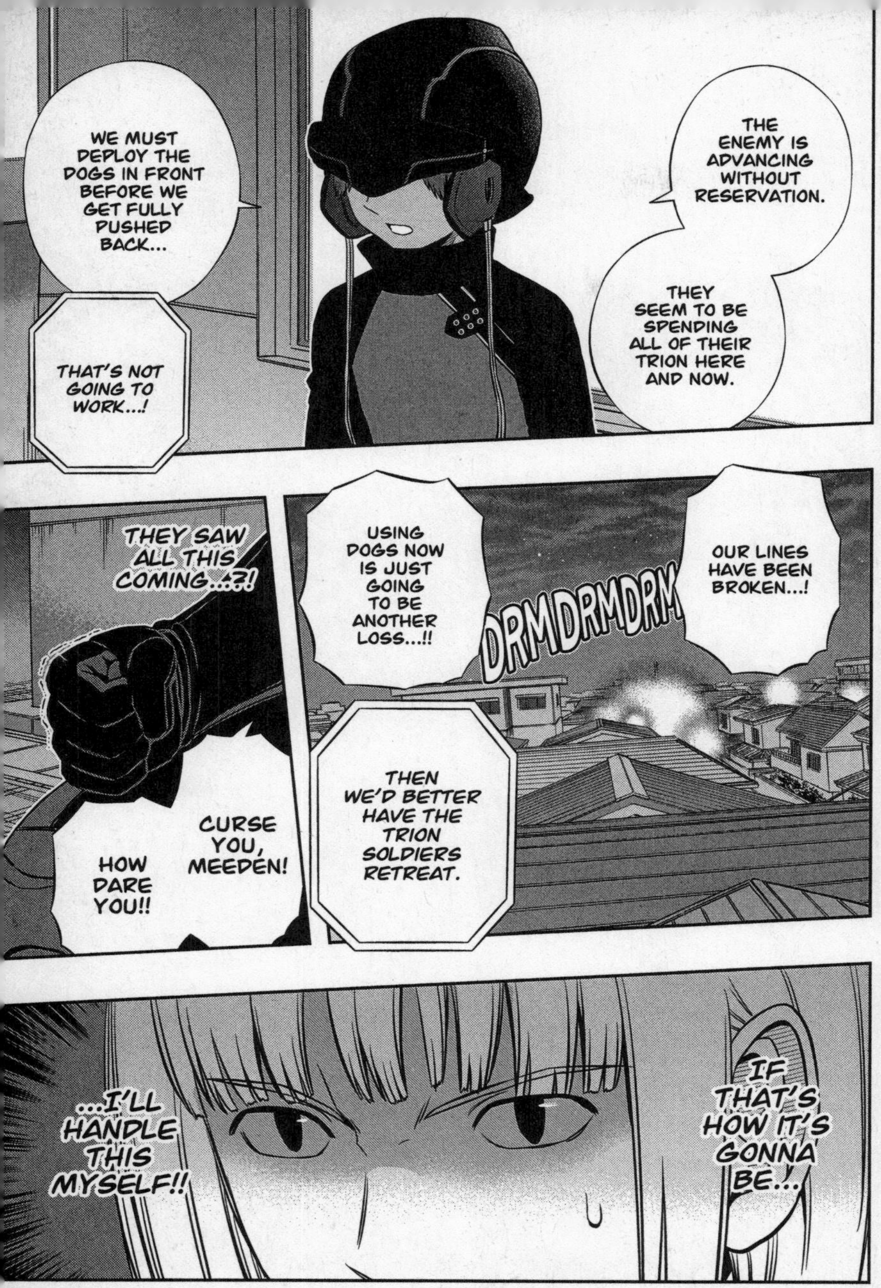

THE ENEMY IS ADVANCING WITHOUT RESERVATION.
THEY SEEM TO BE SPENDING ALL OF THEIR TRION HERE AND NOW.
WE MUST DEPLOY THE DOGS IN FRONT BEFORE WE GET FULLY PUSHED BACK...
THAT'S NOT GOING TO WORK...!
OUR LINES HAVE BEEN BROKEN...!
DRMDRMDRM
USING DOGS NOW IS JUST GOING TO BE ANOTHER LOSS...!!
THEN WE'D BETTER HAVE THE TRION SOLDIERS RETREAT.
THEY SAW ALL THIS COMING...?!
CURSE YOU, MEEDEN!
HOW DARE YOU!!
IF THAT'S HOW IT'S GONNA BE...
...I'LL HANDLE THIS MYSELF!!

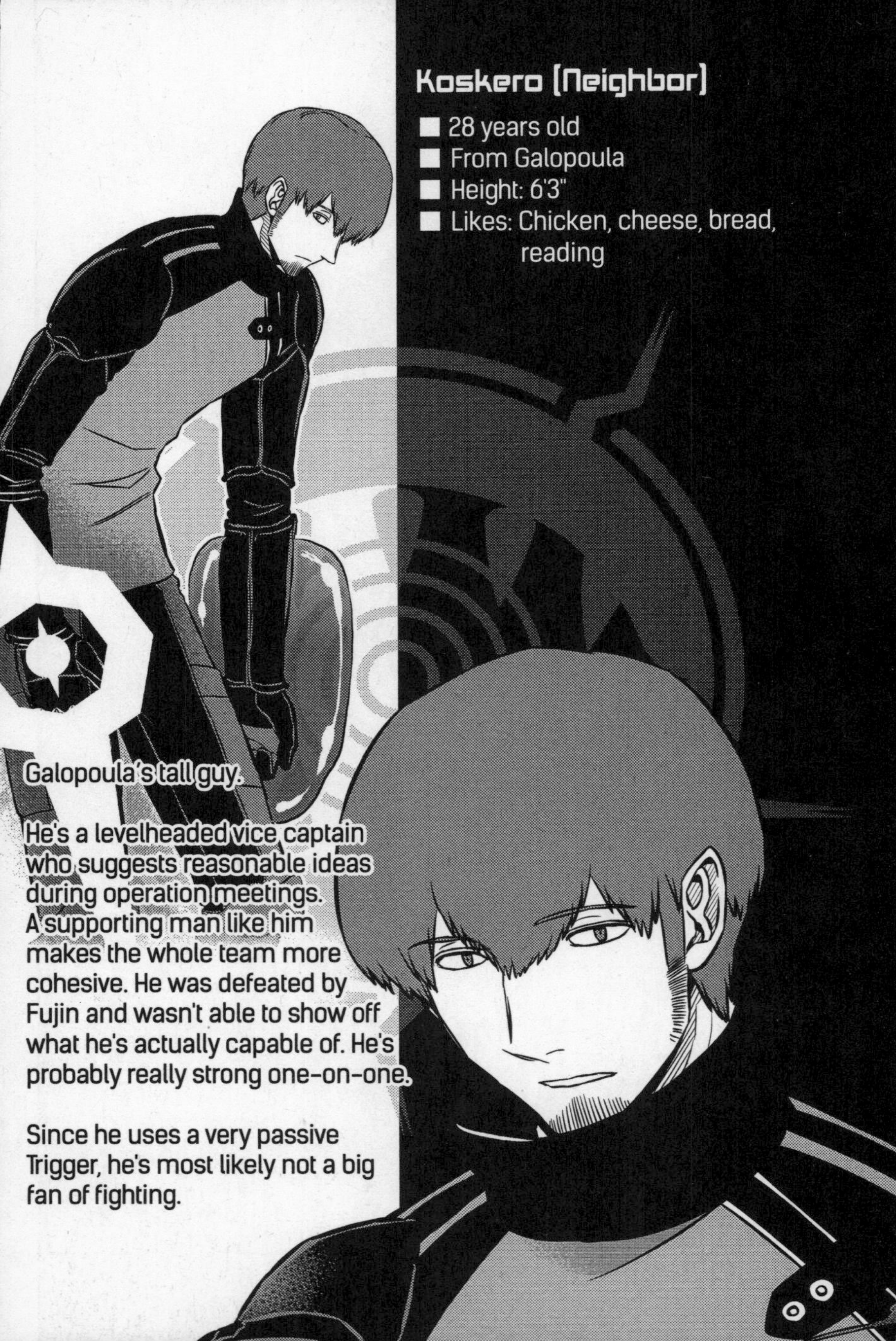

Koskero [Neighbor]

- 28 years old
- From Galopoula
- Height: 6'3"
- Likes: Chicken, cheese, bread, reading

Galopoula's tall guy.

He's a levelheaded vice captain who suggests reasonable ideas during operation meetings. A supporting man like him makes the whole team more cohesive. He was defeated by Fujin and wasn't able to show off what he's actually capable of. He's probably really strong one-on-one.

Since he uses a very passive Trigger, he's most likely not a big fan of fighting.

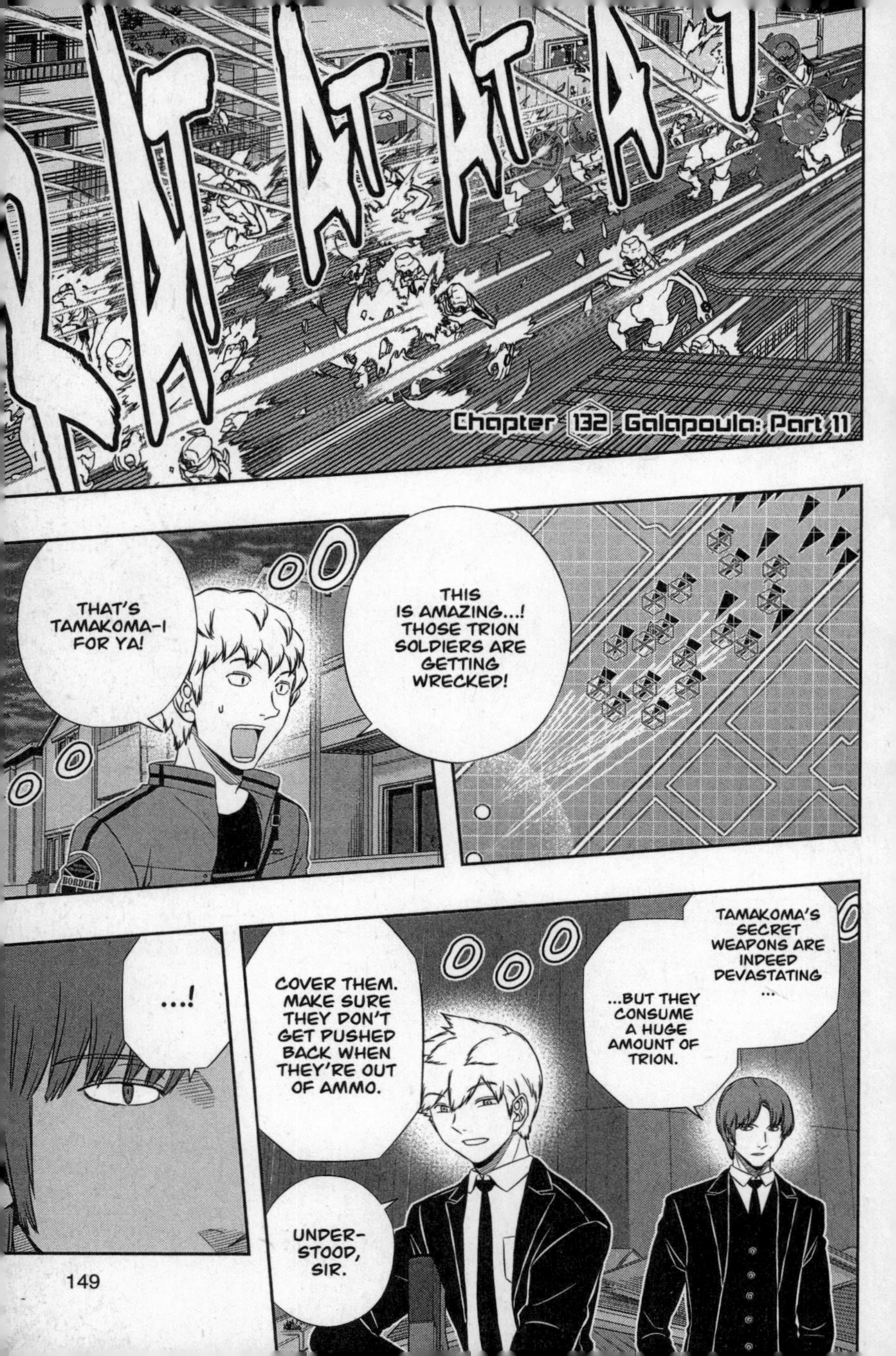
RATATATATA
Chapter 132 Galapoula: Part 11
THIS IS AMAZING...! THOSE TRION SOLDIERS ARE GETTING WRECKED!
THAT'S TAMAKOMA-1 FOR YA!
BORDER
TAMAKOMA'S SECRET WEAPONS ARE INDEED DEVASTATING ...
...BUT THEY CONSUME A HUGE AMOUNT OF TRION.
COVER THEM. MAKE SURE THEY DON'T GET PUSHED BACK WHEN THEY'RE OUT OF AMMO.
UNDER-STOOD, SIR.
...!

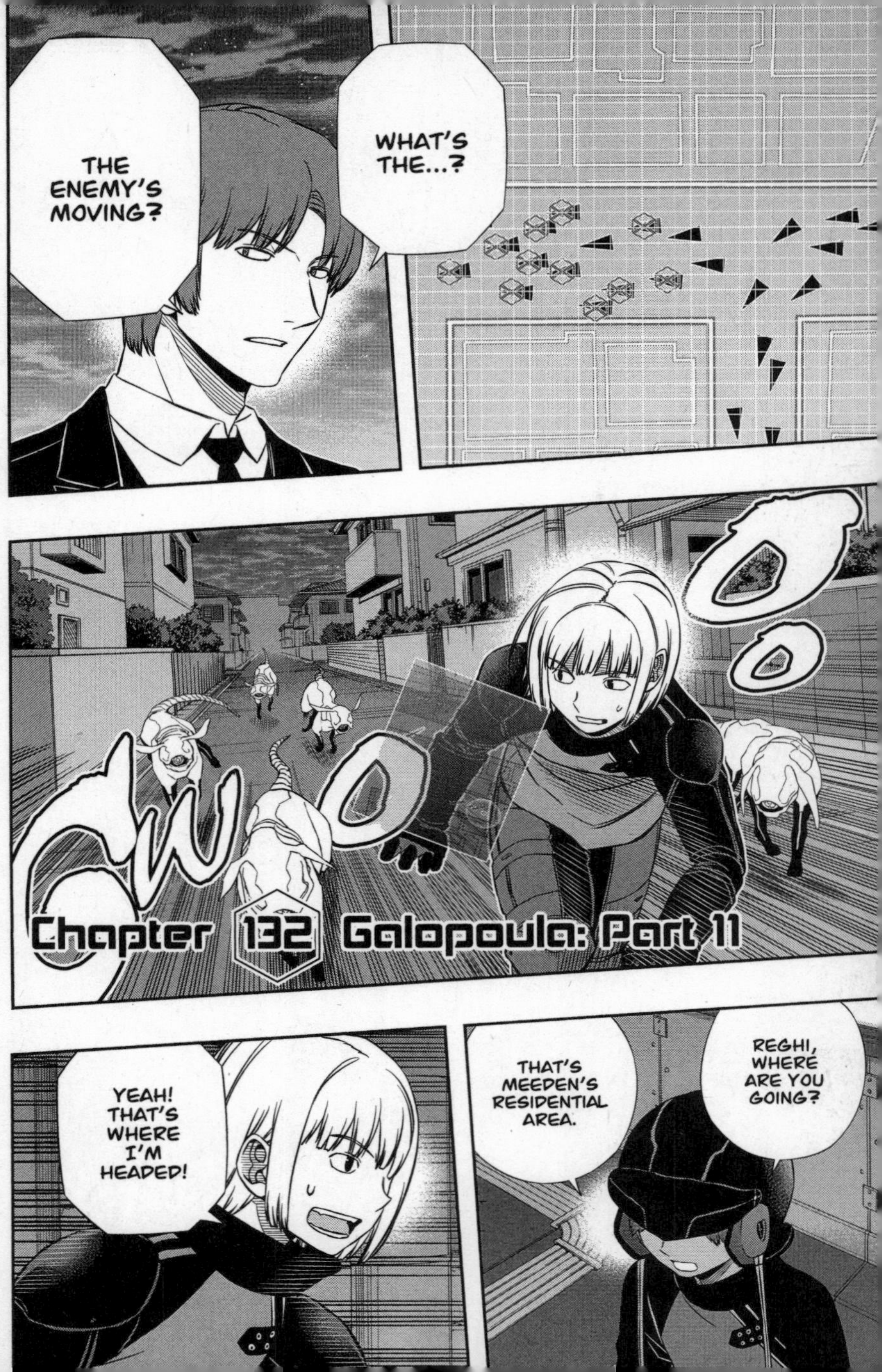
WHAT'S THE...?
THE ENEMY'S MOVING?
Chapter 132 Galopoula: Part 11
REGHI, WHERE ARE YOU GOING?
THAT'S MEEDEN'S RESIDENTIAL AREA.
YEAH! THAT'S WHERE I'M HEADED!

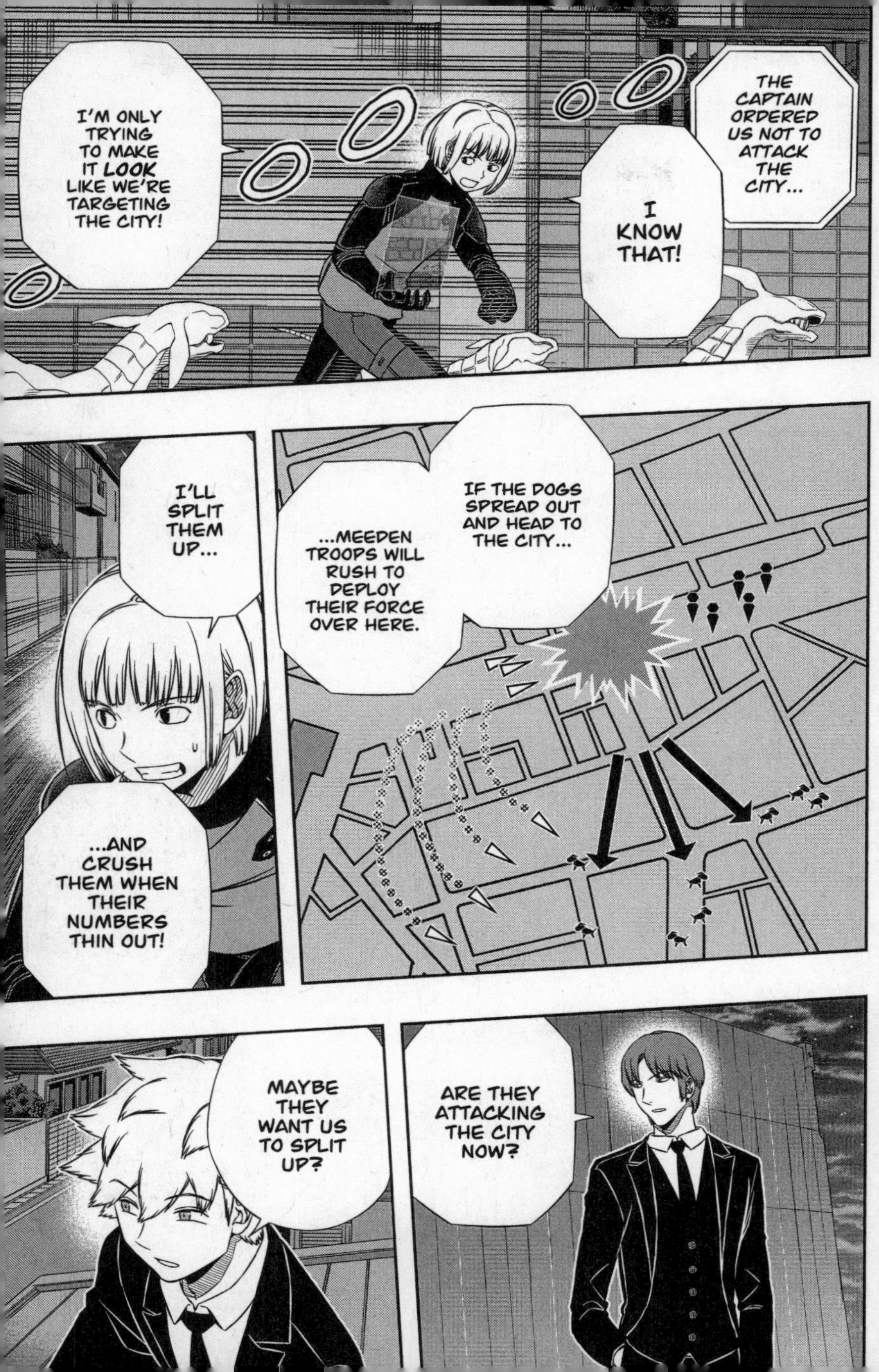
THE CAPTAIN ORDERED US NOT TO ATTACK THE CITY...
I KNOW THAT!
I'M ONLY TRYING TO MAKE IT LOOK LIKE WE'RE TARGETING THE CITY!
IF THE DOGS SPREAD OUT AND HEAD TO THE CITY...
...MEEDEN TROOPS WILL RUSH TO DEPLOY THEIR FORCE OVER HERE.
I'LL SPLIT THEM UP...
...AND CRUSH THEM WHEN THEIR NUMBERS THIN OUT!
ARE THEY ATTACKING THE CITY NOW?
MAYBE THEY WANT US TO SPLIT UP?

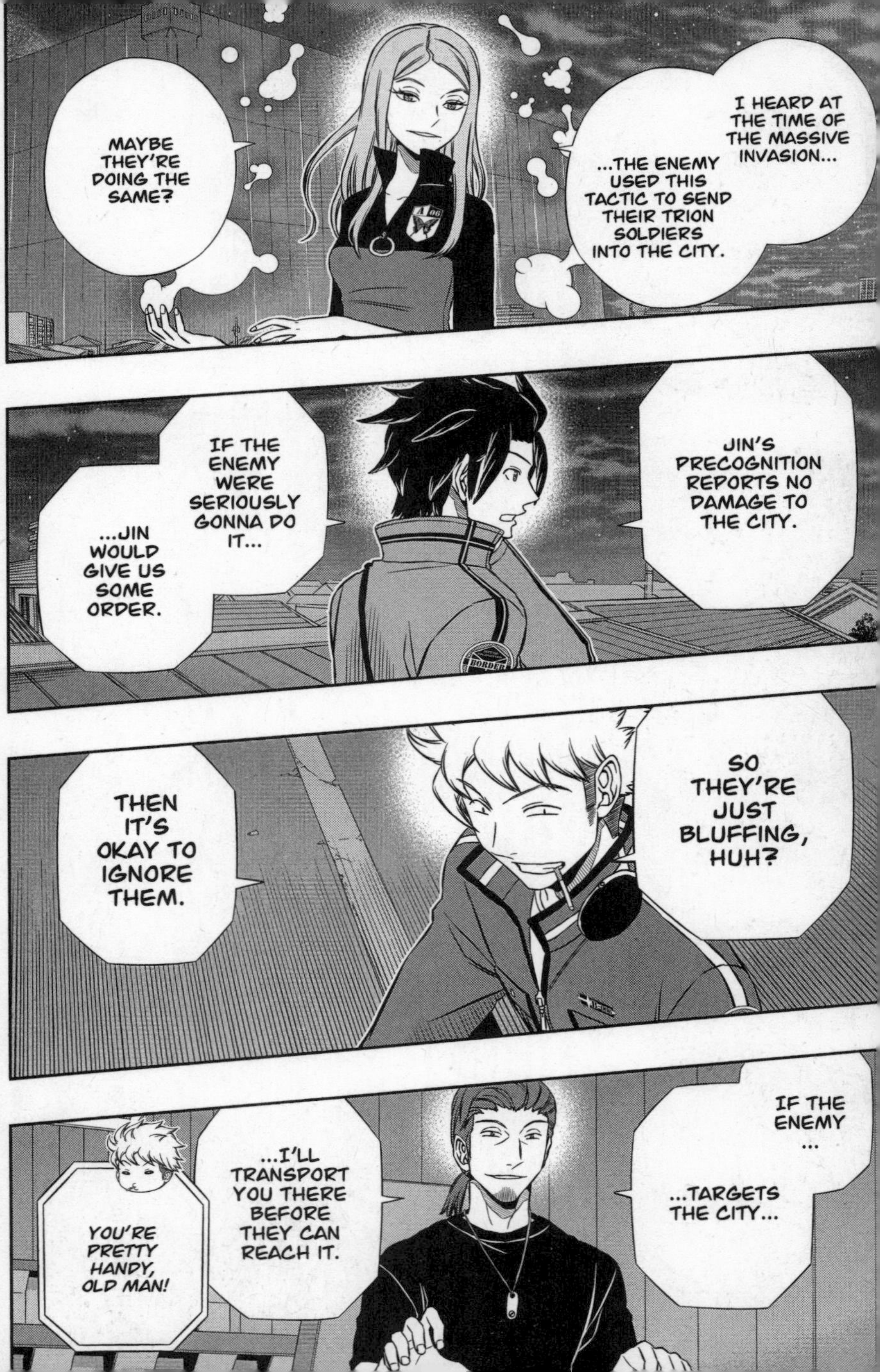
I HEARD AT THE TIME OF THE MASSIVE INVASION...
...THE ENEMY USED THIS TACTIC TO SEND THEIR TRION SOLDIERS INTO THE CITY.
MAYBE THEY'RE DOING THE SAME?
JIN'S PRECOGNITION REPORTS NO DAMAGE TO THE CITY.
IF THE ENEMY WERE SERIOUSLY GONNA DO IT...
...JIN WOULD GIVE US SOME ORDER.
SO THEY'RE JUST BLUFFING, HUH?
THEN IT'S OKAY TO IGNORE THEM.
IF THE ENEMY...
...TARGETS THE CITY...
...I'LL TRANSPORT YOU THERE BEFORE THEY CAN REACH IT.
YOU'RE PRETTY HANDY, OLD MAN!

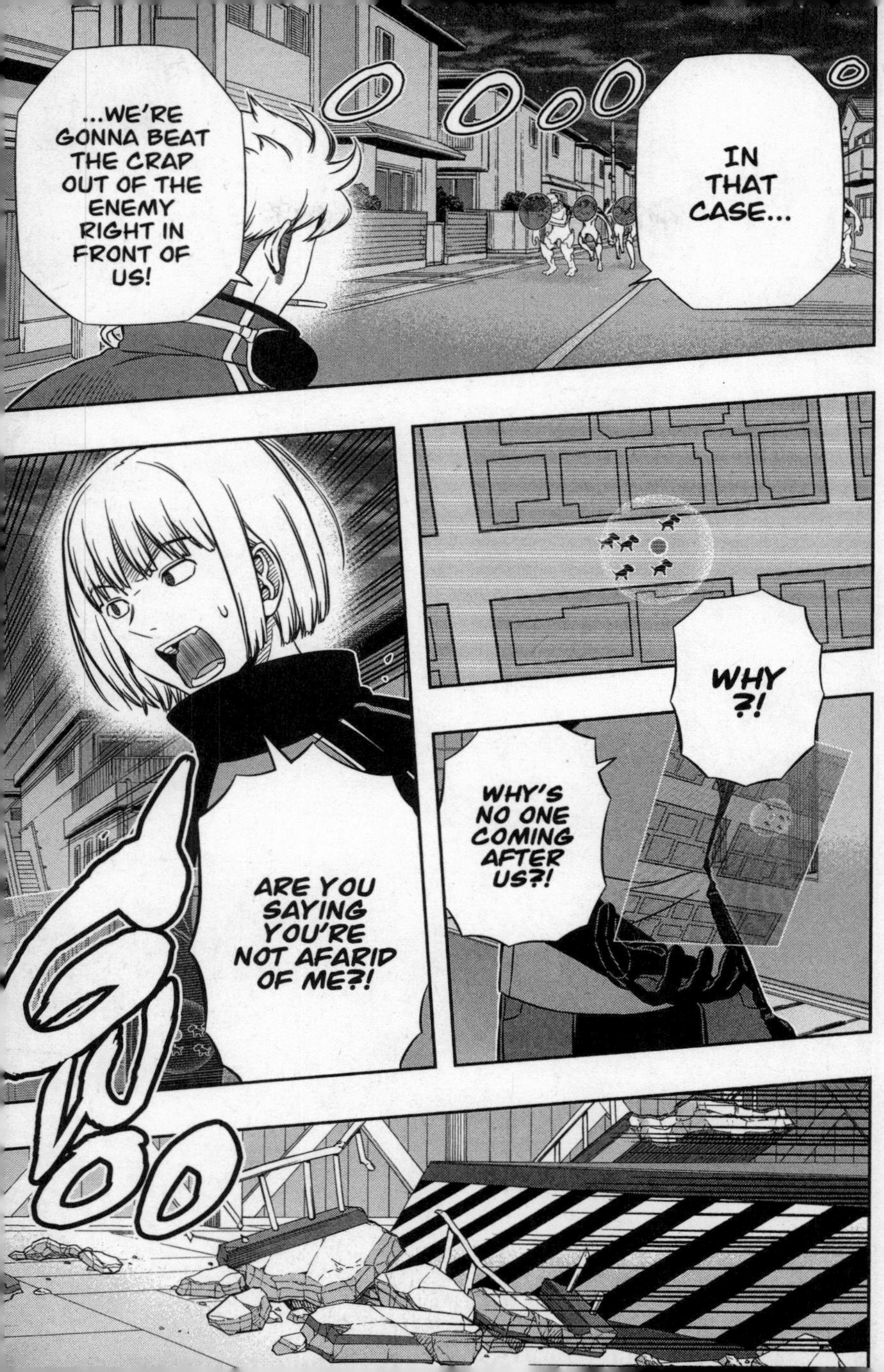
IN THAT CASE...
...WE'RE GONNA BEAT THE CRAP OUT OF THE ENEMY RIGHT IN FRONT OF US!
WHY ?!
WHY'S NO ONE COMING AFTER US?!
ARE YOU SAYING YOU'RE NOT AFARID OF ME?!

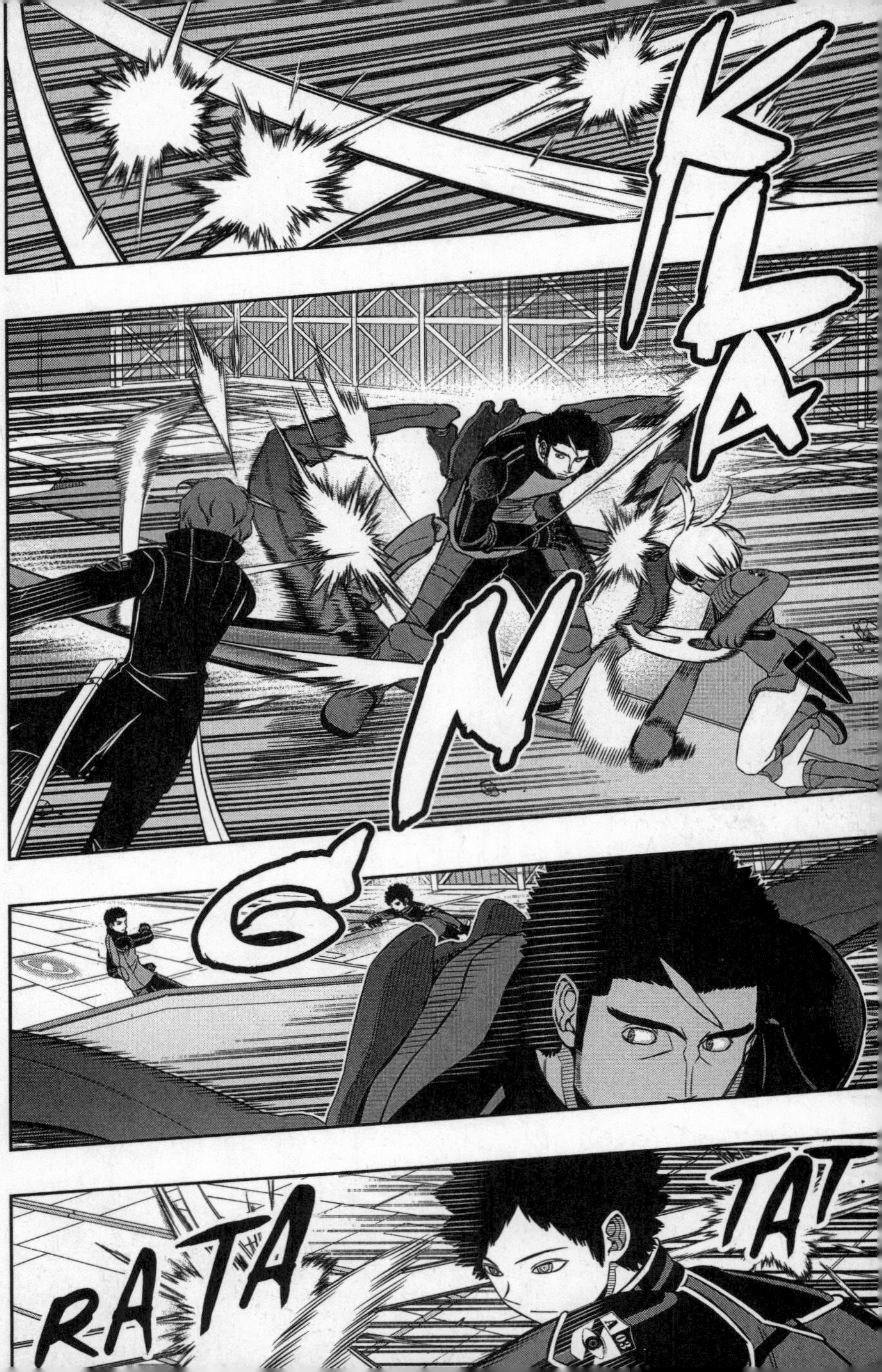
KLANG
RATATAT

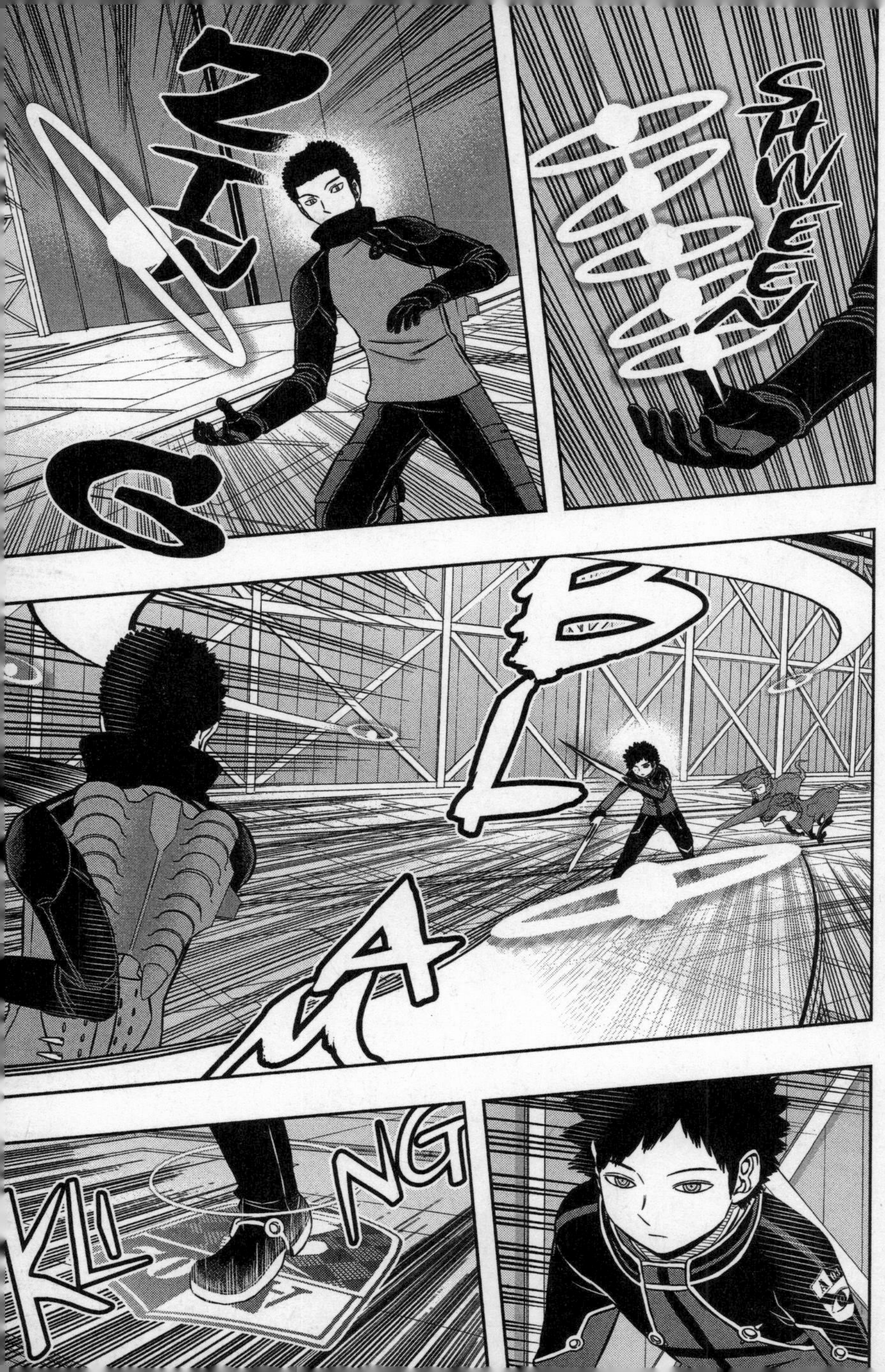
SHWEEN
ZING
BLAM
KLING

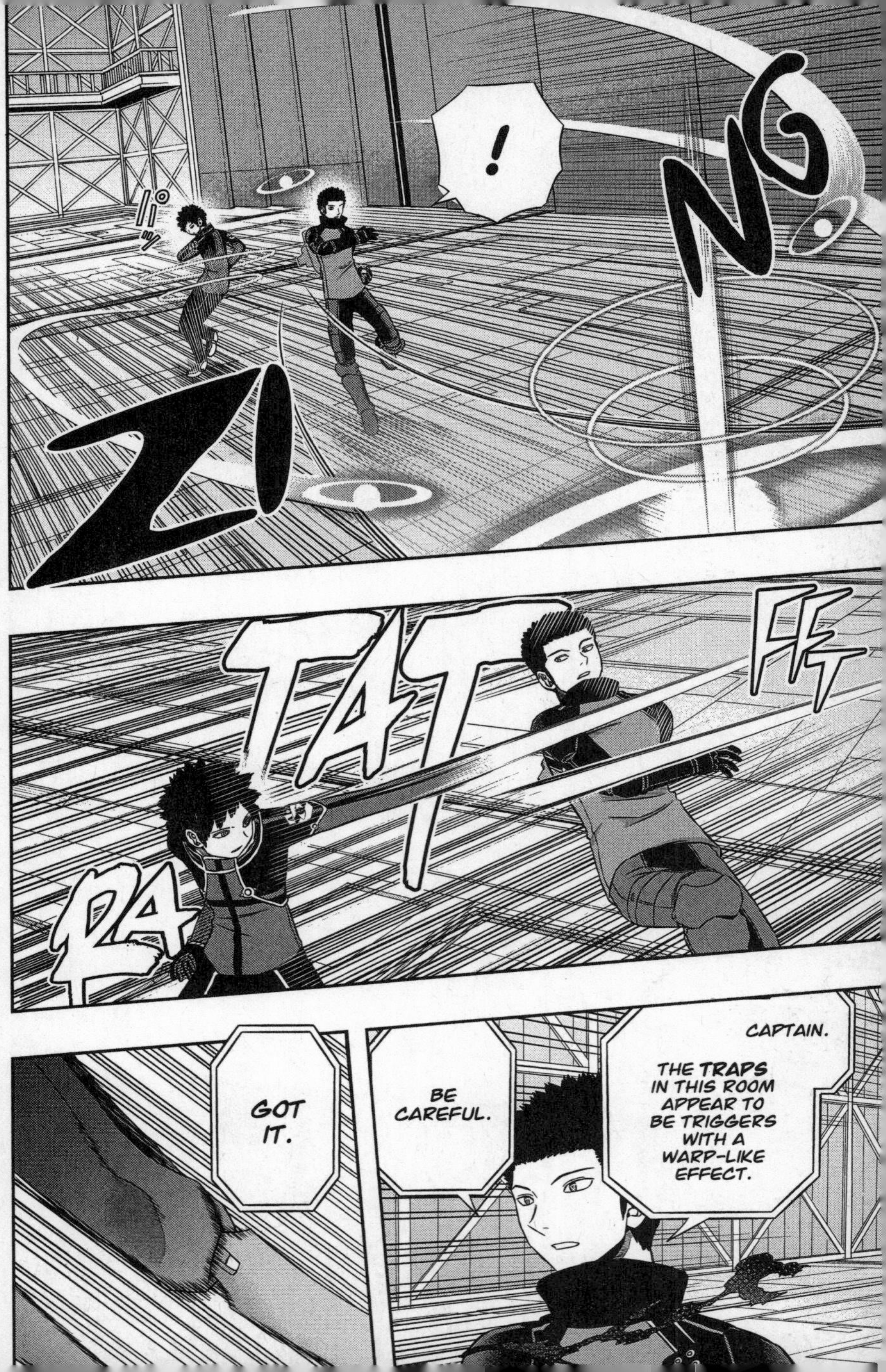
NG
!
パッ
ZI
FFT
TAT
RA
CAPTAIN.
THE TRAPS IN THIS ROOM APPEAR TO BE TRIGGERS WITH A WARP-LIKE EFFECT.
BE CAREFUL.
GOT IT.

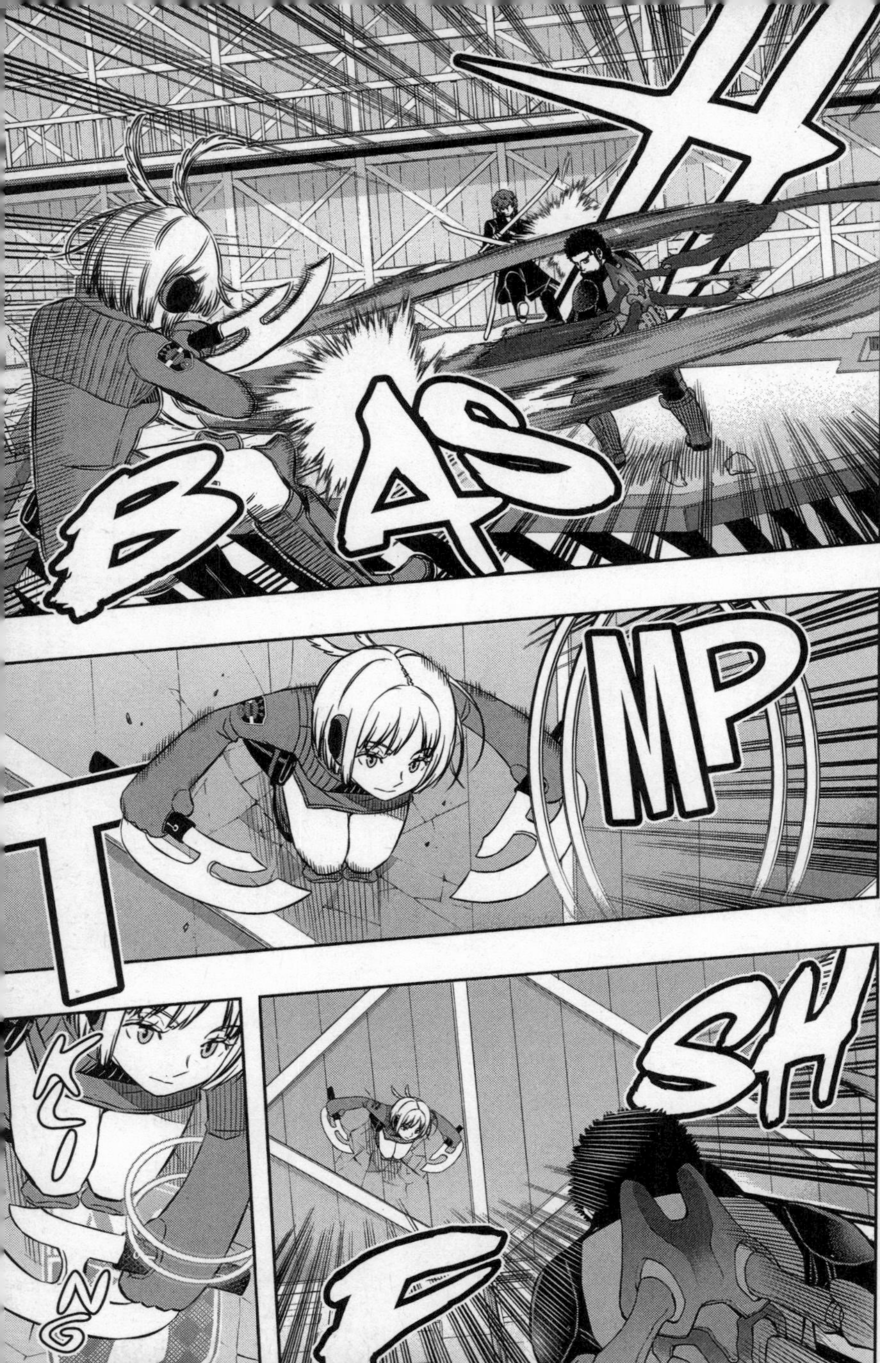
B AS
T MP
SH
KLING

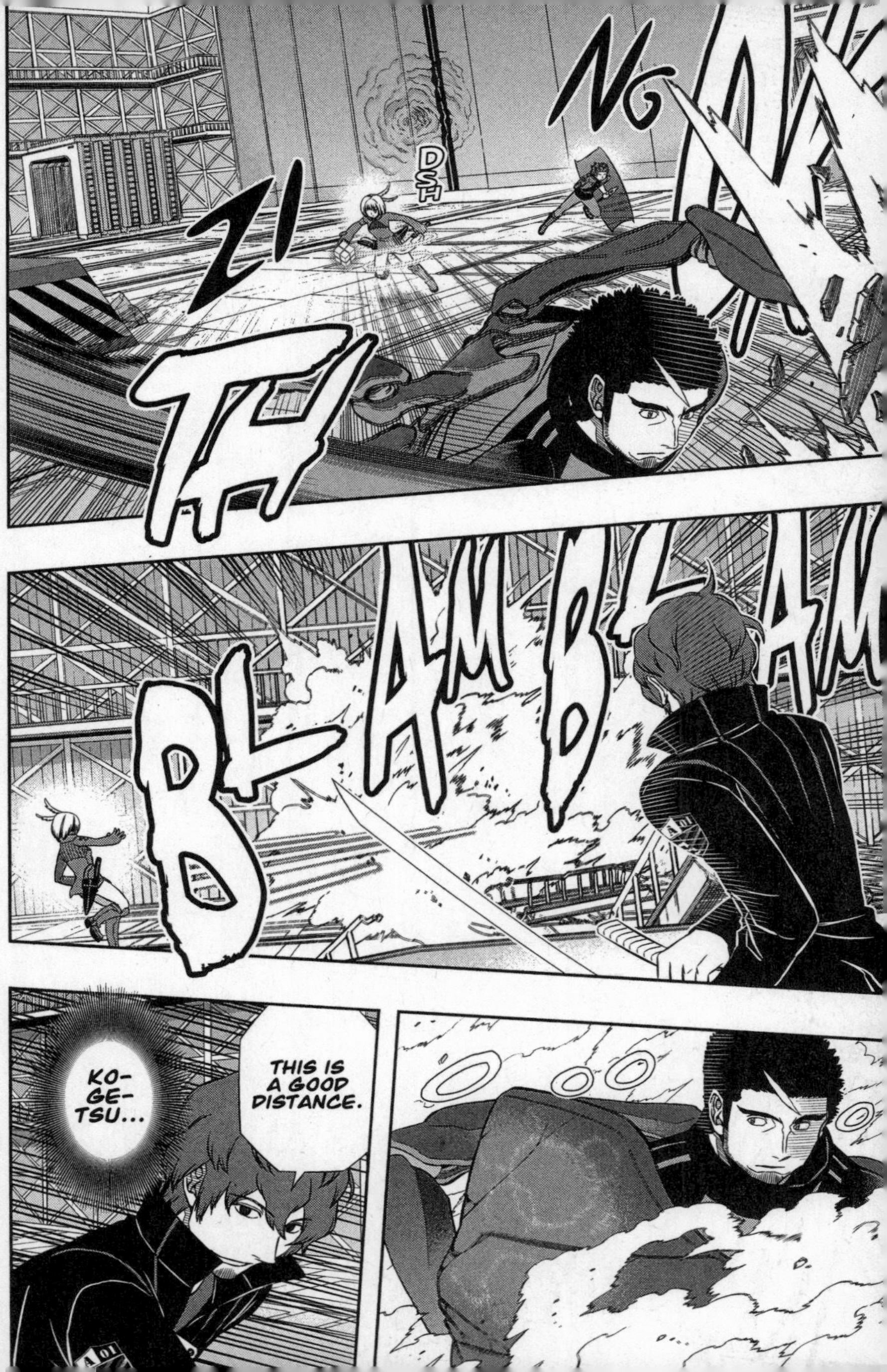
NG
DSH
ZI
TH
BLAM
BLAM
THIS IS A GOOD DISTANCE.
KO-GE-TSU...

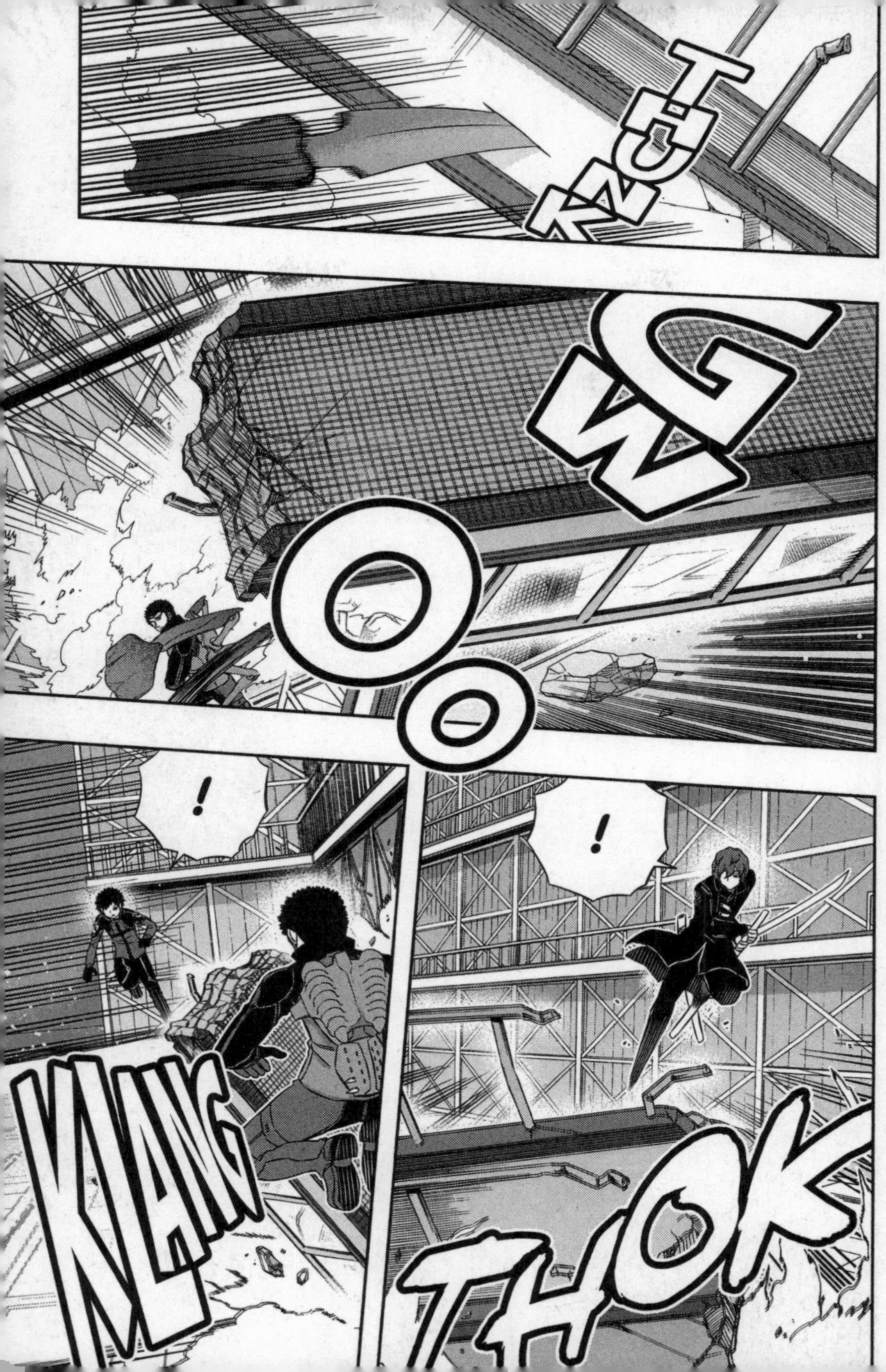
THUNK
GWOOO
!
THOK
!
KLANG

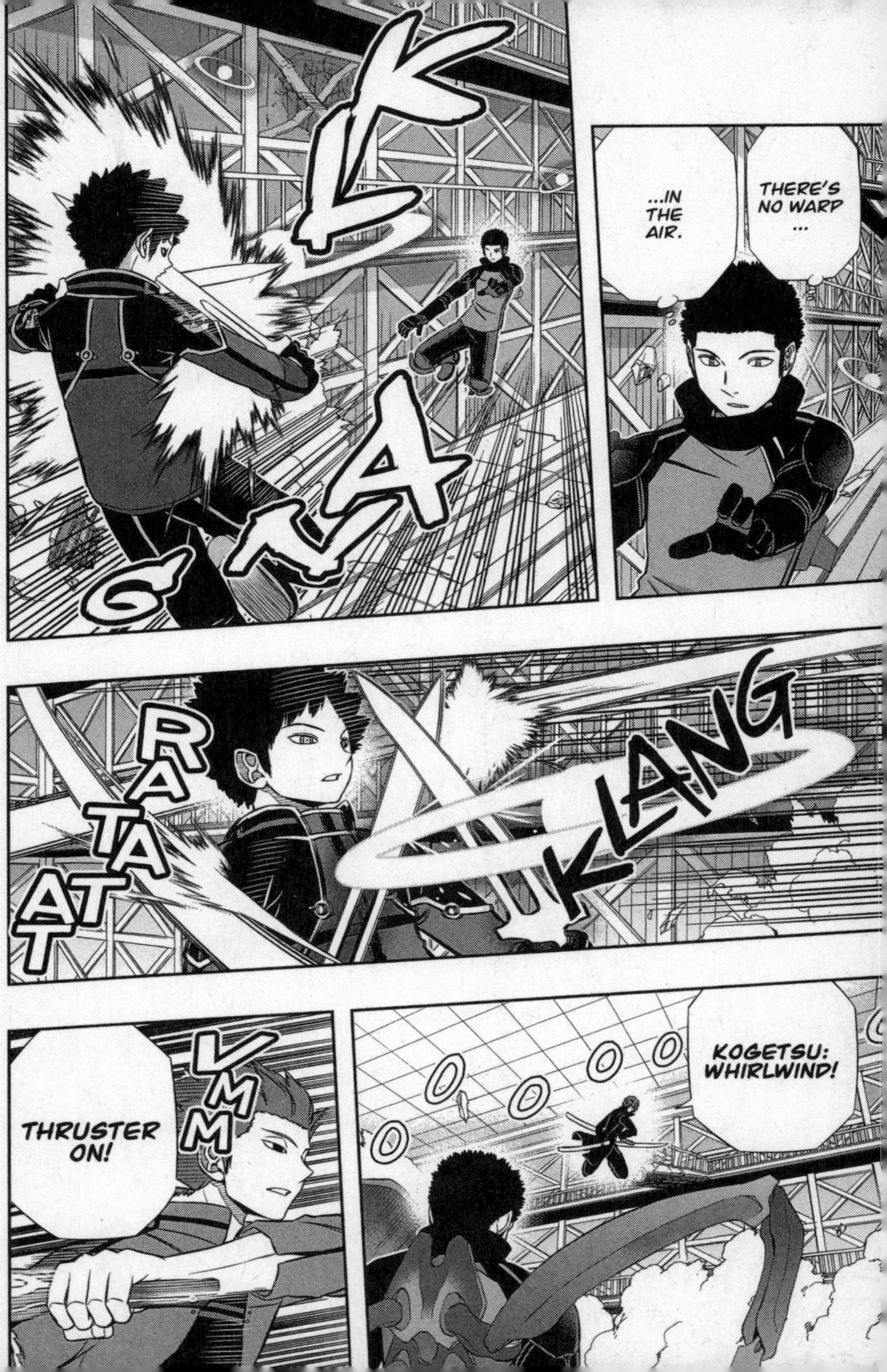
THERE'S NO WARP ...
...IN THE AIR.
KLANG
RATATAT
KOGETSU: WHIRLWIND!
THRUSTER ON!
VMMM

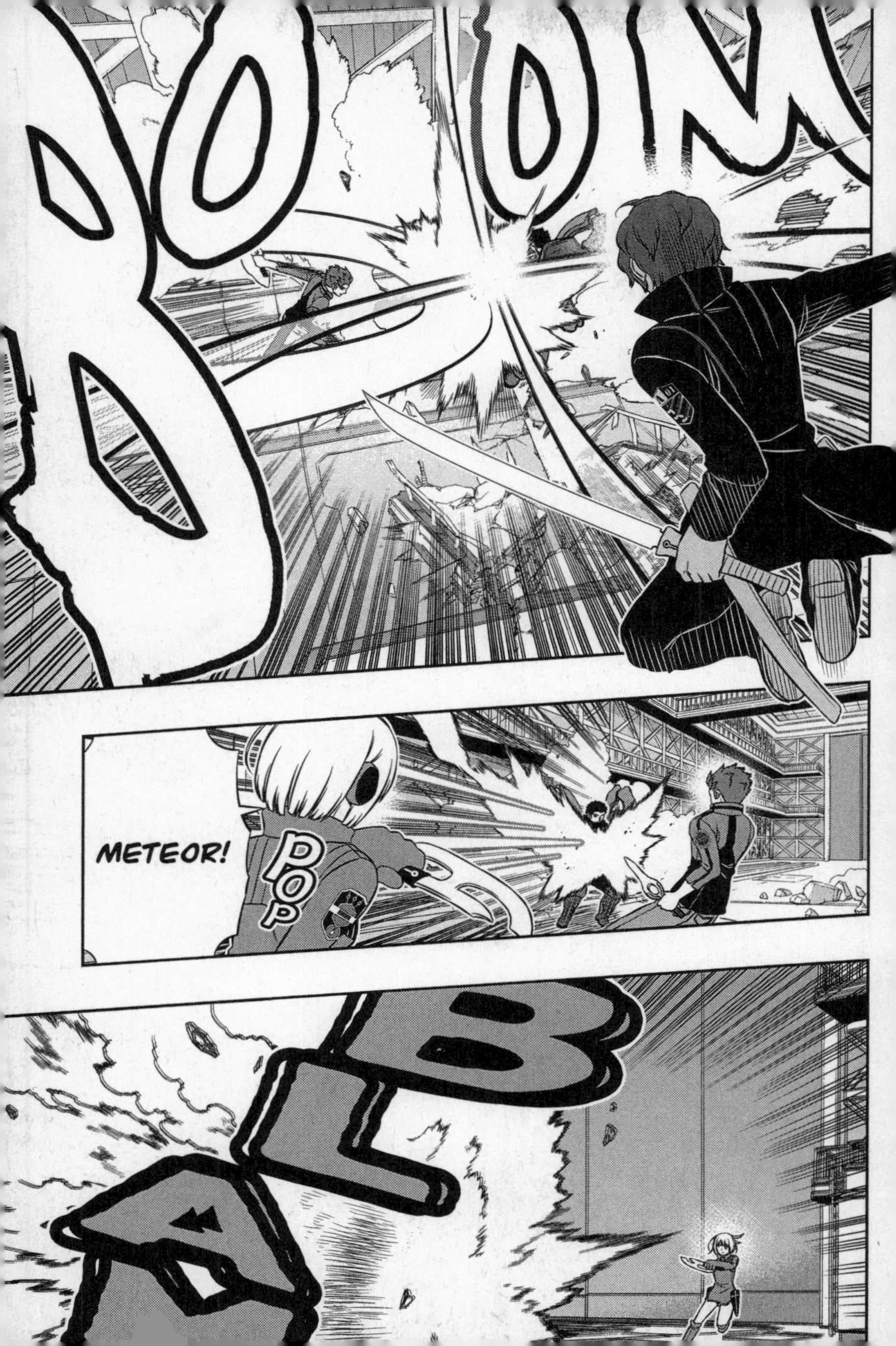
METEOR!
POP

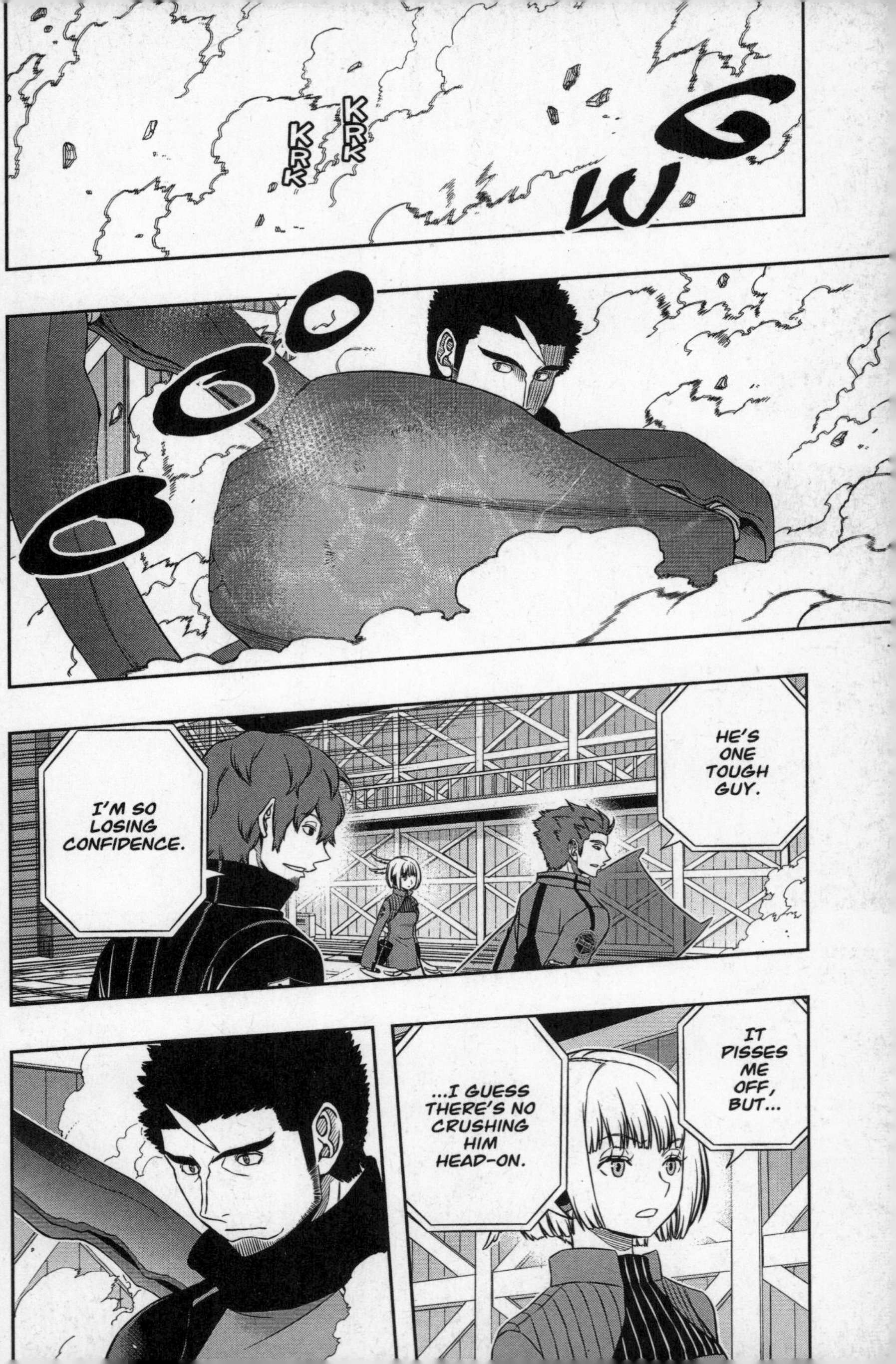
GW
KRK
KRK
OOO
HE'S ONE TOUGH GUY.
I'M SO LOSING CONFIDENCE.
IT PISSES ME OFF, BUT...
...I GUESS THERE'S NO CRUSHING HIM HEAD-ON.

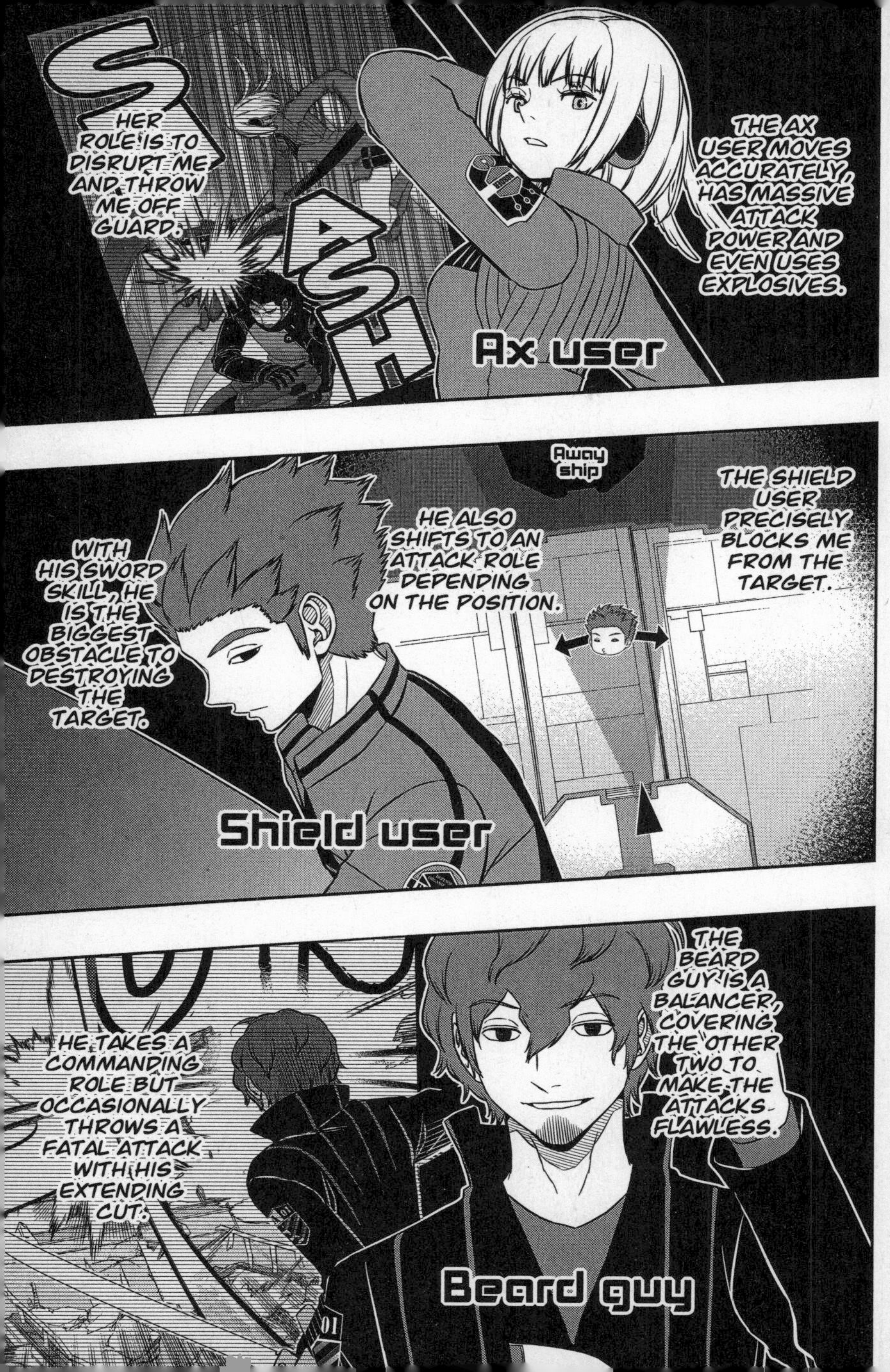
THE AX USER MOVES ACCURATELY, HAS MASSIVE ATTACK POWER AND EVEN USES EXPLOSIVES.
Ax user
HER ROLE IS TO DISRUPT ME AND THROW ME OFF GUARD.
Away ship
THE SHIELD USER PRECISELY BLOCKS ME FROM THE TARGET.
HE ALSO SHIFTS TO AN ATTACK ROLE DEPENDING ON THE POSITION.
WITH HIS SWORD SKILL, HE IS THE BIGGEST OBSTACLE TO DESTROYING THE TARGET.
Shield user
THE BEARD GUY IS A BALANCER, COVERING THE OTHER TWO TO MAKE THE ATTACKS FLAWLESS.
HE TAKES A COMMANDING ROLE BUT OCCASIONALLY THROWS A FATAL ATTACK WITH HIS EXTENDING CUT.
Beard guy

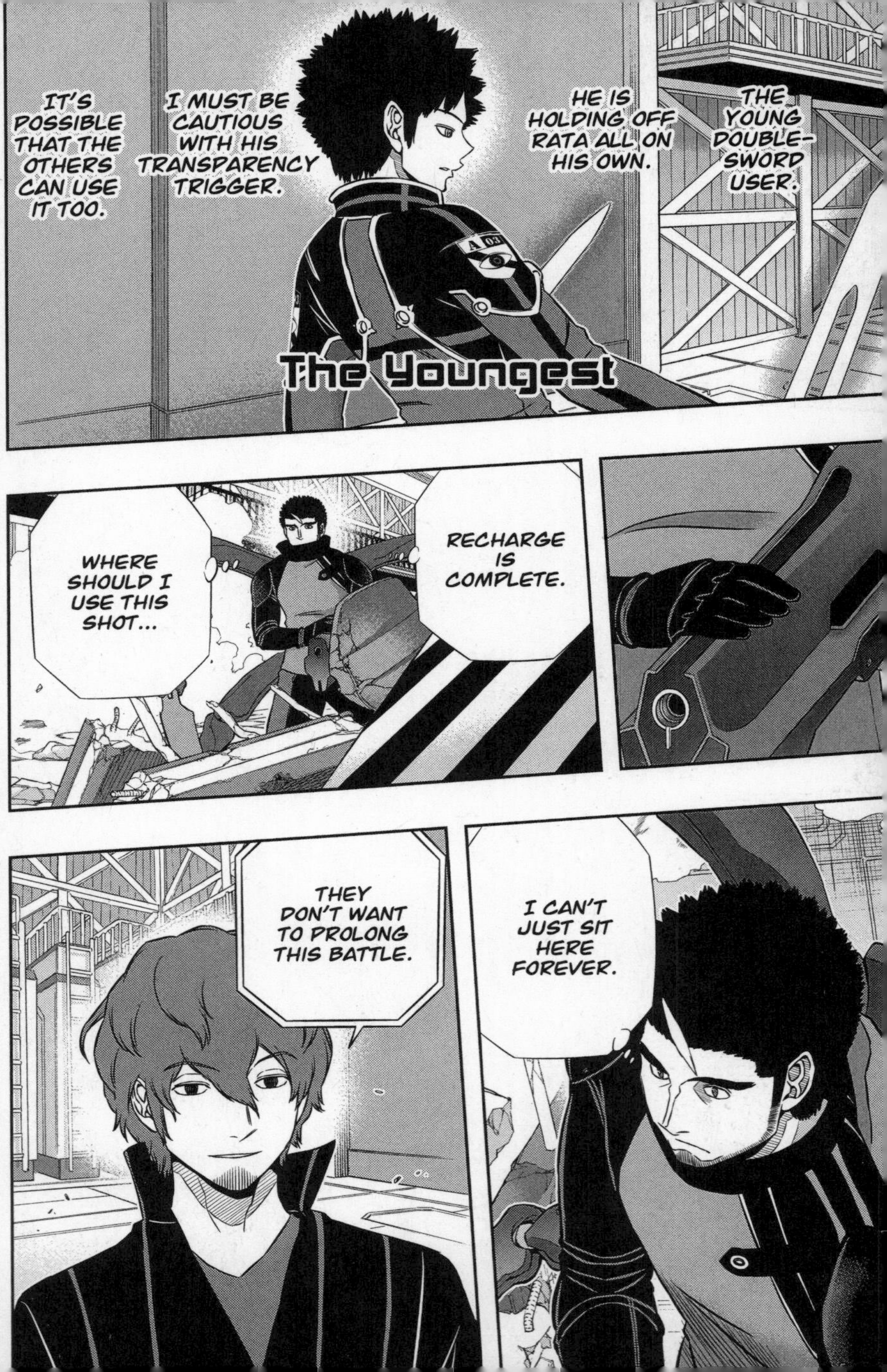
THE YOUNG DOUBLE-SWORD USER.
HE IS HOLDING OFF RATA ALL ON HIS OWN.
I MUST BE CAUTIOUS WITH HIS TRANSPARENCY TRIGGER.
IT'S POSSIBLE THAT THE OTHERS CAN USE IT TOO.
The Youngest
RECHARGE IS COMPLETE.
WHERE SHOULD I USE THIS SHOT...
I CAN'T JUST SIT HERE FOREVER.
THEY DON'T WANT TO PROLONG THIS BATTLE.

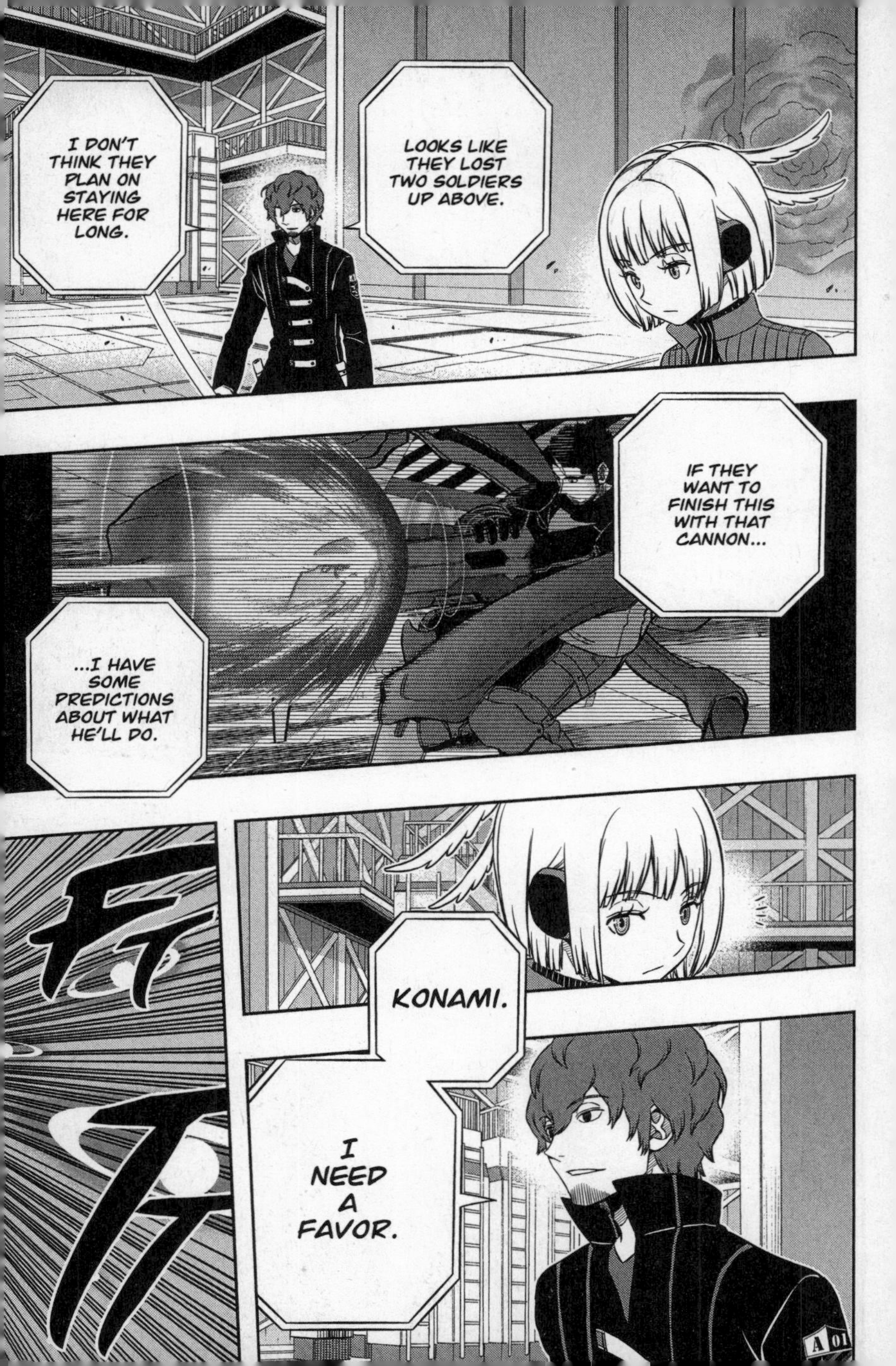

LOOKS LIKE THEY LOST TWO SOLDIERS UP ABOVE.
I DON'T THINK THEY PLAN ON STAYING HERE FOR LONG.
IF THEY WANT TO FINISH THIS WITH THAT CANNON...
...I HAVE SOME PREDICTIONS ABOUT WHAT HE'LL DO.
KONAMI.
I NEED A FAVOR.

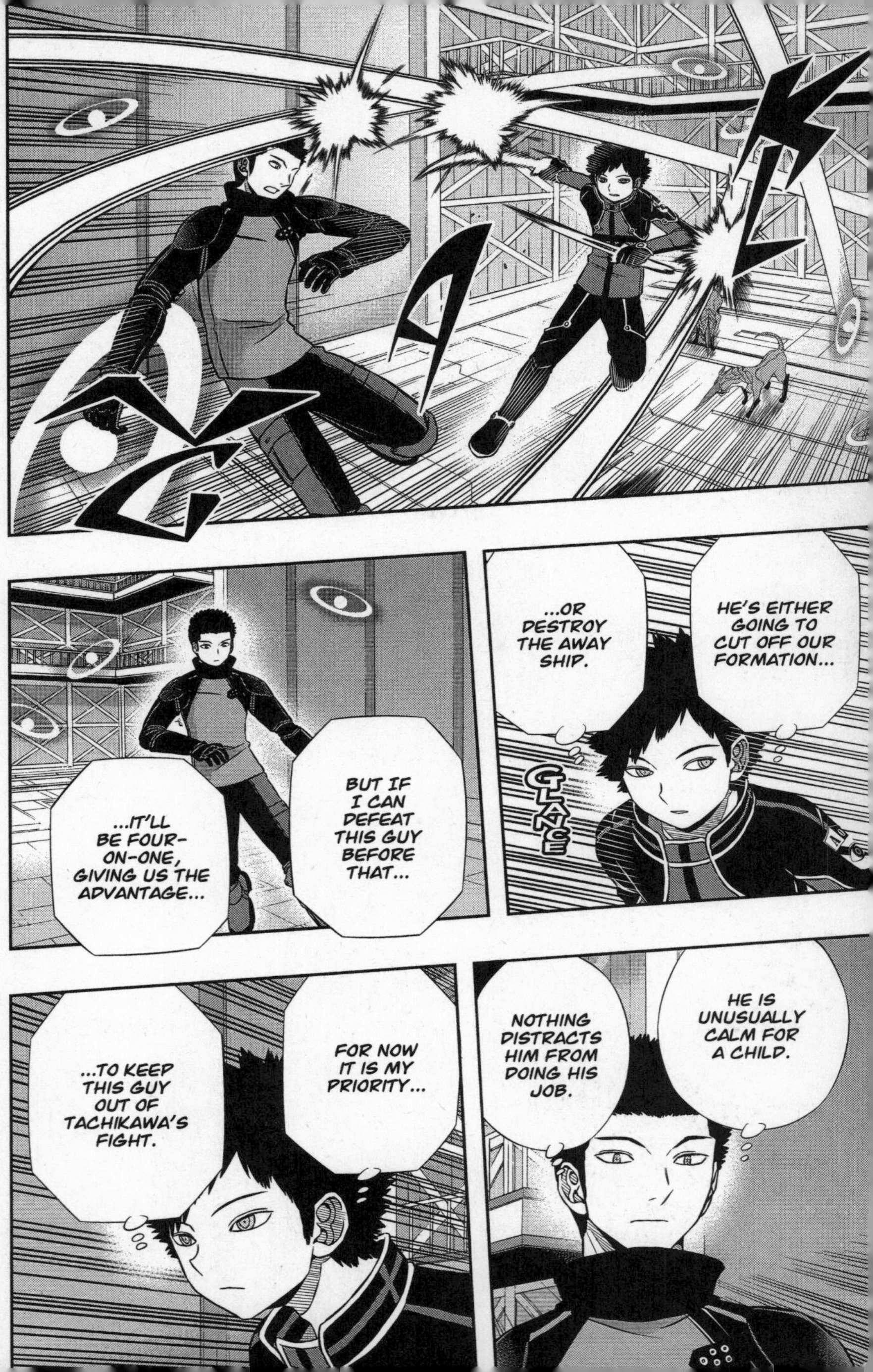
HE'S EITHER GOING TO CUT OFF OUR FORMATION...
...OR DESTROY THE AWAY SHIP.
GLANCE
BUT IF I CAN DEFEAT THIS GUY BEFORE THAT...
...IT'LL BE FOUR-ON-ONE, GIVING US THE ADVANTAGE...
HE IS UNUSUALLY CALM FOR A CHILD.
NOTHING DISTRACTS HIM FROM DOING HIS JOB.
FOR NOW IT IS MY PRIORITY...
...TO KEEP THIS GUY OUT OF TACHIKAWA'S FIGHT.

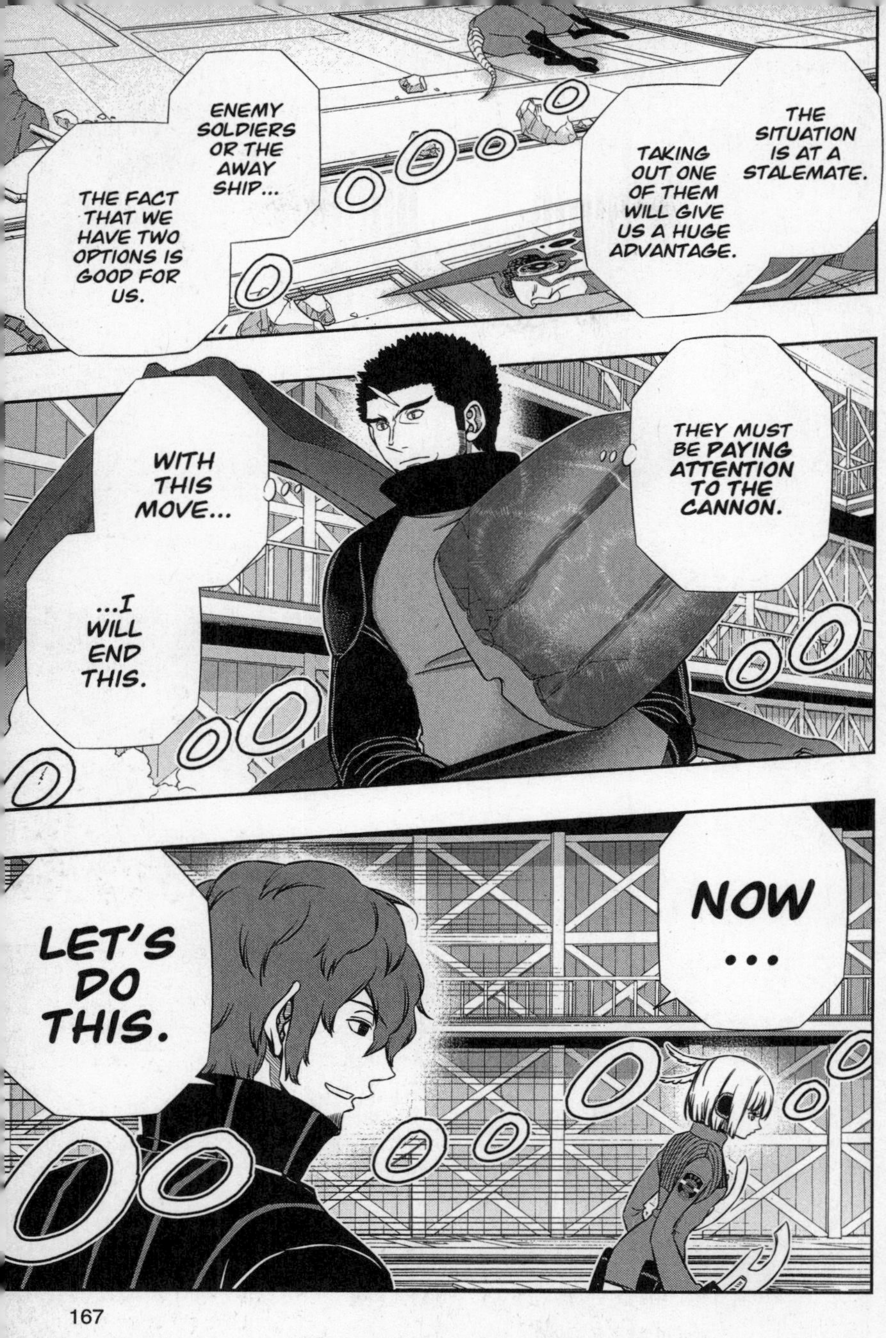
THE SITUATION IS AT A STALEMATE.
TAKING OUT ONE OF THEM WILL GIVE US A HUGE ADVANTAGE.
ENEMY SOLDIERS OR THE AWAY SHIP...
THE FACT THAT WE HAVE TWO OPTIONS IS GOOD FOR US.
THEY MUST BE PAYING ATTENTION TO THE CANNON.
WITH THIS MOVE...
...I WILL END THIS.
NOW...
LET'S DO THIS.

Valentine's Day 2016 Ranking: 1st – 3rd

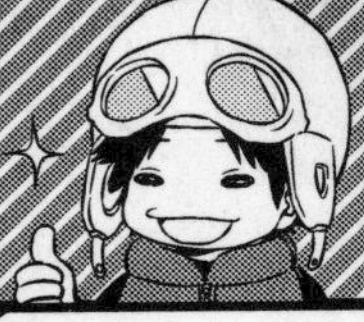

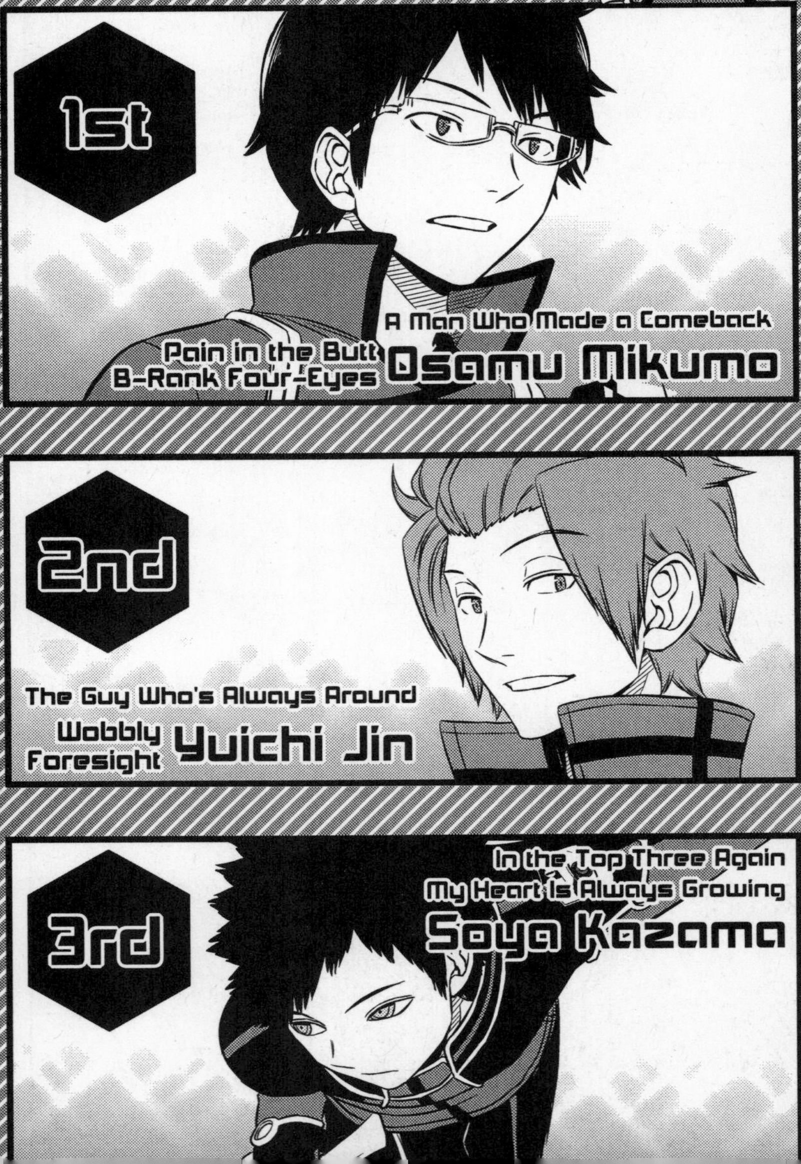
1st
A Man Who Made a Comeback
Pain in the Butt B-Rank Four-Eyes
Osamu Mikumo
2nd
The Guy Who's Always Around
Wobbly Foresight
Yuichi Jin
In the Top Three Again
My Heart Is Always Growing
Soya Kazama
3rd

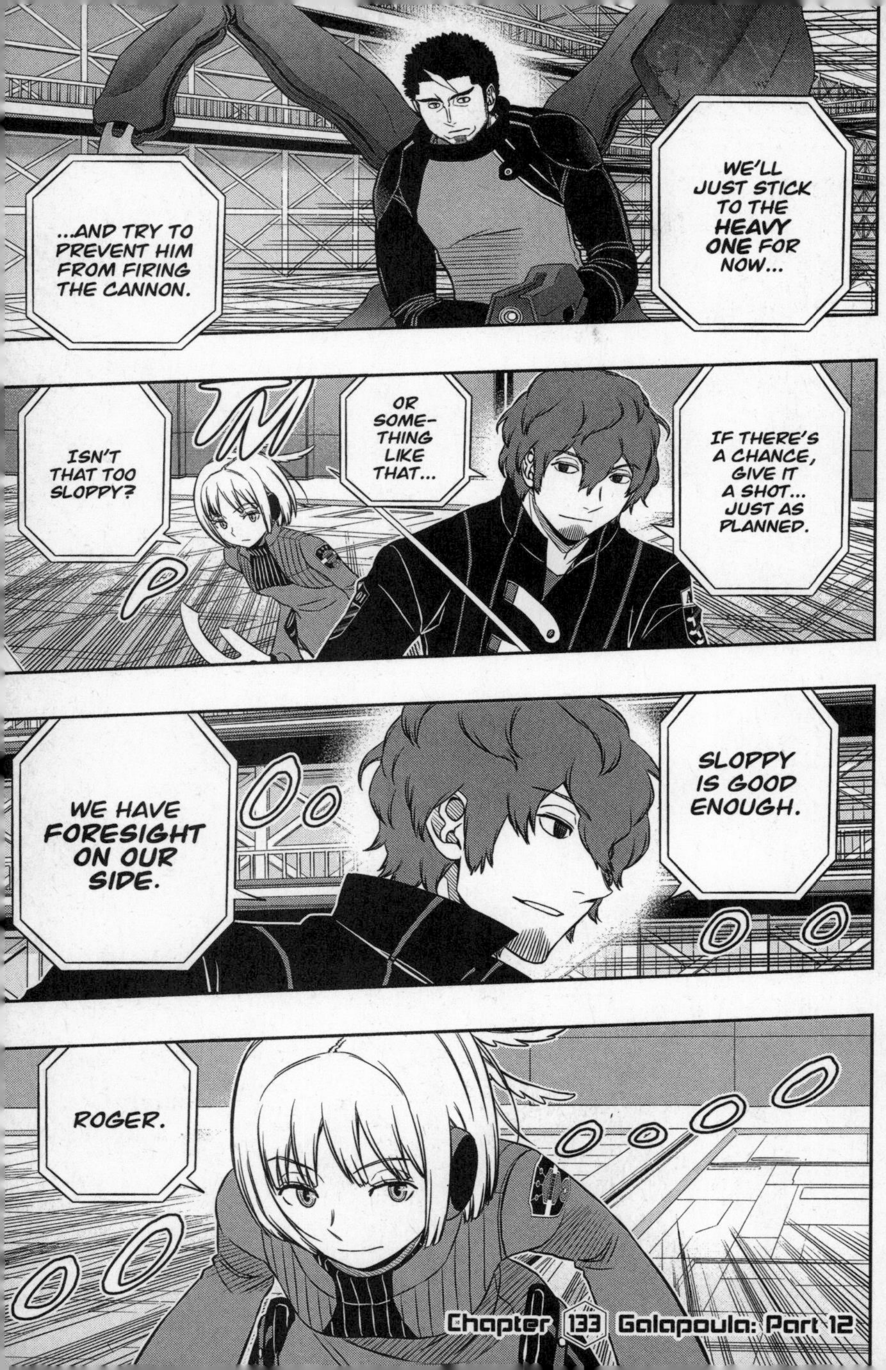
WE'LL JUST STICK TO THE HEAVY ONE FOR NOW...
...AND TRY TO PREVENT HIM FROM FIRING THE CANNON.
IF THERE'S A CHANCE, GIVE IT A SHOT... JUST AS PLANNED.
OR SOMETHING LIKE THAT...
ISN'T THAT TOO SLOPPY?
SLOPPY IS GOOD ENOUGH.
WE HAVE FORESIGHT ON OUR SIDE.
ROGER.
Chapter 133 Galapoula: Part 12

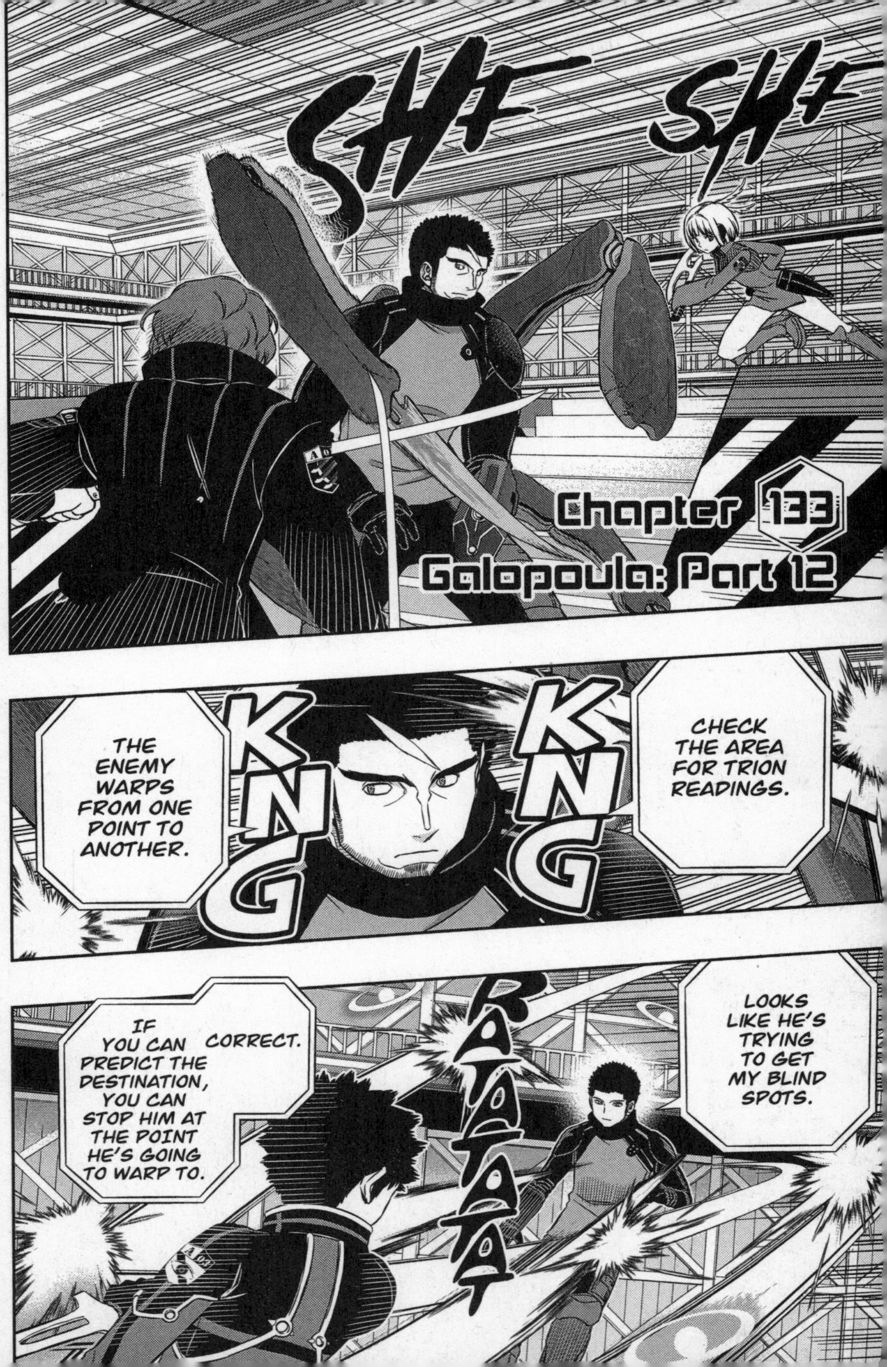
SHF SHF
Chapter 133
Galopoula: Part 12
CHECK THE AREA FOR TRION READINGS.
KNG KNG
THE ENEMY WARPS FROM ONE POINT TO ANOTHER.
LOOKS LIKE HE'S TRYING TO GET MY BLIND SPOTS.
RATATATAT
CORRECT.
IF YOU CAN PREDICT THE DESTINATION, YOU CAN STOP HIM AT THE POINT HE'S GOING TO WARP TO.

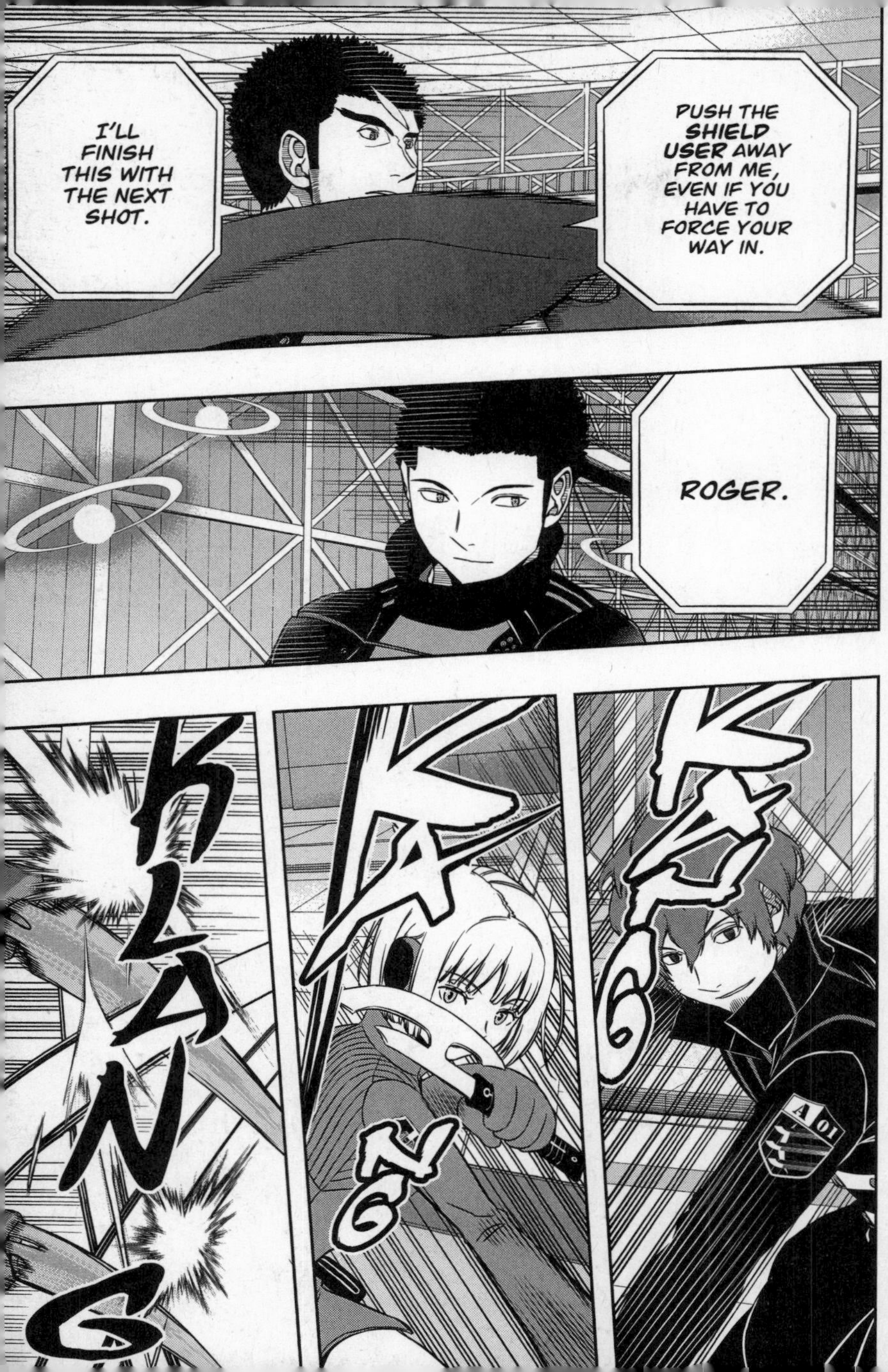
PUSH THE SHIELD USER AWAY FROM ME, EVEN IF YOU HAVE TO FORCE YOUR WAY IN.
I'LL FINISH THIS WITH THE NEXT SHOT.
ROGER.

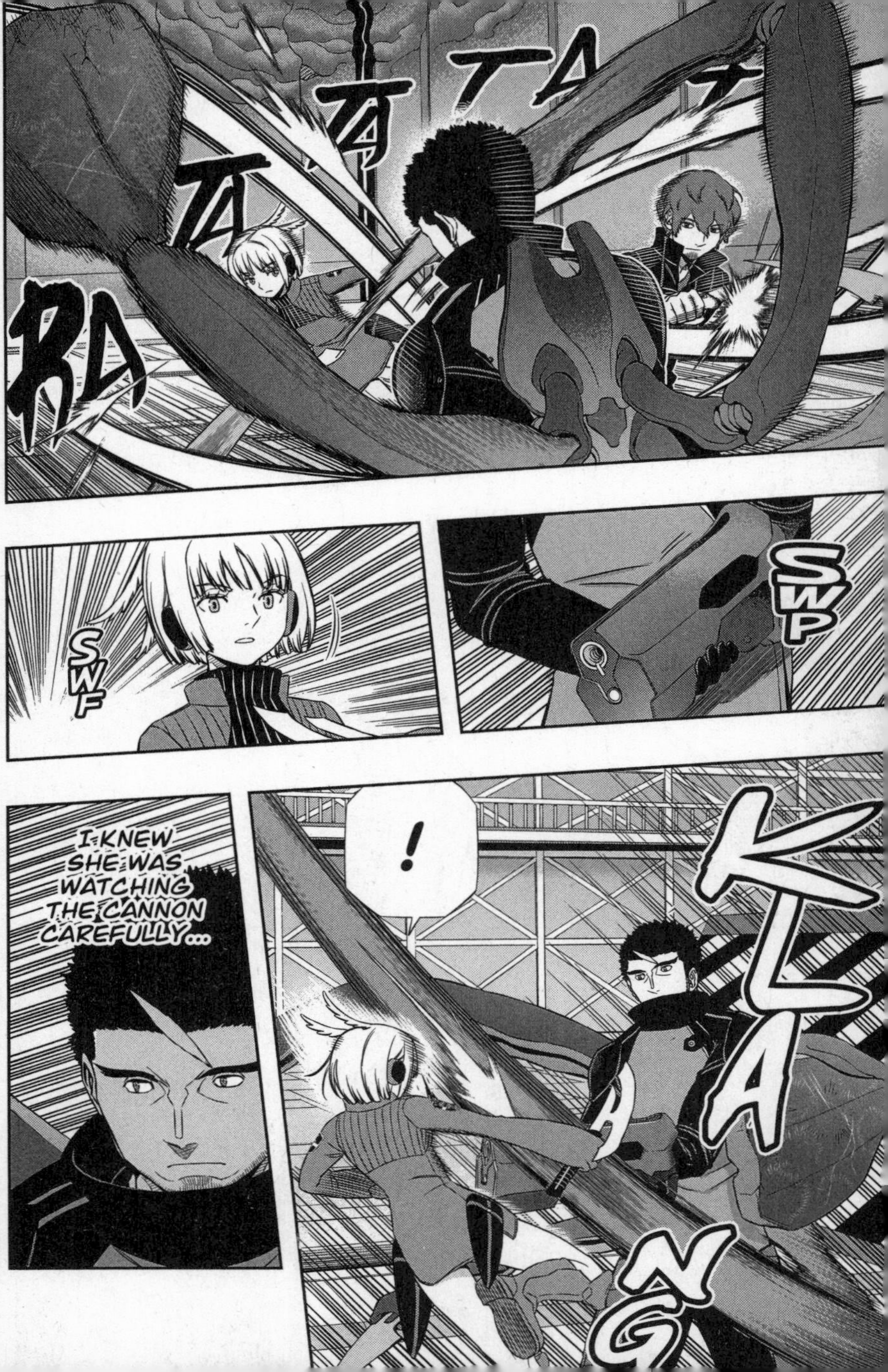
SWP
SWF
!
KLANG
I KNEW SHE WAS WATCHING THE CANNON CAREFULLY...

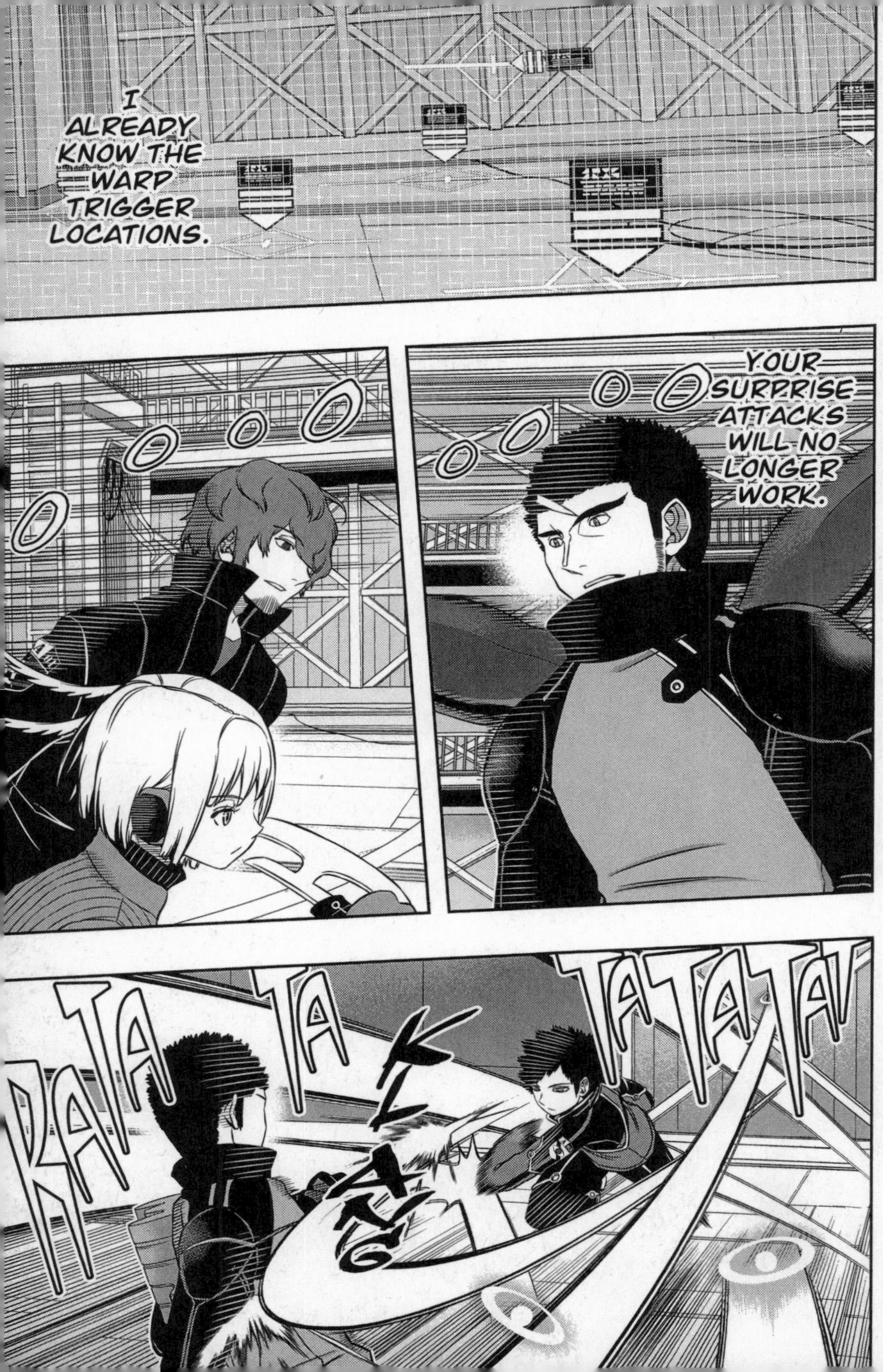
I ALREADY KNOW THE WARP TRIGGER LOCATIONS.
YOUR SURPRISE ATTACKS WILL NO LONGER WORK.
KRATA TA TATATAT

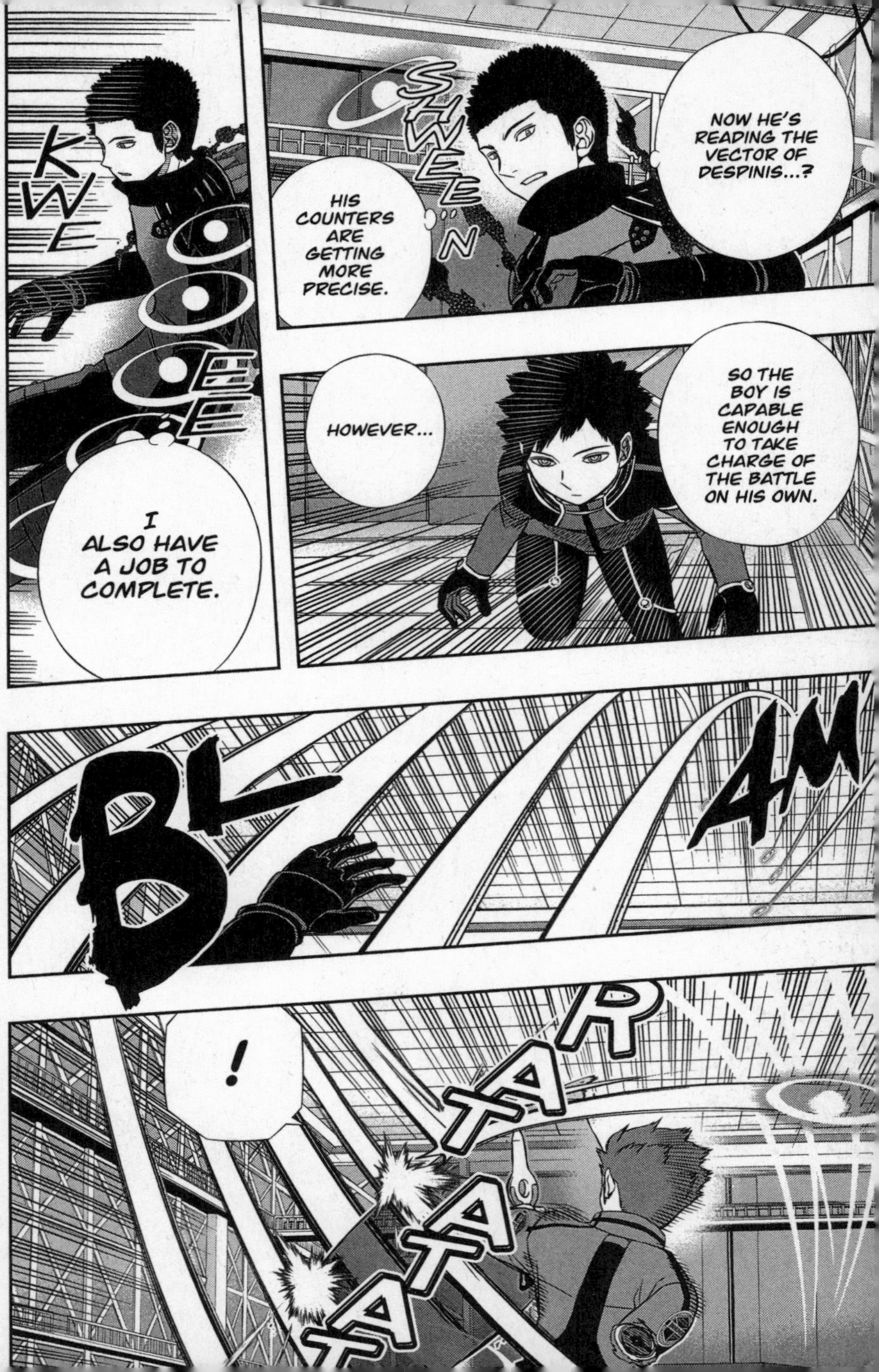
SHWEEN
NOW HE'S READING THE VECTOR OF DESPINIS...?
HIS COUNTERS ARE GETTING MORE PRECISE.
SO THE BOY IS CAPABLE ENOUGH TO TAKE CHARGE OF THE BATTLE ON HIS OWN.
HOWEVER...
KWEE
EEE
I ALSO HAVE A JOB TO COMPLETE.
BLAM
!
RATATAT

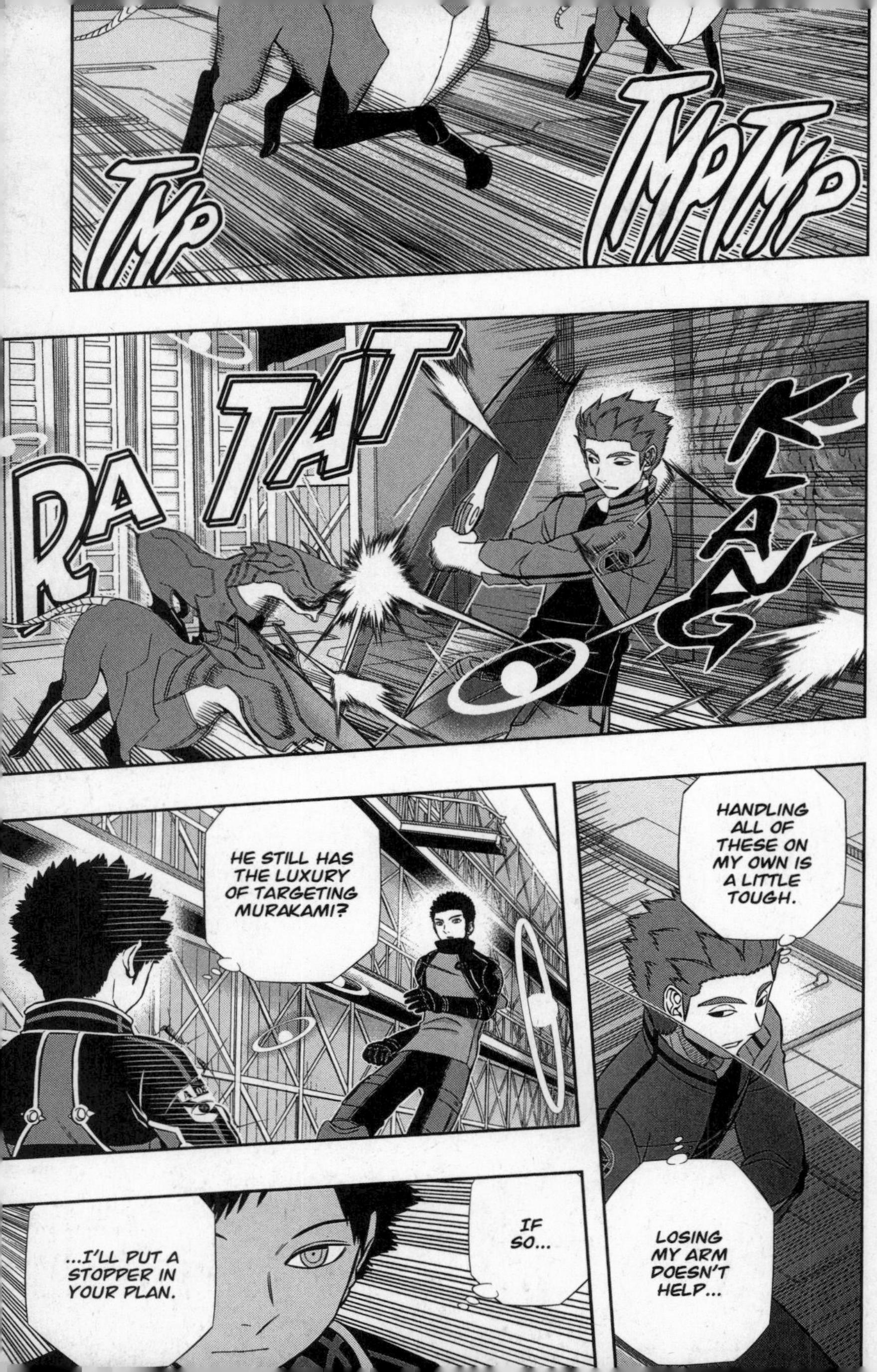
TMPTMP
TMP
KLANG
RATAT
HANDLING ALL OF THESE ON MY OWN IS A LITTLE TOUGH.
LOSING MY ARM DOESN'T HELP...
HE STILL HAS THE LUXURY OF TARGETING MURAKAMI?
IF SO...
...I'LL PUT A STOPPER IN YOUR PLAN.

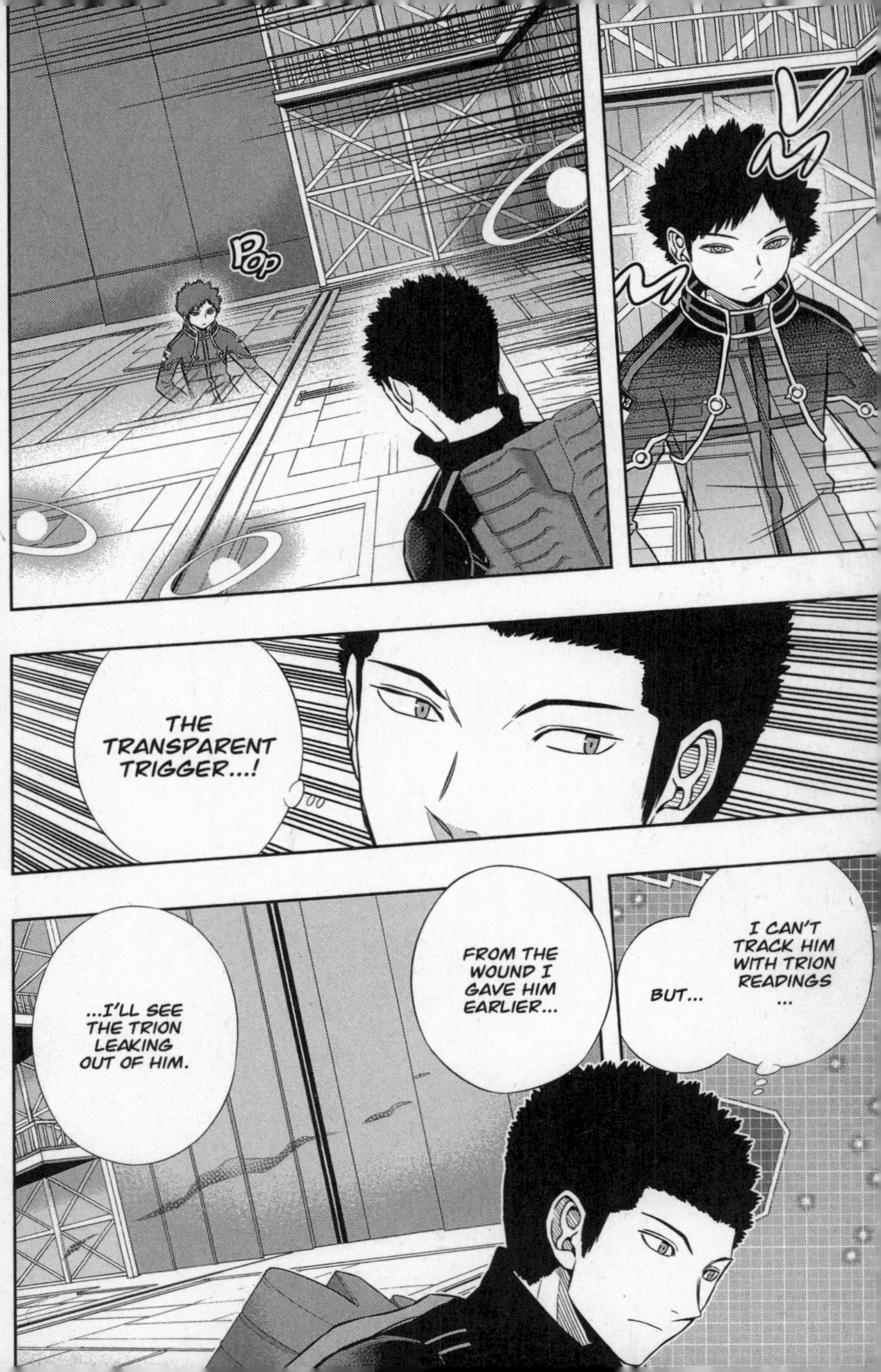

POP
THE TRANSPARENT TRIGGER...!
I CAN'T TRACK HIM WITH TRION READINGS...
BUT...
FROM THE WOUND I GAVE HIM EARLIER...
...I'LL SEE THE TRION LEAKING OUT OF HIM.

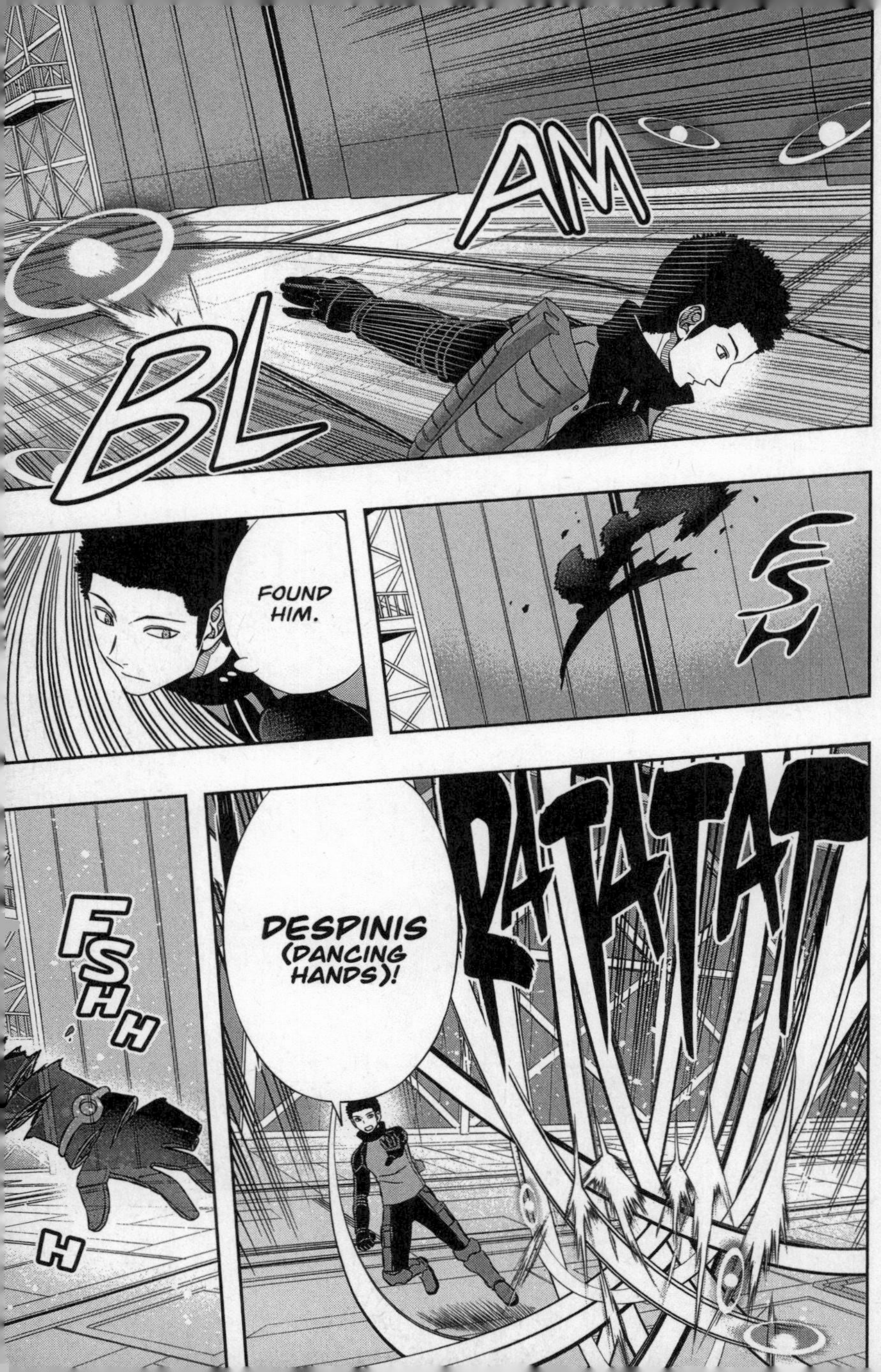

BLAM
FSH
FOUND HIM.
RATATAT
DESPINIS (DANCING HANDS)!
FSHHH
H

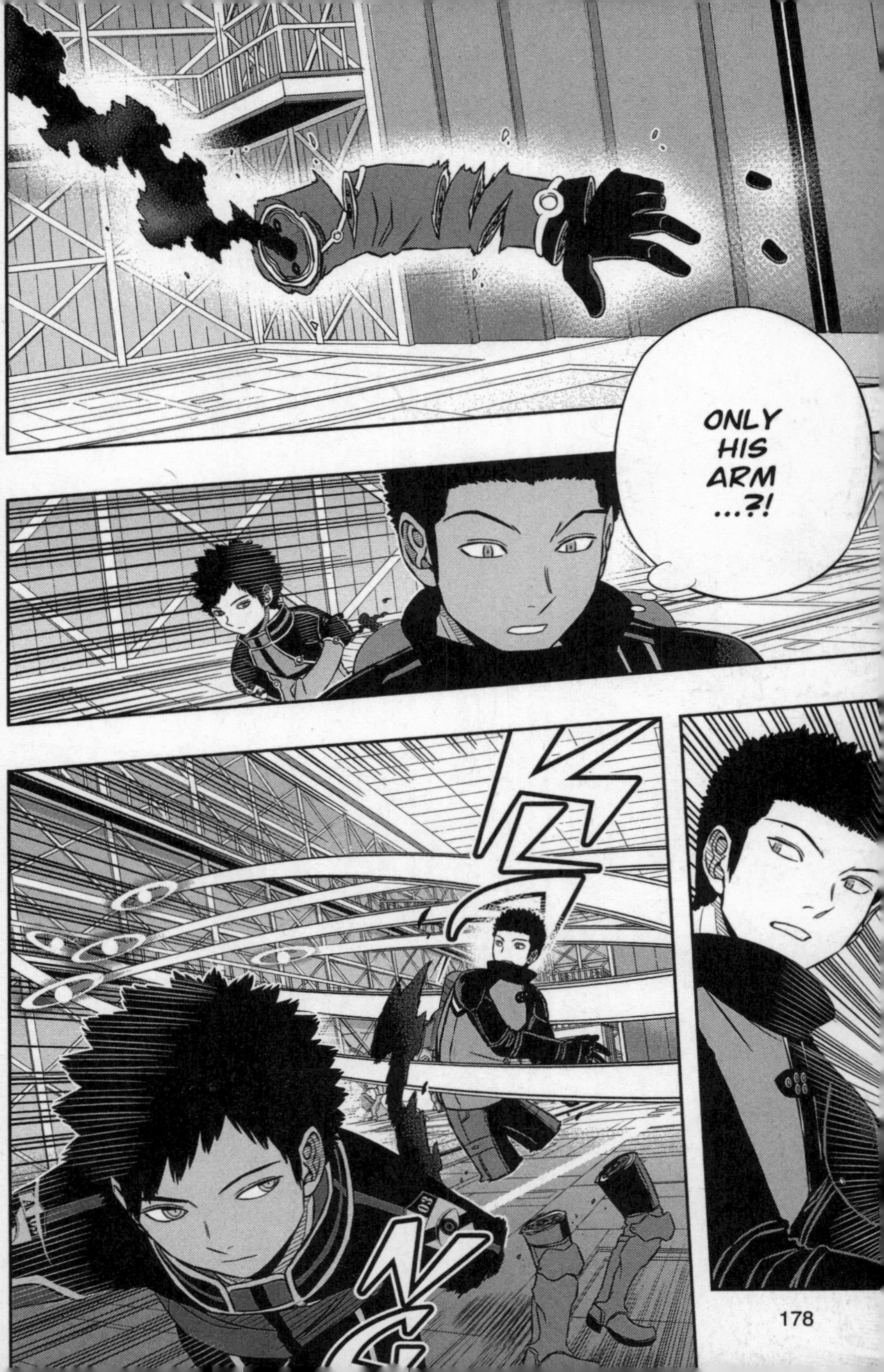
ONLY HIS ARM ...?!

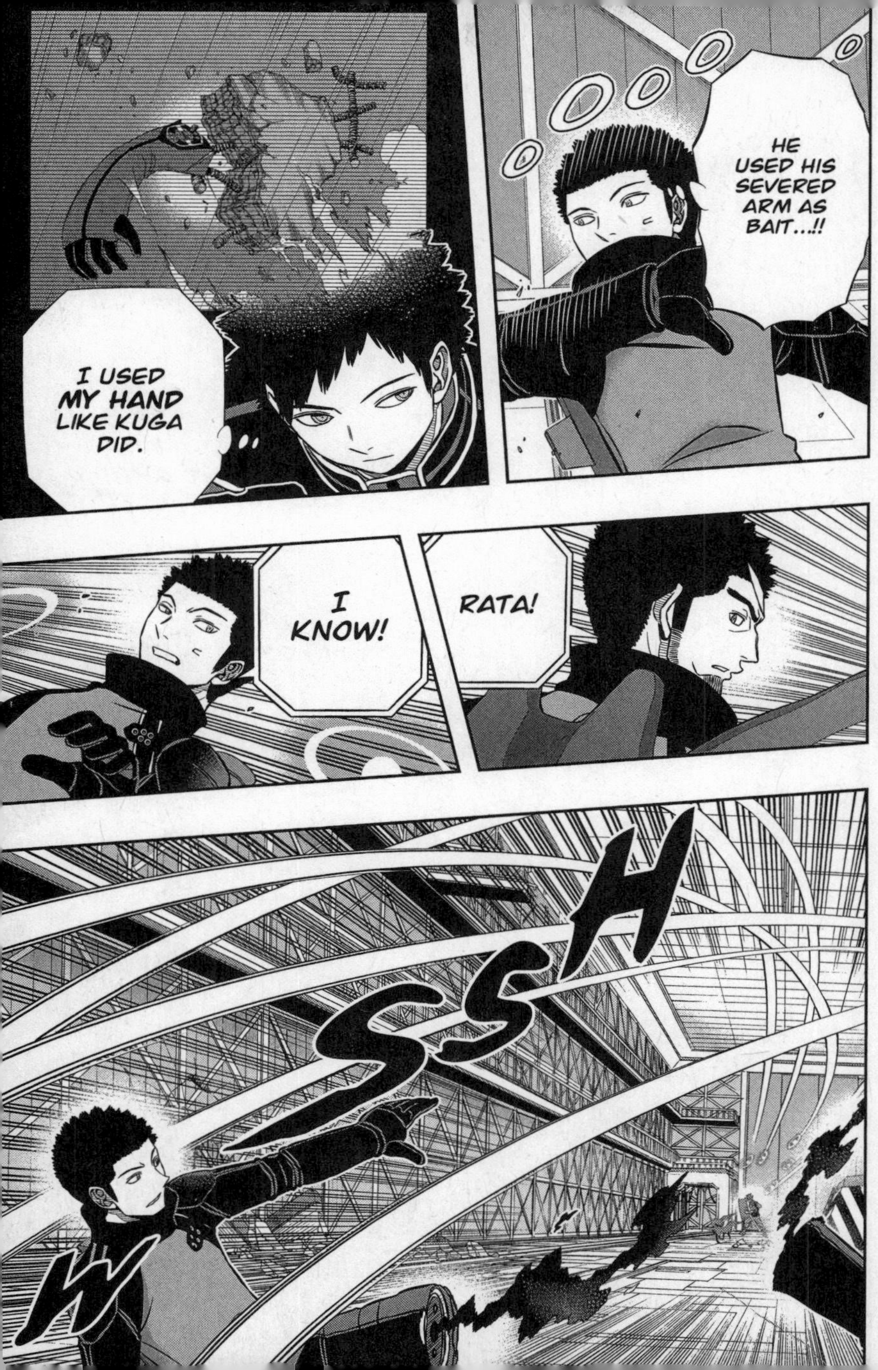
HE USED HIS SEVERED ARM AS BAIT...!!
I USED MY HAND LIKE KUGA DID.
RATA!
I KNOW!
SSH

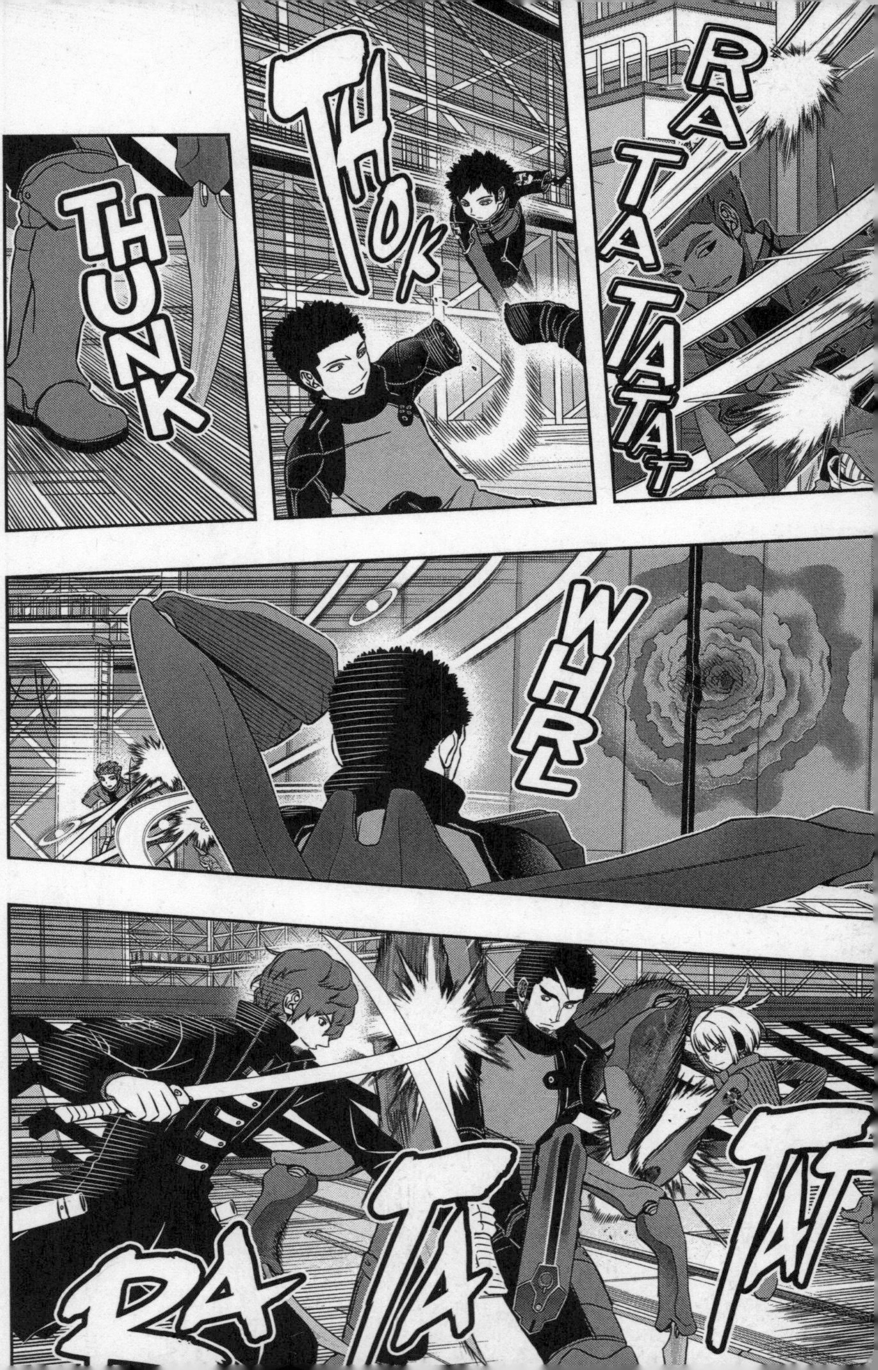
RATATATAT
THOK
THUNK
WHRL
RATATAT

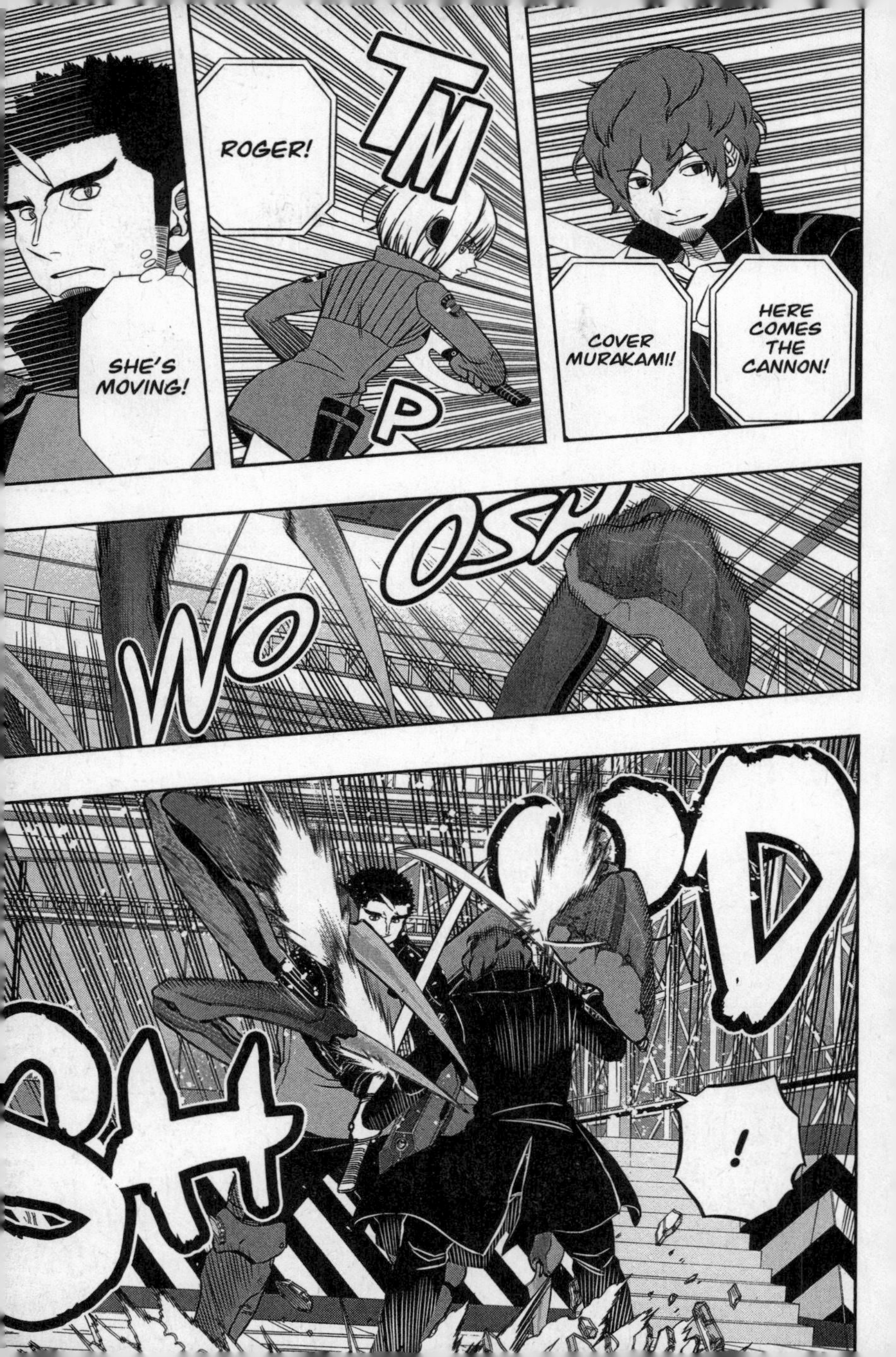
HERE COMES THE CANNON!
COVER MURAKAMI!
ROGER!
TMP
SHE'S MOVING!
WOOSH
!

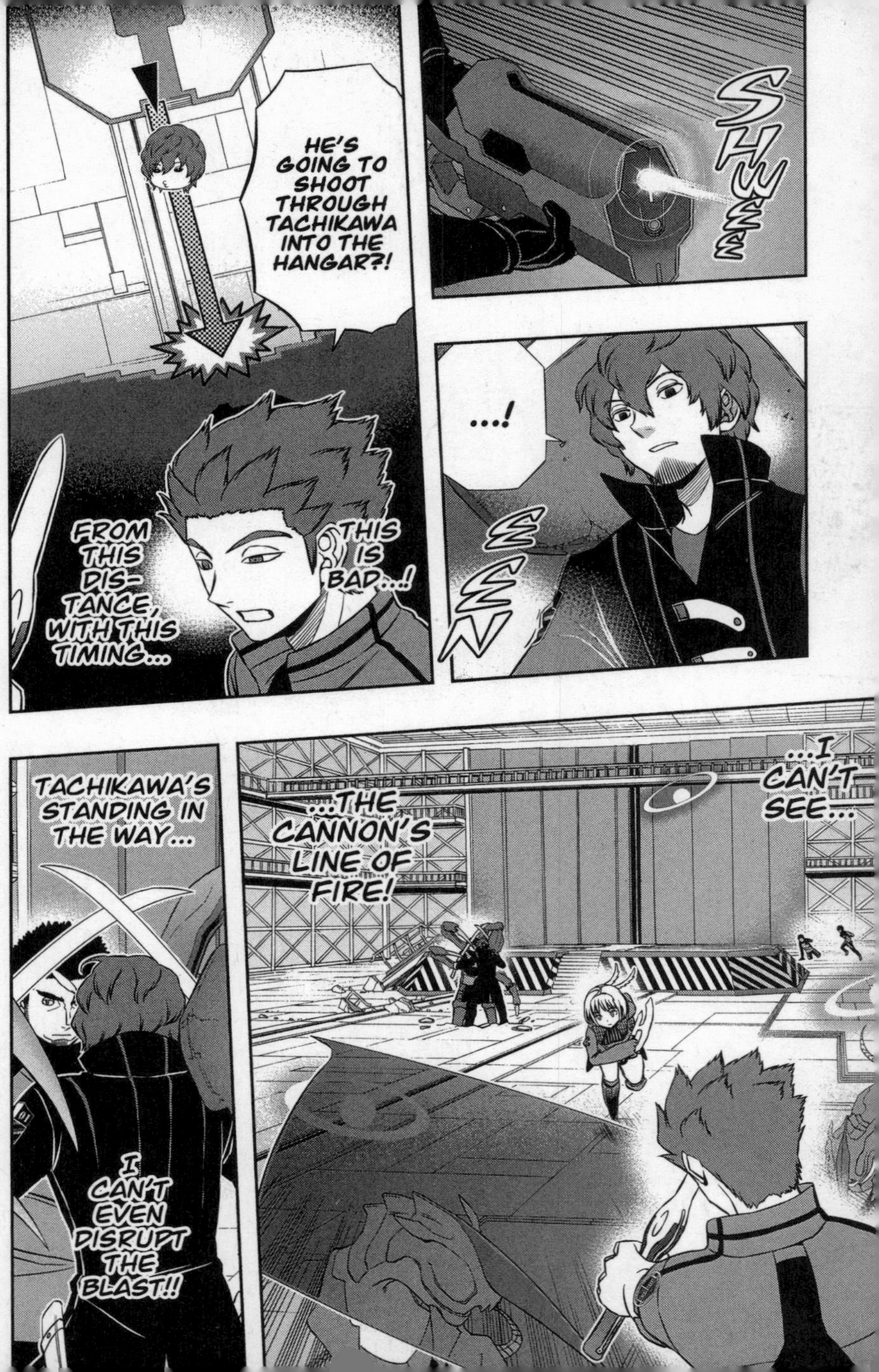
SHUWEEE
...!
EEEN
HE'S GOING TO SHOOT THROUGH TACHIKAWA INTO THE HANGAR?!
THIS IS BAD...!
FROM THIS DIS-TANCE, WITH THIS TIMING...
...I CAN'T SEE...
...THE CANNON'S LINE OF FIRE!
TACHIKAWA'S STANDING IN THE WAY...
I CAN'T EVEN DISRUPT THE BLAST!!

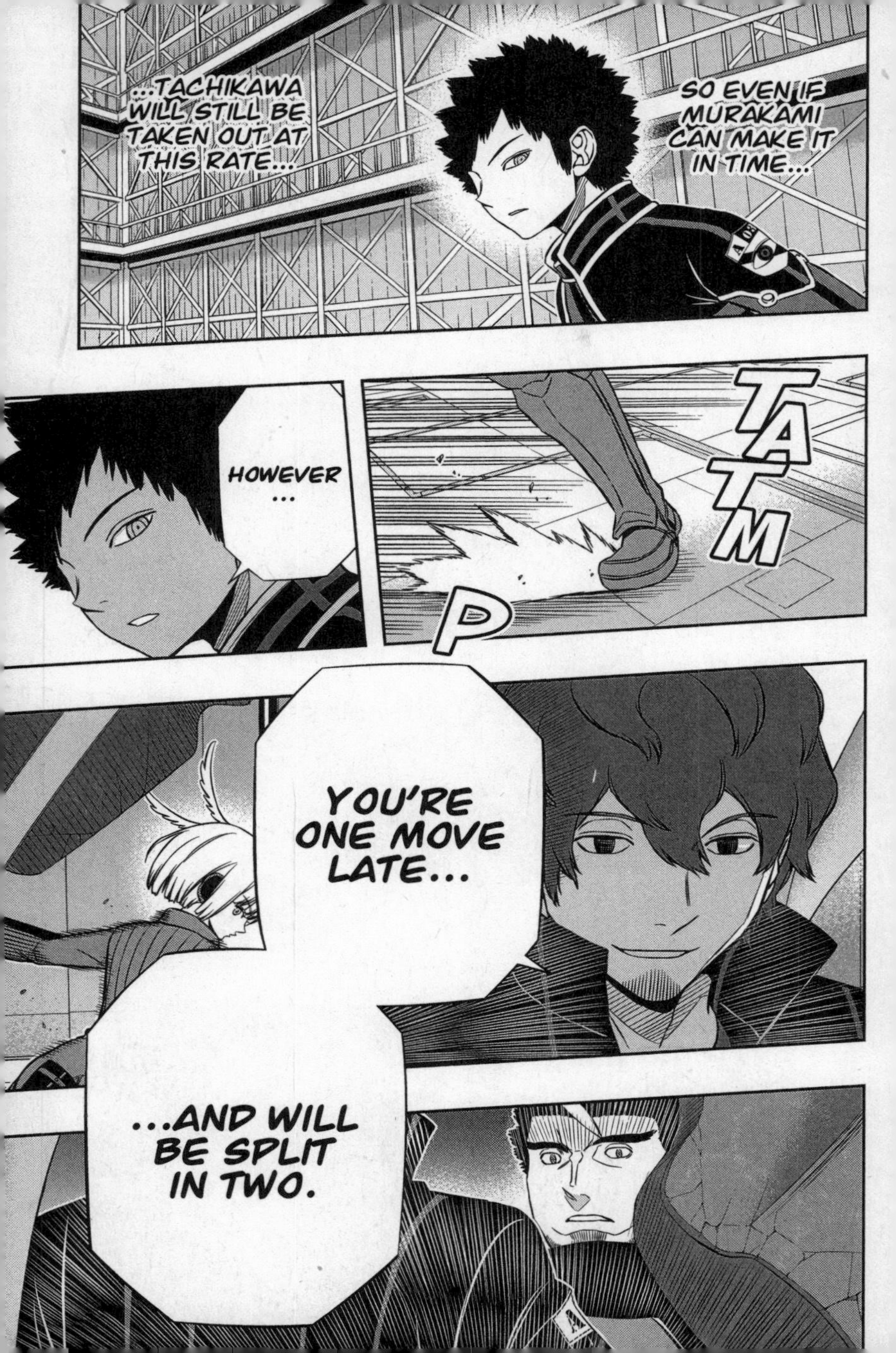
SO EVEN IF MURAKAMI CAN MAKE IT IN TIME...
...TACHIKAWA WILL STILL BE TAKEN OUT AT THIS RATE...
TATMP
HOWEVER ...
YOU'RE ONE MOVE LATE...
...AND WILL BE SPLIT IN TWO.

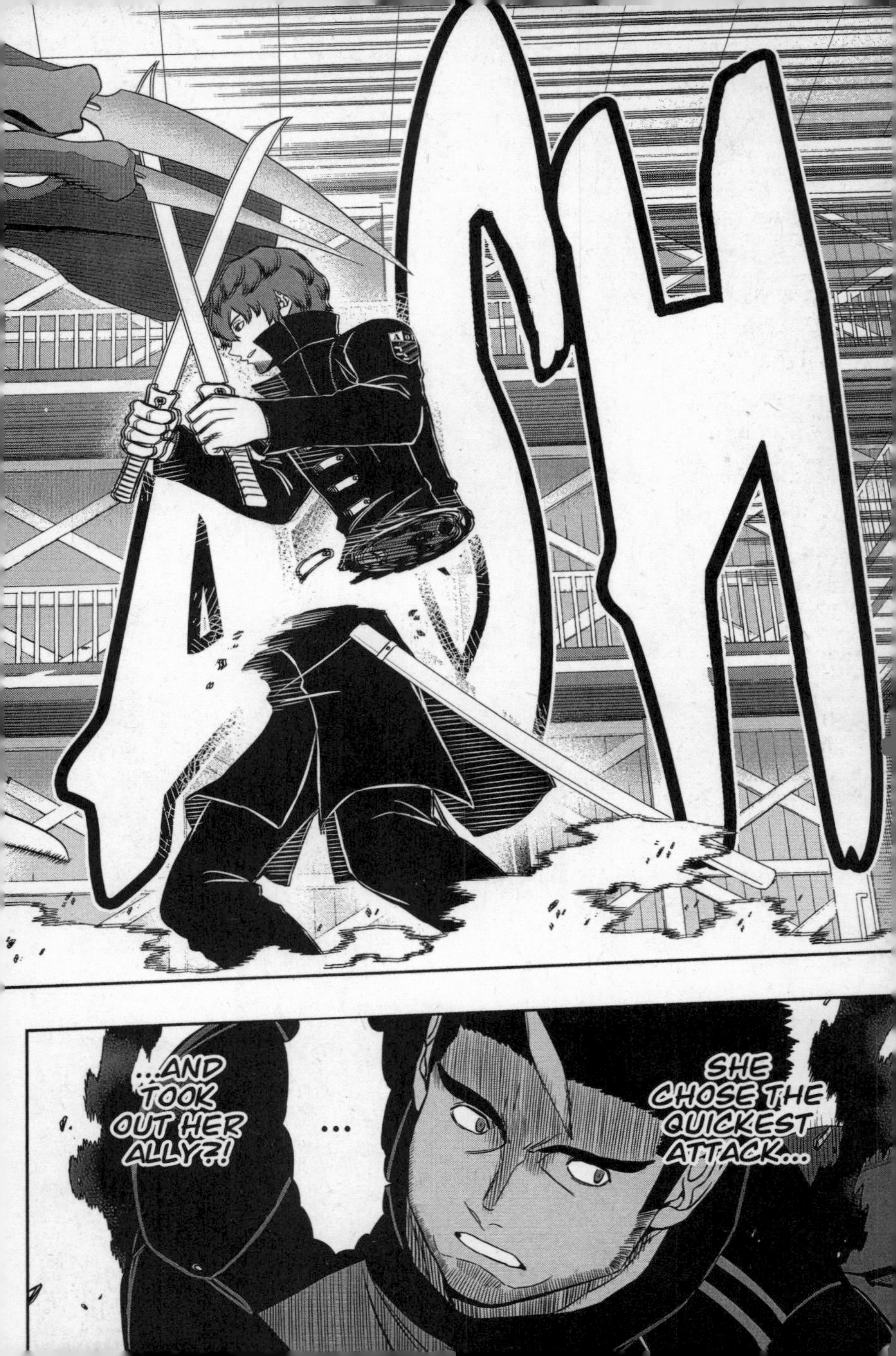
SHE CHOSE THE QUICKEST ATTACK...
...
...AND TOOK OUT HER ALLY?!

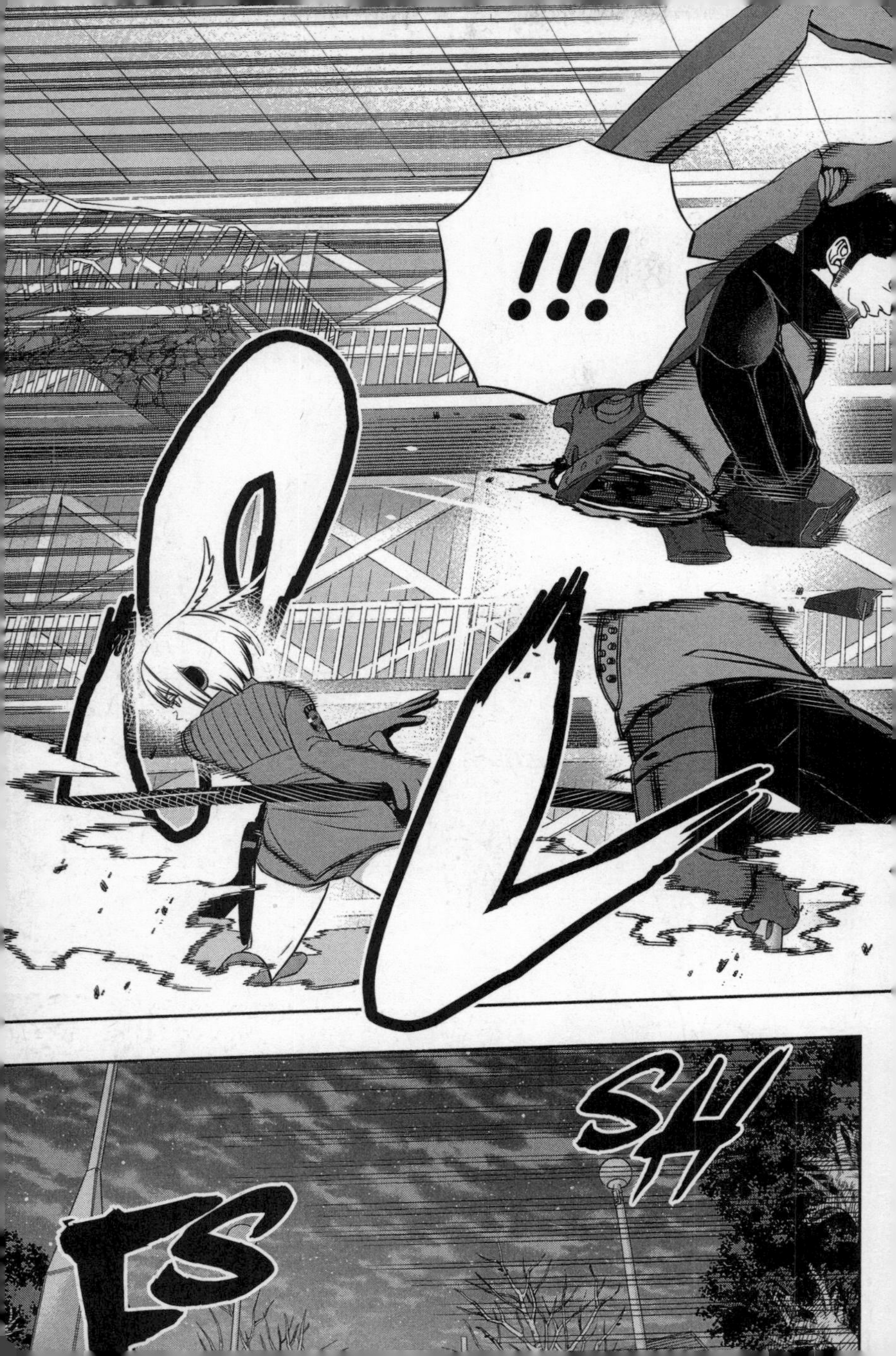
!!!
SH
TS

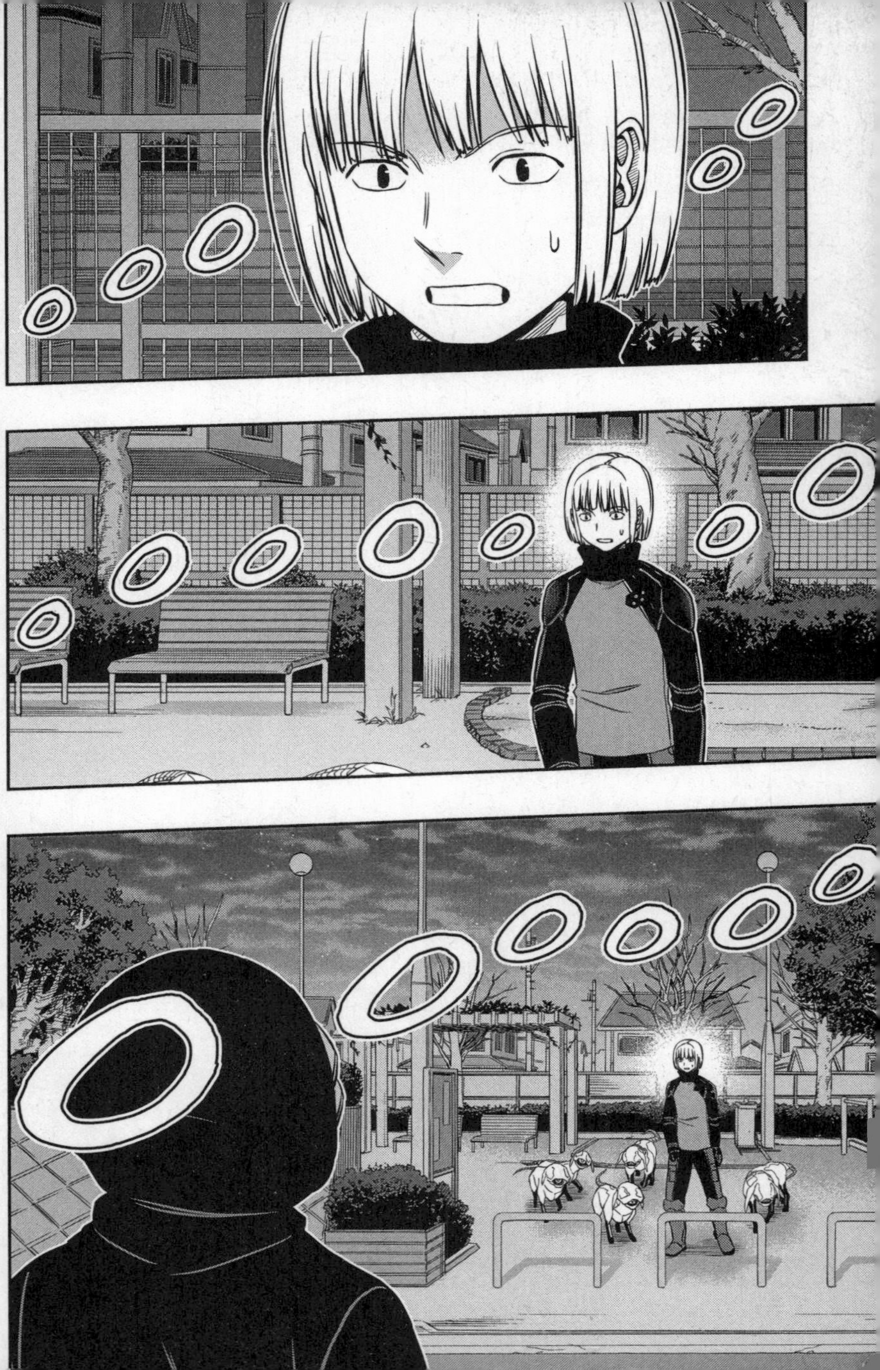

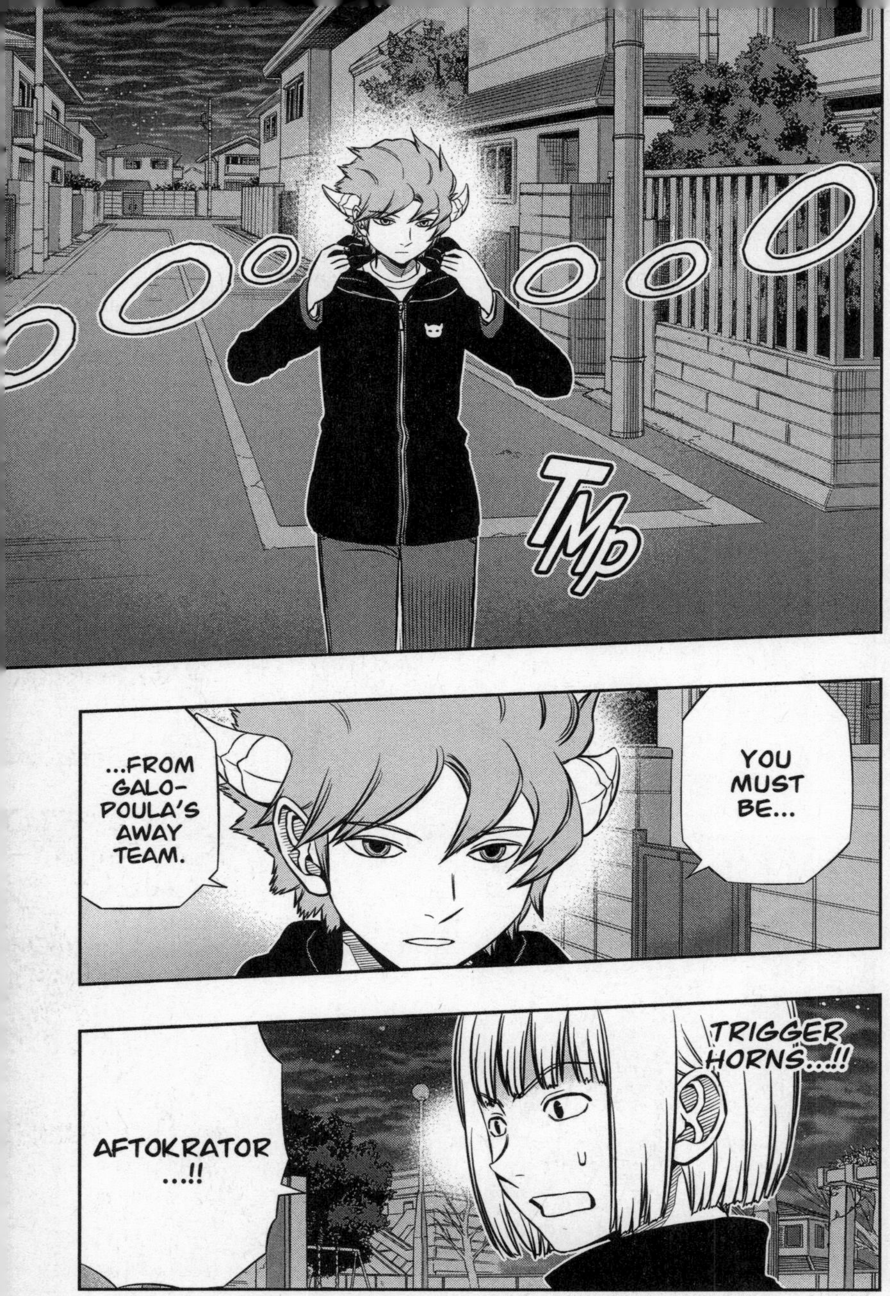
TMP
YOU MUST BE...
...FROM GALO-POULA'S AWAY TEAM.
TRIGGER HORNS...!!
AFTOKRATOR ...!!

To Be Continued in **World Trigger** 16!

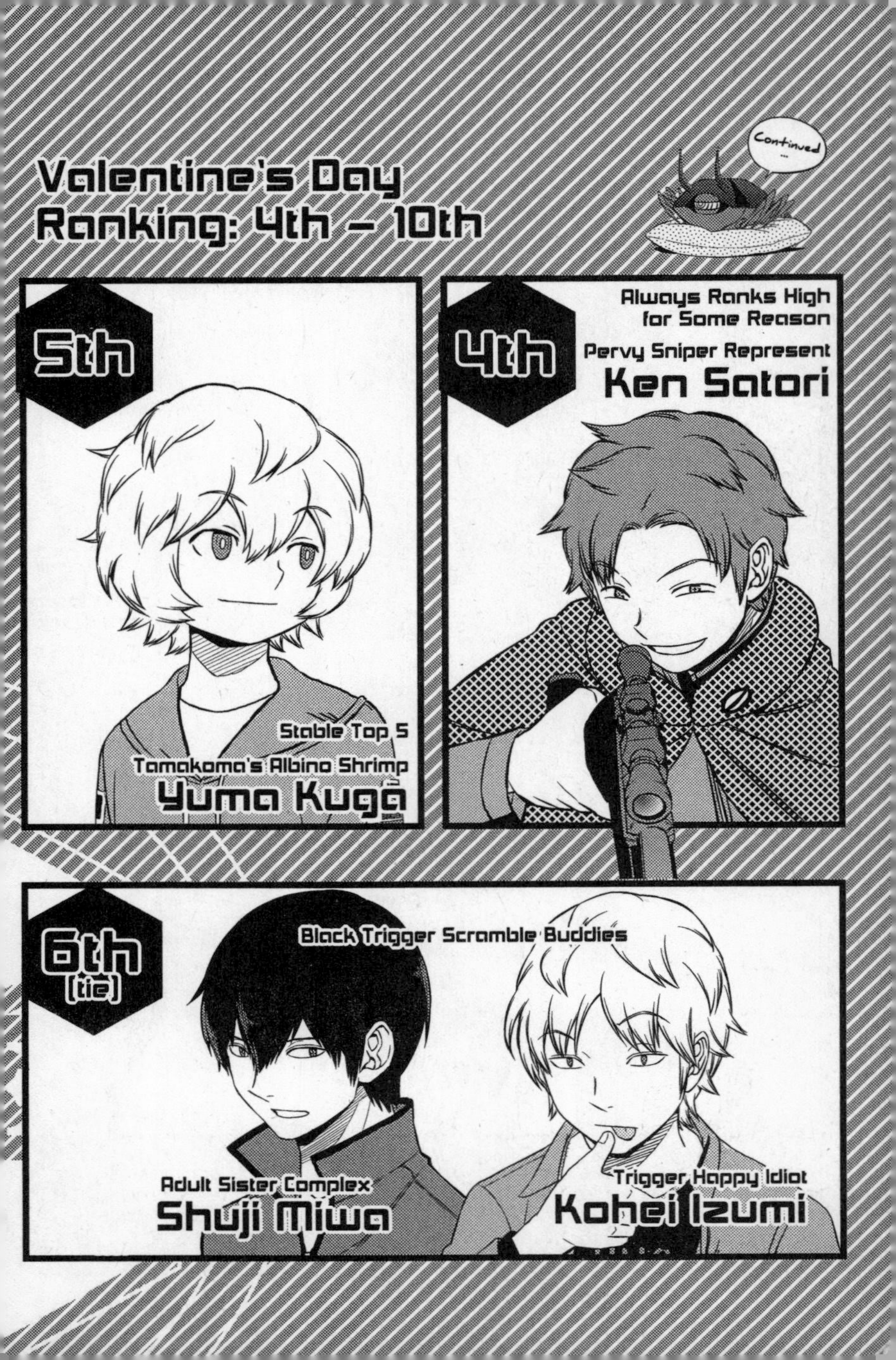

Continued...
Valentine's Day Ranking: 4th - 10th
4th
Always Ranks High for Some Reason
Pervy Sniper Represent
Ken Satori
5th
Stable Top 5
Tamakoma's Albino Shrimp
Yuma Kuga
6th (tie)
Black Trigger Scramble Buddies
Trigger Happy Idiot
Kohei Izumi
Adult Sister Complex
Shuji Miwa

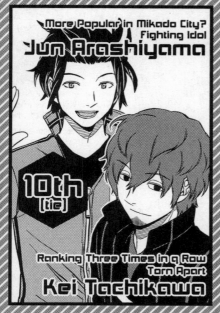

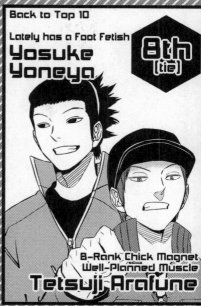

Back to Top 10
Lately has a Foot Fetish
Yosuke Yoneya
8th (tie)
B-Rank Chick Magnet
Well-Planned Muscle
Tetsuji Arafune

More Popular in Mikado City?
Fighting Idol
Jun Arashiyama
10th (tie)
Ranking Three Times in a Row
Torn Apart
Kei Tachikawa

Multiple Votes Top 3

1 Ryo Utagawa

2 Soya Kazama

3 Haruaki Azuma

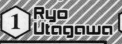

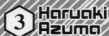

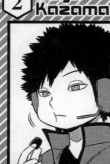

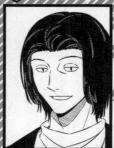

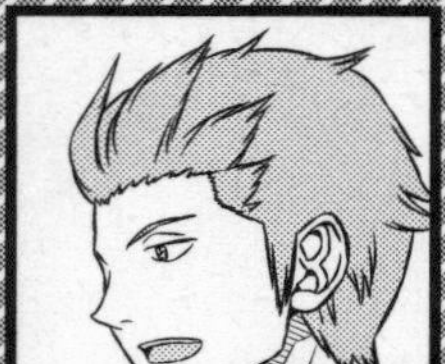

We're back at it again! I'd like to announce that we received a ton of gifts for Utagawa and Azuma from a lot of crazy fans. Thank you very much! Kazama appeared to be popular both in single and multiple votes. I guess he's the most popular overall? The staff really enjoyed all of the gifts. We got so many of them again this year!

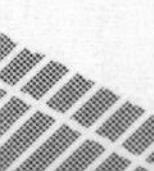

WORLD TRIGGER

Bonus Character Pages

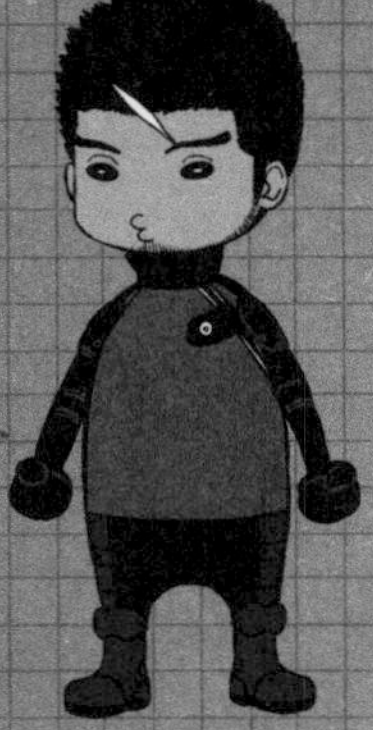

GATTLIN

Corporate Warrior

A subcontracted leader who has to protect his people from crazy jobs dropped on them by the higher-ups by leading with an iron fist. A man with sideburns who worked his way up the ranks to eventually become the captain of the Away Team. A bearer of sideburns that even connect to his beard! If it wasn't for Jin's foresight, his mission would've succeeded. Mr. Dramatic Sideburns...who has a wife and 8-year-old son back home and can easily pull off a dramatic hostage situation.

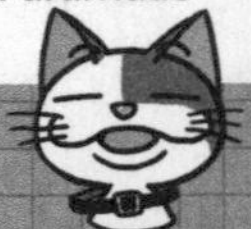

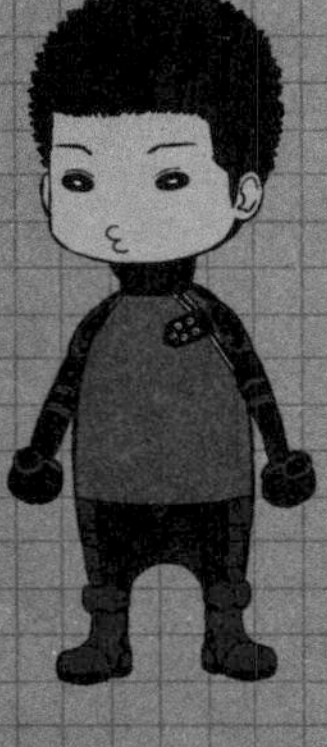

RATA

Poorly Cultivated by Clean Water

A buzz cut with clear eyes who I initially nicknamed "baseball boy"! There's a long and deep story for why his hair is cut this way, but I always wonder if the readers would find it entertaining or not. He originally had Reghi's hair, but they were later switched. He's a very important buzz cut who may play a huge role in things to come.

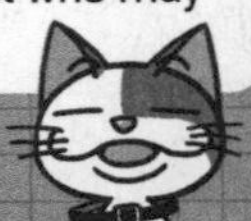